A TRAVELLER'S NARRATIVE

'Abdu'l-Bahá

Translated and edited by Edward G. Browne

A TRAVELLER'S NARRATIVE

WRITTEN TO ILLUSTRATE

THE EPISODE OF THE BÁB

TRANSLATED INTO ENGLISH FROM
THE ORIGINAL PERSIAN

BY

EDWARD G. BROWNE, M.A., M.B., F.B.A., F.R.C.P.
SIR THOMAS ADAMS'S PROFESSOR OF ARABIC,
AND FELLOW OF PEMBROKE COLLEGE,
IN THE UNIVERSITY OF CAMBRIDGE

BAHA'I PUBLISHING COMMITTEE
P.O. BOX 348, GRAND CENTRAL STATION
NEW YORK, N.Y.
1930

TITLE PAGE FROM THE 1930 EDITION

STUDIES IN THE BÁBÍ AND BAHÁ'Í RELIGIONS
Reprint Series

A TRAVELLER'S NARRATIVE

written to illustrate the episode of the Báb

'Abdu'l-Bahá

Translated and edited by Edward G. Browne

Kalimát Press
Los Angeles
2004

STUDIES IN THE BÁBÍ AND BAHÁ'Í RELIGIONS
Reprint Series

A Traveller's Narrative was first published by Cambridge University Press, 1891, in two volumes: Volume One, the Persian text (*Maqálah-i shakhsí-i sayyáh kih dar qazíyah-i Báb nivishtah ast*); Volume Two, Browne's English translation and notes. The English volume was reprinted as a new edition by the Bahá'í Publishing Committee (New York) in 1930. Philo Press (Amsterdam) reprinted the Persian and English as one volume in 1975. The Bahá'í Publishing Trust (Wilmette, Ill.) published the English translation alone, without Browne's introduction and notes—but with occasional new footnotes—in 1980, as a "New and Corrected Edition." This volume is a reprint of the 1930 Bahá'í edition.

Library of Congress Cataloging-in-Publication Data

On file with the Library of Congress

ISBN 1-890688-37-1

Kalimát Press
1600 Sawtelle Boulevard, Suite 310
Los Angeles, CA 90025

www.kalimat.com

CONTENTS OF VOLUME II.

CONTENTS.

PREFACE TO AMERICAN EDITION

Members of the Bahá'í Cause are greatly indebted to Prof. Browne for his scholarly researches into the history and literature of the movement, and most particularly for his dignified and powerful translation of "A Traveller's Narrative." As recounted by Prof. Browne in his own introduction to the edition published under the auspices of Cambridge University, the manuscript of this work was given him by 'Abdu'l-Bahá at the time he visited Bahá'u'lláh and the Bahá'í community in Akká during the year 1891. The accuracy of this historical narrative is therefore fully recognized by all Bahá'ís, who in it possess the only complete and authoritative record of the early days of the Cause yet published in the English language.

The present edition is a reprint from the plates made by Cambridge University Press for the Publishing Committee of the National Spiritual Assembly of the Bahá'ís of the United States and Canada, the English edition having been out of print for many years. It is the understanding of the Committee that the plates are too worn to permit of any further use and also that Cambridge University does not plan to reissue the book in future. The present edition, ordered to meet the demand for copies long felt by American Bahá'ís, consequently represents the only source of supply available at the present time.

In including this important title among the authorized Bahá'í works published or distributed under the auspices of the American National Assembly, the reader's attention is called to the fact that the historical accuracy possessed by the text given to Prof. Browne at Akká does not, unfortunately, extend to the entire body of notes added by the translator himself. As will be only too evident to every student of the Bahá'í Cause who brings to the reading of these notes a knowledge of its history and development during the forty years since 1891, Prof. Browne vastly over-emphasized the significance of the Ezeli movement, attributing to it, in fact, an importance as rival contestant with the movement founded by Bahá'u'lláh which history itself has revealed it never possessed. Today, Subhi-Ezel, the rebellious half-brother of Bahá'u'lláh, stands merely as one of the many figures whose vain attempt to interrupt the progress of the Bahá'í movement and confuse its universal purpose succeeded only in affording the incidents by which the spiritual power of Bahá'u'lláh could be the more clearly vindicated to the world. The error which so lamentably invalidated Prof. Browne's point of view a generation ago arose from the fact that he was unable to follow the stream of Bahá'í history from the Báb to Bahá'u'lláh, failed to perceive that Bahá'u'lláh was the founder of the religion and the Báb his forerunner, and as result devoted his unique resources of scholarship to the sterile task of interpreting the Bahá'í movement in terms of the limited understanding of the very few Bábis whose faces were turned to the past. Prof. Browne's interest in the Báb was so profound, and his researches so ardent, that his inability to readjust his point of view when working upon material created after the Báb's martyrdom is regarded as a tragic loss by every friend of the Cause.

INTRODUCTION.

This book is the history of a proscribed and persecuted sect written by one of themselves. After suffering in silence for nigh upon half a century, they at length find voice to tell their tale and offer their apology. Of this voice I am the interpreter.

So many Persian works of universally acknowledged and incontrovertible merit remain unpublished, not only in Europe but in the East, that one who offers to the public as the result of his study and labour the translation and text of a quite recent compilation, whereof the authorship must remain unknown, and which must therefore rely solely on whatever intrinsic interest and merit it may possess, may reasonably be expected to state the considerations which have led him to select for publication such a work.

This book is, as I have said, recent in composition; for, as appears from a passage which will be found on p. 67, it was written probably during the year 1886. It is also anonymous. This could not well be otherwise; for what Persian could, with ordinary prudence, acknowledge a work written in defence of a faith whereof the name is scarce mentioned in Persia without fear and trembling? So that these two things, which some might incline to account grave defects in the book, and reasons against its publication, are, in truth, inherent in its very nature and character. It is of quite modern origin, because it treats of a recent movement, of which the first beginnings are remembered by many still living; it is anonymous, because every promoter of that movement is, in the country which gave it birth, as a man "sitting beneath a sword suspended by a single hair, who knoweth not when it shall descend upon him, whether it shall descend instantly or after a while[1]."

If, then, the subject treated of in this book be of sufficient interest and importance to merit careful study, and if the book itself, notwithstanding our ignorance of its authorship, can be shewn to proceed from a trustworthy source, I am sufficiently justified in having decided to edit and translate this "Traveller's Narrative."

Now it appears to me that the history of the Bábí movement must be interesting in different ways to others besides those who are directly engaged in the study of Persian. To the student of religious thought it will afford no little matter for reflection; for here he may contemplate such personalities as by lapse of time pass into heroes and demi-gods still unobscured by myth and fable; he may examine by the light of concurrent and independent testimony one of those strange outbursts of enthusiasm, faith, fervent devotion, and indomitable heroism—or fanaticism, if you will—which we are accustomed to associate with the earlier history of the human race; he may witness, in a word, the birth of a faith which may not impossibly win a place amidst the great religions of the world. To the ethnologist also it may yield food for thought as to the character of a people, who, stigmatized as they often have been as selfish, mercenary, avaricious, egotistical, sordid, and cowardly, are yet capable of exhibiting under the

[1] See p. 150 *infra*.

influence of a strong religious impulse a degree of devotion, disinterestedness, generosity, unselfishness, nobility, and courage which may be paralleled in history, but can scarcely be surpassed. To the politician, too, the matter is not devoid of importance; for what changes may not be effected in a country now reckoned almost as a cypher in the balance of national forces by a religion capable of evoking so mighty a spirit? Let those who know what Muhammad made the Arabs, consider well what the Báb may yet make the Persians.

But to myself, and I believe to most others who have been or shall be brought to consider this matter, the paramount interest thereof lies in this, that here is something, whether wise or unwise, whether tending towards the amelioration of mankind or the reverse, which seemed to many hundreds, if not thousands, of our fellow-creatures worth suffering and dying for, and which, on this ground alone, must be accounted worthy of our most attentive study.

I have now to explain how this book came into my hands; what, so far as I have been able to learn, were the causes which led to its composition; and why (with certain reservations which will be presently specified) we are warranted in regarding it as a true and authentic account of the events which it relates. In order to make this explanation clear, it is necessary for me to describe briefly how my attention was first directed towards this subject; how my interest in it was kindled; how the means of investigating it were made available to me; and how the investigation, whereof this book is at present the final outcome, was conducted.

One day some seven years ago I was searching amongst the books in the University Library of Cambridge for fresh materials for an essay on the Ṣúfí philosophy, in the study of which I was then chiefly engaged, when my eye was caught by the title of Count Gobineau's *Religions et Philosophies dans l'Asie Centrale.* I took down the book, glanced through it to discover whether or no it contained any account of the Ṣúfís, and, finding that a short chapter was devoted to them, brought it back with me to my rooms. My first superficial glance had also shewn me that a considerable portion of the book was taken up with an account of the Bábís, of which sect I had at that time no definite knowledge, save a general idea that they had been subjected to a most severe persecution.

The perusal of Gobineau's chapter on the Ṣúfís caused me, I must frankly confess, no small mortification; for I was an ardent admirer of these eloquent mystics, whose spirit has inspired so much of what is best and finest in Persian literature, and a rude shock was inflicted on my susceptibilities by such words as these:—"Le quiétisme, le beng et l'opium, l'ivrognerie la plus abjecte, voilà surtout ce qu'elle [le soufysme] a produit."

When, however, I turned from this mournful chapter to that portion of the book which treated of the Bábí movement, the case was altogether different. To anyone who has already read this masterpiece of historical composition, this most perfect presentation of accurate and critical research in the form of a narrative of thrilling and sustained interest, such as one may, indeed, hope to find in the drama or the romance, but can scarcely expect from the historian, it is needless to describe the effect which it produced on me. To anyone who has not read it, I can only say let him do so forthwith, if he is in any way interested in the history of the Bábís. Many new facts may be added to those recorded by Gobineau, and the history which he carried down to A.D. 1852 needs to be supplemented by an appendix detailing the events of the last thirty-eight years, but the narrative of the first origin of Bábíism can hardly be told better than he has told it; certainly not in a style more eloquent nor in a manner more worthy of the subject.

Count Gobineau's book, then, effected in a certain sense a complete revolution in my ideas and projects. I had long ardently desired to visit Persia and above all Shíráz, and this desire was now greatly intensified. But whereas I had previously wished to see Shíráz because it was the home of Ḥáfiẓ and of Sa'dí, I now wished to see it because it was the birthplace of Mírzá 'Alí Muḥammad the Báb. And, after Shíráz, not Ṭús and Nishápúr, but Zanján, Mázandarán, and Tabríz were the objects of my eager desire. My impatience, too, was greatly increased; for I reflected that although there must be many still living who had witnessed, or even taken part in, the events of which I was so anxious to discover every slightest detail, each year that passed would materially lessen their number, and render ever fainter the possibility of restoring the picture in its entirety. Besides this, I was eager to know more of the doctrines which could inspire such heroism, and to gain this knowledge, as I clearly perceived, there was but one satisfactory and effectual method. As Anquetil du Perron had succeeded in unlocking the secrets of the Zoroastrian religion by going amongst those who professed it, winning their confidence, and eventually, after infinite patience and endeavour, obtaining copies of their sacred books and a clue to their contents, so I, if I were to succeed in fathoming the mysteries of the Bábí faith, must go to the land of its origin, strive to become intimate with some of its votaries, and from these obtain the knowledge which I sought. Let no one suppose that I am so presumptuous as to institute any comparison between Anquetil du Perron and myself. His task was one which only rare courage, perseverance, and genius could bring to a successful issue. He had to induce the suspicious, taciturn, and uncommunicative priests of an ancient national religion actuated by no desire of making proselytes to impart to him a secret doctrine and ritual hitherto most jealously guarded. And when at length the sacred books were gained, they were books written in a language so long dead that over it had formed a deposit of commentaries in a speech which had grown, flourished, and died since it had been a spoken tongue. Added to this, Anquetil's investigations were conducted amidst hardships, privations, and dangers of an exceptional kind. The Bábís, on the contrary, would, I was convinced, be eager to impart their doctrines to any enquirer on whose discretion and fidelity they could place reliance. Their sacred books, moreover, were either in Arabic, or in Persian, and, beyond a certain reserve and obscurity necessitated by prudential motives, and a peculiar terminology such as all sects, whether philosophical or religious, possess, I anticipated no particular difficulty in understanding them. One special obstacle, it was true, did exist in this case to the primary establishment of relations of intimacy. The Bábís were a proscribed sect, whereof every member was practically liable to outlawry and even death should he allow his creed to become known. It seemed probable enough, therefore, that I should at first have some difficulty in discovering them and putting myself into communication with them. Yet, could I but find means of spending a few months in Persia, it would be hard, I thought, if some lucky chance did not bring me in contact with some Bábí who would venture to take me into his confidence. And, if the first step could be won, I relied on the fair knowledge of colloquial Persian which I already possessed, the general acquaintance with the Bábí doctrines which Gobineau's work had given me, the genuine admiration which I felt for the Báb and his apostles, and the close brotherhood which, according to all analogy, must probably exist within the sect, to effect the rest.

Meanwhile the first step was to get to Persia, and of this there seemed to be but little chance. Anquetil du Perron would have gone, chance or no chance, and either attained his object or perished in the search. I, not being fashioned in so heroic a mould, waited for the means. I made several fruitless attempts to obtain some appointment which would take me to the land of my quest, and finally, as a last resource, offered myself as a candidate for a medical post in the realms of the Nizám of Ḥaydar-ábád, on the chance that there I might find means of visiting Persia. Here again I was unsuccessful; and I was beginning to despair of attaining my object when suddenly and unexpectedly that thing befel me which is, as I believe, the greatest good-fortune which can fall to the lot of one eager to pursue a scientific enquiry from which he is debarred by lack of means. A fellowship became vacant at my college, and to this fellowship I was elected. This happened on May 30th, 1887. Five months later I had crossed the Turco-Persian frontier and was within three stages of Tabríz.

Of the disappointments and failures which I at first met with in my attempts to discover and communicate with the Bábís; of the fortunate chance which at length placed the clue in my hand; and of the fulfilment of my hopes in a manner surpassing my most sanguine expectations I have already spoken in another place[1]. Of these and other things incidental to my journey I may perhaps give a fuller account at some future time. Here it is

[1] *Journal of the Royal Asiatic Society*, for 1889, vol. XXI. (New Series), pp. 486—489, 495—496, 501, &c.

sufficient for me to state that I returned to England in October 1888, having visited Zanján, Tabríz, Shíráz, and Sheykh Ṭabarsí, the places most intimately associated with Bábí history; having lived on terms of intimacy for periods varying from a few days to many weeks with the principal Bábís at Isfahán, Shíráz, Yezd, and Kirmán; and bringing with me a number of Bábí books and writings, as well as journals wherein the gist of every important conversation with any member of the sect was carefully recorded.

So soon as I had established myself once more in the college which four years' absence from Cambridge and a year's travelling in Persia had served to render yet more dear to me, I set to work to make a systematic examination of the materials collected during my journey. The *Persian Beyán*, the *Íḳán*, the *Kitáb-i-Aḳdas*, the *Epistles to the Kings*, the *Táríkh-i-Jadíd*, and a host of more or less important letters, memoranda, poems, and abstracts, were read, digested, and indexed; and the outcome of this and my previous labour, together with a brief account of my journey, was laid before the public in two articles, comprising in all 170 pages, of which the first appeared in July, the second in October 1889, in the *Journal of the Royal Asiatic Society*. To these articles I shall continually have occasion to refer in the course of this work, and, for the sake of brevity, I shall henceforth generally denote them as "B. i." and "B. ii."

The preparation of these articles, in conjunction with other work, kept me occupied till the autumn of 1889, when, the main results of my investigations having been satisfactorily recorded, I was left at liberty to turn my attention to matters of detail. It appeared to me extremely desirable that texts or translations of the chief Bábí works should be published *in extenso;* the only question was which to begin with. Inasmuch as it seemed likely that the historical aspects of the movement would prove more generally interesting than its doctrinal aspects, I finally determined to publish first the text and translation of the *Táríkh-i-Jadíd*[1], and this determination was approved by several of my friends and correspondents whose knowledge entitled them to speak with authority. This text and translation I accordingly began to prepare; and the former was completely copied out for the printer (awaiting only collation with the British Museum text)[2], while the latter was in an advanced stage of progress, when circumstances, immediately to be detailed, occurred, which postponed the completion of that work, and substituted for it another, the present.

My researches amongst the Bábís in Persia had, at a comparatively early stage, revealed to me the fact that since Count Gobineau composed his work great changes had taken place in their organization and attitude. I had expected to find Mírzá Yaḥyá *Ṣubḥ-i-Ezel* ("*Ḥaẓrat-i-Ezel*" as Gobineau calls him) universally acknowledged by them as the Báb's successor and the sole head to whom they confessed allegiance. My surprise was great when I discovered that, so far from this being the case, the majority of the Bábís spoke only of *Behá* as their chief and prophet; asserted that the Báb was merely his herald

[1] Concerning the *Táríkh-i-Jadíd* see Note A at end, pp. 192—197 *infra*.

[2] This collation has since been effected, and the variants offered by the British Museum MS. proved to be both numerous and important. Should the publication of the work be proceeded with, it would be necessary to collate also the defective MS. recently acquired by the St. Petersburg Library, the closing words of which occur on p. 235 of my MS. See note 1 at the foot of p. 192 *infra*, and the forthcoming (sixth) vol. of Baron Rosen's *Collections Scientifiques*, p. 244.

and forerunner (those who had read the Gospels, and they were many, likened the Báb to John the Baptist and Behá to Christ); and either entirely ignored or strangely disparaged Mírzá Yaḥyá. It took me some time fully to grasp this new and unexpected position of affairs, and perhaps I should not have succeeded in doing so had it not been for the knowledge of the former state of things which I had obtained from Gobineau's work, and the acquaintance which I subsequently made in Kirmán with five or six persons who adhered to what I may call the "old dispensation" and regarded Mírzá Yaḥyá "*Ṣubḥ-i-Ezel*" as the legitimate and sole successor of the Báb.

To state briefly a long story, the case stands thus:—

(1) Mírzá 'Alí Muḥammad the Báb during his life chose from amongst his most faithful and most gifted disciples 18 persons called "Letters of the Living" (*Ḥurúfát-i-Ḥayy*), who, together with himself the "Point" (*Nuḳṭa*), constituted that sacred hierarchy of 19 called the "First Unity" (*Váḥid-i-Avval*). Of these "Letters" I have not been able to obtain a complete list, and indeed it would appear that the whole hierarchy was never made known. Mírzá Yaḥyá *Ṣubḥ-i-Ezel* held the fourth place in this hierarchy, and, on the death of the "Point" and the two first "Letters," rose, by a natural process of promotion, to the position of chief of the sect[1]. Behá, whose proper name is Mírzá Ḥuseyn 'Alí of Núr, was also, according to Gobineau[2], included in the "Unity." Gobineau has, however, mistaken the relationship which existed between him and Mírzá Yaḥyá. That the two are brothers (or rather half-brothers, born of the same father by different wives) is a fact established by convincing testimony[3].

[1] See note 1 on p. 95 *infra*.

[2] *Religions et Philosophies*, p. 277.

[3] Cf. pp. 56, note 2; 63, top; and 373.

(2) Mírzá 'Alí Muḥammad the Báb declared explicitly and repeatedly in all his works that the religion established by him and the books revealed to him were in no way final; that his followers must continually expect the advent of "Him whom God shall manifest," who would perfect and complete this religion; that, though "He whom God shall manifest" would not, it was hoped, delay his appearance for more than 1511, or, at most, 2001 years (these numbers being represented in cabbalistic fashion by the words *Ghiyáth* and *Mustagháth*), he might appear at any time; and that, whenever one should appear claiming to be "He whom God shall manifest," his very being, together with his power of revealing verses, would be his sufficient signs. All who believed in the Báb were solemnly warned not to reject one so characterized and making such a claim, and were commanded, in case of doubt, to incline towards belief rather than disbelief.

(3) During the sojourn of the Bábí exiles at Adrianople, Behá (according to Nabíl in A.D. 1866—7) suddenly claimed to be "He whom God shall manifest," in proof of which he revealed sundry "signs" (*áyát*) in eloquent Arabic and Persian, wherein he summoned all the Bábís to acknowledge him as their supreme and sole chief and spiritual guide. Most of the Bábís eventually made this acknowledgement, vowed allegiance to Behá, and thereby became *Behá'ís;* some few refused to transfer their allegiance from Mírzá Yaḥyá *Ṣubḥ-i-Ezel* (who himself strenuously resisted Behá's claims, which he regarded in the light of an usurpation and a rebellion), and these were thenceforth known as *Ezelís*.

Thus did the great schism take place which divided the Bábís into two unequal parties: a large majority, of whose unbounded and almost incredible love and reverence the object is Behá; a small minority, whose eager gaze is directed, not to Acre in Syria, but to Famagusta in Cyprus, where dwells the exiled chief whom they refuse to disavow. Needless is it to say how bitter is the animosity which subsists between the Behá'ís and the Ezelís. Amongst both factions I have found good men and faithful friends, and from the chiefs of both and their sons I have met with much kindness; wherefore I would for the present touch as lightly as may be on this painful matter, leaving my readers to draw their own conclusions from what is hereinafter set forth. The general nature of the arguments for and against either side will be found summarized at pp. 514 and 515 of my first and pp. 997—998 of my second article on the Bábís in the *J. R. A. S.*, to which I refer such of my readers as are curious to examine the matter more minutely. Of one thing there can, in my opinion, be but little doubt: the future (if Bábíism, as I most firmly believe, has a future) belongs to Behá and his successors and followers.

With most of the facts summarized above I became acquainted during my sojourn in Persia, but I was unable to learn for certain whether Mírzá Yaḥyá *Ṣubḥ-i-Ezel* was still alive, nor could I ascertain in what part of Cyprus he had fixed his residence. A dervish with whom I became acquainted in Kirmán told me that he had visited him, but could not remember the name of the town wherein he dwelt; and none of the Ezelís whom I saw could give me any more precise information. In my first paper on the Bábís in the *J. R. A. S.* (pp. 516—517) I was therefore compelled to confess my failure in all attempts to elucidate this point. At the same time I pointed out how much precious information might be gained from *Ṣubḥ-i-Ezel* if he were still alive, and how extremely desirable it was in the interests of science that this matter should be cleared up.

After the publication of my first, and during the preparation of my second paper, I began to institute enquiries on this point. My sister, who was then travelling in the East, succeeded in obtaining the first clue from Mr G. L. Houston, who was kind enough to procure for me definite proof that *Ṣubḥ-i-Ezel* was still alive and was residing with his family at Famagusta. Shortly after this, my friend Dr F. H. H. Guillemard, who had spent many months in Cyprus and had friends in all parts of the island, very obligingly wrote to Mr C. D. Cobham, Commissioner at Larnaca, and to Captain Young, Commissioner at Famagusta, asking them to obtain for me the fullest information possible relative to the Bábí exiles in Cyprus. I myself wrote at the same time, stating the nature of the information which I sought. Both Captain Young and Mr Cobham responded to my request with a kindness for which I cannot sufficiently express my gratitude; and so vigorously and energetically did they push their enquiries that I was soon in possession of all the chief facts relating to the Bábí exiles. Captain Young, indeed, spared no pains to clear up every point connected with the enquiry. The day after he received my letter he paid a visit to *Ṣubḥ-i-Ezel*; questioned him concerning his life, his adventures, and his doctrines; asked for information on sundry points mentioned in my paper; and forwarded to me a complete account of all that he had learned. Nor was this all; for he succeeded so well in winning *Ṣubḥ-i-Ezel's* confidence that with this first letter (dated July 28th, 1889) he was able to forward a MS. of one of the Báb's works, whereof, so far as I know, no copy had previously reached Europe. Through Captain Young I was also able to address directly to *Ṣubḥ-i-Ezel* letters containing questions on numerous matters connected with the history, doctrine, and literature of the Bábís, to all of which letters I received most full and courteous replies.

Ṣubḥ-i-Ezel further sent me at different times several other MSS., a complete list of such of the Báb's works as had been in his own possession at Baghdad[1], and a brief history of the Bábí movement written by himself, besides numerous letters, each one of which contained most precious information.

This correspondence, which opened out so rich a mine of new facts, was but in an early stage when my second paper on the Bábís was published in the *J.R.A.S.* for October 1889, but I was able to add to it an appendix (pp. 994—998) embodying the more important results of the enquiry undertaken by Captain Young, Mr Cobham, and Mr Houston. A fuller and more accurate account of *Ṣubḥ-i-Ezel* and the other Bábí exiles in Cyprus, based on the enquiries of the above-mentioned gentlemen, the examination of official documents, and the statements made to me by *Ṣubḥ-i-Ezel*, his sons, and others, will be found in Note W at the end of this book. It is therefore unnecessary for me to allude further to this correspondence at present.

While I was in Persia I had already formed the intention of visiting Acre and learning the doctrine of Behá from the fountain-head. From the moment when I discovered that *Ṣubḥ-i-Ezel* was still alive I further resolved to visit him also, for from repeated personal interviews I anticipated results which could not be obtained by a correspondence, however elaborate. I was also anxious for my own satisfaction to see those who since the Báb's death had been the leaders of the Bábí movement. Without this I felt that my researches would lack that completeness which I wished to give them. The motives which impelled me towards Acre and Famagusta were equally strong, but somewhat different. At the former place I expected to see

[1] See Note U at end.

the mainspring and fulcrum of a mighty force with the astonishing results of which I had become practically acquainted in Persia, and from which I believed (as I still believe) that results yet more wonderful might be expected in the future. At the latter place I hoped to converse with one whom the Báb had recognized as his immediate successor and vicegerent; one who had been personally acquainted with Mullá Ḥuseyn of Bushraweyh, Mullá Sheykh 'Alí, Suleymán Khán, Ḳurratu' l-'Ayn, and, in short, almost all of those whose devoted lives and heroic deaths had first inspired my enthusiasm; one, moreover, who represented the spirit and tradition of the old Bábíism, which, in the hands of Behá, had already undergone important modifications, and, indeed, become almost a new religion. Various considerations decided me to visit Cyprus first, of which two only need be mentioned here:—*firstly*, it was practically certain that no obstacle to my seeing Ṣubḥ-i-Ezel would arise, while it was by no means certain that I should be able to see Behá; *secondly*, the logical order of procedure was to begin with the investigation of the old order of things, and having completed this, to continue the examination of the new. I hoped, however, to make one journey suffice for the attainment of both objects; but, allowing for the time which must be consumed in actual travelling, it was clear that at least two months would be required for the enterprise. The Long Vacation was amply sufficient for the purpose, but the summer was the most unsuitable season for such a journey, and I therefore determined to petition the University for such extension of leave at Easter as would enable me to be absent from England for two months. The University, ever ready to facilitate research of every kind, granted me permission to absent myself from Cambridge from March 4th till May 3rd, 1890, and accordingly, leaving England on the date first mentioned, I landed at Larnaca in Cyprus on March 19th.

Captain Young and Mr Cobham, on becoming acquainted with my intention of visiting Cyprus, had, with that ready kindness and hospitality which, so far as my experience goes, are rarely lacking in Englishmen resident in the East, written to ask me to be their guest during such time as I might desire to remain in Famagusta or Larnaca, so that I was entirely relieved of all anxiety as to the possibility of finding a base of operations for my researches. Captain Young further counselled me, in case I wished to gain access to the official records of the Island Government, to obtain before leaving England such letters of recommendation as might ensure the attainment of this object. I accordingly applied for help in obtaining these to Major-General Sir Frederic Goldsmid, whose long residence in Persia and intimate knowledge of the Persian people and language had led him to take some interest in my communications on the subject of the Bábís to the Royal Asiatic Society. He spared no pains to further my plans, and introduced me to Sir Robert Biddulph, who very kindly gave me a letter to Sir Henry Bulwer, the Governor-General of Cyprus, asking him to allow me, so far as might be permissible or expedient, to inspect such official documents as might throw light on the object of my investigations.

In Larnaca I spent only one day, the shortness of the time at my disposal and my eagerness to see *Ṣubḥ-i-Ezel* compelling me with great reluctance to forego the pleasure which a more prolonged sojourn under Mr Cobham's hospitable roof would have afforded me. That day passed most pleasantly, for in my host I found not only an accomplished Oriental scholar and a traveller to whom few regions of the habitable globe were unknown, but a genial friend and a warm sympathizer in my researches. Mr Cobham had studied Persian for some time with *Mushkín-Ḳalam*, one of the Behá'í exiles sent with Ṣubḥ-i-Ezel to Cyprus[1], and from him had learned much concerning the new religion. *Ṣubḥ-i-Ezel,* however, he had not seen; for *Mushkín-Ḳalam*, as was natural, had spoken only of Behá, and had entirely ignored the existence of a chief whose authority he disavowed.

On the following day (Thursday, March 20th, 1890) I bade farewell to Mr Cobham, and, after some six hours spent in a somewhat antiquated vehicle belonging to a loquacious Italian who had fought for Garibaldi, found myself at Famagusta, or rather its suburb Varoshia, where I met with a most cordial welcome from Captain and Lady Evelyn Young. Captain Young at once sent a message to *Ṣubḥ-i-Ezel's* son 'Abdu'l-'Alí (who keeps a shop in Varoshia) requesting him to come to the *ḳonáḳ*. In a short time he appeared; and I was much struck by the refinement of his manner, the intelligence revealed by his countenance and conversation, and the courteousness of his address. Our conversation was conducted in Persian, which, though he had never been in Persia, he spoke as his mother-tongue. It was soon arranged that I should visit *Ṣubḥ-i-Ezel* on the following day at whatever time he should appoint.

Next morning we received a message to the effect that *Ṣubḥ-i-Ezel* was prepared to receive us as soon as we could come. At about 11 a.m., therefore, Captain Young drove me into the town, which is situated about a mile from the suburb of Varoshia. As I had not entered within the walls of Famagusta on the preceding day I now saw for the first time the massive fortifications, the multitu-

[1] Concerning *Mushkín-Ḳalam* see B. i, p. 516; B. ii, pp. 994—995; and Note W at end.

dinous churches (whereof the number, as is currently reported by the inhabitants, equals the number of days in the year), and the desolate neglected streets of that most interesting relic of the Middle Ages. After Captain Young had transacted some other business we proceeded to *Ṣubḥ-i-Ezel's* abode, in the court-yard of which we were received by his sons 'Abdu'l-'Alí, Riẓván-'Alí, 'Abdu'l-Waḥíd, and Taḳí'u'd-Dín, and an old Bábí of Zanján who had settled in the island so as to be near his master. Accompanied by these (with the exception of the last-mentioned) we ascended to an upper room, where a venerable and benevolent-looking old man of about sixty years of age, somewhat below the middle height, with ample forehead on which the traces of care and anxiety were apparent, clear searching blue eyes, and long grey beard, rose and advanced to meet us. Before that mild and dignified countenance I involuntarily bowed myself with unfeigned respect; for at length my long-cherished desire was fulfilled, and I stood face to face with Mírzá Yaḥyá *Ṣubḥ-i-Ezel* ("the Morning of Eternity"), the appointed successor of the Báb, the fourth "Letter" of the "First Unity."

This my first interview was necessarily short and somewhat formal, for I had yet to win the confidence of *Ṣubḥ-i-Ezel* and induce him little by little to speak without reserve of those things whereof I so earnestly desired to hear. In this, thanks to the confidence with which Captain Young's kindness had already inspired *Ṣubḥ-i-Ezel*, and the very vivid picture of the chief actors in the Bábí movement, which, first derived from the perusal of Count Gobineau's work, had continued to glow and grow in my mind till it became almost as a part of my own personal experience, I was completely successful. During the fortnight which I spent at Famagusta I visited *Ṣubḥ-i-Ezel* daily, remaining with him as a rule from two or three o'clock in the afternoon until sunset. Lack of space forbids me from describing in detail and consecutive order the conversations which took place on these occasions. Note-book and pencil in hand I sat before him day by day; and every evening I returned to Varoshia with a rich store of new facts, most of which will be found recorded in the notes wherewith I have striven to illustrate or check the statements advanced in the following pages. Apart from the delight inseparable from successful research my stay at Famagusta was a very pleasant one, for from every one with whom I came in contact, but most of all from Captain and Lady Evelyn Young, I met with a kindness which I can never forget. Besides my visits to *Ṣubḥ-i-Ezel* in the afternoon I often spent some portion of the morning with his son 'Abdu'-l-'Alí, and we were sometimes joined by Riẓván 'Alí, or by one or other of the few Ezelís who have settled in Famagusta. During these conversations I learned many new facts of greater or less importance. The reserve which had at first been apparent in *Ṣubḥ-i-Ezel* gradually disappeared, and at each successive interview I found him more communicative. Although our conversation was chiefly on religious topics, and the history, biography, doctrine, and literature of the Bábís, other matters were occasionally discussed. Of the Báb and his first apostles and followers, as of his own life and adventures, *Ṣubḥ-i-Ezel* would speak freely, but concerning the origin of the schism which for him had been attended with such disastrous results, and all pertaining to Behá and the Behá'ís, he was most reticent, so that, perceiving this subject to be distasteful, I refrained for the most part from alluding to it. During these conferences *Ṣubḥ-i-Ezel's* sons were always present, though they hardly spoke in the presence of their father, towards whom they observed the utmost deference and respect.

Tea was always served in the Persian fashion, but tobacco in all forms was conspicuous by its absence, the Ezelís, unlike the Behá'ís, following the injunctions of the Báb in this matter. In the course of each visit, or sometimes when I was leaving the house, *Ṣubḥ-i-Ezel's* youngest son Taḳí'u'd-Dín, a pretty, graceful child about thirteen years of age, used to present me with a little bunch of roses or such other flowers as the modest garden attached to the house would afford. On my walk to and from Famagusta I was always accompanied by 'Abdu'l-'Alí and often by one of his brothers.

A few days after my arrival at Famagusta I wrote to Sir Henry Bulwer stating what was my object in desiring to examine the official records concerning the exiles which might be preserved at Nicosia, asking whether I might be permitted to do so, and forwarding the letter of recommendation given me by Sir Robert Biddulph. In response to my request Sir Henry Bulwer, having learnt that the shortness of my stay in the island made it difficult, if not impossible, for me to visit Nicosia, was kind enough to forward for my perusal all the more important papers bearing on the subject. All of these, therefore, I was able to examine at my leisure; and of all of them, with one exception, I received permission to make use. An abstract of the important facts and dates established by these documents will be found in Note W at the end of this book.

The fifth of April, which was the ultimate limit whereunto my stay in Cyprus could be protracted, unless I were prepared to postpone indefinitely my visit to Acre, came at last. On the morning of that day, therefore, having with great reluctance bade farewell to all my kind friends, I left Famagusta, and embarked the same afternoon at Larnaca on the Messageries steamer *Gironde.* I passed a pleasant evening with a Turkish official and a Syrian who were the only other passengers besides myself, and early next morning awoke to find myself at Beyrout.

As I had now but two weeks at my disposal ere I must again turn my face homewards I was naturally anxious to proceed as soon as possible to Acre, especially as I learned that should I fail to find a steamer bound directly for that port, three days at least would be consumed by the journey thither. It was, however, necessary for me first to obtain permission from the Bábí head-quarters; for though I could without doubt proceed to Acre if I so pleased without consulting any one's inclination save my own, it was certain that unless my journey had previously received the sanction of Behá it would in all probability result in naught but failure and disappointment. Now there reside at Beyrout, Port Said, and Alexandria (by one of which places all desirous of proceeding to Acre by sea must of necessity pass) Bábís of consequence to whom all desirous of visiting Behá must in the first instance apply. Should such application prove successful, the applicant is informed that he may proceed on his journey, and receives such instruction, advice, and assistance as may be necessary. To the Bábí agent at Beyrout (whose name I do not feel myself at liberty to mention) I had a letter of recommendation from one of his relatives with whom I had become acquainted in Persia. The first thing which I did on my arrival was to send a messenger to discover his abode. The messenger shortly returned, saying that he had indeed succeeded in finding the place indicated, but that the agent was absent from Beyrout. This was a most serious blow to my hopes, for time was against me, and every day was of vital importance. There was nothing for it, however, but to make the best of the matter, and I therefore went in person to the abode of the absent agent and presented myself to his deputy, who opened and attentively perused my letter of recommendation, and then informed me that his master was at Acre and was not expected back for ten days or a fortnight. In reply to my anxious enquiries as to how I had best proceed, he advised me to write a letter to his master explaining the state of the case, which letter, together with the letter of recommendation, he undertook to forward at once, as the post fortunately chanced to be leaving for Acre that very evening. I at once wrote as he directed, and then returned to my lodging with the depressing consciousness that at least five or six days must elapse ere I could receive an answer to my letter or start for Acre; that even if permission was granted (as no steamer appeared likely to be sailing) three more days would be spent in reaching my goal; and that consequently eight or nine days out of the fourteen still remaining to me would be wasted before I could even set foot in the land of my quest. Altogether I began to fear that the second part of my journey was likely to prove far less successful than the first.

Fortunately matters turned out much better than I expected. In the first place I made the acquaintance of Mr Eyres, the British Vice-Consul, whose kindness and hospitality did much to render my stay at Beyrout pleasant, and who, on learning that I wished to proceed to Acre, told me that he himself intended to start for Acre and Ḥaifa on the following Friday (April 11th), and that I might if I pleased accompany him. In the second place it occurred to me that I might save two or three days' delay by telegraphing to Acre so soon as my letter must, in the natural course of things, have reached its destination, and requesting a telegram in reply to inform me whether I might proceed thither. On Wednesday, April 9th, therefore, I sent a telegram to this effect. On Thursday evening, returning after sunset to my hotel from a ride in the hills, I was met with the welcome news that a Persian had called twice to see me during the afternoon stating that he had important business which would not brook delay, and that he had left a note for me which I should find upstairs. From this note, hurriedly scribbled in pencil on a scrap of paper, I learned that permission had been granted, and that I was free to start as soon as I pleased.

On receiving this intelligence my first action was to verify it beyond all doubt by calling at once on the deputy of the absent agent, whom I fortunately found at home. He congratulated me warmly on the happy issue of my affairs, and handed over to me the original telegram. It was laconic in the extreme, containing, besides the address, two words only:—"*Yatawajjahu 'l-musáfir*" ("Let the traveller approach"). He then informed me that as no steamer was starting for Acre I must of necessity proceed thither by land, and that the reason why he had been so anxious to communicate with me earlier was that the post left that day at sun-down and I might have accompanied it. I then told him of Mr Eyres' kind offer; which, as we agreed, was a most exceptional piece of good-fortune for me, inasmuch as he proposed to start on the following morning, and expected to reach Acre on April 13th.

After bidding farewell to the deputy-agent and thanking him for the effectual aid which he had rendered me, I visited Mr Eyres, and told him that I would accept his kind offer if I could obtain a horse and make the necessary arrangements for my journey on the following morning. He told me that he must start early, but that if I left Beyrout by mid-day I could easily overtake him at Sidon, where he would halt for the night; and he further placed at my disposal the services of one of his *ḳawwáṣes* to assist me in my preparations.

Next morning (Friday, April 11th) I was astir early, for there was much to be done. With the help of my friend Jemálu'd-Dín Bey of the Imperial Ottoman Bank, and the active co-operation of the *ḳawwáṣ* of the Consulate, all was at length satisfactorily arranged; and shortly after midday I found myself on a sturdy, good-looking, but somewhat indolent horse, with a *khurjín* (pair of saddle-bags) containing the most indispensable of my effects behind me, plodding along a sandy road bordered with cactus in the direction of Sidon, where (the road being fortunately easy to follow) I arrived without mishap at sun-down.

To speak of the delights of that three days' journey, the beauty of the scenery, the purity and fragrance of the soft spring air, the pleasant mid-day halts by some rippling stream or in some balmy grove, and the hospitable receptions accorded to me as Mr Eyres' travelling companion by those in whose houses we alighted at Sidon, Tyre, and Acre, would be to wander further than is permissible from the subject in hand. Suffice it to say that, thanks to Mr Eyres' kindness in allowing me to accompany him, a journey, which, if performed in solitude, would have lost more than half its charm, was rendered enjoyable in the highest degree. The last day was perhaps the most delightful of all, and I was greatly astonished on entering the Acre plain to behold a wealth of beautiful gardens and fragrant orange-groves such as I had little expected to find in what Behá has stigmatized as "the most desolate of countries" (*akhrabu'l-bilád*). I subsequently mentioned this feeling of surprise to the Bábís at Acre, who replied that had I seen it when Behá first came there nearly two and twenty years ago I should not have deemed the title misapplied, but that since he had dwelt there it had assumed this fair and comely aspect.

We entered Acre towards sun-down on April 13th, and, wending our way through the fine bazaars, on the smooth stone pavement of which our horses' hoofs slipped as on ice, alighted at the house of a Christian merchant named Ibrahím Khúrí, who accorded to us the usual hospitable reception. That same evening I sent a note to the Bábí agent, which was brought back by the messenger unopened, with the disagreeable news that my mysterious correspondent had gone to Ḥaifá with Behá's eldest son 'Abbás Efendí. This was most unwelcome information; for as Mr Eyres was leaving the next day for Ḥaifá, and I did not wish to trespass further on the hospitality of Ibrahím Khúrí, it was absolutely essential that I should obtain help from the Bábís in finding other quarters. Evidently there was nothing for it but to wait for the morrow and what it might bring forth.

Next morning I enquired if there was any representative of the absent agent who might be cognizant of his movements, and was conducted to a shop in the bazaar, where I found a tall handsome youth clothed entirely in white save for his red fez, from beneath which a mass of glossy black hair swept back behind his ears, at the lower level of which it terminated[1]. This youth, accosting me in Turkish, enquired first somewhat haughtily what might be my business. I answered him in Persian, whereat he appeared surprised; and, after hearing what I had to say, bade me follow him. He led me to a house situated near the seashore, at the door of which we were met by an old Persian

[1] Concerning the characteristic manner in which the Bábís arrange their hair, cf. B. i. pp. 499—500. The wearing of pure white garments was from the first another special feature of theirs. Thus we learn from the *Táríkh-i-Jadíd* that the defenders of Sheykh Ṭabarsí used to issue forth to attack their foes clad in pure white raiment and crying out "*Yá Ṣáḥibu'z-Zamán*" ("O Lord of the Age!").

with long grizzled hair and beard, whose scrutinizing gaze was rendered more rather than less formidable by an enormous pair of spectacles. This man, after conversing for a few moments with my guide in an under tone, led me into a large room devoid of all furniture save a sort of bench or divan which ran round its four sides. I had scarcely seated myself when another Persian, evidently superior in authority to the other two, entered and saluted me. He was a man of middle height and middle age, with a keen and not unpleasing countenance, whereof the lower part was concealed by a short crisp beard. After bidding me reseat myself (for I had of course risen on his entrance) and ordering his servant (for such, I discovered, was the old man who had met me at the door) to give me a cup of coffee, he proceeded to subject me to a most minute cross-examination as to my nationality, my occupation, my travels in Persia, the objects of my present journey, and the like. My answers appeared to satisfy him; and when he had finished his questioning he asked me what I proposed to do. I told him that I would be guided entirely by his advice. He then asked me whether I would proceed to Ḥaifá, where I was certain to find the agent whom I sought with Behá's son 'Abbás Efendí. To this I replied that as I had but a few days at my disposal, and as Acre and not Ḥaifá was the goal of my journey, I would rather remain than depart. "In that case," said he, "I myself will go to Ḥaifá this afternoon and bring back word tomorrow what you must do. Meanwhile will you remain where you stayed last night till I return?" I answered that I would rather not trespass further on a hospitality extended to me solely as Mr Eyres' friend, and that if he could suggest any other lodging for that night I should be glad. I was not, I added, exacting in the matter of comfort, and would be quite content with a caravansary.

He reflected for a few moments and then said, "Very well. If that be your wish you can stay here. I myself shall be absent, but I will give instructions that you shall be looked after. And after all it is only for one night: tomorrow I shall return, and we will, if God please, find you better quarters. When the consul departs for Ḥaifá do you also leave the house where you are staying and bring your effects here." I then took my leave with many expressions of gratitude, and occupied myself during the remainder of the morning in packing my saddle-bags and making arrangements for the stabling of my horse during the time I expected to remain at Acre.

After lunch Mr Eyres departed for Ḥaifá, and I, quitting Ibrahím Khurí's abode, found someone to carry my effects to the house which I had visited in the morning. Here I was received by a sharp-looking boy of about fourteen, who proved to be the son of my interlocutor of the morning, to whom also, as I subsequently discovered, the house which I had now entered belonged. I had expected to receive but the roughest accommodation, the resources of the house being in nowise revealed by the room on the ground-floor where I had been received in the morning. My experience of the hospitality of the Persians in general and the Bábís in particular, and the deceptive exteriors of Oriental houses, might, it is true, have led me to expect tolerable comfort, but could hardly have prepared me for the positive luxury which the thoughtful kindness of my host had provided. During the afternoon I was entertained by my host's son, who showed that admirable courtesy and *savoir faire* with which even quite young Persian boys are capable, in the absence of their elders, of receiving the stranger and doing the honours of the house. As it was Easter Monday the street outside was filled with Syrian Christians, who continued so long as daylight lasted to express their joy in howls, gun-shots, and wild dances, at which we looked on in amazement from the window. A more remarkable and discordant expression of religious fervour it has never been my lot to witness. Towards the latter part of the afternoon my host's son, thinking, I suppose, that I needed further amusement, took me to see an itinerant Greek photographer who was temporarily established in a sort of cellar in the basement of the house. This Greek spoke French tolerably well, and seemed an honest, kindly fellow. He was very anxious to make out that I was a free-mason, and importuned me greatly to tell him the names of the pillars of Solomon's temple. Dim recollections of some book purporting to expose the secrets of that cult prompted me to seek escape from his pertinacity by suggesting "Boaz," whereupon nothing would serve him but I must tell him the name of the other. As I had forgotten this, and begun to weary of the subject, I took my leave.

Towards evening I received another visitor, whose mien and bearing alike marked him as a person of consequence. He was a man of perhaps thirty or thirty-five years of age, with a face which called to one's mind the finest types of Iranian physiognomy preserved to us in the bas-reliefs of Persepolis, yet with something in it beyond this, which involuntarily called forth in my mind the thought, "What would not an artist desirous of painting a saint or an apostle give for such a model!" My visitor (who, as I afterwards discovered, was a son of Behá's deceased brother Músá) was clothed, save for the tall red fez which crowned his head, entirely in pure white; and everything about him, from his short well-trimmed beard and the masses of jet-black hair swept boldly back behind his ears, to the hem of his spotless garment, was characterized by the same scrupulous neatness. He saluted me very graciously, and remained conversing with me all the evening. Shortly after supper he bade me good-night, saying that I must doubtless be fatigued with my journey. I was then conducted by my host's son and the old servant to the room where I had spent the afternoon, where, to my astonishment, I found that a bed provided with the most efficient mosquito-curtains and furnished with fair white sheets and soft mattress had been prepared for me. The arrangement of the mosquito-curtains (called by my new friends *námúsí*) was such as I had not previously seen, and, as it appeared to me perfect in simplicity and efficiency, I shall describe it for the benefit of other travellers. The *námúsí*, then, consists of what may most easily be described as a large box or small chamber of muslin, rectangular in shape, greater in length than in breadth, and furnished with a single funnel-shaped aperture in one of its sides. This muslin chamber is suspended by its corners by cords attached to the wall, and is entered through the funnel-shaped aperture, the mouth of which is encircled by a cord. The bed is laid inside, its component parts being introduced one by one. The occupant on entering draws tight the constricting cord, and is thereby completely cut off from the attacks of gnats, mosquitoes, and the like. The whole structure can, when not in use, be folded up into a very small compass.

I arose next morning (Tuesday, April 14th) after a most refreshing sleep, and was served with tea by the old man with the spectacles. Soon after this a sudden stir without announced the arrival of fresh visitors, and a moment after my companion of the previous evening entered the room accompanied by two other persons, one of whom proved to be the Bábí agent from Beyrout, while the other, as I guessed from the first by the extraordinary deference shewn to him by all present, was none other than Behá's eldest son 'Abbás

Efendí. Seldom have I seen one whose appearance impressed me more. A tall strongly-built man holding himself straight as an arrow, with white turban and raiment, long black locks reaching almost to the shoulder, broad powerful forehead indicating a strong intellect combined with an unswerving will, eyes keen as a hawk's, and strongly-marked but pleasing features—such was my first impression of 'Abbás Efendí, "the master" (*Áḳá*) as he *par excellence* is called by the Bábís. Subsequent conversation with him served only to heighten the respect with which his appearance had from the first inspired me. One more eloquent of speech, more ready of argument, more apt of illustration, more intimately acquainted with the sacred books of the Jews, the Christians, and the Muhammadans, could, I should think, scarcely be found even amongst the eloquent, ready, and subtle race to which he belongs. These qualities, combined with a bearing at once majestic and genial, made me cease to wonder at the influence and esteem which he enjoyed even beyond the circle of his father's followers. About the greatness of this man and his power no one who had seen him could entertain a doubt.

In this illustrious company did I partake of the mid-day meal. Soon after its conclusion 'Abbás Efendí and the others arose with a prefatory "*Bismi'lláh*," and signified to me that I should accompany them, which I did, without having any idea whither we were going. I observed, however, that the saddle-bags containing my effects were carried after us by one of those present; from which I concluded that I was not intended to remain in my present quarters. We left the house, traversed the bazaars, and quitted the town by its solitary gate. Outside this gate near the sea is a large shed which serves as a coffee-house, and here we seated ourselves, my companions evidently awaiting the arrival of something or somebody from a large mansion half-hidden in a grove of trees situated about a mile or a mile and a half inland, towards which they continually directed their glances. While we were waiting thus, a weird-looking old man, who proved to be none other than the famous *Mushkín-Ḳalam*[1], came and seated himself beside us. He told me that he had heard all about me from a relation of his at Isfahán (that same *dallál* who had been the means of my first introduction to the Bábí community[2]), and that he had been expecting to see me at Acre ever since that time.

Presently we discerned advancing towards us along the road from the mansion above mentioned three animals, one of which was ridden by a man. Thereupon we arose and went to meet them; and I soon found myself mounted on one of those fine white asses which, in my opinion, are of all quadrupeds the most comfortable to ride. A quarter of an hour later we alighted in front of the large mansion aforesaid, whereof the name, *Behjé* (Joy), is said to be a corruption (though, as the Bábís do not fail to point out, a very happy corruption) of *Bághcha* (which signifies a garden). I was almost immediately conducted into a large room on the ground-floor, where I was most cordially received by several persons whom I had not hitherto seen. Amongst these were two of Behá's younger sons, of whom one was apparently about twenty-five and the other about twenty-one years of age. Both were handsome and distinguished enough in appearance, and the expression of the younger was singularly sweet and winning. Besides these a very old man with light blue eyes and white beard, whose green turban proclaimed him a descendant of the Prophet, advanced to welcome me, saying, "We know not how we

1 See B. i, p. 516, B. ii, p. 994, and Note W at the end of this book.

2 See B. i, p. 487 *et seq*.

should greet thee, whether we should salute thee with '*as-selámu 'aleykum*' or with '*Alláhu abhá*[1].'" When I discovered that this venerable old man was not only one of the original companions of the Báb but his relative and comrade from earliest childhood, it may well be imagined with what eagerness I gazed upon him and listened to his every utterance.

So here at *Behjé* was I installed as a guest, in the very midst of all that Bábíism accounts most noble and most holy; and here did I spend five most memorable days, during which I enjoyed unparalleled and unhoped-for opportunities of holding intercourse with those who are the very fountain-heads of that mighty and wondrous spirit which works with invisible but ever-increasing force for the transformation and quickening of a people who slumber in a sleep like unto death. It was in truth a strange and moving experience, but one whereof I despair of conveying any save the feeblest impression. I might, indeed, strive to describe in greater detail the faces and forms which surrounded me, the conversations to which I was privileged to listen, the solemn melodious reading of the sacred books, the general sense of harmony and content which pervaded the place, and the fragrant shady gardens whither in the afternoon we sometimes repaired; but all this was as nought in comparison with the spiritual atmosphere with which I was encompassed. Persian Muslims will tell you often that the Bábís bewitch or drug their guests so that these, impelled by a fascination which they cannot resist, become similarly affected with what the aforesaid Muslims regard as a strange and incomprehensible madness. Idle and absurd as this belief is, it yet rests on a basis of fact stronger than that which supports the greater part of what

[1] *i.e.* with the salutation ordinarily used by the Muhammadans, or with that peculiar to the Bábís.

they allege concerning this people. The spirit which pervades the Bábís is such that it can hardly fail to affect most powerfully all subjected to its influence. It may appal or attract: it cannot be ignored or disregarded. Let those who have not seen disbelieve me if they will; but, should that spirit once reveal itself to them, they will experience an emotion which they are not likely to forget.

Of the culminating event of this my journey some few words at least must be said. During the morning of the day after my installation at *Behjé* one of Behá's younger sons entered the room where I was sitting and beckoned to me to follow him. I did so, and was conducted through passages and rooms at which I scarcely had time to glance to a spacious hall, paved, so far as I remember (for my mind was occupied with other thoughts) with a mosaic of marble. Before a curtain suspended from the wall of this great ante-chamber my conductor paused for a moment while I removed my shoes. Then, with a quick movement of the hand, he withdrew, and, as I passed, replaced the curtain; and I found myself in a large apartment, along the upper end of which ran a low divan, while on the side opposite to the door were placed two or three chairs. Though I dimly suspected whither I was going and whom I was to behold (for no distinct intimation had been given to me), a second or two elapsed ere, with a throb of wonder and awe, I became definitely conscious that the room was not untenanted. In the corner where the divan met the wall sat a wondrous and venerable figure, crowned with a felt head-dress of the kind called *táj* by dervishes (but of unusual height and make), round the base of which was wound a small white turban. The face of him on whom I gazed I can never forget, though I cannot describe it. Those piercing eyes seemed to read one's very soul; power and authority sat on that ample brow; while the deep lines on the forehead and face implied an age which the jet-black hair and beard flowing down in indistinguishable luxuriance almost to the waist seemed to belie. No need to ask in whose presence I stood, as I bowed myself before one who is the object of a devotion and love which kings might envy and emperors sigh for in vain!

A mild dignified voice bade me be seated, and then continued:—"Praise be to God that thou hast attained!... Thou hast come to see a prisoner and an exile..... We desire but the good of the world and the happiness of the nations; yet they deem us a stirrer up of strife and sedition worthy of bondage and banishment.... That all nations should become one in faith and all men as brothers; that the bonds of affection and unity between the sons of men should be strengthened; that diversity of religion should cease, and differences of race be annulled—what harm is there in this?... Yet so it shall be; these fruitless strifes, these ruinous wars shall pass away, and the 'Most Great Peace' shall come.... Do not you in Europe need this also? Is not this that which Christ foretold?... Yet do we see your kings and rulers lavishing their treasures more freely on means for the destruction of the human race than on that which would conduce to the happiness of mankind... These strifes and this bloodshed and discord must cease, and all men be as one kindred and one family.... Let not a man glory in this, that he loves his country; let him rather glory in this, that he loves his kind...."

Such, so far as I can recall them, were the words which, besides many others, I heard from Behá. Let those who read them consider well with themselves whether such doctrines merit death and bonds, and whether the world is more likely to gain or lose by their diffusion.

My interview lasted altogether about twenty minutes,

and during the latter part of it Behá read a portion of that epistle (*lawḥ*) whereof the translation occupies the last paragraph on p. 70 and the greater part of p. 71 of this book.

During the five days spent at *Behjé* (Tuesday, April 15th to Sunday, April 20th), I was admitted to Behá's presence four times. These interviews always took place an hour or two before noon, and lasted from twenty minutes to half-an-hour. One of Behá's sons always accompanied me, and once Áḳá Mírzá Aḳá Ján (*Jenáb-i-Khádimu' lláh*)[1] the amanuensis (*kátib-i-áyát*) was also present. In their general features these interviews resembled the first, of which I have attempted to give a description. Besides this, one afternoon I saw Behá walking in one of the gardens which belong to him. He was surrounded by a little group of his chief followers. How the journey to and from the garden was accomplished I know not: probably under cover of the darkness of night.

At length the last day to which my departure could possibly be deferred if I were to reach Cambridge ere the expiration of my leave arrived. Loath as I was to go, there was no help for it; and reluctantly enough I declined the pressing invitations to prolong my stay which the kindness of my friends prompted them to utter. Finding that I was bent on departure, and that I could not remain longer without running a great risk of breaking my promise, they ceased to try to dissuade me from going, and, with most considerate kindness, strove to make such arrangements for my return journey as might most conduce to my comfort. In spite of all my assurances that I could easily return by myself, it was settled that the Bábí agent of Beyrout should accompany me thither. I was very un-

[1] See B. i, p. 519; and pp. 355, n. 2, 358, and 360—362 *infra*.

willing to put him to such inconvenience, but was finally compelled to accede to this arrangement, which, of course, made the return journey far pleasanter than it would otherwise have been.

In the course of a conversation which took place soon after my arrival I had expressed a strong desire to become better acquainted with the later history of the Bábí movement, adding that the only history written in a friendly and sympathetic spirit which I had seen was the *Táríkh-i-Jadíd*, and that this only carried the narrative down to the year A.D. 1850. In reply I was told that a concise and authentic history carried down almost to the present day had been compiled[1]; and that same day this book, of which the text and translation are now published, was placed in my hands. I did not at first understand that this was a gift, for many books were lent to me to read in my room; and consequently I spent much time which, as the event turned out, might have been more profitably employed, in copying out what I deemed the more important passages of the work in question. When, at the moment of my departure, I offered to return the book, I was told that it was a gift which I might take with me in remembrance of my visit; whereat I rejoiced greatly. Besides this I received a fine MS. copy of the *Iḳán* written by the same scribe, "*the Letter Zá*"[2]; for I had mentioned incidentally that the copy of that work which I had obtained in Persia had unfortunately suffered damages which rendered many passages almost illegible.

At length the moment of departure came, and, after taking an affectionate farewell of my kind friends, I once

[1] For a fuller account of the circumstances which led to the compilation of this history see that portion of Note A which is devoted to the *Táríkh-i-Jadíd* (pp. 194—195 *infra*).

[2] See Note Z at end.

more turned my face towards Beyrout. I was accompanied by the Bábí agent; and a servant, who, left fatherless in childhood by one of the Bábí persecutions in Persia, had since remained in the household of Behá, went with us as far as Tyre. I have seldom seen one whose countenance and conversation revealed a more complete contentment with his lot. That night we slept in a caravansaray at Tyre. Next day the servant bade us farewell and turned back towards Acre, while we continued on our way, and shortly after sunset passed through the beautiful gardens which surround Sidon, that fairest and most fragrant of Syria's cities. Here we alighted at the house of a Bábí of Yezd, whose kindly hospitality formed a pleasant contrast to our somewhat dreary lodgings of the previous night.

On the evening of the following day (Tuesday, April 22nd) we entered Beyrout, and halted for a while to rest and refresh ourselves with tea at the house of a Bábí of Baghdad which was situated in the outskirts of the town. This man had as a child gone with his father to Persia in the hope of seeing the Báb. This he was unable to do, the Báb being at that time confined in the fortress of Chihríḳ, but at Teherán he had seen Mullá Ḥuseyn of Bushraweyh. I asked him what manner of man Mullá Ḥuseyn was. "Lean and fragile to look at," he answered, "but keen and bright as the sword which never left his side. For the rest, he was not more than thirty or thirty-five years old, and his raiment was white."

Next day soon after sun-down, the last farewells said, and the precious MSS. carefully concealed about me, I was borne swiftly out of Beyrout harbour by the Egyptian steamer *Raḥmániyya*. Eight days later, on Thursday, May 1st, I was back in Cambridge. So ended a most interesting, most successful, and most pleasant journey.

Shortly after my return to Cambridge I addressed a note to the Syndicate of the University Press, stating in brief outline the course and results of the investigations which had occupied me during the last three years, and my desire to place before the world some portion of these results by publishing the text and translation of one or other of the two Bábí histories which I had obtained. Of these two histories I briefly discussed the respective merits, adding that, although the text of the *Táríkh-i-Jadíd* only awaited collation with the British Museum MS., while the translation thereof was far advanced towards completion, this newer history, owing to its comparatively small bulk, could probably be got ready for publication quite as soon as the larger work, while the MS. of it which I had obtained, being accurate, well written, and, to the best of my knowledge, unique in Europe, might, with perfect propriety, be reproduced in *fac-simile* by some process of photo-lithography. In reply to my application, I was presently informed that the Syndicate was prepared to accept and publish the smaller work so soon as it should be ready, while the expediency of publishing the larger *Táríkh-i-Jadíd* was deferred for future consideration. On learning the favourable result of my application I at once applied myself vigorously to the work of translation and annotation, and by the end of July 1890 the first proof-sheets were already before me. As it had been decided that the text should be reproduced by photo-lithography, I had no anxiety on that score; and the excellence of the *facsimile* produced in the workshops of the Cambridge Engraving Company under the careful supervision of Mr Dew-Smith of Trinity College, will, I am confident, more than reconcile the Persian scholar to the necessity of dealing with a lithographed instead of a printed text.

It remains for me to speak briefly of the peculiarities of this history both as regards tone and style. As to the former, the chief features which will strike the attentive reader are :—

(1) The quite secondary importance accorded to the Báb, whose mission is throughout depicted as a mere preparation for the fuller and more perfect dispensation of Behá. In like manner the deeds and sufferings of the early apostles of Bábíism are passed over very lightly, and many of the most remarkable events of the older dispensation (such as the deaths of the 'Seven Martyrs[1],' and the great massacre at Teherán in 1852 which Renan[2] calls "un jour sans pareil peut-être dans l'histoire du monde") are almost or quite unnoticed. The martyrdoms of Mírzá Badí'[3] and the two Seyyids of Isfahán[4], which belong to the new dispensation, are, on the other hand, treated of very fully.

(2) Mírzá Yaḥyá *Ṣubḥ-i-Ezel* is throughout depicted as a person of no consequence, enjoying for a while a merely nominal supremacy, bestowed upon him, not for any special merit or capacity, but out of regard for certain considerations of expediency[5]. No opportunity is lost of disparaging both his courage and his judgement[6], and of contrasting him in these respects with Behá, who is everywhere described as the true and legitimate chief.

(3) Towards the Sháh of Persia an extraordinarily temperate tone is observed, and in several places apologies are put forward for his justification, the blame for the cruelties inflicted on the Bábís being thrown either on his

[1] See Note B at end.

[2] *Les Apôtres*, p. 378. See also Note T at end.

[3] See pp. 102—106 *infra*.

[4] See pp. 167—169 and 400 *et seq. infra*, and B. i, pp. 489—491.

[5] Cf. pp. 62—63 *infra*.

[6] Cf. pp. 51—52; 63—64; 89—90; and 93—101 *infra*.

ministers and courtiers, or on the Muhammadan doctors, who are repeatedly and strongly denounced[1].

(4) The resistance opposed to the government by the earlier Bábís is deprecated even when evoked by the most wanton acts of aggression and cruelty[2], the attempt on the Sháh's life in particular being alluded to with the utmost horror[3]; and it is implied that, although the Báb's precepts were altogether those of peace, the stronger will and influence of Behá were needed to give them actual currency[4].

The chief peculiarities presented by the style of this work are as follows:—

(1) A remarkable terseness and concision rare in Persian.

(2) An unusual preponderance of the Arabic element, and the frequent employment of many uncommon Arabic words.

(3) An abundant use of the past participle in place of the past tense where we should expect the latter. A good instance of this peculiarity occurs in the first five lines of p. 3 of the text. Of these three peculiarities the second and third are noticed by Gobineau (*Religions et Philosophies*, p. 312) as characteristic of the Bábí style in general. He says:—"C'est un persan où il ne paraît presque que des mots arabes choisis parmi les plus relevés et les plus rares, et où se combinent les formes grammaticales des deux langues de manière à exercer singulièrement la sagacité et, il faut le dire aussi, la patience des lecteurs dévots et confiants. Suivant un usage, qui est du reste assez reçu dans les ouvrages philosophiques, les verbes persans employés se présentent presque toujours sous la

[1] Cf. pp. 20, 32—33, 34—35, 40—41, 52, and 104—106 *infra*.
[2] Cf. p. 35 *infra*.
[3] See pp. 49—51 *infra*.
[4] Cf. pp. 65—69 *infra*.

forme concrète de participes passés, afin de ressembler autant que possible à des verbes arabes."

(4) A very noticeable tendency to omit the Persian auxiliary verb after Arabic participles, whether active or passive, and generally speaking to restrict the employment of the verb as much as possible. The following instances (and the like will be found almost on every page) will suffice to illustrate this feature:—

(On p. 1, last line, and p. 2, first line):—چون این روایات مختلفه در سایر اوراق مذکور و بیانش سبب تطویل لهذا الخ—"Now since these various accounts [are] recorded in other pages, and [since] the setting forth thereof [would be] the cause of prolixity, therefore"...etc.

(On p. 39, last line, and p. 40, first line):—باری ایران در این بحران و علمای اعلام حیران و پریشان که خاقان مغفور محمد شاه مرحوم شد *—"Well, Persia [was] in this critical state and the learned doctors perplexed and anxious, when the late Prince Muḥammad Sháh died."

(On p. 43, last line, and p. 44, first three lines):—تصور و افکارشان بقرار سابق و سلوك و رفتارشان بر حسب قدیم مطابق طریق وصول بباب نیز مسدود و اتش فتنه از هر جهت شعله‌ور و مشهود *—"Their conceptions and ideas [were] after the former fashion, and their conduct and behaviour in correspondence with ancient usage. The way of approach to the Báb [was], moreover, closed, and the flame of trouble visibly blazing on every side."

(5) Two peculiar idioms common to all Bábí compositions remain to be noticed. The *first* of these is the continual use of چه که in the sense of "for," to the almost complete exclusion of چرا که، زیرا, or the simple چه, which are commonly employed in other works. The *second* is the combination of the past and the present or the past and future tenses in general assertions (an idiom which is even more common in the writings of the Báb than in those of Behá). Of this usage the following instances may be cited from the present work:—

(At the bottom of p. 141):—چه که آن سلطان بی مثال لا زال مقدس از صعود و نزول بوده و خواهد بود * ..."for that Peerless King *hath been and will be* for everlasting Holy above ascent or descent."

(In the sentence at the top of p. 142 which follows the above):—پس معنیء نصرت الیوم اعتراض بر احدی و مجادله با نفسی نبوده و نخواهد بود *—"Therefore to-day victory *neither hath been nor will be* interference with any one, nor strife with any person."

The peculiarities of style affected by the Báb have for the most part received the sanction of Behá, and are copied with greater or less fidelity by the majority of Bábís, so that one familiar with them might often succeed in recognizing a letter or other document as of Bábí authorship.

It remains for me to say a few words as to the principles which have guided me in my own work, viz. the translation and notes. As regards the former, I have taken as my guide the canon laid down by the late Dr William Wright, whose death, mourned by all as an irreparable loss, was to such as were like myself privileged to listen to his teaching and feel the genial influence of his constant and unvarying kindness and encouragement, the saddest of bereavements. This canon he states as follows (*Chronicle of Joshua the Stylite*, Cambridge, 1882, pp. vi—vii of the Preface):—"In my translation I have striven to be as literal as the difference between the two idioms will allow. My method is first to translate as closely as I can, and then to try if I can improve the form of expression in any way without the sacrifice of truthfulness to the original. I also endeavour to preserve a somewhat antiquated and Biblical style, as being peculiarly adapted to the rendering into English of Oriental works, whether poetical or historical. The Old Testament and the Ḳo'rân, which are, of course, in many ways strikingly similar in their diction, can both be easily made ridiculous by turning them into our modern vernacular, particularly if we vulgarize with malice prepense." Now though I cannot flatter myself that I have succeeded in making my translation of this history very eloquent English, I can at least conscientiously declare that I have spared no pains to reproduce faithfully not only the thought but also the style and diction of my author. The desire to give a correct impression of the original has even led me to preserve the Persian idiom where a slight alteration would have improved the English. An instance of this occurs in the very first sentence on p. 1, where "on the lips" would undoubtedly have been better English than "on the tongues." Throughout my translation I have unhesitatingly preferred fidelity to elegance; and, even if I have gone too far in this, I trust that at least the English reader will obtain a clearer idea of the peculiarities of the original than would otherwise have been possible. Words of constant recurrence have been, so far as possible, rendered by the same English equivalent, which, according to the canon above referred to, often bears the meaning which it has in the Bible rather than that which is given to it in ordinary usage. Thus by "lawyers" (فقهاء) are intended the expounders of the Sacred Books and of the Law therein contained, and by "doctors" (علماء) those learned in theology and the kindred sciences.

As regards the notes with which I have endeavoured to elucidate, control, and amplify the text, they are of two kinds; foot-notes containing explanations necessary for the proper comprehension of the text, references, supplementary details or varying traditions of events recorded in the body of the work, brief notices of events intentionally or accidentally passed over, comments, and the like; and the final notes designated by capital letters, to which perhaps the term "Excursus" or "Appendix" might more fitly have been given. These latter have, I confess, grown to proportions far exceeding what I originally intended, for the printing of the translation was finished ere half of them was written, and ever as I wrote fresh scraps of information which I could not persuade myself to omit kept coming in. I cannot but feel that, partly in consequence of this, partly because of the very nature of my original plan, portions of my work will appear discursive, desultory, and disconnected, even if it be free (which I can scarcely hope) from contradictions and repetitions. But my aim and object has been chiefly to record, for the benefit of future historians, every fact which I have been able to learn, and every varying tradition which I have heard in Persia, Turkey, Syria, or Cyprus. In the case of divergent traditions I have, so far as was consistent with the safety of my informants, given the *isnád* or chain of authorities by which they reached me. When this could not be done, I have striven to give the reader some means of forming an estimate of the character of my informant. The office of the chronicler and collector of traditions is, in comparison with that of the historian, a humble one; yet the labours of the former are indispensable to those of the latter, and must precede them. The immense superiority of Ṭabarí to all other Oriental historians lies, as Professor Noeldeke observes, in this, that he was content to record the various traditions of diverse events which he learned from this one or that one without seeking prematurely to blend them into one harmonious narrative. Let the oldest traditions of any historical event once be gathered up, the credibility of their narrators being, as far as possible, determined, and the chronicle may without prejudice to itself await in patience, for centuries if need be, the magic touch of the true historian; but if once the old traditions be lost the loss can never be made good. Through a fortunate combination of circumstances unlikely to repeat itself I was placed in a singularly good position for gathering together Bábí traditions from sources many of which will in a few years be no longer available, and I was impatient to place on record the mass of information thus arduously acquired; so that now, as I write the last page of this work, I am conscious of a deep sense of relief and thankfulness that no obstacle has intervened to prevent the conclusion of my labours.

Of the bibliography of Bábíism a full account will be found in Note A at the end of the book; so that I need add nothing further on this subject. My first and second articles on the Bábís in the *J. R. A. S.* for 1889 (vol. xxi, new series, parts iii and iv) are, as already explained, respectively denoted throughout this work as "B. i," and "B. ii." When Gobineau is quoted, his work *Les Religions et les Philosophies dans l'Asie Centrale* (2nd edition, Paris, 1866) is referred to, unless otherwise specified. Mirza

Kazem-Beg's five articles on the Bábís in the *Journal Asiatique*, though all published in 1866, extend through two volumes of that periodical, each of which volumes has a separate pagination. For convenience and brevity, therefore, the first and second of these articles, included in vol. vii (*sixième série*) of the *Journal Asiatique*, are together denoted as "Kazem-Beg i," while the third, fourth, and fifth, contained in vol. viii, are called "Kazem-Beg ii." Any other works whereof the full titles are not given in the notes will be found described in detail in Note A.

Concerning the *fac-simile* of the text some few words are necessary. Thanks to the careful supervision of Mr A. G. Dew-Smith of Trinity College, for whose sympathetic and cordial co-operation I desire to express my warmest gratitude, this leaves little to be desired, reproducing faithfully the features of the original MS. In spite of all care, however, the reproduction of a letter or word here and there would in the first instance prove defective, while now and then points and dots not belonging to the original would creep in. Most of these defects have, I hope, been removed, every page having been subjected two or three times to a careful scrutiny. During this revision the original MS. was always before me, and only when it appeared that a defect observed in the proof already existed there has it been left untouched. In a word, so far as the text is concerned the object has been to reproduce, not to correct or emend. From this general rule, however, I have been compelled to deviate in certain special cases. Throughout the original MS. a somewhat erratic system of punctuation by means of red dots prevails. These red dots necessarily appeared as black dots in the *fac-simile*. Now and then it happened that, owing to their situation, they came to simulate diacritical points, thus creating a confusion, ambiguity, or unsightliness which was foreign to the original MS. In such cases I have considered myself justified in removing these marks of punctuation, but so far as possible they have been allowed to stand. The Persian title-page does not belong to the original, but was subsequently written at Acre by my request in black, and beautifully reproduced in colours by Mr Dew-Smith.

An investigation such as that whereof the course has been above detailed can be brought to a successful issue only by the co-operation and assistance of many persons, without whose kindly aid the desired information could not be obtained. To each and all of those to whose aid I am thus indebted I have striven, even at the risk of repetition, to express my indebtedness as occasion arose. It only remains for me to tender my most sincere thanks to such of my friends as have assisted me in the actual preparation of the work. In the tedious work of revising the proof-sheets I have received most efficient and valuable help from Mr R. A. Neil of this College. To the kindness and learning of Professor Robertson Smith, of Christ's College, and Mr A. A. Bevan, of Trinity College, I am indebted for many suggestions and corrections. To the rare generosity of Baron Victor Rosen of St Petersburg in allowing me to make full and free use of still unpublished work I have had occasion to refer repeatedly in the course of my notes. Lastly, I desire to express my gratitude to the Syndics of the University Press for that liberal assistance without which the publication of this work might have been indefinitely postponed.

ADDENDA.

On p. 132 add the following note to the first sentence of the last paragraph:—In K. the word غیر has been inserted above the line before the words از این طائفه. If we accept this reading (which is, however, unsupported by Rosen's as by the present text) the sentence will translate as follows:—"They have misrepresented matters before the presence of the King in such a way that if any ill deed proceed from anyone not of this sect they account him as [a follower] of the religion of these servants."

On p. 138, l. 5, add the following note after "*Book*":—K., supported by Rosen's text, inserts a sentence whereof this is the translation:—"Some men, when they are unable to answer their opponent, lay hold of the rope of textual corruption; whereas mention of textual corruption occurs [only] in special passages." This Persian sentence, if admitted, would seem to come more naturally at the end of the passage in Persian (omitted in the present text, translated in the foot-notes on pp. 137—138) than where it stands at present in the midst of a piece of Arabic. As regards sequence of ideas, too, it would be much more appropriately placed there than in its present position, where it has no obvious connection with the context.

On p. 141, ll. 5—6, add the following note:—K., as well as Rosen's text, reads "*we have sprinkled*" instead of "*we have made manifest.*"

On p. 142, l. 20, add the following note:—Rosen's text agrees with K. in reading مشهوره (*celebrated, notorious*) instead of مشهوده (*apparent, evident*).

NOTA BENE.

Passages of which the original is in Arabic are printed in italics in the translation. Words supplied to complete the sense are enclosed in square brackets.

CORRIGENDA.

Baron Rosen has kindly called my attention to the following errors:—

On p. 69, n. 1, and again, in a yet more definite manner, on pp. 208 and 211, I have committed the inexcusable blunder of confounding Behá'u'lláh's earlier *Súratu'l-Mulúk* with his later *Alwáḥ-i-Saláṭín*. The former only is described by Baron Rosen in the *first* volume of the *Collections Scientifiques*, and what is there written bears no reference whatever to the *Súra-i-Heykal* or the *Alwáḥ-i-Saláṭín* comprised in it. The MS. described by Baron Rosen on pp. 145—243 of the forthcoming *sixth* volume of the *Collections Scientifiques* contains a series of Behá'u'lláh's writings. The first of these pieces is the *Súratu'l-Mulúk* (previously described in the first volume of the *Collections Scientifiques*) concerning the authorship of which I expressed my doubts on pp. 954—8 of my second article in the *J. R. A. S.* for 1889. In reply to my objections Baron Rosen proves quite conclusively (*Collections Scientifiques*, vol. vi, pp. 145—8) that the *Súratu'l-Mulúk* was written by Behá'u'lláh, and that it was, moreover, written at an earlier date than the *Alwáḥ-i-Saláṭín*. The same MS. contains also the *Súra-i-Heykal* (including, of course, the *Alwáḥ-i-Saláṭín*), and it is of *this* that the full text will appear in vol. vi of the *Collections Scientifiques*. The *Súratu'l-Mulúk* appears to have been written about the end of the Baghdad period, *i.e.* about A.D. 1864; the *Alwáḥ-i-Saláṭín* (or at least the Epistle to the King of Persia, which is the longest and most important of them) during the latter days of the Adrianople period (*cf.* pp. 102, and 119, n. 1 *supra*), *i.e.* about July 1868. The reader is therefore requested to make the following corrections. On p. 69, n. 1, l. 4, for "سورهٔ هيكل" read "سورة الملوك." On p. 208, l. 27, for "a copy of Behá's *Súra-i-Heykal*" read "a copy of Behá's *Súratu'l-Mulúk*," and delete what follows down to the end of l. 2 on p. 209, as well as n. 2 on p. 208. On p. 211, l. 5, for "(or سورهٔ هيكل)" read "and the سورهٔ هيكل."

A TRAVELLER'S NARRATIVE

WRITTEN TO ILLUSTRATE

THE EPISODE OF THE BÁB.

TOUCHING the individual known as the Báb and p. 1.
the true nature of this sect diverse tales are on the tongues and in the mouths of men, and various accounts are contained in the pages of Persian history and the leaves of European chronicles[1]. But because of the variety of their assertions and the diversity of their narratives not one is as worthy of confidence as it should be. Some have loosed their tongues in extreme censure and condemnation; some foreign chronicles have spoken in a commendatory strain; while a certain section have recorded what they themselves have heard without addressing themselves either to censure or approbation.

[1] See Note A at end.

p. 2. Now since these various accounts are recorded in other pages, and since the setting forth thereof would lead to prolixity, therefore what relates to the history of this matter (sought out with the utmost diligence during the time of my travels in all parts of Persia, whether far or near, from those without and those within, from friends and strangers), and that whereon the disputants are agreed, shall be briefly set forth in writing, so that a summary of the facts of the case may be at the disposal of those who are athirst after the fountain of knowledge and who seek to become acquainted with all events.

The Báb was a young merchant of the Pure Lineage[1]. He was born in the year one thousand two hundred and thirty-five [A. H.] on the first day of Muḥarram[2], and when after a few years his father Seyyid Muḥammad Rizá died, he was brought up in
p. 3. Shíráz in the arms of his maternal uncle Mírzá Seyyid 'Alí[3] the merchant. On attaining maturity he engaged in trade in Bushire, first in partnership with his maternal uncle and afterwards independently. On account of what was observed in him he was noted for godliness, devoutness, virtue, and piety, and was regarded in the sight of men as so characterized.

[1] i.e. a Seyyid, or descendant of the family of the Prophet.

[2] October 20th, 1819 A.D. Cf. B. ii, p. 993; and B. i, p. 517–511.

[3] See Note B at end.

In the year one thousand two hundred and sixty [A. H.], when he was in his twenty-fifth year[1], certain signs became apparent in his conduct, behaviour, manners, and demeanour whereby it became evident in Shíráz that he had some conflict in his mind and some other flight beneath his wing. He began to speak and to declare the rank of Báb-hood. Now what he intended by the term *Báb*[2] [Gate] was this, that he was the channel of grace from some great Person still behind the veil of glory, who was the p. 4.
possessor of countless and boundless perfections, by whose will he moved, and to the bond of whose love he clung. And in the first book which he wrote in explanation of the *Súra of Joseph*[3], he addressed himself in all passages to that Person unseen from whom he received help and grace, sought for aid in the arrangement of his preliminaries, and craved the sacrifice of life in the way of his love.

Amongst others is this sentence: '*O Remnant of God*[4], *I am wholly sacrificed to Thee; I am content*

[1] Jamádí-ul-Úlá 5th, 1260 A.H. (May 23rd, 1844 A.D.) is the date given by the Báb himself in the Persian *Beyán* as that whereon his mission commenced. The texts referred to will be found quoted in Note C at end. Cf. also B. i, pp 507–508.

[2] See Note D at end.

[3] Ḳur'an xii. See Gobineau, pp. 146–147; Rosen *MSS. Arabes*, pp. 179–191; B. ii, pp. 904–909.

[4] See Kazem-Beg ii, p. 486 and note.

with curses in Thy way; I crave nought but to be slain in Thy love; and God the Supreme sufficeth as an Eternal Protection.'

He likewise composed a number of works in
explanation and elucidation of the verses of the
p. 5. Ḳur'án, of sermons, and of prayers in Arabic; inciting
and urging men to expect the appearance of that
Person; and these books he named 'Inspired Pages'
and 'Word of Conscience.' But on investigation it
was discovered that he laid no claim to revelation
from an angel.

Now since he was noted amongst the people for
lack of instruction and education, this circumstance
appeared in the sight of men supernatural. Some
men inclined to him, but the greater part manifested
strong disapproval; whilst all the learned doctors
and lawyers of repute who occupied chairs, altars,
and pulpits were unanimously agreed on eradication
and suppression, save some divines of the Sheykhí[1]
party who were anchorites and recluses, and who,
agreeably to their tenets, were ever seeking for
some great, incomparable, and trustworthy person,
p. 6. whom they accounted, according to their own terminology, as the '*Fourth Support*'[2] and the central

[1] See Gobineau, pp. 30–32; Kazem-Beg, pp. 457–464; B. ii, pp. 884–885 and pp. 888–892; and Note E at end.

[2] See Note E at end.

manifestation of the truths of the Perspicuous Religion[1].

Of this number Mullá Ḥuseyn of Bushraweyh, Mírzá Aḥmad of Azghand, Mullá Ṣádiḳ '*Muḳaddas*' ['the Holy'], Sheykh Abú Turáb of Ashtahárd, Mullá Yúsuf of Ardabíl, Mullá Jalíl of Urúmiyya, Mullá Mahdí of Kand, Sheykh Sa'íd the Indian, Mullá 'Alí of Bisṭám, and the like of these came out unto him and spread themselves through all parts of Persia[2].

The Báb himself set out to perform the circumambulation of the House of God[3]. On his return, when the news of his arrival at Bushire reached Shíráz, there was much discussion, and a strange excitement and agitation became apparent in that city. The great majority of the doctors set themselves to p. 7.
repudiate him, decreeing slaughter and destruction, and they induced Ḥuseyn Khán *Ajúdán-báshí*, who was the governor of Fárs, to inflict a beating on the Báb's missionaries, that is on Mullá Ṣádiḳ '*Muḳaddas*'; then, having burnt his moustaches and beard together with those of Mírzá Muḥammad 'Alí of Bárfurúsh and Mullá 'Alí Akbar of Ardistán,

[1] i.e. the religion of Islám.

[2] For a further account of some of these persons see Note F at end.

[3] i.e. the pilgrimage to Mecca. See Kazem-Beg i, p. 344 and note; and also Note G at end.

they put halters on all the three and led them round the streets and bazaars.

Now since the doctors of Persia have no administrative capacity, they thought that violence and interference would cause extinction and silence and lead to suppression and oblivion; whereas interference in matters of conscience causes stability and firmness and attracts the attention of men's sight and souls; which fact has received experimental proof many times and often. So this punishment caused notoriety,
p. 8. and most men fell to making enquiry.

The governor of Fárs, acting according to that which the doctors deemed expedient, sent several horsemen[1], caused the Báb to be brought before him, censured and blamed him in the presence of the doctors and scholars, and loosed his tongue in the demand for reparation. And when the Báb returned his censure and withstood him greatly, at a sign from the president they struck him a violent blow, insulting and contemning him, in such wise that his turban fell from his head and the mark of the blow was apparent on his face. At the conclusion of the meeting they decided to take counsel, and, on receiving bail and surety from his maternal uncle Hájí Seyyid 'Alí, sent him to his house forbidding him to hold intercourse with relations or strangers.

[1] See Note G at end, and Kazem-Beg i, pp. 346–348.

One day they summoned him to the mosque
urging and constraining him to recant, but he
discoursed from the pulpit in such wise as to silence
and subdue those present and to stablish and
strengthen his followers. It was then supposed that p. 9.
he claimed to be the medium of grace from His
Highness the Lord of the Age[1] (upon him be peace);
but afterwards it became known and evident that his
meaning was the Gate-hood [*Bábiyyat*] of another
city and the mediumship of the graces of another
person whose qualities and attributes were contained
in his books and treatises.

At all events, as has been mentioned, by reason
of the doctors' lack of experience and skill in administrative science, and the continual succession
of their decisions, comment was rife; and their
interference with the Báb cast a clamour throughout
Persia, causing increased ardour in friends and the
coming forward of the hesitating. For by reason of
these occurrences men's interest increased, and in
all parts of Persia some [of God's] servants inclined
toward him, until the matter acquired such import- p. 10.
ance that the late king Muḥammad Sháh delegated
a certain person named Seyyid Yaḥyá of Dáráb[2],
who was one of the best known of doctors and
Seyyids as well as an object of veneration and con-

[1] See Kazem-Beg i, p. 345 and note.

[2] See Note H at end.

fidence, giving him a horse and money for the journey so that he might proceed to Shíráz and personally investigate this matter.

When the above-mentioned Seyyid arrived at Shíráz he interviewed the Báb three times. In the first and second conferences questioning and answering took place; in the third conference he requested a commentary on the Súra called *Kawthar*[1], and when the Báb, without thought or reflection, wrote an elaborate commentary on the *Kawthar* in his presence, the above-mentioned Seyyid was charmed and enraptured with him, and straightway, without consideration for the future or anxiety about the results of this affection, hastened to Burújird to
p. 11. his father Seyyid Ja'far, known as *Kashfí*, and acquainted him with the matter. And, although he was wise and prudent and was wont to have regard to the requirements of the time, he wrote without fear or care a detailed account of his observations to Mírzá Luṭf 'Alí the chamberlain in order that the latter might submit it to the notice of the late king, while he himself journeyed to all parts of Persia, and in every town and station summoned the people from the pulpit-tops in such wise that other learned doctors decided that he must be mad, accounting it a sure case of bewitchment.

[1] Ḳur'án, cviii.

Now when the news of the decisions of the doctors and the outcry and clamour of the lawyers reached Zanján, Mullá Muḥammad 'Alí the divine[1], who was a man of mark possessed of penetrating speech, sent one of those on whom he could rely to Shíráz to investigate this matter. This person, having ac- p. 12.
quainted himself with the details of these occurrences in such wise as was necessary and proper, returned with some [of the Báb's] writings. When the divine heard how matters were and had made himself acquainted with the writings, notwithstanding that he was a man expert in knowledge and noted for profound research, he went mad and became crazed as was predestined: he gathered up his books in the lecture-room saying, "The season of spring and wine has arrived," and uttered this sentence:—"*Search for knowledge after reaching the known is culpable.*" Then from the summit of the pulpit he summoned and directed all his disciples [to embrace the doctrine], and wrote to the Báb his own declaration and confession.

The Báb in his reply signified to him the obligation of congregational prayer.

Although the doctors of Zanján arose with heart and soul to exhort and admonish the people they p. 13.
could effect nothing. Finally they were compelled to

[1] Full accounts of this remarkable man will be found in Gobineau (pp. 233–252) and Kazem-Beg ii (pp. 198–224).

go to Teherán and made their complaint before the late king Muḥammad Sháh, requesting that Mullá Muḥammad 'Alí might be summoned to Teherán. So the royal order went forth that he should appear.

Now when he came to Teherán they brought him before a conclave of the doctors; but, so they relate, after many controversies and disputations nought was effected with him in that assembly. The late king therefore bestowed on him a staff and fifty *túmáns*[1] for his expenses, and gave him permission to return.

At all events, this news being disseminated through all parts and regions of Persia, and several proselytes
p. 14. arriving in Fárs, the doctors perceived that the matter had acquired importance, that the power to deal with it had escaped from their hands, and that imprisonment, beating, tormenting, and contumely were fruitless. So they signified to the governor of Fárs, Ḥuseyn Khán, "If thou desirest the extinction of this fire, or seekest a firm stopper for this rent and disruption, an immediate cure and decisive remedy is to kill the Báb. And the Báb has assembled a great host and meditates a rising."

So Ḥuseyn Khán ordered 'Abdu'l-Ḥamíd Khán the high constable to attack the house of the Báb's

[1] At the present time this would be equivalent to about £15, but at the time referred to it would be considerably more —probably more than £20.

maternal uncle at midnight on all sides, and to bring him and all his followers hand-cuffed. But 'Abdu'l-Ḥamíd Khán and his hosts found no one in the house save the Báb, his maternal uncle, and Seyyid Kázim of Zanján; and as it chanced that on that night the sickness of the plague and the extreme heat of the p. 15.
weather had compelled Ḥuseyn Khán to flee, he released the Báb on condition of his quitting the city[1].

On the morning after that night the Báb with Seyyid Káẓim of Zanján set out from Shíráz for Isfahán. Before reaching Isfahán he wrote a letter to the *Mu'tamadu 'd-Dawla*, the governor of the province, requesting a lodging in some suitable place with the sanction of the government. The governor appointed the mansion of the Imám-Jum'a. There he abode forty days; and one day, agreeably to the request of the Imám, he wrote without reflection a commentary on [the Súra of] *Wa'l-'Aṣr*[2] before the company. When this news reached the *Mu'tamad* he sought an interview with him and questioned him concerning the 'Special Mission.' At that same interview an answer proving the 'Special Mission' was written[3].

The *Mu'tamad* then gave orders that all the p. 16.
doctors should assemble and dispute with him in one

[1] See Note I at end.
[2] Ḳur'án, ciii.
[3] See Note I at end.

conclave, and that the discussion should be faithfully recorded without alteration by the instrumentality of his private secretary, in order that it might be sent to Teherán, and that whatever the royal edict and decree should ordain might be carried out.

The doctors, however, considering this arrangement as a weakening of the Law, did not agree, but held a conclave and wrote, "If there be doubt in the matter there is need of assembly and discussion, but as this person's disagreement with the most luminous Law is clearer than the sun therefore the best possible thing is to put in practice the sentence of the Law."

The *Mu'tamad* then desired to hold the assembled conference in his own presence so that the actual truth might be disclosed and hearts be at peace, but these learned doctors and honourable scholars, p. 17. unwilling to bring the Perspicuous Law into contempt, did not approve discussion and controversy with a young merchant, with the exception of that most erudite sage Áḳá Muḥammad Mahdí, and that eminent Platonist Mírzá Ḥasan of Núr[1]. So the conference terminated in questionings on certain points relating to the science of fundamental dogma, and the elucidation and analysis of the doctrines of Mullá Ṣadrá[2]. So, as no conclusion was arrived at

[1] See Note J at end.

[2] For some account of this great philosopher see Gobineau, pp. 80–90, and Note K at end.

by the governor from this conference, the severe sentence and harsh decision of the learned doctors was not carried out; but, anxious to abate the great anxiety quickly and prevent a public tumult effectually, he gave currency to a report that a decree had been issued ordering the Báb to be sent to Teherán in order that some decisive settlement might be arrived at, or that some courageous divine might be able to confute [him].

He accordingly sent him forth from Isfahán with a p. 18.
company of his own mounted body-guard; but when they reached Múrché-Khúr[1] he gave secret orders for his return to Isfahán, where he afforded him a refuge and asylum in his own roofed private quarters[2]; and not a soul save the confidential and trusty dependents of the *Mu'tamad* knew aught of the Báb.

A period of four months passed in this fashion, and the *Mu'tamad* passed away to the mercy of God. Gurgín Khán, the *Mu'tamad's* nephew, was aware of the Báb's being in the private apartments, and represented the matter to the Prime Minister. Hájí Mírzá Áḳásí, that celebrated minister, issued a decisive

[1] Múrche-Khúr is the second stage out from Isfahán on the north road, and is distant about 35 miles therefrom.

[2] The building to which the Báb was thus transferred is called in the Táríkh-i-Jadíd '*the Royal Building of the Sun*' (عمارت خورشيد سلطانى). In the Persian Beyán (*Váḥid* ii, *ch.* 16) the Báb alludes to his dwelling-place at Isfahán under the name of عمارت صدر.

command and gave instructions that they should send the Báb secretly in disguise under the escort of Nuṣeyrí[1] horsemen to the capital.

p. 19. When he reached Kinár-i-gird[2] a fresh order came from the Prime Minister appointing the village of Kalín[3] as an abode and dwelling-place. There he remained for a period of twenty days. After that, the Báb forwarded a letter to the Royal Presence craving audience to set forth the truth of his condition, expecting this to be a means for the attainment of great advantages. The Prime Minister did not admit this, and made representation to the Royal Presence :—"The royal cavalcade is on the point of starting, and to engage in such matters as the present

[1] The Nuṣeyrí religion is prevalent amongst many of the *ílyát* or wandering tribes of Persia. An interesting account of the secret doctrines and practices of this sect by one Suleymán Efendí al-Adhaní, who had withdrawn himself from it subsequently to his initiation, has been published at Beyrout under the title of كتاب الباكورة السليمانيّه فى كشف اسرار الديانة النصيريّة. A very comprehensive account of this work by E. E. Salisbury may be found in the Journal of the American Oriental Society for 1866 (vol. viii, pp. 227—308). See also de Sacy's *Exposé de la Religion des Druzes*, vol. ii, pp. 559—586.

[2] A station on the old Isfahán road (now abandoned for one bearing more towards the west) distant about 28 miles from Teherán.

[3] "Nom de la première station que rencontre le voyageur en allant de Rey à Khowar." Barbier de Meynard, *Dictionnaire Géog. Hist. et Litt. de la Perse* (Paris, 1861).

will conduce to the disruption of the kingdom. Neither is there any doubt that the most notable doctors of the capital also will behave after the fashion of the doctors of Isfahán, which thing will be the cause of a popular outbreak, or that, according to
the religion of the immaculate Imám, they will regard p. 20.
the blood of this Seyyid as of no account, yea, as more lawful than mother's milk. The imperial train is prepared for travel, neither is there hindrance or impediment in view. There is no doubt that the presence of the Báb will be the cause of the gravest trouble and the greatest mischief. Therefore, on the spur of the moment, the wisest plan is this:—to place this person in the Castle of Mákú during the period of absence of the royal train from the seat of the imperial throne, and to defer the obtaining of an audience to the time of return."

Agreeably to this view a letter was issued addressed to the Báb in his Majesty's own writing, and, according to the traditional account of the tenour of this letter, the epitome thereof is this:—

(After the titles). "Since the royal train is on
the verge of departure from Teherán, to meet in a p. 21.
befitting manner is impossible. Do you go to Mákú and there abide and rest for a while, engaged in praying for our victorious state; and we have arranged that under all circumstances they shall shew

you attention and respect. When we return from travel we will summon you specially."

After this they sent him off with several mounted guards (amongst them Muḥammad Beg, the courier) to Tabríz and Mákú[1].

Besides this the followers of the Báb recount certain messages conveyed [from him] by the instrumentality of Muḥammad Beg (amongst which was a promise to heal the foot of the late king, but on condition of an interview, and the suppression of the tyranny of the majority), and the Prime Minister's prevention of the conveyance of these letters to the Royal Presence. For he himself laid claim to be a spiritual guide and was prepared to perform
p. 22. the functions of religious directorship. But others deny these accounts.

At all events in the course of the journey he wrote a letter to the Prime Minister saying, "You summoned me from Isfahán to meet the doctors and for the attainment of a decisive settlement. What has happened now that this excellent intention has been changed for Mákú and Tabríz?"

Although he remained forty days in the city of Tabríz the learned doctors did not condescend to approach him and did not deem it right to meet him. Then they sent him off to the Castle of Mákú, and for nine months lodged him in the inaccessible castle

[1] See Note L at end.

which is situated on the summit of that lofty mountain. And 'Alí Khán of Mákú[1], because of his excessive love for the family of the Prophet, paid him such attention as was possible, and gave permission [to some persons] to converse with him.

Now when the accomplished divines of Ázar- p. 23.
baiján perceived that in all the parts round about Tabríz it was as though the last day had come by reason of the excessive clamour, they requested the government to punish the [Báb's] followers, and to remove the Báb to the Castle of Chihrık. So they sent him to that castle and consigned him to the keeping of Yaḥyá Khán the Kurd[1].

Glory be to God! Notwithstanding these decisions of great doctors and reverend lawyers, and severe punishments and reprimands—beatings, banishments, and imprisonments—on the part of governors, this sect was daily on the increase, and the discussion and disputation was such that in meetings and assemblies in all parts of Persia there was no conversation but on this topic. Great was the commotion which arose: the doctors of the Perspicuous Religion
were lamenting, the common folk clamorous and p. 24.
agitated, and the Friends rejoicing and applauding.

But the Báb himself attached no importance to this uproar and tumult, and, alike on the road and in the castles of Mákú and Chihríḳ, evening and

[1] See Note L at end.

morning, nay, day and night, in extremest rapture and amazement, he would restrict himself to repeating and meditating on the qualities and attributes of that absent-yet-present, regarded-and-regarding Person of his[1]. Thus he makes a mention of him whereof this is the purport:—

"Though the ocean of woe rageth on every side, and the bolts of fate follow in quick succession, and the darknesses of griefs and afflictions invade soul and body, yet is my heart brightened by the remembrance of Thy countenance and my soul is as a rose-garden from the perfume of Thy nature."

In short, after he had remained for three months in the Castle of Chihríḳ, the eminent doctors of
p. 25. Tabríz and scholars of Ázarbaiján wrote to Teherán and demanded a severe punishment in regard to the Báb for the intimidation and frightening of the people. When the Prime Minister Hájí Mírzá Áḳásí beheld the ferment and clamour of the learned doctors in all districts of Persia, he perforce became their accomplice and ordered him to be brought from Chihríḳ to

[1] As I have pointed out in another place (B. ii, pp. 924–927), one of the most striking features of the Persian Beyán, composed by the Báb during his imprisonment at Mákú (which he repeatedly alludes to as '*the Mountain of M*' جبل ميم), is the continual reference to '*Him whom God shall manifest*' (من يظهره الله), whose precursor the Báb considered himself to be. The work translated by Gobineau (*op. cit.* p. 461 *et seq.*) under the title of *Livre des Préceptes* also affords ample evidence of this.

Tabríz. In the course of his transit by Urúmiyya the governor of the district Ḳásim Mírzá treated him with extraordinary deference, and a strange flocking together of high and low was apparent. These conducted themselves with the utmost respectfulness[1].

When the Báb reached Tabríz they brought him after some days before the government tribunal. Of the learned doctors the Niẓámu 'l-'Ulamá, Mullá Muḥammad Mámáḳání, Mírzá Aḥmad the Imám-

[1] Dr Wright of the American Mission at Urúmiyya wrote a brief account of the Báb and his sect which was communicated by Mr Perkins to the German Oriental Society and published in their transactions for the year 1851. This account, dated March 31st, 1851, fully confirms the statement here made. After describing briefly the rise of the sect, the arrest of the Báb, his imprisonment at Mákú (..."a remote district six days' journey from Urúmiyya situated on the Turkish frontier"), his transference to Chihríḳ (..."near Salmás, only two days' journey from Urúmiyya"), and the conflicts between the Bábís and the orthodox party, especially in Mázandarán, he says:—"Die Sache wurde so ernsthaft, dass die Regierung den Befehl erliess, den Sectenstifter nach Tabrîz zu bringen und ihm die Bastonade zu geben, seine Schüler aber überall, wo man sie fände, aufzugreifen und mit Geld- und Körperstrafen zu belegen. Auf dem Wege nach Tabrîz wurde Bâb nach Orumia gebracht, wo ihn der Statthalter mit besonderer Aufmerksamkeit behandelte und viele Personen die Erlaubniss erhielten, ihn zu besuchen. Bei einer Gelegenheit war eine Menge Leute bei ihm, und wie der Statthalter nachher bemerkte, waren diese alle geheimnissvoll bewegt und brachen in Thränen aus." (*Zeitschrift der Deutschen Morgenländischen Gesellschaft*, vol. v, pp. 384–385.)

p. 26. Jum'a, Mírzá 'Alí Aṣghar the Sheykhu 'l-Islám, and several other divines were present[1]. They asked concerning the claims of the Báb. He advanced the claim of Mahdí-hood; whereon a mighty tumult arose. Eminent doctors in overwhelming might compassed him on all sides, and such was the onset of orthodoxy that it had been no great wonder if a mere youth had not withstood the mountain of Elburz. They demanded proof. Without hesitation he recited texts, saying, "This is the permanent and most mighty proof." They criticised his grammar. He adduced arguments from the Ḳur'án, setting forth therefrom instances of similar infractions of the rules of grammar. So the assembly broke up and the Báb returned to his own dwelling.

The heaven-cradled Crown-Prince[2] was at that
p. 27. time governor of Ázarbaiján. He pronounced no sentence with regard to the Báb, nor did he desire to interfere with him. The doctors, however, considered it advisable at least to inflict a severe chastisement, and beating was decided on. But none of the corps of *farráshes*[3] would agree to become the instruments of the infliction of this punishment. So Mírzá 'Alí Aṣghar the Sheykhu 'l-Islám, who was one of the

[1] See Note M at end.

[2] Náṣiru'd-Dín, the present king of Persia.

[3] The *farrásh* (literally *carpet-spreader*) is the lictor of the East.

noble Seyyids, brought him to his own house and applied the rods with his own hand. After this they sent the Báb back to Chihrík̹ and subjected him to a strict confinement.

Now when the news of this beating, chastisement, imprisonment, and rigour reached all parts of Persia, learned divines and esteemed lawyers who were possessed of power and influence girt up the loins of endeavour for the eradication and suppression of this sect, exerting their utmost efforts therefor. And they wrote notice of their decision, to wit "that p. 28. this person and his followers are in absolute error and are hurtful to Church and State." And since the governors in Persia enjoyed the fullest authority, in some provinces they followed this decision and united in uprooting and dispersing the Bábís. But the late King Muḥammad Sháh[1] acted with deliberation in this matter, reflecting, "This youth is of the Pure Lineage and of the family of him addressed with '*were it not for thee*[2].' So long as no offen-

[1] For an admirable sketch of the characters of this monarch and his minister Ḥáji Mírzá Áḳási, see Gobineau, pp. 160–166. Concerning the latter see also Watson's *History of Persia*, p. 288.

[2] See note 1 at foot of p. 2. In a very well-known tradition God is said to have addressed the Prophet Muḥammad as follows:—لولاك لولاك لما خلقت الافلاك '*Were it not for thee I had not created the heavens.*' Hence "the family of him addressed with '*were it not for thee*'" means simply the

sive actions which are incompatible with the public peace and well-being proceed from him, the government should not interfere with him." And whenever the learned doctors appealed to him from the surrounding districts, he either gave no answer, or else commanded them to act with deliberation.

Notwithstanding this, between eminent doctors
p. 29. and illustrious scholars and those learned persons who were followers of the Báb opposition, discussion, and strife did so increase that in some provinces they desired [to resort to] mutual imprecation; and for the governors of the provinces, too, a means of acquiring gain was produced, so that great tumult and disturbance arose. And since the malady of the gout had violently attacked the king's foot and occupied his world-ordering thought, the good judgement of the Chief Minister, the famous Háji Mírzá Ákásí[1], became the pivot of the conduct of affairs, and his incapacity and lack of resource became apparent as the sun. For every hour he formed a new opinion and gave a new order: at one moment he would seek to support the decision of the doctors, accounting the eradication and suppression of the Bábís as necessary: at another time he would charge the
p. 30. doctors with aggressiveness, regarding undue inter-

descendants of the Prophet, amongst whom the Báb, in his capacity of Seyyid, must be reckoned.

[1] See note 1 at foot of preceding page.

ference as contrary to justice: at another time he would become a mystic and say, '*All these voices are from the King*[1],' or repeat with his tongue, '*Moses is at war with Moses*[2],' or recite, '*This is nought but Thy*

[1] The distich of which this is the first hemistich is a great favourite with the Súfís. It occurs in the first book of the *Masnavi* of Jalálu'd-Dín Rúmí in the 8th story (Story of the Harper). Different editions present considerable variants in the first hemistich, and in no one of the four which I have consulted does it stand as here quoted. In the Bombay edition of A. H. 1290 (p. 50, l. 20), the Teherán edition of A.H. 1299 known as 'Alá'ud-Dawla's (p. 51, l. 4), and a Constantinople edition of the first book published in A.H. 1288 (p. 77, l. 20) the entire couplet stands as follows:

مطلق آن آواز خود از شه بود * گرچه از حلقوم عبد الله بود *

"*Indeed that voice is really from the King*
Although [apparently] *it is from the throat of 'Abdu 'lláh.*"

The English reader may consult Redhouse's versified translation of Book i of the *Masnaví*, p. 141, first two lines.

[2] This quotation is also from the *Masnaví* [Teherán edition of 'Alá'ud-Dawla, p. 65, l. 27; Bombay edition, p. 63, l. 16]. The couplet stands in both as follows:—

چونکه بیرنگی اسیر رنگ شد * موسئی با موسئی در جنگ شد *

"*When Colourlessness became the captive of colour*
A Moses is at war with a Moses."

Redhouse's version will be found on p. 180 of his work above quoted, first two lines. A complete treatise on the mysticism of the Súfís might be written on this text, which is pretty fully discussed in Hájí Mullá Hádí's excellent commentary on the *Masnaví* (Teherán edition of A.H. 1285, p. 68 and also in a marginal note in 'Alá'ud-Dawla's Teherán edition (*loc. cit.*). In brief the meaning is this:—that strife and contest

trial[1].' In short this changeable minister, by reason of his mismanagement of important matters and failure to control and order the affairs of the community, so acted that disturbance and clamour arose from all quarters and directions: the most notable and influential of the doctors ordered the common folk to molest the followers of the Báb, and a general onslaught took place. More especially when the claim of Mahdí-hood[2] reached the hearing of eminent divines and profound doctors they began to make lamentation and to cry and complain from their
p. 31. pulpits, saying, "one of the essentials of religion and of the authentic traditions transmitted from the holy Imáms, nay, the chief basis of the foundations of the church of His Highness Ja'far[3], is the Occultation

arise from the imprisonment of the One Absolute Undifferentiated Being ('*Colourlessness*') in the phantasmal appearances ('*colours*') of the World of Plurality. So Jámí says at the close of a very beautiful passage:—

این همه آشوب و غوغا در جهان از عشق اوست *
کشت معلوم این زمان سرفتنه غوغا یکیست *

"*All this tumult and strife in the world are from love of Him;*
It hath become known at this time that the source of the strife is One."

[1] Ḳur'án vii, 154.

[2] See note N at end, and p. 20 *supra*.

[3] The Imám Ja'far-i-Ṣádiḳ, as he is commonly called, was, according to the Shí'ite faith, the sixth of the twelve Imáms,

of the immaculate twelfth Imám (upon both of them be peace). What has happened to Jábulḳá[1]? Where has Jábulsá gone? What was the Minor Occultation? What has become of the Major Occultation? What are the sayings of Ḥuseyn ibn Rúḥ, and what

and succeeded his father, the Imám Muḥammad Báḳir, who was the fifth Imám. Why the Shí'ites should speak of him as in some sort the founder of their church is explained thus in a work called عقائد الشيعة (*Tenets of the Shí'ites*) published in Teherán:—"Since His Holiness [the Imám Ja'far] lived at the end of the Omayyad and the beginning of the 'Abbásid dynasty and these two families were in conflict with one another, he tranquilly engaged in expounding the ordinances of God; therefore do men refer the religion to him, since he gave currency to the true doctrines."

[1] For the explanation of this and the subsequent points of Shí'ite belief alluded to in this passage see Note O at end. The general tenour of the argument here put in the mouths of the Shí'ite doctors is this:—"That certain prodigies and marvellous signs shall usher in the advent of the Imám Mahdí is an essential doctrine of our faith sufficiently confirmed and established by authentic traditions. If we believe this, then we must reject the Báb's claim to be the promised Mahdí, since these signs have not been witnessed: in which case it behoves us to inflict on him the severest punishment. If, on the other hand, we admit the Báb's claim, we thereby renounce our religion and become neither Sunnís nor Shí'as; unless, indeed, we take the view of the Bábís that these signs are to be understood metaphorically, that no literal fulfilment of them is to be looked for, and that to substantiate a claim to Mahdíhood only two things are necessary—that the claimant should belong to the family of the Prophet, and that he should be able to produce revealed verses similar to those in the Ḳur'án." Concerning this view of the Bábís see B. ii, pp. 915—918.

the tradition of Ibn Mihriyár? What shall we make of the flight of the Guardians and the Helpers? How shall we deal with the conquest of the East and the West? Where is the Ass of Antichrist? When will the appearance of Sofyán be? Where are the signs which are in the traditions of the Holy Family? Where is that whereon the Victorious Church is agreed? The matter is not outside one of two alternatives:—either we must repudiate the traditions of
p. 32. the Holy Imáms, grow wearied of the Church of Ja'far, and account the clear indications of the Imám as disturbed dreams; or, in accordance with the primary and subsidiary doctrines of the Faith and the essential and explicit declarations of the most luminous Law, we must consider the repudiation, nay, the destruction of this person as our chief duty. If so be that we shut our eyes to these authentic traditions and obvious doctrines universally admitted, no remnant will endure of the fundamental basis of the Church of the immaculate Imám: we shall neither be Sunnites, nor shall we be of the prevalent sect[1] to continue awaiting the promised Saint and believing in the begotten Mahdí. Otherwise we must regard as admissible the opening of the Gate of Saintship, and consider that He who is to arise[2] of the family of Muḥammad possesses two signs:—the first condition,

[1] i.e. of the Shí'ite church dominant in Persia.
[2] i.e. the Imám-Mahdí. See Note O at end.

Holy Lineage; the second, [that he is divinely] fortified with brilliant verses. What can we do with these thousand-year-old beliefs of the delivered band of the Shi'ites, or what shall we say concerning their p. 33.
profound doctors and pre-eminent divines? Were all these in error? Did they journey in the vale of transgression? What an evidently false assertion is this! *By God, this is a thing to break the back!* O people, extinguish this fire and forget these words! Alas! woe to our Faith, woe to our Law!"

Thus did they make complaint in mosques and chapels, in pulpits and congregations.

But the Bábí chiefs composed treatises against them, and set in order replies according to their own thought[1]. Were these to be discussed in detail it would conduce to prolixity, and our object is the statement of history, not of arguments for believing or rejecting; but of some of the replies the gist is this:—that they held the Proof as supreme, and the evidence as outweighing traditions, considering the p. 34.

[1] Amongst the controversial works of the Bábís may be mentioned especially the دلائل سبعه (Seven Proofs) composed by the Báb himself about the year A.H. 1264–5 (A.D. 1848–49) during his imprisonment at Mákú, and the ایقان (Assurance) composed by Behá'u'lláh in Baghdad in the year A.H. 1278 (A.D. 1861–62). For a brief abstract of the former see B. ii, pp. 912—918: for specimens of the latter carefully and judiciously selected see Rosen's *MSS. Persans*, pp. 32—51, and for some account of the work see B. ii, pp. 944—948.

former as the root and the latter as the branch, and saying, "If the branch agree not with the root it serves not as an argument and is unworthy of reliance; for the reported consequence has no right to oppose itself to the established principle, and cannot argue against it." Indeed in such cases they regarded interpretation as the truth of revelation and the essence of true exegesis[1]: thus, for instance, they interpreted the sovereignty of the *Ḳá'im* as a mystical sovereignty, and his conquests as conquests of the cities of hearts, adducing in support of this the meekness and defeat of the Chief of Martyrs[2] (may the life of all being be a sacrifice for him). For he was the true manifestation of the blessed verse '*And verily our host shall overcome for them*[3],' yet, notwithstanding this, he quaffed the cup of martyrdom with perfect
p. 35. meekness, and, at the very moment of uttermost defeat, triumphed over his enemies and became the most mighty of the troops of the Supreme Host. Similarly they regarded the numerous writings which, in spite of his lack of education, the Báb had composed, as due to the promptings of the Holy Spirit; extracted from books contrary sayings handed down by men of mark; adduced traditions apparently agreeing with their objects; and clung to the an-

[1] See Rosen's *MSS. Persans*, p. 36, and B. ii, pp. 915—916.
[2] Ḥuseyn, son of 'Alí, the third Imám.
[3] Ḳur'án xxxvii, 173.

nouncements of certain notables of yore. They also considered the conversion of austere and recluse doctors and eminent votaries of the Perspicuous Religion [of Islám] as a valid proof[1], deemed the steadfastness and constancy of the Báb a most mighty sign[2], and related miracles and the like; which things, being altogether foreign to our purpose, we have passed by with brevity, and will now proceed with p. 36.
our original topic.

At the time of these events certain persons appeared amongst the Bábís who had a strange ascendancy and appearance in the eyes of this sect. Amongst these was Mírzá Muḥammad 'Alí of Mázandarán, who was the disciple of the illustrious Seyyid (may God exalt his station) Hájí Seyyid Káẓim of Resht, and who was the associate and companion of the Báb in his pilgrimage journey. After a while certain manners and states issued from him such that all, acting with absolute confidence, considered obedience to him as an impregnable stronghold, so that even Mullá Ḥuseyn of Bushraweyh, who was the leader of all and the arbiter appealed to alike by the noble and the humble of this sect, used to behave in his presence with great humility and with the self-abasement of a lowly servant[3].

1 See Rosen's *MSS. Persans*, p. 41.

2 Ibid, p. 43.

3 This statement is confirmed by the Táríkh-i-Jadíd.

This personage set himself to exalt the word of
p. 37. the Báb with the utmost steadfastness, and the Báb did full justice to speech in praising and glorifying him, accounting his uprising as an assistance from the Unseen. In delivery and style[1] he was '*evident magic*,' and in firmness and constancy superior to all. At length in the year [A.H.] 1265 at the sentence of the chief of lawyers the Sa'ídu 'l-'Ulamá the chief divine of Bárfurúsh, he yielded his head and surrendered his life amidst extremest clamour and outcry[2].

And amongst them was she who was entitled Ḳurratu 'l-'Ayn the daughter of Hájí Mullá Ṣáliḥ, the sage of Ḳazvín, the erudite doctor. She, according to what is related, was skilled in diverse arts, amazed the understandings and thoughts of the most eminent masters by her eloquent dissertations on the exegesis and tradition of the Perspicuous Book[3], and was a mighty sign in the doctrines of the glorious Sheykh of Aḥsá[4]. At the Supreme Shrines[5]
p. 38. she borrowed light on matters divine from the lamp

[1] Of the writings of Mullá Muḥammad 'Alí (called آثار قدّوسيّه from the title—جناب قدّوس—borne by their author amongst his co-religionists) six pieces occupying in all 39 pages are contained in a MS. in my possession.

[2] See Note P at end.

[3] The Ḳur'án.

[4] Sheykh Aḥmad Aḥsá'í the founder of the Sheykhí school of theology, concerning which see Note E at end.

[5] Kerbelá and Nejef.

of Káẓim[1], and freely sacrificed her life in the way of the Báb. She discussed and disputed with the doctors and sages, loosing her tongue to establish her doctrine. Such fame did she acquire that most people who were scholars or mystics sought to hear her speech and were eager to become acquainted with her powers of speculation and deduction. She had a brain full of tumultuous ideas, and thoughts vehement and restless. In many places she triumphed over the contentious, expounding the most subtle questions. When she was imprisoned in the house of [Maḥmúd] the *Kalántar* of Teherán[2], and the festivities and rejoicings of a wedding were going on, the wives of the city magnates who were present as guests were so charmed with the beauty of her speech that, forgetting the p. 39.
festivities, they gathered round her, diverted by listening to her words from listening to the melodies, and rendered indifferent by witnessing her marvels to the contemplation of the pleasant and novel sights which are incidental to a wedding. In short in elocution she was the calamity of the age, and in ratiocination the trouble of the world. Of fear or timidity there was no trace in her heart, nor had the admonitions of the kindly-disposed any profit

[1] Hájí Seyyid Káẓim of Resht, the pupil and successor of Sheykh Aḥmad and the Teacher of the Báb. See Note E at end.

[2] See Gobineau, pp. 292—295; Kazem-Beg i, p. 522 and note, and ii, p. 249; and Eastwick's *Diplomate's Residence in Persia*, vol. i, p. 288—290.

or fruit for her. Although she was of [such as are] damsels [meet] for the bridal bower, yet she wrested pre-eminence from stalwart men, and continued to strain the feet of steadfastness until she yielded up her life at the sentence of the mighty doctors in Teherán. But were we to occupy ourselves with these details the matter would end in prolixity[1].

Well, Persia was in this critical state and the learned doctors perplexed and anxious, when the
p. 40. late Prince Muḥammad Sháh died[2], and the throne of sovereignty was adorned with the person of the new monarch. Mírzá Taḳí Khán *Amír-Niẓám*, who was Prime Minister and Chief Regent, seized in the grasp of his despotic power the reins of the affairs of the commonwealth, and urged the steed of his ambition into the arena of wilfulness and sole possession. This minister was a person devoid of experience and wanting in consideration for the consequences of actions; bloodthirsty and shameless; and swift and ready to shed blood[3]. Severity in

[1] For some further account of Ḳurratu'l-'Ayn see Note Q at end.

[2] September 4th, 1848. See Watson's *History*, p. 354.

[3] This is by no means the light in which Mírzá Taḳí Khán is regarded by most historians. See especially the encomiums bestowed on him by Watson (*History of Persia from the beginning of the Nineteenth Century, &ct.* p. 364 and p. 404). Compare also Lady Sheil's *Diary*, pp. 248—253. Yet his cruelty towards the Báb and his followers goes far to justify their opinion of him, and at least fully explains the fact that they

punishing he regarded as wise administration, and harshly entreating, distressing, intimidating, and frightening the people he considered as a fulcrum for the advancement of the monarchy. And as His Majesty the King was in the prime of youthful years the minister fell into strange fancies and sounded the p. 41.
drum of absolutism in [the conduct of] affairs: on his own decisive resolution, without seeking permission from the Royal Presence or taking counsel with prudent statesmen, he issued orders to persecute the Bábís, imagining that by overweening force he could eradicate and suppress matters of this nature, and that harshness would bear good fruit; whereas [in fact] to interfere with matters of conscience is simply to give them greater currency and strength; the more you strive to extinguish the more will the flame be kindled, more especially in matters of faith and religion, which spread and acquire influence so soon as blood is shed, and strongly affect men's hearts. These things have been put to the proof, and the greatest proof is this very transaction. Thus they relate that the possessions of a certain Bábí in p. 42.
Káshán were plundered, and his household scattered and dispersed. They stripped him naked and scourged him, defiled his beard, mounted him face backwards

regard the cruel fate which befel him at the hands of the king as a signal instance of Divine vengeance. See Gobineau, p. 253—254.

on an ass, and paraded him through the streets and bazaars with the utmost cruelty, to the sound of drums, trumpets, guitars, and tambourines. A certain guebre[1] who knew absolutely nought of the world or its denizens chanced to be seated apart in a corner of a caravansaray. When the clamour of the people rose high he hastened into the street, and, becoming cognizant of the offence and the offender, and the cause of his public disgrace and punishment in full detail, he fell to making search, and that very day entered the society of the Bábís, saying, "This very ill-usage and public humiliation is a proof of
p. 43. truth and the very best of arguments. Had it not been thus it might have been that a thousand years would have passed ere one like me became informed."

At all events the minister with the utmost arbitrariness, without receiving any instructions or asking permission, sent forth commands in all directions to punish and chastise the Bábís. Governors and magistrates sought a pretext for amassing wealth, and officials a means of [acquiring] profits; celebrated doctors from the summits of their pulpits incited men to make a general onslaught; the powers of the

[1] It is almost unnecessary to remark that the word *guebre* (more correctly *gabr*) is always used in a contemptuous if not in an offensive sense. It is never used by the Zoroastrians in speaking of themselves.

religious and the civil law linked hands and strove to eradicate and destroy this people.

Now this people had not yet acquired such knowledge as was right and needful of the fundamental principles and hidden doctrines of the Báb's teachings, and did not recognise their duties. Their conceptions and ideas were after the former fashion, and their conduct and behaviour in correspondence with p. 44. ancient usage. The way of approach to the Báb was, moreover, closed, and the flame of trouble visibly blazing on every side. At the decree of the most celebrated of the doctors, the government, and indeed the common people, had, with irresistible power, inaugurated rapine and plunder on all sides, and were engaged in punishing and torturing, killing and despoiling, in order that they might quench this fire and wither these [poor] souls. In towns where these were but a limited number all of them with bound hands became food for the sword, while in cities where they were numerous they arose in self-defence agreeably to their former beliefs, since it was impossible for them to make enquiry as to their duty, and all doors were closed.

In Mázandarán amongst other places the people of p. 45. the city of Bárfurúsh at the command of the chief of lawyers the Sa'ídu'l-'Ulamá made a general attack on Mullá Ḥuseyn of Bushraweyh and his followers, and slew six or seven persons. They were busy compassing

the destruction of the rest also when Mullá Ḥuseyn ordered the *azán*[1] to be sounded and stretched forth his hand to the sword, whereupon all sought flight, and the nobles and lords coming before him with the utmost penitence and deference agreed that he should be permitted to depart. They further sent with them as a guard Khusraw of Ḳádí-kalá with horsemen and footmen, so that, according to the terms of agreement, they might go forth safe and protected from the territory of Mázandarán. When they, being ignorant of the fords and paths, had emerged from the city, Khusraw dispersed his horsemen and footmen and set them in ambush in the
p. 46. forest of Mázandarán, scattered and separated the Bábís in that forest on the road and off the road, and began to hunt them down singly. When the reports of muskets arose on every side the hidden secret became manifest, and several wanderers and other persons were suddenly slain with bullets. Mullá Ḥuseyn ordered the *azán*[1] to be sounded to assemble his scattered followers, while Mírzá Luṭf-'Alí[2] the secretary drew his dagger and ripped open Khusraw's vitals. Of Khusraw's host some were slain and others wandered distractedly over the field

[1] The call to prayer.

[2] According to the *Táríkh-i-Jadíd* it was a Bábí named Mírzá Muḥammad Taḳí who, exasperated by Khusraw's insolences towards Mullá Ḥuseyn slew the treacherous guide.

of battle. Mullá Ḥuseyn quartered his host in a fort near the burial-place of Sheykh Ṭabarsí[1], and, being aware of the wishes of the community, relaxed and interrupted the march. This detachment was p. 47. subsequently further reinforced by Mírzá Muḥammad 'Alí of Mázandarán with a number of other persons, so that the garrison of the fort numbered three hundred and thirteen souls. Of these, however, all were not capable of fighting, only one hundred and ten persons being prepared for war. Most of them were doctors or students whose companions had been during their whole life books and treatises; yet, in spite of the fact that they were unaccustomed to war or to the blows of shot and sword, four times were camps and armies arrayed against them and they were attacked and hemmed in with cannons, muskets, and bomb-shells, and on all four occasions they inflicted defeat, while the army was completely routed and dispersed[2]. On the occasion of the fourth defeat

[1] The tomb of Sheykh Ṭabarsí—ever memorable for the gallant defence of the Bábís—is situated about fourteen miles SE. of Bárfurúsh and can only be reached by traversing swampy rice-fields and dense forests which in wet weather must be almost impassable. I visited the spot on September 26th 1888, and could perceive no trace of the strong ramparts described by the Musulmán historians and by Gobineau as having been erected by the Bábís.

[2] Kazem-Beg enumerates four sorties made by the Bábís, of which the first three were successful, although in the second Mullá Ḥuseyn was killed. Kazem-Beg's *second sortie* there-

'Abbás-Ḳulí Khán of Láríján was captain of the forces and Prince Mahdí-Ḳulí Mírzá commander in the camp.
p. 48. The Khán above mentioned used at nights to conceal and hide himself in disguise amongst the trees of the forest outside the camp, while during the day he was present in the encampment. The last battle took place at night and the army was routed. The Bábís fired the tents and huts, and night became bright as day. The foot of Mullá Ḥuseyn's horse caught in a noose, for he was riding, the others being on foot. 'Abbás-Ḳulí Khán recognised him from the top of a tree afar off, and with his own hand discharged several bullets. At the third shot he threw him from his feet. He was borne by his followers to the fort, and there they buried him. Notwithstanding this event [the troops] could not

fore corresponds to the *fourth* Bábí victory mentioned above. Considerable confusion exists as to the successive incidents of the siege, but after comparing the different accounts and especially that of the *Táríkh-i-Jadíd* I should suppose the four successes here alluded to to be as follows:—(1) Rout of some of the comrades of the deceased Khusraw who attacked the Bábís some three weeks after they had taken up their quarters at Sheykh Ṭabarsí. (2) Repulse of a larger force of local volunteers and sack of Faráhil (Kazem-Beg i, p. 491—492; Gobineau, p. 197—199). (3) Surprise of Mahdí-Ḳulí Mírzá and rout of his troops with great loss (Kazem-Beg i, p. 495—499; Gobineau, p. 201—206). (4) The successful sortie wherein Mullá Ḥuseyn's gallant career was brought to a close in the very hour of victory (Kazem-Beg i, p. 499—504; Gobineau, p. 210—215).

prevail by superior force. At length the Prince
made a treaty and covenant, and sware by the Holy
Imáms, confirming his oath by vows plighted on the p. 49.
glorious Ḳur'án, to this effect: "You shall not be
molested; return to your own places." Since their
provisions had for some time been exhausted, so that
even of the skins and bones of horses nought remained, and they had subsisted for several days on
pure water, they agreed. When they arrived at the
army food was prepared for them in a place outside
the camp. They were engaged in eating, having
laid aside their weapons and armour, when the soldiers
fell on them on all sides and slew them all. Some
have accounted this valour displayed by these people
as a thing miraculous, but when a band of men are
besieged in some place where all avenues and roads
are stopped and all hope of deliverance is cut off
they will assuredly defend themselves desperately
and display bravery and courage. p. 50.

In Zanján and Níríz likewise at the decree of erudite doctors and notable lawyers a bloodthirsty military force attacked and besieged. In Zanján the chief was Mullá Muḥammad 'Alí the *mujtahid*, while in Níríz Seyyid Yaḥyá of Dáráb was the leader and arbiter[1]. At first they sought to bring about a

[1] For full accounts of the siege of Zanján see Gobineau, p. 233—254; Kazem-Beg ii, p. 196—224; and compare Watson, p. 387—392; Lady Sheil's *Diary*, p. 181. Kazem-Beg alone of

reconciliation, but, meeting with cruel ferocity, they reached the pitch of desperation; and, the overpowering force of the victorious troops having cut off every passage of flight, they unclosed their hands in resistance. But although they were very strong in battle and amazed the chiefs of the army by their steadfastness and endurance, the overwhelming military force closed the passage of flight and broke
p. 51. their wings and feathers. After numerous battles they too at last yielded to covenants and compacts, oaths and promises, vows registered on the Ḳur'án, and the wonderful stratagems of the officers, and were all put to the edge of the sword.

Were we to occupy ourselves in detail with the wars of Níríz and Zanján, or to set forth these events from beginning to end, this epitome would become a bulky volume. So, since this would be of no advantage to history, we have passed them over briefly.

During the course of the events which took place at Zanján the Prime Minister devised a final and trenchant remedy. Without the royal command, without consulting with the ministers of the subject-

these four authorities gives an account of the events at Níríz (ii, p. 224—239), but, as it appears to me, he deals very unjustly with the character of Seyyid Yaḥyá of Dáráb. This much at least is certain, that the Bábís still regard him as one of their saints, which at any rate shews that they entertain no doubts either of his sincerity or his loyalty. See Note H at end.

protecting court, he, acting with arbitrary disposition,
fixed determination, and entirely on his own authority,
issued commands to put the Báb to death. This
befel in brief as follows. The governor of Ázar- p. 52.
baiján, Prince Ḥamzé Mírzá, was unwilling that the
execution of this sentence should be at his hands[1],
and said to the brother of the Amír, Mírzá Ḥasan
Khán, "This is a vile business and an easy one; anyone is capable and competent. I had imagined that
His Excellency the Regent would commission me
to make war on the Afghans or Uzbegs or appoint
me to attack and invade the territory of Russia or
Turkey." So Mírzá Ḥasan Khán wrote his excuse
in detail to the Amír.

Now the Seyyid Báb had disposed all his affairs
before setting out from Chihríḳ towards Tabríz, had
placed his writings and even his ring and pen-case
in a specially prepared box, put the key of the box
in an envelope, and sent it by means of Mullá Báḳir,
who was one of his first associates, to Mullá 'Abdu'l- p. 53.
Karím of Ḳazvín[2]. This trust Mullá Báḳir delivered

[1] According to Gobineau (p. 259 *et seq.*), however, Ḥamzé Mírzá took the leading part in the examination and condemnation of the Báb.

[2] Mullá 'Abdu'l-Karím was also known amongst the Bábís by the name of Mírzá Aḥmad-i-*Kátib* (the Scribe), inasmuch as he acted as amanuensis to the Báb and later to Mírzá Yaḥyá, Ṣubḥ-i-Ezel. He was one of the twenty-eight victims put to death in August 1852 in Teherán, and fell by the hands

over to Mullá 'Abdu'l-Karím at Ḳum in presence of a numerous company. At the solicitations of those present he opened the lid of the box and said, "I am commanded to convey this trust to Behá'u'lláh: more than this ask not of me, for I cannot tell you." Importuned by the company, he produced a long epistle in blue, penned in the most graceful manner with the utmost delicacy and firmness in a beautiful minute *shikasta* hand, written in the shape of a man so closely that it would have been imagined that it was a single wash of ink on the paper[1]. When they had read this epistle [they perceived that] he had produced three hundred and sixty derivatives from the word *Behá*. Then Mullá 'Abdu'l-Karím con-
p. 54. veyed the trust to its destination.

Well, we must return to our original narrative. The Prime Minister issued a second order to his brother Mírzá Ḥasan Khán, the gist of which order was this:—"Obtain a formal and explicit sentence from the learned doctors of Tabríz who are the firm support of the Church of Ja'far (upon him be peace)

of the artillerymen, apparently without having undergone previous torture which he had much feared and wherefrom he had prayed frequently to be delivered.

[1] An epistle of this sort written by the Báb I have seen. It was in the form of a pentacle, and most beautifully executed as above described. Cf. Kazem-Beg ii, p. 498. For a specimen of the 'derivatives' produced by the Báb from the word *Behá* see Note R at end.

and the impregnable stronghold of the Shi'ite faith; summon the Christian regiment of Urúmiyya; suspend the Báb before all the people; and give orders for the regiment to fire a volley."

Mírzá Ḥasan Khán summoned his chief of the *farráshes*, and gave him his instructions. They removed the Báb's turban and sash which were the signs of his Seyyid-hood, brought him with four of his followers[1] to the barrack square of Tabríz, confined him in a cell, and appointed forty of the Christian soldiers of Tabríz to guard him. p. 55.

Next day the chief of the *farráshes* delivered over the Báb and a young man named Áḳá Muḥammad 'Alí who was of a noble family of Tabríz to Sám Khán, colonel of the Christian regiment of Urúmiyya, at the sentences of the learned divine Mullá Muhammad of Mámáḳán, of the second ecclesiastical authority Mírzá Báḳir, and of the third ecclesiastical authority Mullá Murtaẓá-Ḳulí and others. An iron nail was hammered into the middle of the staircase of the very cell wherein they were imprisoned, and two ropes were hung down. By one rope the Báb was suspended and by the other rope Áḳá Muḥammad 'Alí, both being firmly bound in such wise that the

[1] These four would seem to have been—(1) Áḳá Muḥammad 'Ali of Tabriz; (2) Áḳá Seyyid Ḥuseyn of Yezd, the Báb's amanuensis; (3) Áḳá Seyyid Ḥasan of Yezd, his brother; (4) Áḳá Seyyid Aḥmad of Tabríz. See Note S at end.

head of that young man was on the Báb's breast. The surrounding house-tops billowed with teeming crowds. A regiment of soldiers ranged itself in three files. The first file fired; then the second file, and
p. 56. then the third file discharged volleys. From the fire of these volleys a mighty smoke was produced. When the smoke cleared away they saw that young man standing and the Báb seated by the side of his amanuensis Áḳá Seyyid Ḥuseyn in the very cell from the staircase of which they had suspended them. To neither one of them had the slightest injury resulted.

Sám Khán the Christian asked to be excused; the turn of service came to another regiment, and the chief of the *farráshes* withheld his hand. Áḳá Ján Beg of Khamsa, colonel of the body-guard, advanced; and they again bound the Báb together with that young man to the same nail. The Báb uttered certain words which those few who knew Persian understood[1], while the rest heard but the sound of his voice.

p. 57. The colonel of the regiment appeared in person: and it was before noon on the twenty-eighth of Sha'bán in the year [A.H.] one thousand two hundred

[1] The Ázarbaiján dialect of Turkish is the language generally spoken in Tabríz, and only persons who have either received some education or travelled in other parts of Persia understand Persian. Indeed Turkish prevails as far east as Ḳazvín, is widely spoken in Teherán, and is understood by many even as far south as Ḳum.

and sixty-six[1]. Suddenly he gave orders to fire. At this volley the bullets produced such an effect that the breasts [of the victims] were riddled, and their limbs were completely dissected, except their faces, which were but little marred.

Then they removed those two bodies from the square to the edge of the moat outside the city, and that night they remained by the edge of the moat. Next day the Russian consul came with an artist and took a picture of those two bodies in the posture wherein they had fallen at the edge of the moat.

On the second night at midnight the Bábís carried away the two bodies.

On the third day the people did not find the bodies, and some supposed that the wild beasts had p. 58.
devoured them, so that the doctors proclaimed from the summits of their pulpits saying, "The holy body of the immaculate Imám and that of the true Shi'ite are preserved from the encroachments of beasts of prey and creeping things and wounds, but the body of this person have the wild beasts torn in pieces." But after the fullest investigation and enquiry it hath

[1] July 9th 1850. I have already pointed out (B. i, p. 512) that Kazem-Beg is in error in placing the Báb's death in 1849. As to the events contemporary with the Founder's martyrdom, the siege of Zanján was in progress, while the Níríz insurrection had just been quelled. Indeed Áḳá Seyyid Yaḥyá of Dáráb according to reliable tradition suffered martyrdom on the same day as the Báb.

been proved that when the Báb had dispersed all his writings and personal properties and it had become clear and evident from various signs that these events would shortly take place[1], therefore, on the second day of these events, Suleymán Khán[2] the son of Yaḥyá Khán, one of the nobles of Ázarbaiján devoted to the Báb, arrived, and proceeded straightway to the house of the mayor of Tabríz. And since the mayor was an old friend, associate, and confidant of
p. 59. his; since, moreover, he was of the mystic temperament and did not entertain aversion or dislike for any sect, Suleymán Khán divulged this secret to

[1] There is no doubt that, as Gobineau states (p. 258), the Báb fully expected to suffer martyrdom. He even issued instructions as to the disposal of his remains, which he desired should be placed near the shrine of Sháh 'Abdu'l-'Aẓím some five miles to the south of Teherán. "*The place of Sháh-'Abdu'l-'Aẓím,*" he wrote, "*is a good land, by reason of the proximity of Waḥíd*" (i.e. Ṣubḥ-i-Ezel, whose name, Yaḥyá, is equivalent numerically to *Waḥíd*, cf. B. ii, 997) "*for keeping; and God is the Best of Keepers.*" The body, as here stated, was presently sent along with that of Áḳá Muḥammad 'Alí, the Báb's fellow-sufferer, from Tabríz to Teherán. It was committed to the care of Áḳá Mahdí of Káshán, who deposited it in a little shrine called *Imám-zádé-i-Ma'ṣúm* situated near the *Imám-zádé-i-Ḥasan* on the road from Teherán to Ribáṭ-Karím. Here it remained in charge of the custodian of the shrine (who was paid to keep watch over it) till about the year 1867, when it was removed elsewhere by command of Behá'u'lláh.

[2] Concerning Suleymán Khán's martyrdom in August 1852 at Teherán see Note T at end.

him saying, "To-night I, with several others, will endeavour by every means and artifice to rescue the body. Even though it be not possible, come what may we will make an attack, and either attain our object or pour out our lives freely in this way." "Such troubles," answered the mayor, "are in no wise necessary." He then sent one of his private servants named Hají Alláh-yár, who, by whatever means and proceedings it was, obtained the body without trouble or difficulty and handed it over to Hájí Suleymán Khán. And when it was morning the sentinels, to excuse themselves, said that the wild beasts had devoured it. That night they sheltered the body in the workshop of a Bábí of Mílán: next p. 60.
day they manufactured a box, placed it in the box, and left it as a trust. Afterwards, in accordance with instructions which arrived from Teherán, they sent it away from Ázarbaiján. And this transaction remained absolutely secret.

Now in these years [A.H. one thousand two hundred and] sixty-six and sixty-seven throughout all Persia fire fell on the households of the Bábís, and each one of them, in whatever hamlet he might be, was, on the slightest suspicion arising, put to the sword. More than four thousand souls were slain[1], and a great multitude of women and children,

[1] The most notable massacres during this period were at Zanján and Níríz. Concerning the martyrdom of the "Seven

left without protector or helper, distracted and confounded, were trodden down and destroyed. And all
these occurrences were brought about solely by the
arbitrary decision and command of Mírzá Taḳí Khán,
p. 61. who imagined that by the enactment of a crushing
punishment this sect would be dispersed and disappear in such wise that all sign and knowledge of
them would be cut off. Ere long had passed the
contrary of his imagination appeared, and it became
certain that [the Bábís] were increasing. The flame
rose higher and the contagion became swifter: the
affair waxed grave and the report thereof reached
other climes. At first it was confined to Persia:
later it spread to the rest of the world. Quaking
and affliction resulted in constancy and stability,
and grievous pains and punishment caused acceptance
and attraction. The very events produced an impression; impression led to investigation; and investigation resulted in increase. Through the ill-
considered policy of the Minister this edifice became
fortified and strengthened, and these foundations
firm and solid. Previously the matter used to be
p. 62. regarded as commonplace: subsequently it acquired
a grave importance in men's eyes. Many persons
from all parts of the world set out for Persia, and

Martyrs" at Teherán (amongst whom was the Báb's maternal uncle Mírzá Seyyid 'Alí) which likewise took place at this time some information will be found in Note B at end.

began to seek with their whole hearts. For it hath been proved by experience in the world that in the case of such matters of conscience laceration causeth healing; censure produceth increased diligence; prohibition induceth eagerness; and intimidation createth avidity. The root is hidden in the very heart, while the branch is apparent and evident. When one branch is cut off other branches grow. Thus it is observed that when such matters occur in other countries they become extinct spontaneously through lack of attention and exiguity of interest. For up to the present moment of movements pertaining to religion many have appeared in the countries of Europe, but, non-interference and absence of bigotry p. 63.
having deprived them of importance, in a little while they became effaced and dispelled.

After this event there was wrought by a certain Bábí a great error and a grave presumption and crime, which has blackened the page of the history of this sect and given it an ill name throughout the civilized world. Of this event the marrow is this, that during the time when the Báb was residing in Ázarbaiján a youth, Ṣádiḳ by name, became affected with the utmost devotion to the Báb, night and day was busy in serving him, and became bereft of thought and reason. Now when that which befel the Báb in Tabríz took place, this servant, actuated by his own fond fancies, fell into thoughts of seeking blood-

revenge. And since he knew naught of the details of the events, the absolute autocracy of the *Amír-Nizám*, his unbridled power, and sole authority; nor
p. 64. [was aware] that this sentence had been promulgated absolutely without the cognizance of the Royal Court, and that the Prime Minister had presumptuously issued the order on his own sole responsibility; since, on the contrary, he supposed that agreeably to ordinary custom and usage the attendants of the court had had a share in, and a knowledge of this sentence, therefore, [impelled] by folly, frenzy, and his evil star, nay, by sheer madness, he rose up from Tabríz and came straight to Teherán, one other person being his accomplice. Then, since the Royal Train had its abode in Shimrán, he thither directed his steps. God is our refuge! By him was wrought a deed so presumptuous that the tongue is unable to declare and the pen loath to describe it. Yet to God be praise and thankfulness that this madman had charged his pistol with shot, imagining this to be preferable and superior to all projectiles[1].

p. 65. Then all at once commotion arose, and this sect became of such ill repute that still, strive and struggle as they may to escape from the curse and disgrace

[1] Of the attempt on the Sháh's life a very graphic account is given by Gobineau (chapter xi). See also Watson's *History of Persia, &c.* pp. 407—410, Lady Sheil's *Diary*, pp. 273—282, and Note T at end.

and dishonour of this deed, they are unable to do so. They will recount from the first manifestation of the Báb until the present time; but when the thread of the discourse reaches this event they are abashed and hang their heads in shame, repudiating the presumptuous actor and accounting him the destroyer of the edifice and the cause of shame to mankind.

Now after the occurrence of this grave matter all of this sect were suspected. At first there was neither investigation nor enquiry[1], but afterwards in mere justice it was decided that there should be investigation, enquiry, and examination. All who were known to be of this sect fell under suspicion. Behá'u'lláh was passing the summer in the village of p. 66.
Afcha situated one stage from Teherán. When this news was spread abroad and punishment began, every one who was able hid himself in some retreat or fled the country. Amongst these Mírzá Yaḥyá[2], the brother of Behá'u'lláh, concealed himself, and, a bewildered fugitive, in the guise of a dervish, with *kashkúl*[3] in hand, wandered in mountains and plains

[1] i.e. at first everyone who was suspected of belonging to the Bábí community was put to death without enquiring as to whether he had any share in the conspiracy against the king.

[2] See Gobineau, pp. 277—279, and Note W at end.

[3] A hollow receptacle of about the size and shape of a cocoa-nut, round the orifice of which two chains are attached at four points to serve as a handle. It is used by dervishes as an alms-basket.

on the road to Resht. But Behá'u'lláh rode forth with perfect composure and calmness from Afcha, and came to Niyávarán, which was the abode of the Royal Train and the station of the imperial camp. Immediately on his arrival he was placed under arrest, and a whole regiment guarded him closely.
p. 67. After several days of interrogation they sent him in chains and fetters from Shimrán to the gaol of Teherán. And this harshness and punishment was due to the immoderate importunity of Hájí 'Alí Khán, the Ḥájibu'd-Dawla[1], nor did there seem any hope of deliverance, until His Majesty the King, moved by his own kindly spirit, commanded circumspection, and ordered this occurrence to be investigated and examined particularly and generally by means of the ministers of the imperial court.

Now when Beha'u'lláh was interrogated on this matter he answered in reply, "The event itself indicates the truth of the affair and testifies that this is the action of a thoughtless, unreasoning, and igno-

[1] Concerning this infamous monster who, amongst innumerable other wickednesses and cruelties, *volunteered* to carry out the sentence of death on his fallen benefactor, Mírzá Taḳí Khán, see Watson's *History of Persia*, &c. pp. 403—404. Dr Polak (*Persien; das Land und seine Bewohner*, Leipsic, 1865, vol. 1, p. 352) describes him as "*ein Mann ohne Herz und auf Commando zu jeder Grausamkeit bereit*," and then proceeds to enumerate the ghastly tortures which he devised for the Bábís.

rant man. For no reasonable person would charge his pistol with shot when embarking on so grave an enterprise. At least he would so arrange and plan it that the deed should be orderly and systematic. From the very nature of the event it is clear and evident as the sun that it is not the act of such as myself." p. 68.

So it was established and proven that the assassin had on his own responsibility engaged in this grievous action and monstrous deed with the idea and design of taking blood revenge for his Master, and that it concerned no one else[1]. And when the truth of the matter became evident the innocence of Behá'u'lláh from this suspicion was established in such wise that no doubt remained for anyone; the decision of the court declared his purity and freedom from this charge; and it became apparent and clear that what had been done with regard to him was due to the

[1] According to Gobineau (p. 280) three Bábís actually took part in the attempt on the Sháh's life and others were concerned in the plot. According to the *Násikhu't-Tawáríkh*, which gives the most circumstantial account of the occurrence, Mullá Sheykh 'Alí (called by the Bábís *Jenáb-i-'Azím*) first proposed the attempt, for the carrying out of which twelve persons volunteered. Of these twelve, however, there were but three—Ṣádiḳ of Zanján (or Mílán), Mullá Fatḥu'lláh of Ḳum, and Mírzá Muḥammad of Níríz—whose hearts did not fail them at the last. Of these three the first was killed on the spot, the other two were put to death afterwards. See Note T at end.

efforts of his foes and the hasty folly of the Ḥájibu'd-Dawla. Therefore did the government of eternal
p. 69. duration desire to restore certain properties and estates which had been confiscated, that thereby it might pacify him. But since the chief part of these was lost and only an inconsiderable portion was forthcoming, none came forward to claim them. Indeed Behá'u'lláh requested permission to withdraw to the Supreme Shrines [of Kerbelá and Nejef] and, after some months[1], by the royal permission and with the leave of the Prime Minister, set out accompanied by one of the King's messengers for the Shrines.

Let us return, however, to our original subject. Of the Báb's writings many remained in men's hands. Some of these were commentaries on, and interpretations of the verses of the Ḳur'án; some were prayers, homilies, and hints of [the true significance of certain] passages; others were exhortations, admonitions, dissertations on the different branches of the doctrine of the Divine Unity, demonstrations of the special prophetic mission of the Lord of existing things [Muḥammad], and (as hath been understood) encouragements to amendment of character, severance from worldly states,
p. 70. and dependence on the inspirations of God[2]. But

[1] According to Nabíl's chronological poem (B. ii, p. 983, 987) Behá'u'lláh was imprisoned in Teherán for four months.

[2] For an enumeration of the Báb's writings see Note U at end.

the essence and purport of his compositions were the praises and descriptions of that Reality soon to appear which was his only object and aim, his darling, and his desire. For he regarded his own appearance as that of a harbinger of good tidings, and considered his own real nature merely as a means for the manifestation of the greater perfections of that One. And indeed he ceased not from celebrating Him by night or day for a single instant, but used to signify to all his followers that they should expect His arising: in such wise that he declares in his writings, "I am a letter out of that most mighty book and a dew-drop from that limitless ocean, and, when He shall appear, my true nature, my mysteries, riddles, and intimations will become evident, and the embryo of this religion shall develop through the grades of its being and ascent, attain to the station of '*the most comely of forms*[1],' and become adorned with the p. 71.
robe of '*blessed be God, the Best of Creators*[2].' And this event will disclose itself in the year [A.H. one thousand two hundred and] sixty-nine, which corresponds to the number of the year of '*after a while*[3],'

[1] Ḳur'án, xcv. 4.

[2] Ḳur'án, xxiii. 14. For texts from Beyán illustrating this passage, see Note V at end.

[3] The year of '*a while*' (سنه، حين) is 68 (ح=8, ی=10, ن=50), and the year of '*after a while*' therefore corresponds to 69, which is the number *after* 68. It was not, however, till A.H. 1283 (A.D. 1866—67) that, according to Nabíl (B. ii. pp. 984,

and '*thou shalt see the mountains which thou thinkest so solid passing away like the passing of the clouds*[1]' shall be fulfilled." In short he so described Him that, in his own expression, he regarded approach to the divine bounty and attainment of the highest degrees of perfection in the worlds of humanity as dependent on love for Him, and so inflamed was he with His flame that commemoration of Him was the bright candle of his dark nights in the fortress of Mákú, and remembrance of Him was the best of companions in the straits of the prison of Chihrík. Thereby he obtained spiritual enlargements; with His wine was he inebriated; and at remembrance of Him did he rejoice. All of his followers too were in
p. 72. expectation of the appearance of these signs, and each one of his intimates was seeking after the fulfilment of these forecasts.

Now from the beginning of the manifestation of the Báb there was in Teherán (which the Báb called the *Holy Land*) a youth of the family of one of the ministers and of noble lineage[2], gifted in every way,

988), Behá openly declared himself as 'He whom God shall manifest.'

[1] Ḳur'án, xxvii. 90.

[2] Behá'u'lláh (Mírzá Ḥuseyn 'Alí) and Ṣubḥ-i-Ezel (Mírzá Yaḥyá) were both sons of Mírzá 'Abbás (better known as Mírzá Buzurg) but by different mothers. This is confirmed beyond all doubt by Ṣubḥ-i-Ezel and others who have the best means of knowing, though Gobineau (p. 277) gives a different

and adorned with purity and nobility. Although he combined lofty lineage with high connection, and although his ancestors were men of note in Persia and universally sought after[1], yet he was not of a race of doctors or a family of scholars. Now this youth was from his earliest adolescence celebrated amongst those of the ministerial class, both relatives and strangers, for single-mindedness, and was from childhood pointed out as remarkable for sagacity, and held in regard in the eyes of the wise. He did not, however, after the fashion of his ancestors, desire elevation to lofty ranks nor seek advancement to splendid but transient positions. His extreme aptitude was nevertheless admit- p. 73.
ted by all, and his excessive acuteness and intelligence were universally avowed. In the eyes of the common folk he enjoyed a wonderful esteem, and in all gatherings and assemblies he had a marvellous speech and delivery. Notwithstanding lack of instruction and education[2] such was the keenness of his penetration

account. There was another brother called Músá, now deceased, one of whose sons is at present residing at Acre.

[1] Lit. "the place where the camels' saddles are put down," i.e. people whose houses are frequented by guests and visitors. See Lane's *Lexicon*, Book I. Part III. p. 1053.

[2] Behá himself says in the earlier portion of his *Epistle to the King of Persia* not included in the extract therefrom given further on:—ما قرأتُ ما عند النّاس من العلوم و ما دخلتُ المدارس فاسئل المدينة التى كنت فيها لتوقن بانّى لستُ من الكاذبين ✱ "*I have not studied the sciences which men have, neither have I entered*

and the readiness of his apprehension that when during his youthful prime he appeared in assemblies where questions of divinity and points of metaphysic were being discussed, and, in presence of a great concourse of doctors and scholars loosed his tongue, all those present were amazed, accounting this as a sort of prodigy beyond the discernment natural to the human race. From his early years he was the hope of his kindred and the unique one of his family and race, nay, their refuge and shelter.

However, in spite of these conditions and circum-
p. 74. stances, as he wore a *kuláh*[1] on his head and locks flowing over his shoulder, no one imagined that he would become the source of such matters, or that the waves of his flood would reach the zenith of this firmament.

When the question of the Báb was noised abroad signs of partiality appeared in him. At the first he apprized his relatives and connections, and the children and dependents of his own circle; subsequently he occupied his energies by day and night in

the colleges: ask the city wherein I was that thou mayest be sure that I am not of those who lie."

[1] The Persian lamb-skin hat worn by Government employés and civilians. The words مکلّه (hatted) and معمّم (turbaned) are commonly used to distinguish the laity or civilian class from the clergy or learned class. The latter usually shave the head, while the former wear their hair in *zulf* descending below the level of the ears.

inviting friends and strangers [to embrace the new faith]. He arose with mighty resolution, engaged with the utmost constancy in systematizing the principles and consolidating the ethical canons of that society in every way, and strove by all means to protect and guard these people.

When he had [thus] established the foundations
in Teherán he hastened to Mázandarán, where he
displayed in assemblies, meetings, conferences, inns, p. 75.
mosques, and colleges a mighty power of utterance
and exposition. Whoever beheld his open brow or
heard his vivid eulogies perceived him with the
eye of actual vision to be a patent demonstration, a
latent magnetic force, and a pervading influence. A
great number both of rich and poor and of erudite
doctors were attracted by his preaching and washed
their hands of heart and life, being so enkindled that
they laid down their lives under the sword dancing
[with joy].

Thus, amongst many instances, one day four
learned and accomplished scholars of the divines of
Núr were present in his company, and in such wise
did he expound that all four were involuntarily con-
strained to entreat him to accept them for his service.
For by dint of his eloquence, which was like 'evident sorcery,' he satisfied these eminent doctors p. 76.
that they were in reality children engaged in the
rudiments of study and the merest tyros, and that

therefore they must read the alphabet from the beginning. Several protracted conferences were passed in expounding and elucidating the *Point*[1] and the *Alif* of the Absolute, wherein the doctors present were astounded, and filled with amazement and astonishment at the seething and roaring of the ocean of his utterance. The report of this occurrence reached the hearing of far and near, and deep despondency fell on the adversaries. The regions of Núr were filled with excitement and commotion at these events, and the noise of this mischief and trouble smote the ears of the citizens of Bárfurúsh. The chief divine of Núr, Mullá Muḥammad, was in Ḳishláḳ[2]. When

[1] The '*Point*' (نقطه), '*Point of Revelation*' (نقطهٔ بیان), and '*First Point*' (نقطهٔ اولی) were the titles assumed by the Báb during the latter part of his mission, and it is by one of these titles, or by the phrases حضرت اعلی ('*His Highness the Supreme*'), حضرت ربّی الاعلی ('*His Highness my Lord the Supreme*'), that he is mentioned amongst the Bábís. (See Gobineau, p. 156.) The *Alif*, in the phraseology of the mystics, indicates the unmanifested Essence of God.

[2] *Ḳishláḳ* is a word of Turkish origin (from قِش winter) applied generally to the warmer low-lying districts where the winter is passed, the highlands where the summer is spent being called *Yiláḳ* or *Yilágh*. It is also applied as a proper name to several places in the north of Persia. *Kishláḳ of Núr* is, as appears from the Sháh's Diary of his journey through Mázandarán, a district bordering on the coast, of which the chief town is Khurramábád. Núr itself is situated in the mountains.

he heard of these occurrences he sent two of the most distinguished and profound of the doctors, who were possessed of wondrous eloquence, effective oratorical p. 77.
talent, conclusiveness of argument, and brilliant powers of demonstration, to quench this fire, and to subdue and overcome this young man by force of argument, either reducing him to penitence, or causing him to despair of the successful issue of his projects. Glory be to God for His wondrous decrees! When those two doctors entered the presence of that young man, saw the waves of his utterance, and heard the force of his arguments, they unfolded like the rose and were stirred like the multitude, and, abandoning altar and chair, pulpit and preferment, wealth and luxury, and evening and morning congregations, they applied themselves to the furtherance of the objects of this person, even inviting the chief divine to tender his allegiance. So when this young man with a faculty p. 78.
of speech like a rushing torrent set out for Ámul and Sárí he met with that experienced doctor and that illustrious divine in Ḳishláḳ of Núr. And the people assembled from all quarters awaiting the result. His accomplished reverence the divine, although he was of universally acknowledged excellence, and in science the most learned of his contemporaries, nevertheless decided to have recourse to augury as to [whether he should engage in] discussion and disputation. This did not prove favourable and he therefore excused

himself, deferring [the discussion] until some other time. His incompetency and shortcoming thereby became known and suspected, and this caused the adherence, confirmation, and edification of many.

In brief outline the narrative is this. For some while he wandered about in those districts. After the death of the late prince Muḥammad Sháh he returned to Teherán, having in his mind [the intention of] corresponding and entering into relations
p. 79. with the Báb. The medium of this correspondence was the celebrated Mullá 'Abdu'l-Karím of Ḳazvín[1], who was the Báb's mainstay and trusted intimate. Now since a great celebrity had been attained for Behá'u'lláh in Teherán, and the hearts of men were disposed towards him, he, together with Mullá 'Abdu'l-Karím, considered it as expedient that, in face of the agitation amongst the doctors, the aggressiveness of the greater part of [the people of] Persia, and the irresistible power of the *Amír-Niẓám*, whereby both the Báb and Behá'u'lláh were in great danger and liable to incur severe punishment, some measure should be adopted to direct the thoughts of men towards some absent person, by which means Behá'u'lláh would remain protected from the interference of all men. And since further, having regard to sundry considerations, they did not consider an outsider as suitable, they cast the lot of this

[1] See above, p. 41 and note.

augury to the name of Behá'u'lláh's brother Mírzá Yaḥyá[1].

By the assistance and instruction of Behá'u'lláh, p. 80.
therefore, they made him notorious and famous on the tongues of friends and foes, and wrote letters, ostensibly at his dictation, to the Báb. And since secret correspondences were in process the Báb highly approved of this scheme. So Mírzá Yaḥyá was concealed and hidden while mention of him was on the tongues and in the mouths of men. And this mighty plan was of wondrous efficacy, for Behá'u'lláh, though he was known and seen, remained safe and secure, and this veil was the cause that no one outside [the sect] fathomed the matter or fell into the idea of molestation, until Behá'u'lláh quitted Teherán at the permission of the King and was permitted to withdraw to the Supreme Shrines.

When he reached Baghdad and the crescent moon of the month of Muḥarram of the year [A. H. one p. 81.
thousand two hundred and] sixty-nine (which was termed in the books of the Báb "the year of '*after a while*[2]'" and wherein he had promised the disclosure of the true nature of his religion and its mysteries) shone forth from the horizon of the world, this covert secret, as is related, became apparent amongst all within and without [the society]. Behá'u'lláh with mighty steadfastness became a target for the arrows

[1] See Note W at end. [2] See note 3 at foot of p. 55.

of all amongst mankind, while Mírzá Yaḥyá in disguise passed his time, now in the environs and vicinity of Baghdad engaged for better concealment in various trades, now in Baghdad itself in the garb of the Arabs.

Now Behá'u'lláh so acted that the hearts of this sect were drawn towards him, while most of the inhabitants of 'Iráḳ[1] were reduced to silence and speechlessness, some being amazed and others an-
p. 82. gered. After remaining there for one year he withdrew his hand from all things, abandoned relatives and connections, and, without the knowledge of his followers, quitted 'Iráḳ[1] alone and solitary, without companion, supporter, associate, or comrade. For nigh upon two years he dwelt in Turkish Kurdistán, generally in a place named Sarkalú, situated in the mountains, and far removed from human habitations. Sometimes on rare occasions he used to frequent Suleymániyyé. Ere long had elapsed the most eminent doctors of those regions got some inkling of his circumstances and conditions, and conversed with him on the solution of certain difficult questions connected with the most abstruse points of theology. Having witnessed on his part ample signs and satisfactory explanations they observed towards him the

[1] Here and in subsequent passages where 'Iráḳ is mentioned *'Iráḳ-i-'Arab* (especially Baghdad) is intended, not *Iráḳ-i-'Ajam*.

utmost respectfulness and deference. In consequence of this he acquired a great fame and wonderful p. 83. reputation in those regions, and fragmentary accounts of him were circulated in all quarters and directions, to wit that a stranger, a Persian, had appeared in the district of Suleymániyyé (which hath been, from of old, the place whence the most expert doctors of the Sunnites have arisen), and that the people of that country had loosed their tongues in praise of him. From the rumour thus heard it was known that that person was none other than Behá'u'lláh. Several persons, therefore, hastened thither, and began to entreat and implore, and the urgent entreaty of all brought about his return.

Now although this sect had not been affected with quaking or consternation at these grievous events, such as the slaughter of their chief and the rest, but did rather increase and multiply; still, since the Báb was but beginning to lay the founda- p. 84. tions when he was slain, therefore was this community ignorant concerning its proper conduct, action, behaviour, and duty, their sole guiding principle being love for the Báb. This ignorance was the reason that in some parts disturbances occurred; for, experiencing violent molestation, they unclosed their hands in self-defence. But after his return Behá'u'lláh made such strenuous efforts in educating, teaching, training, regulating, and reconstructing this com-

munity that in a short while all these troubles and mischiefs were quenched, and the utmost tranquillity and repose reigned in men's hearts; so that, according to what hath been heard, it became clear
p. 85. and obvious even to statesmen that the fundamental intentions and ideas of this sect were things spiritual, and such as are connected with pure hearts; that their true and essential principles were to reform the morals and beautify the conduct of the human race, and that with things material they had absolutely no concern.

When these principles, then, were established in the hearts of this sect they so acted in all lands that they became celebrated amongst statesmen for gentleness of spirit, steadfastness of heart, right intent, good deeds, and excellence of conduct. For this people are most well-disposed towards obedience and submissiveness, and, on receiving such instruction, they conformed their conduct and behaviour thereto. Formerly exception was taken to the words, deeds, de-
p. 86. meanour, morals, and conduct of this sect: now objection is made in Persia to their tenets and spiritual state. Now this is beyond the power of man, that he should be able by interference or objection to change the heart and conscience, or meddle with the convictions of any one. For in the realm of conscience nought but the ray of God's light can command, and on the throne of the heart none

but the pervading power of the King of Kings should rule. Thus it is that one can arrest and suspend [the action of] every faculty except thought and reflection; for a man cannot even by his own volition withhold himself from reflection or thought, nor keep back his musings and imaginings.

At all events the undeniable truth is this, that for nigh upon thirty-five years[1] no action opposed to the government or prejudicial to the nation has p. 87.
emanated from this sect or been witnessed [on their part], and that during this long period, notwithstanding the fact that their numbers and strength are double what they were formerly, no sound has arisen from any place, except that every now and then learned doctors and eminent scholars (really for the extension of this report through the world and the awakening of men) sentence some few to death. For such interference is not destruction but edification when thou regardest the truth, which will not thereby become quenched and forgotten, but rather stimulated and advertised.

I will at least relate one short anecdote of what

[1] This passage clearly shews that our history was composed not more than four or five years ago, probably during the year 1886. For since the attempt on the Sháh's life in the month of Shawwál, A.H. 1268 (August 1852), the Bábís have taken no action hostile to the Persian government, and the month of Shawwál, A.H. 1303 (35 years from this date) began in July, 1886.

actually took place. A certain person violently molested and grievously injured a certain Bábí.
p. 88. The victim unclosed his hand in retaliation and arose to take vengeance, unsheathing his weapon against the aggressor. Becoming the object of the censure and reprimand of this sect, however, he took refuge in flight. When he reached Hamadán his character became known, and, as he was of the clerical class, the doctors vehemently pursued him, handed him over to the government, and ordered chastisement to be inflicted. By chance there fell out from the fold of his collar a document written by Behá'u'lláh, the subject of which was reproof of attempts at retaliation, censure and reprobation of the search after vengeance, and prohibition from following after lusts. Amongst other matters they found these expressions contained in it :—" *Verily God is quit of the sedi-*
p. 89. *tious*," and likewise :—" *If ye be slain it is better for you than that ye should slay. And when ye are tormented have recourse to the controllers of affairs and the refuge of the people*[1]; *and if ye be neglected then entrust your affairs to the Jealous Lord. This is the mark of the sincere, and the characteristic of the*

[1] i.e. " If you be wronged or persecuted, appeal for protection and redress to the legally constituted authorities ; and if they will not help you, then be patient and put your trust in God, but do not attempt by force to obtain redress for yourselves."

assured." When the governor became cognizant of this writing he addressed that person saying, "By the decree of that chief whom you yourself obey correction is necessary and punishment and chastisement obligatory." "If," replied that person, "you will carry out all his precepts I shall have the utmost pleasure in [submitting to] punishment and death." The governor smiled and let the man go.

So Behá'u'lláh made the utmost efforts to educate [his people] and incite [them] to morality, the acquisition of the sciences and arts of all countries, kindly dealing with all the nations of the earth, desire for the welfare of all peoples, sociability, concord, obedience, submissiveness, instruction of [their] p. 90.
children, production of what is needful for the human race, and inauguration of true happiness for mankind; and he continually kept sending tracts of admonition to all parts, whereby a wonderful effect was produced. Some of these epistles have, after extreme search and enquiry, been examined, and some portions of them shall now be set down in writing[1].

[1] For some account of Behá's various writings see B. ii. pp. 942—981. A specimen of the ایقان in the original may be found in Rosen's *MSS. Persans*, pp. 32—51, and a part of the سورهٔ هیکل in his *MSS. Arabes*, pp. 191—212. Baron Rosen intends shortly to publish the whole of the سورهٔ هیکل including the *Epistles to the Kings* (الواح سلاطین), and he has been kind enough to send me the proof-sheets of this

All these epistles consisted of [exhortations to] purity of morals, encouragement to good conduct, reprobation of certain individuals, and complaints of the seditious. Amongst others this sentence was recorded:—

"*My captivity is not my abasement: by my life, it is indeed a glory unto me! But the abasement is the ac-*
p. 91. *tion of my friends who connect themselves with us and follow the devil in their actions. Amongst them is he who taketh lust and turneth aside from what is commanded; and amongst them is he who followeth the truth in right guidance. As for those who commit sin and cling to the world they are assuredly not of the people of Behá.*"

So again:—

"*Well is it with him who is adorned with the decoration of manners and morals: verily he is of those who help their Lord with clear perspicuous action.*"

"*He is God, exalted is His state, wisdom and utterance.* The True One (glorious is His glory) for the shewing forth of the gems of ideals from the mine of man, hath, in every age, sent a trusted one. The primary foundation of the faith of God and the religion of God is this, that they should not make diverse sects and various paths the cause and reason of hatred. These principles and laws and firm sure roads

important work as they are printed off. Further information will be found in a subsequent foot-note.

appear from one dawning-place and shine from one dayspring, and these diversities were out of regard for the requirements of the time, season, ages, and epochs. p. 92.
O unitarians, make firm the girdle of endeavour, that perchance religious strife and conflict may be removed from amongst the people of the world and be annulled. For love of God and His servants engage in this great and mighty matter. Religious hatred and rancour is a world-consuming fire, and the quenching thereof most arduous, unless the hand of Divine Might give men deliverance from this unfruitful calamity. Consider a war which happeneth between two states: both sides have foregone wealth and life: how many villages were beheld as though they were not! This precept is in the position of the light in the lamp of utterance."

"O people of the world, ye are all the fruit of one tree and the leaves of one branch. Walk with perfect charity, concord, affection, and agreement. I swear p. 93.
by the Sun of Truth, the light of agreement shall brighten and illumine the horizons. The all-knowing Truth hath been and is the witness to this saying. Endeavour to attain to this high supreme station which is the station of protection and preservation of mankind. This is the intent of the King of intentions, and this the hope of the Lord of hopes."

"We trust that God will assist the kings of the earth to illuminate and adorn the earth with the refulgent light of the Sun of Justice. At one time we spoke in the language of the Law, at another time in the language of the Truth and the Way; and the ultimate object and remote aim was the shewing forth of this high supreme station. *And God sufficeth for witness.*"

p. 94. "O friends, consort with all the people of the world with joy and fragrance. If there be to you a word or essence whereof others than you are devoid, communicate it and shew it forth in the language of affection and kindness: if it be received and be effective the object is attained, and if not leave it to him, and with regard to him deal not harshly but pray[1]. The language of kindness is the lodestone of hearts and the food of the soul; it stands in the relation of ideas to words, and is as an horizon for the shining of the Sun of Wisdom and Knowledge."

"If the unitarians had in the latter times acted according to the glorious Law [which came] after His Highness the Seal [of the Prophets[2]] (may the life of all beside him be his sacrifice!), and had clung to its skirt, the foundation of the fortress of religion

[1] i.e. "If you have a message or gospel wherein others are not partakers, then convey it to those about you in kind and gentle words. If they accept it you have gained your object; if not, leave it to ripen and bear fruit, and pray that it may do so, but on no account strive to force its acceptance on any one."

[2] Muḥammad.

would not have been shaken, and populous cities would not have been ruined, but rather cities and p. 95. villages would have acquired and been adorned with the decoration of peace and serenity."

"Through the heedlessness and discordance of the favoured people and the smoke of wicked souls the Fair Nation is seen to be darkened and enfeebled. Had they acted [according to what they knew] they would not have been heedless of the light of the Sun of Justice."

"This victim hath from earliest days until now been afflicted at the hands of the heedless. They exiled us without cause at one time to 'Irák[1], at another time to Adrianople, and thence to Acre, which was a place of exile for murderers and robbers; neither is it known where and in what spot we shall take up our abode after this greatest prison-house. *Knowledge is with God, the Lord of the Throne and of the dust and the Lord of the lofty seat.* In whatever place we may be, and whatever befal us, the saints must gaze with perfect steadfastness and confidence towards the Supreme Horizon and occupy p. 96. themselves in the reformation of the world and the education of the nations. What hath befallen and shall befal hath been and is an instrument and means for the furtherance of the Word of Unity. *Take*

[1] See note on p. 64.

hold of the command of God and cling thereto: verily it hath been sent down from beside a wise Ordainer."

"With perfect compassion and mercy have we
guided and directed the people of the world to that
whereby their souls shall be profited. I swear by
the Sun of Truth which hath shone forth from the
highest horizons of the world that the people of Behá
had not and have not any aim save the prosperity
and reformation of the world and the purifying
of the nations. With all men they have been in
sincerity and charity. Their outward [appearance] is
one with their inward [heart], and their inward [heart]
identical with their outward [appearance]. The truth
p. 97. of the matter is not hidden or concealed, but plain
and evident before [men's] faces. Their very deeds are
the witness of this assertion. To-day let every one
endowed with vision win his way from deeds and signs
to the object of the people of Behá and from their
speech and conduct gain knowledge of their intent.
The waves of the ocean of divine mercy appear at
the utmost height, and the showers of the clouds
of His grace and favour descend every moment.
During the days of sojourn in 'Irák[1] this oppressed
one sat down and consorted with all classes without
veil or disguise. How many of the denizens of the

[1] See note on p. 64.

horizons[1] entered in enmity and went forth in sympathy! The door of grace was open before the faces of all. With rebellious and obedient did we outwardly converse after one fashion, that perchance the evil-doers might win their way to the ocean of boundless forgiveness. The splendours of the Name of the Concealer[2] were in such wise manifested that the evil-doer imagined that he was accounted of the good. No messenger was disappointed and no enquirer was turned back. The causes of the aversion and avoidance of men were certain of the doctors of Persia and the unseemly deeds of the ignorant. By [the term] 'doctors' in these passages are signified those persons who have withheld mankind from the shore of the Ocean of Unity; but as for the learned who practise [their knowledge] and the wise who act justly, they are as the spirit unto the body of the world. Well is it with that learned man whose head is adorned with the crown of justice, and whose body glorieth in the ornament of honesty. The Pen of Admonition p. 98.

[1] i.e. The people of all lands.

[2] 'The Concealer' (الستّار) is one of the Names of God (see Redhouse's *Most Comely Names*, p. 38, No. 236), of which Names the Prophets are the mirrors or places of manifestation (مظاهر). In their actions the Divine Attributes whether '*beautiful*' (جمالی) or '*terrible*' (جلالی) are displayed. So Behá's concealment of his feelings is here described as a manifestation of the 'Name of the Concealer.'

exhorteth the friends and enjoineth on them charity, pity, wisdom, and gentleness. The oppressed one[1] is this day a prisoner; his allies are the hosts of good deeds and virtues; not ranks, and hosts, and guns,
p. 99. and cannons. One holy action maketh the world of earth highest paradise.

"O friends, help the oppressed one with well-pleasing virtues and good deeds! To-day let every soul desire to attain the highest station. He must not regard what is in him, but what is in God. *It is not for him to regard what shall advantage himself, but that whereby the Word of God which must be obeyed shall be upraised.* The heart must be sanctified from every form of selfishness and lust, for the weapons of the unitarians and the saints were and are the fear of God. That is the buckler which guardeth man from the arrows of hatred and abomination. Unceasingly hath the standard of piety been victorious, and accounted amongst the most puissant hosts of the world. *Thereby do the saints subdue the*
p. 100. *cities of* [men's] *hearts by the permission of God, the Lord of hosts.* Darkness hath encompassed the earth: the lamp which giveth light was and is wisdom. The dictates thereof must be observed under all circumstances. And of wisdom is the regard of place and the utterance of discourse according to measure and

[1] Throughout his writings by the terms '*the oppressed one*,' '*this oppressed one*,' '*this servant*,' &c., Behá intends himself.

state. And of wisdom is decision; for man should not accept whatsoever anyone sayeth[1].

"Under all circumstances desire of the True One (glorious is His glory) that He will not deprive His servants of the sealed wine[2] and the lights of the Name of the Self-subsistent.

"*O friends of God, verily the Pen of Sincerity enjoineth on you the greatest faithfulness. By the Life of God, its light is more evident than the light of the sun! In its light and its brightness and its radiance every light is eclipsed.* We desire of God that He p. 101.
will not withhold from His cities and lands the radiant effulgence of the Sun of Faithfulness. We have directed all in the nights and in the days to faithfulness, chastity, purity, and constancy; and have enjoined good deeds and well-pleasing qualities. In

[1] i.e. Of the dictates of wisdom one is this, that the believer should in speaking have regard to fitness of time and place and not with undiscriminating zeal lay bare his convictions to all persons or in all companies; and another is this, that he should be firmly established in his belief and not be 'tossed to and fro and carried about with every wind of doctrine.'

[2] By the '*sealed wine*' are meant the ordinances of God. Thus in the '*Most Holy Book*' (كتاب اقدس rather than لوح اقدس by which name I formerly described it, B. ii. 972—981) it is written:—لا تحسبنّ انّا نزّلنا لكم الاحكام بل فتحنا ختم الرّحيق المختوم باصابع القدرة و الاقتدار * "*Do not consider that we have revealed unto you ordinances, but rather that we have opened the seal of the sealed wine with the fingers of might and power.*"

the nights and in the days the shriek of the pen ariseth and the tongue speaketh, that against the sword the word may arise, and against fierceness patience, and in place of oppression submission, and at the time of martyrdom resignation. For thirty years and more, in all that hath befallen this oppressed community they have been patient, referring it to God. Every one endowed with justice and fairness hath testified and doth testify to that which hath been said. During this period this oppressed one was engaged in good exhortations and efficacious and sufficient admonitions, till it became
p. 102. established and obvious before all that this victim had made himself a target for the arrows of calamity unto the shewing forth of the treasures deposited in [men's] souls. Strife and contest were and are seemly in the beasts of prey of the earth, [but] laudable actions are seemly in man.

"*Blessed is the Merciful One: Who created man: and taught him utterance.* After all these troubles, neither are the ministers of state content, nor the doctors of the church. Not one soul was found to utter a word for God before the court of His Majesty the King (*may God perpetuate his kingdom*). *There shall not befal us aught save that which God hath decreed unto us.* They acted not kindly, nor was there any shortcoming in the display of evil. Justice became like the phœnix[1], and faithfulness like the philosopher's stone: none spake for the right. It would seem that justice had become hateful to men and cast p. 103. forth from all lands like the people of God. Glory be to God! In the episode of the land of Ṭá[2] not one spoke for that which God had commanded. Having regard to the display of power and parade of service in the presence of the King (*may God perpetuate his kingdom*) they have called good evil and the reformer a sedition-monger. The like of these persons would depict the drop as an ocean, and the mote as a sun. They call the house at Kalín[3] 'the strong fortress,' and close their eyes to the perspicuous truth. They have attacked a number of reformers of the world with the charge

[1] The *'Anḳá* (in Persian *Símurgh*), a mythical bird dwelling in the mountains of *Ḳáf*, which bound the world according to the old Arabian cosmography. Hence anything very rare or hard to find or of which the name is heard but the form is not seen (موجود الاسم مفقود الجسم) is compared to it.

[2] '*The land of Ṭá*' (ارض طا) means Teherán. So in the *Kitáb-i-Aḳdas* Khurásán is called ارض الخاء and Kirmán ارض الكاف و الراء; while in the Persian Beyán we find mention of the *land of Alif* (Ázarbaiján), the *land of 'Ayn* ('Iráḳ), *the land of Fá* (Fárs), and the *land of Mím* (Mázandarán). This use of the letters of the alphabet to designate places and people is very common amongst the Bábís. See the note on the colophon at the end of the book.

[3] Concerning Kalín (less correctly Kuleyn) see p. 14 *supra* and note 3 thereon.

of seditiousness. As God liveth, these persons had and have no intent nor hope save the glory of the state and service to their nation! For God they spoke and for God they speak, and in the way of God do they journey.

p. 104. "O friends, ask of Him who is the Desire of the denizens of earth that He will succour His Majesty the King (*may God perpetuate his kingdom*) so that all the dominions of Persia may by the light of the Sun of Justice become adorned with the decoration of tranquillity and security. According to statements made, he, at the promptings of his blessed nature, loosed those who were in bonds, and bestowed freedom on the captives. The representation of certain matters before the faces of [God's] servants is obligatory, and natural to the pious, so that the good may be aware and become cognizant [thereof]. *Verily He inspireth whom He pleaseth with what He desireth, and He is the Powerful, the Ordainer, the Knowing, the Wise.*

"A word from that land hath reached the oppressed one which in truth was the cause of wonder. His Highness the Mu'tamadu 'd-Dawla, Farhád Mírzá[1], said concerning the imprisoned one that whereof the
p. 105. repetition is not pleasing. This victim consorted very little with him or the like of him. So far as is

[1] Farhád Mírzá was the uncle of the Sháh. He died in 1888.

recollected on [only]' two occasions did he visit Murgh-Maḥalla in Shimírán[1] where was the abode of the oppressed one. On the first occasion he came one day in the afternoon, and on the second one Friday morning, returning nigh unto sundown. He knows and is conscious that he should not speak contrary to the truth. If one enter his presence let him repeat these words before him on behalf of the oppressed one:—'*O Prince! I ask justice and fairness from your Highness concerning that which hath befallen this poor victim.*' Well is it for that soul whom the doubts of the perverse withhold not from the display of justice, and deprive not of the lights of the luminary of equity. *O saints of God!* p. 106.
at the end of our discourse we enjoin on you once again chastity, faithfulness, godliness, sincerity, and purity. Lay aside the evil and adopt the good. This is that whereunto ye are commanded in the Book of God, the Knowing, the Wise. Well is it with those who practise [this injunction]. At this moment the pen crieth out, saying, 'O saints of God, regard the horizon of uprightness, and be quit, severed, and free from what is beside this. *There is no strength and no power save in God.*'"

[1] Shimírán or Shimrán (sometimes used in the plural, Shimránát) is the name applied generally to the villages and mansions situated on the lower slopes descending from Elburz which serve as summer residences to the wealthier inhabitants of Teherán.

In short, formerly in all provinces in Persia accounts and stories concerning this sect diverse and discordant, yea, incompatible with the character of the human race and opposed to the divine endowment, passed on the tongues and in the mouths of men and obtained notoriety. But when their prin-
p. 107. ciples acquired fixity and stability and their conduct and behaviour were known and appreciated, the veil of doubt and suspicion fell, the true character of this sect became clear and evident, and it reached the degree of certainty that their principles were unlike men's fancies, and that their foundation differed from [the popular] opinion and estimate. In their conduct, action, morality, and demeanour was no place for objection; the objection in Persia is to certain of the ideas and tenets of this sect. And from the indications of various circumstances it hath been observed that the people have acquired belief and confidence in the trustworthiness, faithfulness, and godliness of this sect in all transactions.

Let us return to our original topic. During the period of their sojourn in 'Iráḳ these persons became notorious throughout the world. For exile resulted
p. 108. in fame, in such wise that a great number of other parties sought alliance and union, and devised means of [acquiring] intimacy [with them]. But the chief of this sect, discovering the aims of each faction, acted with the utmost consistency, circumspection, and

firmness. Reposing confidence in none, he applied himself as far as possible to the admonition of each, inciting and urging them to good resolutions and aims beneficial to the state and the nation. And this conduct and behaviour of the chief acquired notoriety in 'Irák.

So likewise during the period of their sojourn in 'Irák certain functionaries of foreign governments were desirous of intimacy, and sought friendly relations [with them]; but the chief would not agree. Amongst other strange haps was this, that in 'Irák p. 109.
certain of the Royal Family came to an understanding with these [foreign] governments, and, [induced] by promises and threats, conspired with them. But this sect unloosed their tongues in reproach and began to admonish them, saying, "What meanness is this, and what evident treason; that man should, for worldly advantages, personal profit, easy circumstances, or protection of life and property, cast himself into this great detriment and evident loss, and embark in a course of action which will conduce to the greatest abasement and involve the utmost infamy and disgrace both here and hereafter! One can support any baseness save treason to one's country, and every sin admits of pardon and forgiveness save [that of] dishonouring one's government and injuring one's nation." And they imagined that they were acting patriotically, displaying sincerity and loyalty, and p. 110.

accounting sacred the duties of fidelity; which noble aim they regarded as a moral obligation. So rumours of this were spread abroad through 'Irák-i-'Arab, and such as wished well to their country loosed their tongues in uttering thanks, expressing approval and respect. And it was supposed that these events would be represented in the Royal Presence; but after a while it became known that certain of the Sheykhs at the Supreme Shrines[1] who were in correspondence with the court, yea, even with the King, were in secret continually attributing to this sect strange affinities and relations, imagining that such attempts would conduce to favour at the Court and cause
p. 111. advancement of [their] condition and rank. And since no one could speak freely on this matter at that court which is the pivot of justice, whilst just ministers aware [of the true state of the case] also regarded silence as their best policy, the 'Irák question, through these misrepresentations and rumours, assumed gravity in Teherán, and was enormously exaggerated. But the consuls-general, being cognizant of the truth, continued to act with moderation, until Mírzá Buzurg Khán of Ḳazvín[2] became consul-

[1] Kerbelá and Nejef.

[2] According to Ṣubḥ-i-Ezel's statement, Mírzá Buzurg Khán became incensed against the Bábís, partly because they would not consent to secure his goodwill by a bribe, partly because Behá'u'lláh took to wife the daughter of a merchant whom he wished to marry. At all events his enmity was such

general in Baghdad. Now since this person was wont to pass the greater portion of his time in a state of intoxication and was devoid of foresight, he became the accomplice and confederate of those Sheykhs in 'Irák, and girded up his loins stoutly to destroy and demolish. Such power of description and [strength] of fingers as he possessed he employed in p. 112.
making representations and statements. Each day he secretly wrote a dispatch to Teherán, made vows and compacts with the Sheykhs, and sent diplomatic notes to His Excellency the Ambassador-in-chief[1] [at Constantinople]. But since these statements and depositions had no basis or foundation, they were all postponed and adjourned; until at length these Sheykhs convened a meeting to consult with the [Consul-] General, assembled a number of learned doctors and great divines in the [mosque of the] 'two Káẓims'[2] (upon them be peace), and, having come to

that he strove to incite the '*Ulamá* of Baghdad to declare a *jihád* or religious war against the Bábís, and this, according to Ṣubḥ-i-Ezel, they would have done, had not Námiḳ Páshá, then governor of Baghdad, prevented them, saying, 'These are not rebels, and you shall not kill them'.

[1] Mírzá Ḥuseyn Khán was at this time Persian ambassador at Constantinople.

[2] 'The tombs of the '*two Káẓims*' (i.e. the seventh Imám, Músá Káẓim, and the ninth Imám, Muḥammad Taḳí) are situated about 3 miles N. of Baghdad, and constitute one of the principal places of pilgrimage of the Shí'ites. Around them has grown up a considerable town, chiefly inhabited by Persians, known as *Káẓimeyn*.'

an unanimous agreement, wrote to the divines of Kerbelá the exalted and Nejef the most noble, convoking them all. They came, some knowing, others not knowing. Amongst the latter the illustrious and expert doctor, the noble and celebrated scholar, the
p. 113. seal of seekers after truth, Sheykh Murtaẓá[1], now departed and assoiled, who was the admitted chief of all, arrived without knowledge [of the matter in hand]. But, so soon as he was informed of their actual designs, he said, "I am not properly acquainted with the essential character of this sect, nor with the

[1] In the *Epistle to the King of Persia* (لوح سلطان) Sheykh Murtaẓá is especially exempted from the condemnation pronounced against the majority of the Shi'ite doctors, and held up as an example of a truly pious and God-fearing divine (see p. 129 *infra*). I was informed by Ṣubḥ-i-Ezel that he not only refused to pronounce sentence against the Bábís or sanction a *jihád* against them, but that he also withheld the Sháh from persecuting the Sheykhís (concerning whom see Note E at end) saying, "May it not become like the affair of the Bábís!" The book called قصص العلما, (*Stories of Divines*), published at Teherán A.H. 1304, gives a brief account of Sheykh Murtaẓá, whose lectures, as it appears, the author of the work in question attended for a while. According to this account Sheykh Murtaẓá was a native of Shushtar, but spent the greater part of his life at Nejef, where, at the age of 80, he died and was buried. Neither the date of his birth nor that of his death is given. His works—not very numerous—are mentioned, and his remarkable piety and learning highly praised. Indeed it is stated that after Sheykh Muḥammad Ḥasan he was the most eminent of all the Shi'ite doctors.

secret tenets and hidden theological doctrines of this community; neither have I hitherto witnessed or perceived in their demeanour or conduct anything at variance with the Perspicuous Book which would lead me to pronounce them infidels. Therefore hold me excused in this matter, and let him who regards it as his duty take action." Now the design of the Sheykhs and the Consul was a sudden and general attack, but, by reason of the non-compliance of the departed Sheykh, this scheme proved abortive, resulting, indeed, only in shame and disappointment. So that concourse of Sheykhs, doctors, and common folk which had come from Kerbelá dispersed. p. 114.

Just at this time mischievous persons—[including] even certain dismissed ministers—endeavoured on all sides so to influence this sect that they might perchance alter their course and conduct. From every quarter lying messages and disquieting reports continually followed one another in uninterrupted and constant succession to the effect that the deliberate intention of the court of Persia was the eradication, suppression, annihilation, and destruction of this sect; that correspondence was continually being carried on with the local authorities; and that all [the Bábís] in 'Irák̤ would shortly be delivered over with bound hands to Persia. But the Bábís passed the time in calmness and silence, without in any way altering their behaviour and conduct.

So when Mírzá Buzurg Khán failed to effect and accomplish the designs of his heart by such actions also, he ill-advisedly fell to reflecting how he might
p. 115. grieve and humiliate [the Bábís]. Every day he sought some pretext for offering insult, aroused some disturbance and tumult, and raised up the banner of mischief, until the matter came nigh to culminating in the sudden outbreak of a riot, the lapse of the reins of control from the hand, and the precipitation of [men's] hearts into disquietude and perturbation and [their] minds into anguish and agony.

Now when [the Bábís] found themselves unable to treat this humour by any means (for, strive as they would, they were foiled and frustrated), and when they failed to find any remedy for this disorder or any fairness in this flower, they deliberated and hesitated for nine months, and at length a certain number of them, to stop further mischief, enrolled themselves as subjects of the Sublime Ottoman Government, that [thereby] they might assuage this tumult. By means
p. 116. of this device the mischief was allayed, and the consul withdrew his hand from molesting them; but he notified this occurrence to the Royal Court in a manner at variance with the facts and contrary to the truth, and, together with the confederate Sheykhs, applied himself in every way to devices for distracting the senses [of the Bábís]. Finally, however, being

dismissed, and overwhelmed with disaster, he became penitent and sorry.

Let us proceed with our original topic. For eleven years and somewhat over, Behá'u'lláh abode in 'Irák-i-'Arab. The behaviour and conduct of the sect were such that [his] fame and renown increased. For he was manifest and apparent amongst men, consorted and associated with all parties, and would converse familiarly with doctors and scholars concerning the solution of difficult theological questions and the verification of the true sense of abstruse points of divinity. As is currently reported by p. 117.
persons of every class, he used to please all, whether inhabitants or visitors, by his kindly intercourse and courteous address; and this sort of demeanour and conduct on his part led them to suspect sorcery and account him an adept in the occult sciences.

During this period Mírzá Yaḥyá remained concealed and hidden, continuing and abiding in his former conduct and behaviour, until, when the edict for the removal of Behá'u'lláh from Baghdad[1] was issued by His Majesty the Ottoman monarch, Mírzá Yaḥyá would neither quit nor accompany [him]: at one time he meditated setting out for India, at another, settling in Turkistán[2]; but, being unable to

[1] It would seem that the departure of the Bábís from Baghdad took place during the summer of 1864.

[2] Perhaps *Turkistán* is here intended to signify, not the

decide on either of these two plans, he finally, at his
p. 118. own wish, set out before all in the garb of a dervish, in disguise and change of raiment, for Karkúk and Arbíl. Thence, by continuous advance, he reached Mosul, where, on the arrival of the main body, he took up his abode and station alongside their caravan[1]. And although throughout this journey the governors and officials observed the utmost consideration and respectfulness, while march and halt were alike dignified and honourable, nevertheless was he always concealed in change of raiment, and acted cautiously, on the idea that some act of aggression was likely to occur.

In this fashion did they reach Constantinople, where they were appointed quarters in a guest-house on the part of the glorious Ottoman monarchy. And at first the utmost attention was paid to them in
p. 119. every way. On the third day, because of the straitness of their quarters and the greatness of their

country properly so called, but merely the country of the Turks, in which case we should rather translate 'remaining in Turkey.'

[1] Mírzá Yaḥyá, according to his own account, went from Baghdad to Karkúk in 8 days; thence to Mosul in 4 days; thence to Diyár Bekr in 20 days; thence to Kharpút in 7 or 8 days. From Kharpút he went to Sívás, thence to Samsún, and thence by sea to Constantinople. The whole journey from Baghdad to Constantinople, including halts, occupied between three and four months. By Nabíl also the duration of this exodus is stated as four months (B. ii. pp. 984, 987, v. 8).

numbers, they migrated and moved to another house. Certain of the nobles came to see and converse with them, and these, as is related, behaved with moderation. Notwithstanding that many in their assemblies and gatherings continued to condemn and vilify them, saying, "This sect are a mischief to all the world and destructive of treaties and covenants; they are a source of trouble and baleful to all lands; they have kindled a fire and consumed the earth; and though they be outwardly fair-seeming yet are they deserving of every chastisement and punishment," yet still the Bábís continued to conduct themselves with patience, calmness, deliberation, and constancy, so that they did not, even in self-defence, importune [the occupants of] high places or frequent the houses of any of the magnates of that kingdom. Whomsoever amongst the great he [Behá] interviewed on his p. 120.
own account, they met, and no word save of sciences and arts passed between them; until certain noblemen sought to guide him, and loosed their tongues in friendly counsel, saying, "To appeal, to state your case, and to demand justice is a measure demanded by custom." He replied in answer, "Pursuing the path of obedience to the King's command we have come to this country. Beyond this we neither had nor have any aim or desire that we should appeal and cause trouble. What is [now] hidden behind the veil of destiny will in the future become manifest.

There neither has been nor is any necessity for supplication and importunity. If the enlightened-minded leaders [of your nation] be wise and diligent, they will certainly make enquiry, and acquaint themselves with the true state of the case; if not, then
p. 121. [their] attainment of the truth is impracticable and impossible. Under these circumstances what need is there for importuning statesmen and supplicating ministers of the Court? We are free from every anxiety, and ready and prepared for the things predestined to us. '*Say, all is from God*[1]' is a sound and sufficient argument, and '*If God toucheth thee with a hurt there is no dispeller thereof save Him*[2]' is a healing medicine."

After some months a royal edict was promulgated appointing Adrianople in the district of Roumelia as their place of abode and residence. To that city the Bábís, accompanied by [Turkish] officers, proceeded all together, and there they made their home and habitation. According to statements heard from sundry travellers and from certain great and learned men of that city, they behaved and conducted themselves there also in such wise that the inhabitants of the district and the government officials used to
p. 122. eulogize them, and all used to shew them respect and deference. In short, since Behá'u'lláh was wont

1 Ḳur'án, iv, 80.

2 Ḳur'án, vi, 17; x, 107.

to hold intercourse with the doctors, scholars, magnates, and nobles, [thereby] obtaining fame and celebrity throughout Roumelia, the materials of comfort were gathered together, neither fear nor dread remained, they reposed on the couch of ease, and passed their time in quietude, when one Seyyid Muḥammad[1] by name, of Isfahán, one of the followers

[1] Hájí Seyyid Muḥammad Isfahání was, together with his nephew Mírzá Riẓá-Ḳulí, amongst the *Ezelís* (followers of Mírzá Yaḥyá, Ṣubḥ-i-Ezel) killed at Acre by some of Behá's followers. (See B. i. p. 517). His death is evidently alluded to in a passage of the كتاب اقدس addressed to Mírzá Yaḥyá which runs as follows:—قل يا مطلع الاعراض دع الاغماض ثمّ انطق بالحقّ بين الخلق تالله قد جرت دموعى على خدودى بما اراك مقبلاً الى هواك و معرضاً عمّن خلقك و سوّاك ان اذكر فضل مولاك اذ ربّيناك فى الليالى و الايّام لخدمة الامر اتّق الله و كن من التّائبين هبنى اشتبه على النّاس امرك هل يشتبه على نفسك خف عن الله ثمّ اذكر اذ كنت قائماً لدى العرش و كتبت ما القيناك من آيات الله المهيمن المقتدر القدير ايّاك ان تمنعك الحميّة عن شطر الاحديّة توجّه اليه و لا تخف من اعمالك انّه يغفر من يشاء بفضل من عنده لا اله الّا هو الغفور الكريم انّما ننصحك لوجه الله ان اقبلت فلنفسك و ان اعرضت انّ ربّك غنى عنك و عن الّذين اتّبعوك بوهم مبين قد اخذ الله من اغواك اذاً فارجع اليه خاضعاً خاشعاً متذلّلاً انّه يكفّر عنك سيّئاتك انّ ربّك لهو التّواب العزيز الرّحيم *

"Say, 'O Source of Perversion, cease closing thy eyes; then

[of the Báb], laid the foundations of intimacy and familiarity with Mírzá Yaḥyá, and [thereby] became the cause of vexation and trouble. In other words, he commenced a secret intrigue and fell to tempting Mírzá Yaḥyá, saying, "The fame of this sect hath risen high in the world, and their name hath become noble: neither dread nor danger remaineth, nor is there any fear or [need for] caution
p. 123. before you. Cease, then, to follow, that thou mayest be followed by the world; and come out from amongst adherents, that thou mayest become celebrated

confess to the truth amongst mankind. By God, my tears have flowed over my cheeks for that I behold thee advancing toward thy lust and turning aside from Him who created thee and fashioned thee. Remember the favour of thy master when we brought thee up during the nights and days for the service of the Religion. Fear God, and be of those who repent. Grant that thine affair is dubious unto men: is it dubious unto thyself? Fear God: then remember when thou didst stand before the Throne and write what we did propose to thee of the verses of God, the Protecting, the Powerful, the Mighty. Beware lest jealousy withhold thee from the shore of [the Divine] Unity: turn unto Him, and fear not because of thy deeds: verily He pardoneth whom He pleaseth by a favour on His part: there is no God but Him, the Forgiving, the Kind. Verily we do but advise thee for the sake of God: if thou advancest, it is for thyself; and if thou turnest aside, verily thy Lord needeth not thee, nor such as follow thee in evident error. *God hath taken away him who led thee astray:* return then unto Him humble, contrite, abased: verily He will put away from thee thy sins: verily thy Lord He is the Repenter, the Mighty, the Merciful.'"

throughout the horizons." Mírza Yaḥyá, too, through lack of reflection and thought as to consequences, and want of experience, became enamoured of his words and befooled by his conduct. This one was [like] the sucking child, and that one became as the much-prized breast. At all events, how much soever some of the chiefs of the sect wrote admonitions and pointed out to him the path of discretion saying, "For many a year hast thou been nurtured in thy brother's arms and hast reposed on the pillow of ease and gladness; what thoughts are these which are the results of madness? Be not beguiled by this empty name,[1] which, out of regard for certain con-

[1] The name alluded to is of course that of *Ezel* (the Eternal) bestowed on Mírzá Yaḥyá by the Báb. Gobineau (p. 277) calls him *Ḥaẓrat-i-Ezel* ('l'Altesse Éternelle'), but his correct designation, that which he himself adopts, and that whereby he is everywhere known, is *Ṣubḥ-i-Ezel* ('the Morning of Eternity'). The epistles addressed to him by the Báb (of some of which copies are in my possession) invoke him either as '*Ismu'l-Ezel*' ('Name of the Eternal') or '*Ismu'l-Waḥíd*' ('Name of the One')—for the latter and the reason of its employment, see B. ii. 996–997. According to his own statement he was the fourth in the Bábí hierarchy (واحد) of 19. The first was of course the Báb himself; next in rank was Mullá Muḥammad 'Alí Bárfurúshí (*Jenáb-i-Ḳuddús*); then Mullá Ḥuseyn of Bush-raweyh (*Jenáb-i-Bábu'l-Báb*); then Mírzá Yaḥyá (*Ṣubḥ-i-Ezel*). After the fall of Sheykh Ṭabarsí and the death of the two 'Letters' who intervened between him and the Báb, he attained the second place in the hierarchy, and, on the Báb's death, became the recognized chief of the sect. The 'considerations'

siderations and as a matter of expediency, was bestowed [upon thee]; neither seek to be censured by the community. Thy rank and worth depend on a
p. 124. word[1], and thine exaltation and elevation were for a

which, according to the somewhat different account of our historian, rendered the recognition 'expedient' will be seen on pp. 62—63 above.

[1] A passage in the لوح نصیر illustrates this expression. It runs as follows:—

اکر تفکّر مینمودند در ظهور ثانیم باسمی از اسمایم از
جمالم محتجب نمیماندند این است شأن این عباد و رتبه و مقام ایشان دع ذکرهم
و ما یجری من قلمهم و یخرج من فمهم با اینکه در جمیع الواح بیان جمیع
عبادرا مأمور فرمودم که از ظهور بعدم غافل نمانند و بحجبات اسماء و
اشارات از ملیك صفات محتجب نکردند و حال تو ملاحظه کن که باحتجاب
کفایت نشده چه مقدار از احجار ظنون بر شجرهٔ عزّ مکنون من غیر تعطیل
و تعویق انداخته و باین هم کفایت ننموده تا آنکه اسمی از اسمایم که بحرفی
اورا خلق فرمودم و بنفخهٔ حیات بخشیدم بمحاربه بر جمالم بر خاست

"Had they reflected, they would not on my second manifestation have been veiled from my Beauty by a Name amongst my Names. This is the state of these men and their rank and station! *Cease to mention them and what flows from their pens and comes forth from their mouths.* Although I commanded all my servants in all the tablets of the Beyán not to continue heedless of my subsequent manifestation or be veiled by the veils of Names and signs from the Lord of Attributes, consider now, not satisfied with being veiled, how many stones of doubt they cast without cessation or interruption at the tree of my hidden Glory! *And even this did not suffice, till a* protection and a consideration," yet still, the more they admonished him, the less did it affect him; and how much soever they would direct him, he continued to account opposition as identical with advantage. Afterwards, too, the fire of greed and avarice was kindled, and although there was no sort of need, their circumstances being easy in the extreme, they fell to thinking of salary and stipend, and certain of the women dependent on Mírzá Yaḥyá went to the [governor's] palace and craved assistance and charity. So when Behá'u'lláh beheld such conduct and behaviour on his part he dismissed and drove away both [him and Seyyid Muḥammad] from himself.

Then Seyyid Muḥammad set out for Constantinople to get his stipend, and opened the door of suffering. According to the account given, this matter caused

Name amongst my Names, whom I created by a word, and on whom I bestowed life with a breath, arose in war against my Beauty." I have already pointed out in another place (B. ii. 949—953) the important position occupied by the epistle above cited, since it appears to be one of the earliest of Behá's writings wherein he distinctly claims to be a new 'manifestation' of the divinity, and it, more than any other writing which I have seen, throws light on that period of conflict and travail in the Bábí church which made so memorable the latter days of the Adrianople period and marked a new development in the short but eventful history of the new faith. When I wrote the passage above referred to, I believed that the only copy of this epistle in Europe was in my possession, but I have since learned from Baron Rosen that another copy is included in his own library at St Petersburg.

p. 125. the greatest sorrow and brought about cessation of intercourse. In Constantinople, moreover, he presumptuously set afloat certain reports, asserting, amongst other things, that the notable personage who had come from 'Irák was Mírzá Yaḥyá. Sundry individuals, perceiving that herein was excellent material for mischief-making and a means for the promotion of mutiny, ostensibly supported and applauded him, and stimulated and incited him, saying, "You are really the chief support and acknowledged successor: act with authority, in order that grace and blessing may become apparent. The waveless sea hath no sound, and the cloud without thunder raineth no rain." By such speech, then, was that unfortunate man entrapped into his course of action, and led to utter vain words which caused the disturbance of [men's] thoughts. Little by little those who were
p. 126. wont to incite and encourage began without exception to utter violent denunciations in every nook and corner, nay in the court itself, saying, "The Bábís say thus, and expound in this wise: [their] behaviour is such, and [their] speech so-and-so." Such mischief-making and plots caused matters to become misapprehended, and furthermore certain schemes got afloat which were regarded as necessary measures of self-protection; the expediency of banishing the Bábís came under consideration; and all of a sudden an order came, and Behá'u'lláh was removed from

Roumelia; nor was it known for what purpose or whither they would bear him away[1]. Diverse ac-

[1] It is difficult amidst the conflicting statements of the two parties and the silence of disinterested historians to discover precisely what were the causes which led to the removal of the Bábís from Adrianople. Further investigation inclines me to abandon the view (B. i. p. 515) that overt acts of hostility between the two factions made it necessary to separate them, for Mírzá Yaḥyá appears to have been almost without supporters at Adrianople, so that, according to his own account, he and his little boy were compelled to go themselves to the market to buy their daily food. His version of the events which led the Turkish government to change their place of exile is this:—that two of the followers of Behá set out from Adrianople for Constantinople, ostensibly to sell horses, but really to carry controversial books. The Páshá of Adrianople, being apprized of their object, telegraphed to the first halting-place on the road which they had to traverse and caused them to be arrested. The followers of Behá, believing that Mírzá Yaḥyá had given information to the Páshá, retaliated by lodging information against Áḳá Ján Beg, one of Mírzá Yaḥyá's followers then in Constantinople—the same who was afterwards killed in Acre (B. i. 517)—who was at this time, though a Persian, serving in the Turkish artillery. Áḳá Ján Beg had in his possession certain Bábí books destined for Baghdad. Unable to find means for transporting them thither and apparently warned in some way of impending danger, he was contemplating the advisability of destroying them by burying them or throwing them into the sea when he was arrested. He appears to have been examined both by the Turkish authorities and the representatives of the Persian government in Constantinople, particularly by a certain Mírzá Aḥmad then attached to the Persian legation. Áḳá Ján Beg—an honest straightforward man incapable of concealing the truth by falsehood—frankly admitted his connection with "the people at Adrianople," his belief in

counts were current in [men's] mouths, and many exaggerations were heard [to the effect] that there was no hope of deliverance.

Now all those persons who were with him with one accord entreated and insisted that they should [be permitted to] accompany him, and, how much soever the
p. 127. government admonished and forbade them, it was fruitless. Finally one Hájí Ja'far[1] by name was moved

the Bábí doctrines, and the existence of certain of their books in his possession. These books were thereupon seized and laid before the Sheykhu 'l-Islám, who, it would seem, hesitated to pronounce sentence of heresy against their author, but desired to see him himself. However in this wish he was not gratified, for he was soon after dismissed, and the books passed into the hands of another Sheykhu 'l-Islám, who, after carefully examining them, declared that they did not contain actual heresy, although they had a very heretical look. Áḳá Ján Beg, however, was, in spite of his former good services to the Turkish government (he had, I believe, distinguished himself at the recapture of Damascus), dismissed the army and imprisoned for four and a half months. From this imprisonment he went forth with hair and beard whitened by premature old age an exile to Acre, there shortly to meet with a violent death. Whatever may be the respective values of these two accounts, they both point to this, that the detection of some fresh attempt at propagandism on the part of the Bábís impelled the Turkish government to change their place of exile once more.

[1] Hájí Muḥammad Ja'far of Tabríz is twice referred to, though not by name, in my first paper on the Babís; first at p. 493, where he is simply mentioned as 'a Persian merchant belonging to the sect' to whom two Bábí missionaries were forbidden to speak during their voyage to Alexandria; and

to lamentation, and with his own hand cut his throat. When the government beheld it thus, it gave permission to all of them to accompany him, conveyed them from Adrianople to the sea-shore[1], and thence transported them to Acre[2]. Mirzá Yaḥyá they sent in like manner to Famagusta[3].

again at p. 516, where the episode here related is briefly mentioned. Space does not allow me to do more than refer to the first incident here. As regards the second it is, as I have already pointed out (B. ii. p. 962), alluded to in the Epistle from Behá known as لوح رئیس. I here quote the passage in the original:—و فدی احد من الاحبّاء نفسه لنفسی و قطع حنجره بیده حبّاً لله هذا ما لا سمعنا به من القرون الاوّلین هذا ما اختصّه الله بهذا الظّهور اظهاراً لقدرته و انّه لهو المقتدر القدیر ✱ "*And one from amongst the Friends sacrificed himself for myself, and cut his throat with his own hand for the love of God. This is that* [*the like of*] *which we have not heard from former ages. This is that which God hath set apart for this dispensation as a shewing forth of His Power: verily He is the Powerful, the Mighty.*" It appears that the Turkish government at first intended to send only Behá and his family to Acre, and to give his followers passports and money to return to their homes, but the unforeseen determination of the Behá'ís not to be separated from their chief compelled it to change its plans.

1 Gallipoli was the port whence they embarked. It seems that they were first taken direct to Alexandria, and there, without being permitted to land, transhipped into vessels bound for their respective places of exile.

2 They arrived at Acre on August 31st, 1868 (see B. i. p. 526, and B. ii. pp. 984 and 988, v. 12).

3 See Note W at end. An official document, dated De-

During the latter days [passed] in Adrianople Behá'u'lláh composed a detailed epistle setting forth all matters clearly and minutely. He unfolded and expounded the main principles of the sect, and made clear and plain its ethics, manners, course, and mode of conduct: he treated certain political questions in detail, and adduced sundry proofs of his truthfulness: he declared the good intent, loyalty, and
p. 128. sincerity of the sect, and wrote some fragments of prayers, some in Persian, but the greater part in Arabic. He then placed it in a packet and adorned its address with the royal name of His Majesty the King of Persia, and wrote [on it] that some person pure of heart and pure of life, dedicated to God, and prepared for martyr-sacrifice, must, with perfect resignation and willingness, convey this epistle into the presence of the King. A youth named Mírzá Badí'[1], a native of Khurásán, took the epistle, and

cember 9th, 1884, from the *Muḥásebejí's* (Accountant's) office in Cyprus, and embodying information relative to the Bábí exiles required by the Receiver General, states that the original *fermán* of banishment cannot be found, but that "from an unofficial copy of the *fermán* received at the time of banishment of these exiles it appears that the date of their banishment is 5th Rabí'ul-Ákhir, 1285 A.H. (26th July, 1868 A.D.)." According to other documents, the date of the arrival in the island of Ṣubḥ-i-Ezel and those with him was August 20th.

[1] Cf. B. ii. pp. 956–957. I have not been able to learn the proper name of Mírzá Badí'. His father was named Hájí 'Abdu 'l-Majíd. After the martyrdom of his son he visited

hastened toward the presence of His Majesty the King. The Royal Train had its abode and station outside Teherán, so he took his stand alone on a rock in a place far off but opposite to the Royal Pavilion, and awaited day and night the passing of the Royal p. 129. escort or the attainment of admission into the Imperial Presence. Three days did he pass thus in a state of fasting and vigilance: an emaciated body and enfeebled spirit remained. On the fourth day the

Acre, and on one occasion during this visit Behá addressed him in these strange words—این روغن چراغ ریخته‌را نذر امامزاده بکن "*Make this lamp-spilt oil an offering for the Imámzádé*," which, as I understand, are applied proverbially to one who offers up that which has become of little value to him, as the oil which has been upset from the lamp. Some time afterwards he suffered martyrdom in Khurásán, and it was this which Behá's words were believed to have shadowed forth. For by the death of his son in whom his hopes centred had Hájí 'Abdu 'l-Majíd's life lost its sweetness for him and become a thing of little worth, and this life thus marred did he offer up. Mírzá Badí' was not more than 20 or 21 years of age. He had left Acre after accomplishing his pilgrimage thither when news reached him of the letter to be carried to Teherán and of the conditions under which it must be taken. These were, that the bearer must refrain from speaking to or visiting any of his co-religionists during the whole journey, proceed directly and alone to Teherán, and give the letter himself into the hands of the king. The letter was written on one side of a large sheet of paper with the conditions incumbent on the bearer inscribed on the back. The text of these conditions, published by Rosen, will appear in vol. vi. of the *Collections Scientifiques, &c.*, p. 192–193.

Royal Personage was examining all quarters and directions with a telescope when suddenly his glance fell on this man who was seated in the most respectful attitude on a rock. It was inferred from the indications [perceived] that he must certainly have thanks [to offer], or some complaint or demand for redress and justice [to prefer]. [The King] commanded one of those in attendance at the court to enquire into the circumstances of this youth. On interrogation [it was found that] he carried a letter which he desired to convey with his own hand into the Royal Presence. On receiving permission to
p. 130. approach, he cried out before the pavilion with a dignity, composure, and respectfulness surpassing description, and in a loud voice, "*O King, I have come unto thee from Sheba with a weighty message*[1]*!*" [The King] commanded to take the letter and arrest the bearer. His Majesty the King wished to act with deliberation and desired to discover the truth, but those who were present before him loosed their tongues in violent reprehension, saying, "This person has shewn great presumption and amazing audacity, for he hath without fear or dread brought the letter of him against whom all peoples are angered, of him who is banished to Bulgaria and Sclavonia, into the

[1] Cf. Ḳur'án, xxvii, 22, where, however, the words addressed to Solomon by the hoopoe differ slightly from those uttered by Mírzá Badí'.

presence of the King. If so be that he do not instantly suffer a grievous punishment there will be an
increase of this great presumption." So the ministers
of the court signified [that he should suffer] punishment and ordered the torture. As the first torment p. 131.
they applied the chain and rack, saying, "Make
known thy other friends that thou mayest be delivered
from excruciating punishment, and make thy comrades captive that thou mayest escape from the
torment of the chain and the keenness of the sword."
But, torture, brand, and torment him as they might,
they saw nought but steadfastness and silence, and
found nought but dumb endurance [on his part]. So,
when the torture gave no result, they [first] photo-
graphed him (the executioners on his left and
on his right, and he sitting bound in fetters and
chains beneath the sword with perfect meekness and
composure), and then slew and destroyed him. This
photograph I sent for, and found worthy of contemplation, for he was seated with wonderful humility
and strange submissiveness, in utmost resignation.

Now when His Majesty the King had perused p. 132.
certain passages and become cognizant of the contents
of the epistle, he was much affected at what had
taken place and manifested regret, because his
courtiers had acted hastily and put into execution a
severe punishment. It is even related that he said
thrice, "Doth any one punish [one who is but] the

channel of correspondence?" Then the Royal Command was issued that their Reverences the learned doctors and honourable and accomplished divines should write a reply to that epistle. But when the most expert doctors of the capital became aware of the contents of the letter they ordained:—"That this person, without regarding [the fact] that he is at variance with the Perspicuous Religion, is a meddler with custom and creed, and a troubler of kings and
p. 133. emperors. Therefore to eradicate, subdue, repress, and repel [this sect] is one of the requirements of the Well-established Path[1], and indeed the chief of obligations."

This answer was not approved before the [Royal] Presence, for the contents of this epistle had no obvious discordance with the Law or with reason, and did not meddle with political or administrative matters, nor interfere with or attack the Throne of Sovereignty. They ought, therefore, to have discussed the real points at issue, and to have written clearly and explicitly such an answer as would have caused the disappearance of doubts and the solution of difficulties, and would have become a fulcrum for discussion to all.

Now of this epistle sundry passages shall be set forth in writing to conduce to a better understanding [of the matter] by all people. At the beginning of

[1] The religion of Islám. Cf. Ḳur'án, v, 52.

the epistle was a striking passage in the Arabic language [treating] of questions of faith and assurance; p. 134.
the sacrifice of life in the way of the Beloved; the state of resignation and contentment; the multiplicity of misfortunes, calamities, hardships, and afflictions; the falling under suspicion of seditiousness through the machinations of foes; the establishment of his innocence in the presence of His Majesty the King; the repudiation of seditious persons and disavowal of the rebellious party; the conditions of sincere belief in the verses of the Ḳur'án; the needfulness of godly virtues, distinction from all other creatures in this transitory abode, obedience to the commandments, and avoidance of things prohibited; the evidence of divine support in the affair of the Báb; the inability of whosoever is upon the earth to withstand a heavenly thing; his own awakening at the divine afflux, and his falling thereby into unbounded calamities; his acquisition of the divine gift, his p. 135.
participation in spiritual God-given grace, and his illumination with immediate knowledge without study; the excusableness of his [efforts for the] admonition of mankind, their direction toward the attainment of human perfections, and their enkindlement with the fire of divine love; encouragements to the directing of energy towards the attainment of a state greater than the degree of earthly sovereignty; eloquent prayers [written] in the utmost self-abasement, devo-

tion, and humility; and the like of this. Afterwards he discussed [other] matters in the Persian language. And the form of it is this[1]:

"*O God, this is a letter which I wish to send to the King; and Thou knowest that I have not desired*

[1] This letter to the Sháh of Persia I discussed briefly in my second paper on the Bábís (pp. 954—960). Therein I expressed a doubt as to whether another letter, addressed in part to the King of Persia, which had been minutely described by Baron Rosen (*MSS. Arabes*, p. 191 *et seq.*), was to be attributed to Behá. I am now convinced, however, both by Baron Rosen's reasonings and my own further enquiries, that I was wrong. However we may account for the undoubted difference of tone between the two letters—a difference marked and striking—there is no doubt that both of them emanated from the pen of Behá. Baron Rosen is about to publish not only the letter to the King of Persia and the other '*Epistles to the Kings*' but the whole of the سورهٔ هیکل of which (though, as it would seem, originally written separately) they now form a part. To the publication of Baron Rosen's edition of these Epistles (which will appear in the sixth volume of the *Collections Scientifiques de l'Institut des Langues Orientales* of St. Petersburg) all interested in the elucidation of Bábí doctrine and history must look forward anxiously. Baron Rosen has kindly continued to forward to me the proof-sheets of his work as they are printed off, and, therefore, knowing as I do that in a short while a reliable text of this epistle will be available to students, I have not thought it necessary, as I might otherwise have done, to mention in my notes all the variants from the present text presented by another MS. which I obtained in Kirmán. The variants presented by the Kirmán MS. (henceforth denoted by K.) are numerous; in one page of 25 lines there are no less than 32. As a rule the readings of

aught of him save the display of his justice to Thy people, and the shewing forth of his favours to the dwellers in Thy Kingdom. And verily, by my soul, I have not desired aught save what Thou hast desired, neither, by Thy Might, do I desire aught save what Thou desirest. Perish that being which desireth of p. 136.
Thee aught save Thyself! And, by Thy Glory, Thy good pleasure is the limit of my hope, and Thy Will the extremity of my desire! Be merciful then, O God, to this poor [soul] who hath caught hold of the skirt of Thy richness, and to this humble [suppliant] who calleth on Thee, for Thou art indeed the Mighty, the Great. Help, O God, His Majesty the King to execute Thy laws amongst Thy servants and to shew forth Thy justice amidst Thy creatures, that he may rule over this sect as he ruleth over those who are beside them. Verily Thou art the Potent, the Mighty, the Wise.

the present text are preferable, but not always; *e.g.* in several cases what is in K. a rhyming clause is altered here to one not rhyming. But it is the *omissions* of the present text that are most significant, inasmuch as they often consist of clauses which either give a greater force and precision to the passages wherein they occur, or else imply in a more unequivocal manner the position claimed by the writer. Such divergences between the two texts—whether it be a question of omission or alteration—will be noted at the foot of each page as they occur, but only in English. As regards the Arabic exordium (which in K. occupies 5 pages of the 17 filled by the whole epistle) a translation of it (based on the text of K.) will be found in Note X at end.

"Agreeably to the permission and consent of the King of the age, this servant turned from the place of the Royal Throne[1] toward 'Irák-i-'Arab, and in that land abode twelve years. During the period of [his] sojourn [there] no description of his condition was

p. 137. laid before the Royal Presence, neither did any representation go to foreign states. Relying upon God did he abide in that land, until a certain functionary[2] came to 'Irák, who, on his arrival, fell to designing the affliction of a company of poor unfortunates. Every day, beguiled by certain of the doctors of Persia, he persecuted these servants; although nothing prejudicial to Church or State, or at variance with the principles and customs of their country-men had been observed in them. So this servant [was moved] by this reflection:—'May it not be that by reason of the deeds of the transgressors some action at variance with the world-ordering counsel of the King should be engendered!' Therefore was an epitome [of the matter] addressed to Mírzá Sa'íd Khán[3], the Minister for Foreign Affairs, that he might

---

[1] Teherán. Cf. p. 54 *supra*.

[2] Evidently Mírzá Buzurg Khán of Ḳazvín. See above, p. 84 *et seq*.

[3] It was at the hands of this minister and his myrmidons that Mullá Ḥuseyn of Khurásán (who, with Áḳá Muḥammad of Isfahán, had been entrusted with the conveyance of the Báb's remains from Tabríz to Teherán) met his death in August 1852. See Note T at end.

submit it to the [Royal] Presence, and that it might
be done according to that which the Royal command p. 138.
might promulgate. A long while elapsed, and no
command was issued; until matters reached such a
state that it was to be feared that sedition might
suddenly break out and the blood of many be shed.
Of necessity, for the protection of the servants of
God, a certain number [of the Bábís] appealed to the
governor of 'Iráḳ[1]. If [the King] will consider what
has happened with just regard, it will become clear in
the mirror of his luminous heart that what occurred
was [done] from considerations of expediency, and
that there was apparently no resource save this. The
Royal Personage can bear witness and testify to this,
that in whatever land there were some few of this
sect the fire of war and conflict was wont to be
kindled by reason of the aggression of certain
governors. But this transient one after his arrival
in 'Iráḳ withheld all from sedition and strife; and the p. 139.
witness of this servant is his action, for all are aware
and will testify that the multitude of this faction in

[1] i.e. the Turkish governor of Baghdad and ' Iráḳ-i-'Arab,
probably the same Námiḳ Páshá mentioned in the third line of
the foot-notes on p. 84. In this passage it is explained to the
King that the Bábís were compelled to enrol themselves as
subjects of the Ottoman Empire in order to escape the malice
of the Persians, especially that of Mírzá Buzurg-Khán the
Persian Consul at Baghdad.

Persia at that time[1] was more than [it had been] before, yet, notwithstanding this, none transgressed his proper bounds nor assailed any one. It is nigh on fifteen years[2] that all continue tranquil, looking unto God and relying on Him, and bear patiently what hath come upon them, casting it on God. And after the arrival of this servant in this city which is called Adrianople certain of this community enquired concerning the meaning of '*victory*[3].' Diverse answers were sent in reply, one of which answers will be submitted on this page, so that it may become clear
p. 140. before the [Royal] Presence that this servant hath in view naught save peace and reform. And if some of the divine favours, which, without merit [on my part], have been graciously bestowed [on me], do not become evident and apparent, this much [at least] will be known, that [God], in [His] abounding grace and

[1] i.e. at the time Behá was in Baghdad (A.D. 1853—1864). K. reads here "that the multitude of this faction was more in 'Irák than in all [other] countries."

[2] Taking the attempt on the Sháh's life in August 1852 as the last act hostile to the Persian government for which the Bábis can be held in any way responsible, full 16 solar years must have elapsed between that date and the composition—or at any rate the completion—of this epistle, since allusion is made in it to the impending banishment to Acre, which did not occur till August 1868.

[3] K. reads "certain of the people of 'Irák and elsewhere asked concerning the meaning of the 'victory' which hath been revealed in the Books of God."

undeserved[1] mercy, hath not deprived this oppressed one[2] of the ornament of reason. The form of words which was set forth on the meaning of '*victory*' is this:—

"'*He is God, exalted is He.*

"'It hath been known that God (glorious is His mention) is sanctified from the world and what is therein, and that the meaning of "victory" is not this, that any one should fight or strive with any one. The Lord of *He doeth what He will*[3] hath committed the kingdom of creation, both land and sea, into the hand of kings, and they are the manifestations of the p. 141.
Divine Power according to the degrees of their rank: *verily He is the Potent, the Sovereign*[4]. But that which God (glorious is His mention) hath desired for Himself is the hearts of His servants, which are treasures of praise and love of the Lord and stores of divine knowledge and wisdom. The will of the Eternal King hath ever been to purify the hearts of [His] servants from the promptings of the world and what is therein, so that they may be prepared for illumination by the effulgences of the Lord of the Names and

[1] Lit. 'preceding mercy,' i.e. mercy not earned or deserved by previous good actions at the time it is bestowed.

[2] K. reads "the heart" instead of "this oppressed one."

[3] Ḳur'án, iii, 35; xxii, 19.

[4] K. substitutes here, "if they happen [to be] in the shadow of God, they are accounted of God; *and if not, then verily thy Lord is knowing and informed.*"

Attributes. Therefore must no stranger find his way into the city of the heart, so that the Incomparable Friend may come unto His own place—that is, the effulgence of His Names and Attributes, not His Essence (exalted is He), for that Peerless King hath been and will be holy for everlasting above ascent or
p. 142. descent[1]. Therefore to-day[2] "victory" neither hath been nor will be opposition to any one, nor strife with any person; but rather what is well-pleasing is that the cities of [men's] hearts, which are under the dominion of the hosts of selfishness and lust, should be subdued by the sword of the Word, of Wisdom, and of Exhortation. Every one, then, who desireth "victory" must first subdue the city of his own heart with the sword of spiritual truth and of the Word,

[1] Behá here guards himself from the doctrines of حلول, اتّحاد, and the like, held by certain heretical sects, viz. the belief that God can pass into man, or man become essentially one with God. Jámi very beautifully distinguishes the doctrine of *annihilation in God* from that of *identification with God* in the following verse:—

چندان برو این ره که دوئی بر خیزد * ور هست دوئی بره روئی بر خیزد *

تو او نشوی و لیك اگر جهد کنی * جائی رسی کز تو توئی بر خیزد *

"So tread this path that duality may disappear,
For if there be duality in the path, falsity will arise:
Thou wilt not become *He;* but, if thou strivest,
Thou wilt reach a place where *thou-ness* shall depart from thee."

[2] K. inserts "the meaning of."

and must protect it from remembering aught beside God: afterwards let him turn his regards towards the cities of [others'] hearts. This is what is intended by "victory:" sedition hath never been nor is pleasing to God, and that which certain ignorant persons formerly wrought was never approved. *If ye be slain for His good pleasure verily it is better for you than that ye should slay.* To-day the friends of God must p. 143.
appear in such fashion amidst [God's] servants that by their actions they may lead all unto the pleasure of the Lord of Glory. I swear by the Sun of the Horizon of Holiness that the friends of God never have regarded nor will regard the earth or its transitory riches. God hath ever regarded the hearts of [His] servants, and this too is by reason of [His] most great favour, that perchance mortal souls may be cleansed and sanctified from earthly states and may attain unto everlasting places. But that Real King is in Himself sufficient unto Himself [and independent] of all: neither doth any advantage accrue to Him from the love of contingent[1] beings, nor doth any hurt befal Him from their hatred. All earthly places appear through Him and unto Him return, and

[1] By 'contingent' or 'possible' being is meant the material or phenomenal world, of which the being or not-being are alike possible and conceivable, as contrasted with 'Necessary Being' (God) of which the not-being is inconceivable and impossible.

p. 144. God singly and alone abideth in His own place which is holy above space and time, mention and utterance, sign, description, and definition, height and depth. *And none knoweth this save Him and whosoever hath knowledge of the Book. There is no God but Him, the Mighty, the Bountiful.' Finis.*

"But good deeds depend on this[1], that the Royal Person should himself look into that [matter] with just and gracious regard, and not be satisfied with the representations of certain persons unsupported by proof or evidence. *We ask God to strengthen the King unto that which He willeth: and what He willeth should be the wish of the worlds.*

"Afterwards they summoned this servant to Constantinople. We reached that city along with a number of poor unfortunates, and after our arrival did
p. 145. not hold intercourse with a single soul, for we had nought to say [unto them], and there was no wish save that it should be clearly demonstrated by proof to all that this servant had no thought of sedition and had never associated with the seditious. *And, by Him in praise of whose spirit the tongues of all things speak,*

[1] This sentence is rather ambiguous, and would at first sight appear to signify that the continuance of the Bábís' good conduct depends on their being treated with more justice and fairness than they have hitherto met with on the part of the Persian government. But I think the real meaning is rather that the attribution of good actions to the Sháh depends on his now acting justly.

to turn in any direction was difficult in consideration of certain circumstances; but these things were done for the protection of lives[1]. *Verily my Lord knoweth what is in my soul, and verily He is witness unto what I say.* The just king is the shadow of God in the earth; all should take refuge under the shadow of his justice and rest in the shade of his favour. This is not the place for personalities, or censures [directed] specially against some apart from others; for the shadow tells of him who casteth the shadow[2]. God (*glorious is His mention*) hath called Himself the *Lord of the worlds*[3] for that He hath nurtured and p. 146.
doth nurture all; *exalted is His favour which hath preceded*[4] *contingent beings and His mercy which hath preceded the worlds.*

"This is sufficiently clear, that, [whether] right or wrong according to the imagination of the people, this community have accepted as true and adopted the religion for which they are notorious, and that on this account they have foregone *what they had, seeking after what is with God.* And this same renunciation of life in the way of love for the Merciful

1 Allusion is made to the action of the Bábís in enrolling themselves as Turkish subjects. See p. 88, *supra*.

2 i.e. the action of subordinates reveals the temper of their masters.

3 As, for example, in the first verse of the opening chapter of the Ḳu'rán.

4 See note 1 on p. 113, *supra*.

[God] is a faithful witness and an eloquent attest *unto that whereunto they lay claim.* Hath it [ever] been beheld that a reasonable man renounced his life without proof or evidence [of the truth of that for which he died]? And if it be said, 'This people are mad,' this [too] is very improbable, for it is not [a thing] confined to one or two persons, but rather
p. 147. have a great multitude of every class, inebriated with the *Kawthar*[1] of divine wisdom, hastened with heart and soul to the place of martyrdom in the way of the Friend. If these persons, who for God have foregone all save Him, and who have poured forth life and wealth in His way, can be belied, then by what proof and evidence shall the truth of that which others assert concerning that wherein they are[2] be established in the presence of the King?

"The late Hájí Seyyid Muḥammad[3] *(may God*

[1] *Kawthar* primarily signifies *abundance*, but it is also the name of a river in Paradise.

[2] That is, the religion which they profess.

[3] The event here alluded to occurred in the year A. H. 1241 (A.D. 1825). The Persians, exasperated by rumours of oppression and insult on the part of the Russians towards their Musulmán subjects, especially in the then recently ceded provinces of the Caucasus, were incited by the clergy headed by Áḳá (here called Hájí) Seyyid Muḥammad of Isfahán to declare a *jihád* or holy war against their northern enemies, in which, though at first encouraged by some measure of success, they were eventually totally vanquished, the campaign ending in the capture of Tabríz by the Russians and the treaty of

exalt his station and overwhelm him in the depth of the ocean of His mercy and forgiveness), although he was of the most learned of the doctors of the age and the most pious and austere of his contemporaries, and although the splendour of his worth was of such a degree that the tongues of all creatures spoke in praise and eulogy of him and confidently asserted his asceticism and godliness, did nevertheless in the war against the Russians forego much good and turn back p. 148.
after a little contest, although he himself had decreed a holy war, and had set out from his native country with conspicuous ensign in support of the Faith. *O would that the covering might be withdrawn, and that what is hidden from* [men's] *eyes might appear!*

"But as to this sect, it is twenty years[1] and more that they have been tormented by day and by night with the fierceness of the Royal anger, and that they have been cast each one into a [different] land by the blasts of the tempests of the King's wrath. How

Turkmánchây. See Watson's *History of Persia*, pp. 207—238. Watson, however, credits Áḳá Seyyid Muḥammad with some degree of moderation, observing (p. 209) that "he seems to have retained some slight remnant of prudence, after that quality was no longer discernible in the conduct and language of his professional brethren."

[1] The first interference with the Báb and his followers took place in August 1845, so that if we suppose this letter to have been written near the end of the Adrianople period (which came to a close in August 1868) nearly 23 years of persecution had then been endured by the Bábís.

many children have been left fatherless! How many fathers have become childless! How many mothers have not dared, through fear and dread, to mourn over their slaughtered children[1]! Many [were] the servants [of God] who at eve were in the utmost
p. 149. wealth and opulence, and at dawn were beheld in the extreme of poverty and abasement! *There is no land but hath been dyed with their blood and no air whereunto their groanings have not arisen.* And during these few years the arrows of affliction have rained down without intermission from the clouds of fate. Yet, notwithstanding all these visitations and afflictions, the fire of divine love is in such fashion kindled in their hearts that, were they all to be hewn in pieces, they would not forswear the love of the Beloved of

[1] This is no mere figure of speech. Ussher writes in his *Journey from London to Persepolis* (London 1865), p. 629, "It was enough to be suspected of Babeeism to be at once put to death, and many old feuds and injuries were avenged by denouncements and accusation of being tainted by the fatal doctrines. No time was lost between apprehension and execution. Death was the only punishment known; the headless bodies lay in the streets for days, the terrified relatives fearing to give them burial, and the dogs fought and growled over the corpses in the deserted thoroughfares. At last the European missions remonstrated, the reign of terror ceased, and although still proscribed and put to death without mercy whenever discovered, the Babees are supposed yet to reckon many seeming orthodox Moslems among their numbers, the southern parts of the country being thought to be the most tainted with the detested heresy."

all the dwellers upon earth; nay rather with their whole souls do they yearn and hope for what may befal [them] in the way of God.

"O King! The gales of the mercy of the Merciful One have converted these servants and drawn them to the region of the [Divine] Unity—

'The witness of the faithful lover is in his sleeve'[1]—

but some of the doctors of Persia[2] have troubled the most luminous heart of the King of the age with p. 150.
regard to those who are admitted into the Sanctuary of the Merciful One and those who make for the Ka'ba of Wisdom. O would that the world-ordering judgement of the King might decide that this servant should meet those doctors[3], and, in the presence of His Majesty the King, adduce arguments and proofs! This servant is ready, and hopeth of God that such a conference may be brought about, so that the truth of the matter may become evident and apparent before His Majesty the King. *And afterwards the decision is in thy hand, and I am ready to confront the throne of thy sovereignty; then give judgement for me or against me.* The Merciful Lord saith in the Furḳán[4], which is the enduring proof amidst the host

[1] i.e. the faithful lover carries his life in his hand, or, as the Persians say, in his sleeve.

[2] K. reads 'outward [or formal] doctors.'

[3] K. reads 'the doctors of the age.'

[4] i.e. the Ḳur'án, the supernatural eloquence of which is

of existences, '*Desire death, then, if ye be sincere*[1].' He hath declared the desiring of death to be the
p. 151. proof of sincerity; and it will be apparent in the mirror of the [King's] luminous mind which party it is that hath this day foregone life in the way of Him [who is] adored by the dwellers upon earth. Had the doctrinal books of this people, [composed] in proof of that wherein they are[2], been written with the blood which has been shed in His way (exalted is He), books innumerable would assuredly have been apparent and visible amongst mankind.

"How, then, can one repudiate this people, whose words and deeds are consistent, and accept those persons who neither have foregone nor will forego one atom of the consideration [which they enjoy] in the way of [God] the Sovereign?

"Some of the doctors of Persia who have denounced this servant have never either met or seen him, nor [even] become cognizant of [his] intent:
p. 152. *nevertheless they said what they desired and do what they will.* Every statement requires proof, and is not [established] merely by assertion or by outward gear of asceticism.

"A translation of some passages from the con-

the 'permanent miracle' and 'enduring proof' of its divine origin.

[1] Ḳur'án, ii, 88; lxii, 6.

[2] i.e. 'that which they believe.'

tents of the *Hidden Book of Fáṭima*[1] (upon her be

[1] I was at first doubtful as to whether the passages here cited were really translated by Behá from some Arabic work bearing this name, or whether they were in truth extracts from a work of his own called '*Hidden Words*' (كلمات مكنونه) whereof I had heard frequent mention amongst the Bábís. The following passage on p. 379 of Mr Merrick's translation of a work on Shi'ite theology called حيوة القلوب seemed to bear on the question:—"After the Prophet's death Fáṭima was affected in spirit to a degree which none but God knew. Jebrá'íl was sent down daily to comfort her, and 'Alí wrote what the angel said, and this is the Book of Fáṭima which is now with the Imám Mahdí." On consulting Rieu's *Catalogue of the Persian MSS. in the British Museum*, I found mention (vol. ii, p. 829 b.) of a work entitled كلمات مكنونه، فاطميه composed by Mullá Muḥsin-i-Feyz of Káshán, and described as consisting of "one hundred sayings of Imáms and Ṣúfís in Arabic, with Persian commentary." I seized the first opportunity of examining this work, but a search of about two hours through its pages revealed nothing resembling the passages in the text before us. Finally I wrote to Acre, asking, amongst other questions, what might be the true nature of the work here alluded to. The following answer (which is authoritative) was returned:—[Translation] "*Fifth Question.* Concerning the mention of the matters in the *Hidden Book of Fáṭima* (upon her be the peace of God). The answer is this, that the sect of Persia, that is the Shi'ites, who regard themselves as pure, and the [rest of the] world (we take refuge with God!) as unclean, believe that after His Highness the Seal of the Prophets [Muḥammad] Her Highness Fáṭima (upon her be the blessings of God) was occupied night and day in weeping, wailing, and lamenting over the fate of her illustrious father. Therefore was Jebrá'íl commanded by the Lord Most Glorious to commune, converse, and associate with Her Highness Fáṭima; and

the blessings of God) which are apposite to this place will [now] be submitted in the Persian language, in order that some things [now] concealed may be revealed before the [Royal] Presence. Those addressed in these utterances in the above-mentioned book (which is to-day known as '*Hidden Words*') are those people who are outwardly notable for

he used to speak words causing consolation and quietude of heart. These words were collected and named '*The Book of Fáṭima*' (صحيفهٔ فاطمه). And they [i.e. the Shí'ites] believe that this *Book* is with His Highness the Ḳá'im [i.e. the Imám Mahdí] and shall appear in the days of his appearance. But of this *Book* nought is known save the name, and indeed it is a name without form and a title without reality. And His Highness the Existent [i.e. Behá'u'lláh] willed to make known the appearance of the Ḳá'im by intimation and implication; therefore was it mentioned in this manner for a wise reason which he had. And that which is mentioned under the name of the *Book* in the Epistle to His Majesty the King [of Persia] (may God assist him) is from the '*Hidden Words*' [كلمات مكنونه] which was revealed before the Epistle to His Majesty the King. The '*Hidden Words*' was revealed in the languages of eloquence (Arabic) and of light (Persian). It hath been commanded that some portion of it shall be written and sent specially for you, that you may become cognizant of the truth of the matter. At all events both the Persian and the Arabic thereof were revealed in *this* manifestation. As to the pronoun" [I had asked whether the pronoun in ميفرمايد referred to God, or to Gabriel, or to Fátima, i.e. whether its subject was masculine or feminine] "he says, 'It refers to the Hidden Unseen, from the heaven of whose Grace all verses are revealed.'"

science and piety, but who are inwardly subservient to their passions and lust. He says :—

"'O faithless ones! Why do ye outwardly claim to be shepherds, while inwardly ye have become the wolves of my sheep? Your likeness is like unto the p. 153.
star before the morning[1], which is apparently bright and luminous, but really causeth the misguidance and destruction of the caravans of my city and country.'

"So likewise he saith —

'O outwardly fair and inwardly faulty! Thy likeness is like unto clear bitter water, wherein outwardly the utmost sweetness and purity is beheld, but when it falleth into the assaying hands of the taste of the [Divine] Unity He doth not accept a single drop thereof. The radiance of the sun is on the earth and on the mirror alike; but regard the difference as from the guard-stars[2] to the earth; nay, between them is a limitless distance.'

[1] There is a star which appears before the morning star and resembles it, and this the Persians call *káraván-kush* (the caravan-killer) or *charvadár-kush* (the muleteer-killer), because it entices the caravan to start from its halting-place in the belief that the dawn is at hand, and so causes it to lose its way and perish.

[2] *Farḳadán*, the two *Farḳads*, are two bright stars near the pole-star (β and γ of Ursa Minor). See Lane's *Arabic-English Lexicon* s.v. فرقد. In English they are properly called the "Guards" or "Guardians"—"'of the Spanish word *guardare*,' saith Hood, 'which is to beholde, because they are diligently

"So likewise he saith :—

'O child of the world! Many a morning hath the effulgence of my grace come unto thy place from the day-spring of the place-less, found thee on the
p. 154. couch of ease busied with other things, and returned like the lightning of the spirit to the bright abode of glory. And I, desiring not thy shame, declared it not in the retreats of nearness to the hosts of holiness.'

"So likewise he saith :—

'O pretender to my friendship! In the morning the breeze of my grace passed by thee, and found thee sleeping on the bed of heedlessness, and wept over thy condition, and turned back.'

Finis.

"In the presence of the King's justice, therefore, the statement of an adversary ought not to be accepted as sufficient. And in the Furḳán, which distinguisheth between truth and falsehood, He says, '*O ye who believe, if there come unto you a sinner with a message, then discriminate, lest you fall upon a people in ignorance and on the morrow repent of*
p. 155. *what ye have done*[1].' And it hath come down in holy

to be looked unto, in regard of the singular use which they have in navigation.'" (Smyth and Chambers' *Cycle of Celestial Objects*, Oxford, 1881.)

[1] Ḳur'án, XLIX, 6. Concerning the occasion of the revelation of this passage see the notes on it in Sale's and Palmer's translations of the Ḳur'án.

tradition, '*Credit not the calumniator.*' The matter hath been misapprehended by certain doctors, neither have they seen this servant. But those persons who have met [him] testify that this servant hath not spoken *contrary to that which God hath ordained in the Book*, and recite this blessed verse:—He saith (exalted is He) '*Do ye disavow us for aught save that we believe in God, and what hath been sent down unto us, and what was sent down before*[1]*?*'

"O King of the age! The eyes of these wanderers turn and gaze in the direction of the mercy of the Merciful One, and assuredly to these afflictions shall the greatest mercy succeed, and after these most grievous hardships shall follow great ease. But [our] hope is this, that His Majesty the King will himself turn his attention to [these] matters, which thing will be the cause of hope in [our] hearts[2]. And p. 156.
this is unmixed good which hath been submitted, *and God sufficeth for a witness.*

"*Glory be to Thee, O God! O God, I bear witness that the heart of the King is between the fingers of Thy power: if Thou pleasest, turn it, O God, in the direction of mercy and kindliness: verily Thou art the Exalted, the Potent, the Beneficent: there is no God but Thee, the Mighty from whom help is sought.*

[1] Ḳur'án, v, 64.

[2] K. reads سبب رضای محبوب ("the cause of the good pleasure of the Belovéd") in place of سبب رجای قلوب.

"Concerning the qualifications of the doctors, he saith[1]:—'*But amongst the lawyers he who guardeth himself, observeth his religion, opposeth his lust, and obeyeth the command of his Lord—it is incumbent on the people to follow him*...' unto the end. And if the King of the age will regard this utterance, which proceeded from the tongue of the recipient of divine inspiration, he will observe that those characterized
p. 157. by the qualities transmitted in the afore-mentioned tradition are rarer than the philosopher's stone. Therefore the claim of every person pretending to science neither hath been nor is heard.

"So likewise in describing the lawyers of the latter time he says:—'*The lawyers of that time are the most evil of lawyers under the shadow of heaven: from them cometh forth mischief, and unto them it returneth*[2].'

"And if any person deny these traditions, the establishing thereof is [incumbent] on this servant; but since [our] object is brevity therefore the detail of the authorities[3] hath not been submitted.

"Those doctors who have indeed drunk of the

[1] The preposition appears to refer to the Prophet Muḥammad.

[2] K. here adds, "So likewise he saith, '*when the standard of the Truth appeareth the people of the East and of the West curse it.*'"

[3] i.e. the اسناد, or chain of narrators whereby a reliable tradition is substantiated, is omitted for lack of space.

cup of renunciation never interfered with this servant, even as the late Sheykh Murtaẓá[1] (*may God exalt his station and cause him to dwell under the shadow of the domes of His grace*) used to shew [us] affection during the days of [our] sojourn in 'Iráḳ, and used not to speak concerning this matter *other-* p. 158. *wise than God hath permitted. We ask God to help all* [men] *unto that which He loveth and approveth.*

"Now all people have shut their eyes to all [these] matters, and are bent on the persecution of this sect; so that should it be demanded of certain persons, who (after God's grace) rest in the shadow of the King's clemency and enjoy unbounded blessings, 'In return for the King's favour what service have ye wrought? Have ye by wise policy added any country to [his] countries? Or have ye applied yourselves to aught which would cause the comfort of the people, the prosperity of the kingdom, and the continuance of fair fame for the state?', they have no reply save this, that, falsely or truly, they designate a number of persons in the presence of the King by the name of Bábís, and forthwith engage in slaughter and plunder; p. 159. even as in Tabríz and elsewhere[2] they sold certain

[1] See note 1 on p. 86 *supra*.

[2] K. reads "and Manṣúriyya of Egypt." The only record I can find of any of the Bábís being sold into slavery is in the *Táríkh-i-Jadíd*, which, after describing the massacre of most of those who surrendered at Sheykh Ṭabarsí, continues—"The remainder of the companions who were left alive they carried

ones, and received much wealth; and this was never represented before the presence of the King. All these things have occurred because of this, that they have found these poor people without a helper. They have foregone matters of moment, and have fallen upon these poor unfortunates.

"Many sects and diverse tribes rest tranquil in the shadow of the King, and of these sects one is this people. Were it not best that the lofty endeavour and magnanimity of those who surround the King should so be witnessed: that they should be scheming for all factions to come under the King's shadow, and that they should govern amidst all with justice? To put in force the ordinances of God is unmixed justice,
p. 160. and with this all are satisfied; nay, the ordinances of God [ever] have been and will be the instrument and means for the protection of [His] creatures, *as He saith (exalted is He) 'And in retaliation ye have*

in fetters and chains to Bárfurúsh. *Several they sold*, such as Akhúnd-i-Mullá Muḥammad Ṣádiḳ of Khurásán, Áḳá Seyyid 'Aẓím the Turk, Hájí Naṣír of Ḳazvín, and Mírzá Ḥuseyn of Ḳum. And some they sent to Sárí, and there martyred them." But it is not clear that these were *sold into slavery:* they may have been ransomed by their friends, as certainly happened in some cases. More recent instances are evidently alluded to here. Probably the Bábís sent to Khartúm in the Soudan about the period when this letter was written, and afterwards released by General Gordon, were sold as slaves. (See B. i, pp. 493–495.)

life, O people of understanding[1].' [But] it is far from the justice of His Majesty the King that, for the fault of one person, a number of persons should become the objects of the scourges of wrath. God (glorious is His mention) saith:—'*None shall bear the burden of another*[2].' And this is sufficiently evident, that in every community there have been and will be learned and ignorant, wise and foolish, sinful and pious. And to commit abominable actions is far from the wise man. For the wise man either seeketh the world or abandoneth it. If he abandoneth it, assuredly he will not regard aught save God, and, apart from this, the fear of God will withhold him from committing forbidden and culpable actions. And if he seeketh the world, he will as- p. 161.
suredly not commit deeds which will cause and induce the aversion of [God's] servants and produce horror in those who are in all lands; but rather will he practise such deeds as will cause the adhesion of mankind. So it hath been demonstrated that detestable actions have been and will be [wrought only] by ignorant persons[3]. *We ask God to keep His servants from regarding aught but Him, and to*

[1] Ḳur'án, ii. 175.

[2] Ḳur'án, vi. 164; xvii. 16; xxxv. 19; xxxix. 9; liii. 39.

[3] Compare the argument on pp. 52–53 wherewith Behá meets the charge brought against him of complicity in the attempted assassination of the Sháh.

bring them near to Him: verily He is potent over all things.

"*Glory be to Thee, O God! O my God, Thou hearest my groaning, and seest my state and my distress and my affliction, and knowest what is in my soul. If my cry be sincerely for Thy sake, then draw thereby the hearts of Thy creatures unto the horizon of the heaven of Thy recognition, and turn the King unto the right hand of the throne of Thy Name the Merciful;*
p. 162. *then bestow on him, O my God, the blessing which hath descended from the heaven of Thy favour and the clouds of Thy mercy, that he may sever himself from that which he hath and turn toward the region of Thy bounties. O Lord, help him to support the oppressed amongst* [Thy] *servants*[1], *and to raise up Thy Word amidst Thy people; then aid him with the hosts of the unseen and the seen, that he may subdue cities in Thy Name and rule over all who are upon the earth by Thy power and authority, O Thou in whose hand is the Kingdom of creation: and verily Thou art He who ruleth at the beginning and in the end: there is no God save Thee, the Potent, the Mighty, the Wise.*

"They have misrepresented matters before the presence of the King in such a way that if any ill deed proceed from any one of this sect they account it as [a part] of the religion of these servants. *But,*

[1] K. reads "to support Thy religion."

by God, beside whom there is none other God, this servant hath not sanctioned the committing of sins, p. 163. much less that whereof the prohibition hath been explicitly revealed in the Book of God! God hath prohibited unto men the drinking of wine[1], and the unlawfulness thereof hath been revealed and recorded in the Book of God[2], and the doctors of the age (*may God multiply the like of them*) have unanimously

[1] The Muhammadans are in the habit of alleging against the Bábís (of whose tenets they are, with very rare exceptions, perfectly ignorant) sundry false and malicious charges calculated to discredit them in the eyes of the world, as, for instance, that they are communists; that they allow nine husbands to one woman; that they drink wine and are guilty of other unlawful practices. These statements have been repeated by many European writers deriving their information either directly or indirectly from Muhammadan sources, and especially from the Persian state chronicles called *Násikhu't-Tawáríkh* and *Rawẓatu'ṣ-Ṣafá*. Of these somewhat partial and one-sided records the former has the following passage:—"In every house where they [i.e. the Bábís] assembled they used to drink wine and commit other actions forbidden by the Law; and they used to order their women to come unveiled into the company of strangers, engage in quaffing goblets of wine, and give to drink to the men in the company." Anyone knowing what reliance can be placed on the statements of the work in question, when any motive for misrepresentation exists, will learn without astonishment that the Báb absolutely forbade the use of wine, opium, and even tobacco, and that the Bábís observe the obligations laid upon them at least as well as the Muhammadans. The prohibition of tobacco has, however, been withdrawn by Behá.

[2] Ḳur'án, v. 92.

prohibited unto men this abominable action; yet withal do some commit it. Now the punishment of this action falls on these heedless persons, while those manifestations of the glory of sanctity [continue] holy and undefiled: *unto their sanctity all Being, whether of the unseen or the seen, testifieth.*

"Yea, these servants [of God] regard God as '*doing what He pleaseth and ordering what He willeth*[1].' *There is no retreat nor way of flight for any one save unto God, and no refuge nor asylum but in Him.* And at no time hath the cavilling of men, whether learned or unlearned, been a thing to rely on, nor
p. 164. will it be so[2]. The [very] prophets, who are the pearls of the Ocean of Unity and the recipients of Divine Revelation, have [ever] been the objects of men's aversion and cavilling; much more these

[1] Ḳur'án, ii. 254; iii. 35; xxii. 14, 19. K. inserts here:—"But they have considered the [further] appearances of the Manifestations of Unity in the World of dominion [i.e. the phenomenal world] as impossible; whereas if anyone regards this as impossible wherein does he differ from those people who regard the Hand of God as passive? If they regard God (glorious is His mention) as Sovereign, then all must accept a matter which appeareth from the Source of command of that King of Pre-existence."

[2] K. has this sentence differently as follows:—"That thing which is necessary is the production on the claimant's part of proof and demonstration of that which he says and that whereunto he lays claim: else at no time hath the cavilling of men" &c.

servants. Even as He saith:—'*Every nation schemed against their apostle to catch him. And they contended with falsehood therewith to refute the truth*[1].' So likewise He saith, '*There came not unto them any apostle but they mocked at him*[2].' Consider the appearance of the Seal of the Prophets[3], the King of the Elect (the soul of the worlds be his sacrifice); after the dawning of the Sun of Truth from the horizon of the Ḥijáz what wrongs befel that Manifestation of the Might of the Lord of Glory at the hands of the people of error! So heedless were men that they were wont to consider the vexation of that holy one as one of the greatest of good works and as the means of approaching God Most High. For in the first years p. 165.
the doctors of that age, whether Jews or Christians, turned aside from that Sun of the Highest Horizon; and, at the turning aside of those persons, all, whether humble or noble, girt up their loins to quench the radiance of that Light of the Horizon of Ideals. The names of all are recorded in books: amongst them were Wahb ibn Ráhib, Ka'b ibn Ashraf, 'Abdu'lláh [ibn] Ubayy[4], and the like of these persons; till at

[1] Ḳur'án, xl. 5.

[2] Ḳur'án, xv. 11, xxxvi. 29.

[3] Muḥammad.

[4] I can find no mention of Wahb ibn Ráhib. Perhaps Wahb ibn Yahudhá, one of the Jewish tribe of the Bani Ḳuraydha who strenuously opposed Muḥammad and denied the Ḳur'án, is intended; or perhaps Wahb ibn Zayd of the

length the matter reached such a point that they convened a meeting to take counsel as to the shedding of the most pure blood of that holy one, as God (glorious is His mention) hath declared:—'*And when those who misbelieved plotted against thee to confine thee, or slay thee, or drive thee out; and they plotted, and God plotted; and God is the best of plotters*[1].' So likewise He saith:—'*And if their aversion be grievous unto thee, then, if thou art able to seek out*
p. 166. *a hole down into the earth, or a ladder up into the sky, that thou mayest shew them a sign*—[do so]: *but if God pleased He would assuredly bring them all to the true guidance: be not therefore one of the ignorant*[2].' By God, the hearts of those near [unto God] are scorched at the purport of these two blessed verses; but the like of these matters certainly transmitted [to us] are blotted out of sight, and [men] have not reflected, neither do reflect, what was the

same tribe, who said that he would believe if Muḥammad would bring down a book from heaven, and whose name is mentioned as one of the "enemies amongst the Jews." Ka'b ibn Ashraf of the tribe of Ṭayy went with forty Jews from Medína to Mecca and conspired with the arch-enemy of the Prophet, Abú Sofyán, to compass the death of Muḥammad. He was subsequently slain by Muḥammad ibn Maslama at the command of the Prophet. 'Abdu'lláh ibn Ubayy ibn Salúl of the tribe of 'Awf was called "the chief of hypocrites." [See Ibn Hishám's *Life of Muḥammad*, ed. Wüstenfeld.]

[1] Ḳur'án, viii. 30.

[2] Ḳur'án, vi. 35.

reason of the turning aside of [God's] servants at the appearance of the day-springs of divine lights.

"So too, before the Seal of the Prophets, consider Jesus the Son of Mary. After the appearance of that Manifestation of the Merciful One all the doctors charged that Quintessence of Faith with misbelief and rebelliousness; until at length, with the consent of Annas, who was the chief of the doctors of that age, and likewise Caiaphas[1], who was the most learned of the judges, they wrought upon that Holy One that which the pen is ashamed and unable to repeat. *The earth with its amplitude was* p. 167.
too strait for Him, until God took Him up into the heaven. But were a detailed account of the prophets to be submitted it is feared that weariness might result[2].

[1] John xi. 49, 50; xviii. 13–28; Acts iv. 6–10.

[2] K. inserts a long passage here as follows:—"And the Jewish doctors especially hold that after Moses no plenipotentiary prophet possessed of a [new] Law shall come, [but that] one from amongst the children of David shall appear, who shall give currency to the Law of the Pentateuch, until, by his help, the ordinances of the Pentateuch shall become current and effective between the East and the West. So too the people of the Gospel regard it as impossible that after Jesus the Son of Mary any Founder of a new religion should shine forth from the day-spring of the Divine Will; and they seek a proof in this verse which is in the Gospel:—'*Verily it may be that the heaven and the earth should pass away, but the word of the Son of Man shall never pass away.*' And they hold that what Jesus the Son of Mary hath said and commanded shall not

"*O would that thou mightest permit, O King, that we should send unto Thy Majesty that whereby eyes would be refreshed, souls tranquillized, and every just person assured that with him* [i.e. Behá'u'lláh] *is knowledge of the Book. Were it not for the turning aside of the ignorant and the wilful blindness of the doctors, verily I would utter a discourse whereat hearts would be glad and would fly unto the air from the murmur of whose winds is heard, 'There is no God but He.' But now, because the time admitteth it not, the tongue is withheld from utterance, and the vessel of declaration is sealed until God shall unclose it by His power: verily He is the Potent, the Powerful.*

p. 168. "*Glory be to Thee, O God! O my God, I ask of Thee in Thy Name, whereby Thou hast subdued whomsoever is in the heavens and the earth, that Thou wilt keep the lamp of Thy religion with the glass of Thy power and Thy favours, so that the winds of denial pass not by it from the region of those who are heedless of the mysteries of Thy Sovereign Name: then increase*

suffer change, whereas He saith in one place in the Gospel, '*Verily I go and come* [again]'; and in the Gospel of John likewise He giveth tidings of 'the Comforting Spirit which shall come after me'; while in the Gospel of Luke also certain signs are mentioned. But, because some of the doctors of that faith have propounded for each utterance an explanation after their own lusts, therefore have they remained veiled from the meaning intended."

its light by the oil of Thy wisdom: verily Thou art Potent over whomsoever is in Thy earth and Thy heaven.

"O Lord, I ask of Thee by the Supreme Word, whereat whosoever is in the earth and the heaven feareth save him who taketh hold of the 'Most Firm Handle[1]*,' that Thou wilt not abandon me amongst Thy creatures: lift me up unto Thee, and make me to enter in under the shadow of Thy mercy, and give me to drink of the pure wine of Thy grace, that I may dwell under the canopy of Thy glory and the domes of Thy favours: verily Thou art powerful unto that Thou wishest, and verily Thou art the Protecting, the Self-Sufficing.*

"O King! The lamps of justice are extinguished, p. 169. *and the fire of persecution is kindled on all sides, until that they have made my people captives*[2]*. This is not the first honour which hath been violated in the way of God. It behoveth every one to regard and recall what befell the kindred of the Prophet until that the people made them captives and brought them in unto Damascus the spacious; and amongst them was the Prince of Worshippers*[3]*, the Stay of the elect, the Sanctuary of the eager (the soul of all beside*

[1] Kur'án, ii. 257; xxxi. 21.

[2] K. inserts here:—"*from Zawrá* [Baghdad] *unto Mosul 'the prominent'*" (*el-ḥadbá*).

[3] i.e. Zeynu'l-'Ábidín, the fourth Imám, son of Imám Ḥuseyn and Shahrbánú the daughter of Yezdigird. Being ill in his bed at the time of the massacre of Kerbelá his life was,

him be his sacrifice). It was said unto them, 'Are ye seceders?' He said, 'No, by God, we are servants who have believed in God and in His signs, and through us the teeth of faith are disclosed in a smile, and the sign of the Merciful One shineth forth; through our mention spreadeth Al-Baṭḥá[1]*, and the darkness which intervened between earth and heaven is dispelled.' It was said, 'Have ye forbidden what*
p. 170. *God hath sanctioned, or sanctioned what God hath forbidden?' He said, 'We were the first who followed the commandments of God: we are the source of command and its origin, and the first-fruits of all good and its consummation: we are the sign of the Eternal, and His commemoration amongst the nations.' It was said, 'Have ye abandoned the Ḳur'án?' He said, 'Through us did the Merciful One reveal it; and we are gales of the All-glorious amidst* [His] *creatures; we are streams which have arisen from the most mighty Ocean whereby God revived the earth after its death; from us His signs are diffused, His evidences are manifested, and His tokens appear; and with us are His mysteries and His secrets.' It was said, 'For what fault* [then] *were ye afflicted?'*

after some deliberation, spared, and he was sent with the women taken captive to the court of Yezíd at Damascus, where the discussion here recorded is supposed to have taken place. (Cf. Aṭ-Ṭabarí's *Annales*, ed. de Goeje, secunda series, v. i. pp. 367, et seq.)

[1] Mecca.

He said, 'For the love of God and our severance from all beside Him.'

"*Verily we have not repeated his expressions (upon him be peace), but rather we have made manifest a spray from the Ocean of Life which was deposited in his words, that by it those who advance may live and be aware of what hath befallen the* p. 171.
trusted ones of God on the part of an evil and most reprobate people. And to-day we see the people censuring those who acted unjustly of yore, while they oppress more vehemently than those oppressed, and know it not. By God, I do not desire sedition, but the purification of [God's] *servants from all that withholdeth them from approach to God, the King of the Day of Invocation*[1].

"*I was asleep on my couch: the breaths of my Lord the Merciful passed over me and awakened me from sleep*[2]*: to this bear witness the denizens* [of the realms] *of His Power and His Kingdom, and the dwellers in the cities of His Glory, and Himself, the True. I am not impatient of calamities in His*

[1] i.e. the Day of Judgement, "so called," says the Arabic-Turkish dictionary called *Akhtarí Kabír*, "because thereon the people of paradise and the people of hell shall call to one another." The expression occurs once in the Ḳur'án, ch. xl. v. 34.

[2] K. inserts:—"*and commanded me to proclaim betwixt earth and heaven: this was not on my part but on His part, and to this...*" &c.

*way, nor of afflictions for His love and at His good
pleasure. God hath made affliction as a morning
shower to this green pasture, and as a match for*
p. 172. *His lamp whereby earth and heaven are illumined.*

"*Shall that which any one hath of wealth endure unto him, or avail him to-morrow with him who holdeth his forelock*[1]*? If any should look on those who sleep under slabs*[2] *and keep company with the dust, can he distinguish the bones of the king's skull from the knuckles of the slave? No, by the King of Kings! Or doth he know governors from herdsmen, or discern the wealthy and the rich from him who was without shoes or carpet? By God, distinction is removed, save for him who fulfilled righteousness and judged uprightly. Where are the doctors, the scholars, the nobles? Where is the keenness of their glances, the sharpness of their sight, the subtlety of their thoughts, the soundness of their understandings? Where are their hidden treasures and their apparent
gauds, their bejewelled thrones and their ample*
p. 173. *couches? Alas! All have been laid waste, and
the decree of God hath rendered them as scattered dust! Emptied is what they treasured up, and dissipated is what they collected, and dispersed is what they concealed: they have become* [such that] *thou*

[1] See Ḳur'án, xcvi. 15, 16, and cxi. 2 *passim.*

[2] K. reads تحت الرخام "*under marble.*"

seest nought but their empty places, their gaping roofs, their uprooted beams, their new things waxed old. As for the discerning man, verily wealth will not divert him from regarding the end; and for the prudent man, riches will not withhold him from turning toward [God] *the Rich, the Exalted. Where is he who held dominion over all whereon the sun arose, and who spent lavishly and sought after curious things in the world and what is therein created? Where is the lord of the swarthy squadron and the yellow standard? Where is he who ruled in Zawrá*[1], *and where he who wrought injustice in* [Damascus] *the spacious*[2]? *Where are they at whose bounty treasures were afraid,* p. 174. *at whose open-handedness and generosity the ocean was dismayed? Where is he whose arm was stretched forth in rebelliousness, whose heart turned away from the Merciful One? Where is he who used to make choice of pleasures and cull the fruits of desires? Where are the dames of the bridal chambers, and the possessors of beauty? Where are their waving branches and their spreading boughs, their lofty*

[1] Baghdad. The name (or rather epithet) of *Zawrá* ("the crooked") is applied to no less than ten different places. (See Yáḳút's *Mushtarik*, ed. Wüstenfeld, p. 235.) But in this and similar places Baghdad, the capital of the perfidious 'Abbásids so detestable to every true Shí'ité, is intended.

[2] *Al-Feyḥá* ("the spacious") is an epithet designating Damascus. Mu'áwiya, Yezíd, and the Omeyyad caliphs generally are here alluded to.

palaces and trellised gardens? Where is the smoothness of the expanses thereof and the softness of their breezes, the rippling of their waters and the murmur of their winds, the cooing of their doves and the rustling of their trees? Where are their laughing hearts and their smiling teeth?[1] *Woe unto them! They have descended to the abyss and become companions to the pebbles; to-day no mention is heard of them nor any sound; nothing is known of them*
p. 175. *nor any hint. Will the people dispute it while they behold it? Will they deny it when they know it? I know not in what valley they wander erringly: do they not see that they depart and return not? How long will they be famous in the low countries and in the high*[2], *descend and ascend? 'Is not the time yet come to those who believe for their hearts to become humble for the remembrance of God*[3]*?' Well is it with that one who hath said or shall say, 'Yea, O Lord, the time is ripe and hath come,' and who severeth himself from all that is*[4]. *Alas! nought is reaped but what is sown, and nought is taken but what is laid up, save by the grace of God and His favour. Hath the earth conceived him whom the veils*

[1] Or perhaps "*their heaving bosoms* [lit. "dilated lungs"] *and their smiling mouths.*"

[2] Concerning the expression غار و انجد see Lane's *Arabic-English Lexicon*, Bk. i. Pt. vi. p. 2306, column 3.

[3] Ḳur'án, lvii. 15.

[4] K. inserts "*unto the King of beings.*"

of glory prevent not from ascending into the Kingdom of his Lord, the Mighty, the Supreme? Have we any good works whereby defects shall be removed or which shall bring us near unto the Lord of causes? We ask God to deal with us according to His grace, not His justice, and to make us of those who turn toward p. 176.
Him and sever themselves from all beside Him.

"*O King, I have seen in the way of God what no eye hath seen and no ear hath heard. Friends have disclaimed me; ways are straitened unto me; the pool of safety is dried up; the plain of ease is* [scorched] *yellow*[1]. *How many calamities have descended, and how many will descend! I walk advancing toward the Mighty, the Bounteous, while*

[1] I am uncertain as to this line, and incline to think (though both MSS. agree in the pointing of the first and the spelling of the second doubtful word) that we should read ضحضاح in the first clause (which signifies *shallow water* or a *pool*, and agrees in sense with the verb نضب *to dry up* or *sink into the ground*), and صحصاح ('*a flat, even plain, destitute of herbage and containing small pebbles*') in the second. At any rate I can find no other meaning of ضحضاح which would seem appropriate to the verb اصفرّ. However, Baron Rosen's text (*Collections Scientifiques, etc.*, vol. vi. p. 213) agrees with the two MSS. in my possession, and a gloss therein appended to the passage before us explains ضحضاح as meaning 'a pool of water' (ماء القليل), and ضحضاح as meaning 'garden' (الروضة).

behind me glides the serpent. My eyes rain down tears until my bed is drenched; but my sorrow is not for myself. By God, my head longeth for the spears for the love of its Lord, and I never pass by a tree but my heart addresseth it [saying], *'O would that thou wert cut down in my name and my body were crucified upon thee in the way of my Lord;' yea, because I see mankind going astray in their intoxication, and*
p. 177. *they know it not: they have exalted their lusts, and put aside their God, as though they took the command of God for a mockery, a sport, and a plaything; and they think that they do well, and that they are harboured in the citadel of security. The matter is not as they suppose: to-morrow they shall see what they* [now] *deny.*

"*We are about to shift from this most remote place of banishment*[1] *unto the prison of Acre. And, according to what they say, it is assuredly the most desolate of the cities of the world, the most unsightly of them in appearance, the most detestable in climate, and the foulest in water; it is as though it were the metropolis of the owl; there is not heard from its regions aught save the sound of its hooting. And in it they intend to imprison the servant, and to*

[1] Adrianople. In K. this sentence runs as follows:—"*The lords of command and wealth are about to send us forth from this land, which is named Edirné* [Adrianople], *unto the city of Acre,*" etc.

shut in our faces the doors of leniency and take away from us the good things of the life of the world during what remaineth of our days. By God, though weariness should weaken me, and hunger should destroy me, though my couch should be made of the hard rock and my associates of the beasts of the desert, I will not p. 178.
blench, but will be patient, as the resolute and determined are patient, in the strength of God, the King of Pre-existence, the Creator of the nations; and under all circumstances I give thanks unto God. And we hope of His graciousness (exalted is He) the freedom of our necks from chains and shackles in this imprisonment: and that He will render [all men's] *faces sincere toward Him, the Mighty, the Bounteous. Verily He answereth him who prayeth unto Him, and is near unto him who calleth on Him. And we ask Him to make this dark calamity a buckler for the body of His saints, and to protect them thereby from sharp swords and piercing blades. Through affliction hath His light shone and His praise been bright unceasingly: this hath been His method through past ages and bygone times.*

"*The people shall know what to-day they understand not when their steeds shall stumble, their beds be* p. 179
rolled up, their swords be blunted, and their footsteps slip. I know not how long they shall ride the steed of desire and wander erringly in the desert of heedlessness and error. Of glory shall any glory endure, or of

abasement any abasement? Or shall he endure who used to stay himself on high cushions, and who attained in splendour the utmost limit? No, by my Lord the Merciful! 'All that is thereon[1] *is transient, and there remaineth* [only] *the face of my Lord' the Mighty, the Beneficent. What buckler hath not the arrow of destruction smitten, or what pinion hath not the hand of fate plucked? From what fortress hath the messenger of death been kept back when he came? What throne hath not been broken, or what palace hath not been left desolate? Did men but know what pure wine*[2] *of the mercy of their Lord, the Mighty, the All-knowing, was beneath the seal, they would certainly cast*
p. 180. *aside reproach and seek to be satisfied by this servant; but now have they veiled me with the veil of darkness which they have woven with the hands of doubts and fancies. The White Hand*[3] *shall cleave an opening to this sombre night*[4]. *On that day the servants* [of God] *shall say what those cavilling women said of yore*[5], *that there may appear in the*

[1] i.e. on the earth. See Ḳur'án, lv. 26, and cf. 27.

[2] See above, p. 77, note 2.

[3] Alluding to the miracle of Moses. See Ḳur'án, vii. 105; xxvi. 32; xx. 23; xxvii. 12; and xxviii. 32, especially the two last passages.

[4] K. inserts, "*and God will open into His city a gate* [hitherto] *shut* [or, *a great gate*]. *On that day men shall enter in in crowds, and shall say what the cavilling women said,*" etc.

[5] Alluding to what was said by the women who had censured Potiphar's wife Zuleykhá for her love of Joseph when

end what began in the beginning. Do they desire to tarry when their foot is in the stirrup? Or do they see any return in their going? No, by the Lord of Lords, save in the Resurrection! On that day men shall arise from the tombs and shall be questioned concerning their riches. Happy that one whom burdens shall not oppress on that day whereon the mountains shall pass away and all shall appear for the questioning in the presence of God the Exalted! Verily He is severe in punishing.

"*We ask God to sanctify the hearts of certain of* p. 181.
the doctors from rancour and hatred that they may regard things with eyes which closure overcometh not; and to raise them unto a station where the world and the lordship thereof shall not turn them aside from looking toward the Supreme Horizon, and where [anxiety for] *gaining a livelihood and* [providing] *household goods shall not divert them from* [the thought of] *that day whereon the mountains shall be made like carpets. Though they rejoice at that which hath befallen us of calamity, there shall come a day whereon they shall wail and weep. By my Lord, were I given the choice between the glory and opulence, the wealth and dignity, the ease and luxury wherein they are, and the distress and affliction wherein I am, I would certainly choose that wherein I am to-*

they afterwards beheld the latter:—"*This one is none other than a gracious angel!*" See Ḳur'án xii. especially v. 31–32.

day, and I would not now exchange one atom of these afflictions for all that hath been created in the kingdom of production! Were it not for afflictions in the way
p. 182. *of God my continuance would have no sweetness for me, nor would my life profit me. Let it not be hidden from the discerning and such as look towards the chiefest outlook that I, during the greater part of my days, was as a servant sitting beneath a sword suspended by a single hair who knoweth not when it shall descend upon him, whether it shall descend instantly or after a while. And in all this we give thanks to God the Lord of the worlds, and we praise Him under all circumstances: verily He is a witness unto all things.*

"*We ask God to extend His shadow*[1], *that the unitarians may haste thereto, and that the sincere may take shelter therein; and to bestow on* [these] *servants flowers from the garden of his grace and stars from the horizon of his favours; and to assist him in that which he liketh and approveth; and to help him unto that which shall bring him near to the Day-spring of His Most Comely Names, that he may not shut his eyes to the wrong which he seeth, but*
p. 183. *may regard his subjects with the eye of favour and preserve them from violence*[2]. *And we ask Him*

[1] By "the Shadow of God" is meant the King of Persia.

[2] K. inserts here:—"*And we ask Him (exalted is He) to gather all together by the gulf of the Most Mighty Ocean where-*

(exalted is He) to make thee a helper[1] *unto His religion and a regarder of His justice, that thou mayest rule over* [His] *servants as thou rulest over those of thy kindred, and mayest choose for them what thou wouldest choose for thyself. Verily He is the Potent, the Exalted, the Protecting, the Self-subsistent.*"

Now since suitable occasion hath arisen it hath been considered appropriate that some of the precepts of Behá'u'lláh which are contained in tracts and epistles should also be inserted briefly in this treatise, so that the main principles and practice and [their] foundations and basis may become clear and apparent. And these texts have been copied from numerous tracts.

Amongst them [is this]:—"*Consort with* [people of all] *religions with spirituality and fragrance*[2]...

of each drop crieth, 'Verily He is the giver of good tidings to the Worlds and the quickener of the worlds; and praise be to God the King of the Day of Judgement.'"

1 Perhaps there is an allusion here to the name of the Sháh of Persia—*Náṣiru'd-Dín*—'the helper of religion' or 'defender of the faith,' and a prayer is uttered that he may indeed become that which his name implies.

2 The words "*that they may perceive in you the scent of the Merciful One*" (ليجدوا منكم عرف الرحمن) proper to this passage are, whether intentionally or accidentally, omitted in the text, but they occur in all MSS. of the *Kitáb-i-Aḳdas*, from which this quotation is taken.

p. 184. *Beware lest the zeal of ignorance possess you amongst mankind. All originated from God and returneth unto Him: verily He is the Source of creation and the Goal of the worlds.*"

And amongst them [is this]:—"*Ye are forbidden sedition and strife in the books and epistles; and herein I desire nought save your exaltation and elevation, whereunto beareth witness the heaven and its stars, the sun and its radiance, the trees and their leaves, the seas and their waves, and the earth and its treasures. We ask God to continue His saints and strengthen them unto that which befitteth them in this blessed, precious, and wondrous station, and we ask Him to assist those who surround me to act according to that whereunto they have been commanded on the part of the Supreme Pen.*"

And amongst them [is this]:—"The fairest tree of knowledge is this sublime word:—'Ye are all the fruit of one tree and the leaves of one branch.' *Pride is not for him who loves his country, but for him who loves the* [whole] *world.*"

p. 185. And amongst them [is this]:—"*Verily he who educateth his son, or one of the sons* [of another], *it is as though he educated one of my sons. Upon him be the splendour of God, and His grace, and His mercy which preceded the worlds*[1]."

[1] This quotation is also from the *Kitáb-i-Aḳdas.*

Amongst them [is this]:—"O people of Behá! Ye have been and are the dawnings of affection and the day-springs of divine grace: defile not the tongue with cursing or execration of any one, and guard the eye from that which is not seemly. Shew forth that which ye have: if it be accepted, the object is attained; if not, interference is vain[1]: *leave him to himself,* [while] *advancing toward God, the Protecting, the Self-subsistent.* Be not a cause of grief, much less of strife and sedition. It is hoped that ye will be nurtured in the shade of the lote-tree of Divine Grace, and practise that which God desireth.
Ye are all leaves of one tree and drops of one sea." p. 186.

Amongst them [is this]:—"The faith of God and religion of God hath been revealed and manifested from the heaven of the Will of the King of Pre-existence only for the union and concord of the dwellers upon earth: make it not a cause of discord and dissension. The principal means and chief instrument for [bringing about] the appearance and irradiance of the luminary of concord is the religion of God and the Law of the Lord; while the growth of the world, the education of the nations, and the peace and comfort of those in all lands are through the divine ordinances and decrees. This is the principal means for this most great gift; it giveth

[1] Cf. p. 72 *supra*.

the cup of life, bestoweth everlasting life, and conferreth eternal blessedness. The chiefs of the earth, especially the exemplars of divine justice, must make strenuous efforts to guard this state and to upraise
p. 187. and preserve it. So likewise that which is necessary is enquiry into the condition of the people, and cognizance of the deeds and circumstances of each one of the different classes. We desire of the exemplars of God's power, namely of kings and chiefs, that they will make endeavour: perchance discord may depart out of [their] midst, and the horizons may be illumined with the light of concord. All must hold to that which floweth from the Pen of Reminder, and practise it. God witnesseth and [all] the atoms of existences testify that we have mentioned that which will be the cause of the exaltation, elevation, education, preservation, and reformation of the dwellers upon earth. We desire of God that He will strengthen [His] servants. That which this oppressed one seeketh of all is justice and fairness: let them not be satisfied with listening; let them ponder on what hath become manifest from this oppressed one. I swear by the Sun of Revelation, which hath shone forth from the
p. 188. horizon of the heaven of the Kingdom of the Merciful One, that, if any [other] expositor or speaker had been beheld, I would not have made myself an object for the malevolence and the calumnies of mankind."
Finis.

By these sentences a clue to the principles, ideas, line of conduct, behaviour, and intentions of this sect is placed in the hand; whereas if we seek to become acquainted with the truth of this matter through the accounts and stories which are in the mouths of men, the truth will be entirely concealed and hidden by reason of their manifold differences and contrariety. It is therefore best to discover the principles and objects of this sect from the contents of their teachings, tracts, and epistles. There is no authority nor are there any proofs or texts superior to these, for this is the foundation of foundations and the ultimate criterion. One cannot judge of the generality by the speech or action of individuals, for diversity of states p. 189.
is one of the peculiarities and concomitants of the human race.

At all events, in the beginning of the year one thousand two hundred and eighty-five [A.H.] they transferred Behá'u'lláh and all those persons who were with him from Adrianople to the prison of Acre, and Mírzá Yaḥyá to the fortress of Famagusta, and there they remained[1]. But in Persia after a while sundry persons who were discerning in matters, notable for wise policy, and aware and cognizant of the

[1] According to Nabíl's chronological poem, Behá'u'lláh and his companions left Adrianople on the 20th of *Rabí' II.* A.H. 1285 (August 10th, A.D. 1868) and reached Acre on the 12th of *Jemádí I.* (August 31st). See notes 2 and 3 on p. 101, and note W at end.

truth of the earlier and later events, made representation before the presence of His Majesty the King saying, "What has hitherto been reported, related, asserted, and alleged concerning this sect in the Royal Presence was either an exaggeration, or else [the speakers] fabricated statements with a view to [their
p. 190. own] individual designs and the attainment of personal advantages. If so be that His Majesty the King will investigate matters in his own noble person, it is believed that it will become clear before his presence that this sect have no worldly object nor any concern with political matters. The fulcrum of their motion and rest and the pivot of their cast and conduct is restricted to spiritual things and confined to matters of conscience; it has nothing to do with the affairs of government nor any concern with the powers of the throne; its principles are the withdrawal of veils, the verification of signs, the education of souls, the reformation of characters, the purification of hearts, and illumination with the gleams of enlightenment. That which befits the kingly dignity
p. 191. and beseems the world-ordering diadem is this, that all subjects of every class and creed should be the objects of bounty, and [should abide] in the utmost tranquillity and prosperity under the wide shadow of the King's justice. For the divine shadow[1] is the refuge

[1] i.e. "the royal protection"; for a King is called "the shadow of God on the earth."

of all the dwellers upon earth and the asylum of all mankind; it is not limited to one party. In particular, the true nature and real doctrine of this sect have [now] become evident and well known: all their writings and tracts have repeatedly and frequently fallen into [our] hands, and are to be found preserved in the possession of the government. If they be perused, the actual truth and inward verity will become clear and apparent. These pages are entirely taken up with prohibitions of sedition, [recommendations of] upright conduct amongst mankind, obedience, submission, loyalty, conformity[1], and acquisition of laudable qualities, and encouragements p. 192. to become endowed with praiseworthy accomplishments and characteristics. They have absolutely no reference to political questions, nor do they treat of that which could cause disturbance or sedition. Under these circumstances a just government can [find] no excuse, and possesses no pretext [for further persecuting this sect] except [a claim to the right of] interference in thought and conscience, which are the private possessions of the heart and soul. And, as regards this matter, there has [already] been much interference, and countless efforts have been made. What blood has been shed! What heads have been hung up! Thousands of persons have been slain;

[1] i.e. conformity to the royal commands, civil laws, and all such observances and customs as are harmless, even if useless.

thousands of women and children have become wanderers or captives; many are the buildings which have been ruined; and how many noble races and families have become headless and homeless! Yet nought has been effected and no advantage has been
p. 193. gained; no remedy has been discovered for this ill, nor any easy salve for this wound. [To ensure] freedom of conscience and tranquillity of heart and soul is one of the duties and functions of government, and is in all ages the cause of progress in development and ascendency over other lands. Other civilized countries acquired not this pre-eminence, nor attained unto these high degrees of influence and power, till such time as they put away the strife of sects out of their midst, and dealt with all classes according to one standard. All are one people, one nation, one species, one kind. The common interest is complete equality; justice and equality amongst mankind are amongst the chief promoters of empire and the principal means to the extension of the skirt
p. 194. of conquest. From whatever section of earth's denizens signs of contentiousness appear, prompt punishment is required by a just government; while any person who girds up the loins of endeavour and carries off the ball of priority is deserving of royal favours and worthy of splendid and princely gifts. Times are changed, and the need and fashion of the world are changed. Interference with creed and faith in every

country causes manifest detriment, while justice and equal dealing towards all peoples on the face of the earth are the means whereby progress is effected. It is right to exercise caution and care with regard to political factions, and to be fearful and apprehensive of materialist sects; for the subjects occupying the thoughts of the former are [designs of] interference in political matters and [desire of] ostentation, while the actions and conduct of the latter are subversive p. 195.
of safety and tranquillity. But this sect are steadfast in their own path and firmly established in conduct and faith; they are pious, devoted, tenacious, and consistent in such sort that they freely lay down their lives, and, after their own way, seek to please God; they are strenuous in effort and earnest in endeavour; they are the essence of obedience and most patient in hardship and trouble; they sacrifice their existence and raise no complaint or cry; what they utter is in truth the secret longing of the heart, and what they seek and pursue is by the direction of a leader. It is therefore necessary to regard their principles and their chief, and not to make a trivial thing a pretext. Now since the conduct of the chief, the teachings of his epistles, and the purport of his writings are apparent and well known, the line of action of this p. 196.
sect is plain and obvious as the sun. Of whatever was possible and practicable by way of discouragement, determent, eradication, intimidation, repre-

hension, slaughter, banishment, and stripes there was no lack, yet nothing was thereby effected. In other countries when they perceived severity and persecution in such instances to be identical with stimulation and incitement, and saw that paying no attention was more effectual, they abated the fire of revolution. Therefore did they universally proclaim the equal rights of all denominations, and sounded the liberty of all classes from east to west. This clamour and outcry, this uproar and conflagration, are the consequences of instigation, temptation, incitement, and provocation. For thirty years there has been no
p. 197. rumour of disturbance or rebellion, nor any sign of sedition. Notwithstanding the duplication of adherents and the increase and multiplication of this body, through many admonitions and encouragements to virtue this sect are all in the utmost repose and stability: they have made obedience their distinctive trait, and in extreme submissiveness and subordination are the loyal subjects of the King. On what lawful grounds can the government further molest them, or permit them to be slighted? Besides this, interference with the consciences and beliefs of peoples, and persecution of diverse denominations of men is an obstacle to the expansion of the kingdom, an impediment to the conquest of other countries, an obstruction to multiplication of subjects, and contrary to the established principles of monarchy. In the time when

the mighty government of Persia did not interfere with [men's] consciences, diverse sects entered in and abode beneath the banner of the great king, and p. 198. [many] different peoples reposed and served under the shadow of that mighty government's protection. The extent of the empire increased from day to day; the greater portion of the continent of Asia was under the just rule of its administration; and the majority of the different religions and races were [represented] amongst the subjects of him who wore its crown. But when the custom of interference with the creeds of all sects arose, and the principle of enquiring into men's thoughts became the fashion and practice, the extensive dominions of the empire of Persia diminished, and many provinces and vast territories passed out of her hands, until it reached such a point that the great provinces of Túrán, Assyria, and Chaldæa were lost; until—what need of prolixity?—the greater part of the regions of Khurásán likewise passed out of the control of the government of Persia by reason of the interference with matters of conscience and the p. 199. fanaticism of its governors. For the cause of the Afghan independency and the revolt of the Turcoman tribes was in truth this thing, else were they at no time or period separate from Persia. In face of its evident harmfulness what necessity is there for persecuting the harmless? But if we desire to put in force the sentence [of the doctors of religion] no one will escape

fetters and chains and the keenness of the sword, for in Persia, apart from this sect, there exist diverse sects, such as the Mutasharri's, the Sheykhís, the Ṣúfís, the Nuṣeyrís[1], and others, each one of whom regards the other as infidels and accuses them of crime. Under these circumstances what need that the government should persecute this one or that one,
p. 200. or disturb itself about the ideas and consciences of its subjects and people? All are the subjects of the king, and are under the shadow of the royal protection. Every one who hears and obeys should be undisturbed and unmolested, while every one who is rebellious and disobedient deserves punishment at the hands of his Majesty the King. Above all, the times are completely changed, while principles and institutions have undergone alteration. In all countries such actions hinder development and progress, and cause decline and deterioration. Of the violent agitation which has befallen the supports of Oriental government the chief cause and principal factor are in truth these laws and habits of interference; while that state the seat of whose dominion over the Atlantic and the Baltic is in the furthest regions of

[1] Concerning the Sheykhís see Note E at end. Concerning the Nuṣeyrís see note 1 on p. 14. The Mutasharri's are those who conform to the *Sharí'at* or Sacred Law founded on the Ḳur'án and traditions, or, in other words, the orthodox party. The Ṣúfís—those mystical pantheists of Persia—are too well known to need description.

the North has, by reason of equal dealing with its
different subjects and the establishment of the uniform political rights of diverse nationalities, acquired p. 201.
extensive colonies in each of the five continents of
the world. Where is this little island in the North
Atlantic, and where the vast territory of the East
Indies? Can such extension be obtained save by
equal justice to all peoples and classes? At all
events, by means of just laws, freedom of conscience,
and uniform dealing and equity towards all nationalities and peoples, they have actually brought under
their dominion nearly all of the inhabited quarter
of the world, and by reason of these principles
of freedom they have added day by day to the
strength, power, and extent of their empire, while
most of the peoples on the face of the earth celebrate
the name of this state for its justice. As regards
religious zeal and true piety, their touchstone and
proof are firmness and steadfastness in noble qualities,
virtues, and perfections, which are the greatest p. 202.
blessings of the human race; but not interference
with the belief of this one or that one, demolition of
edifices, and cutting off of the human race. In the
middle ages, whereof the beginning was the time of
the fall of the Roman Empire, and the end the
capture of Constantinople at the hands of [the
followers of] Islám, fierce intolerance and molestation
of far and near arose in [all] the countries of Europe

by reason of the paramount influence of religious leaders. The matter came to such a pass that the edifice of humanity seemed tottering to its fall, and the peace and comfort of chief and vassal, king and subject, became hidden behind the veil of annihilation. Night and day all parties were slaves to apprehension and disquietude: civilization was utterly destroyed:
p. 203. the control and order of countries was neglected: the principles and essentials of the happiness of the human race were in abeyance: the supports of kingly authority were shaken: but the influence and power of the heads of religion and of the monks were in all parts complete. But when they removed these differences, persecutions, and bigotries out of their midst, and proclaimed the equal rights of all subjects and the liberty of men's consciences, the lights of glory and power arose and shone from the horizons of that kingdom in such wise that those countries made progress in every direction; and whereas the mightiest monarchy of Europe had been servile to and abased before the smallest government of Asia, now the great states of Asia are unable to oppose the small states of Europe. These are effectual and sufficient proofs
p. 204. that the conscience of man is sacred and to be respected; and that liberty thereof produces widening of ideas, amendment of morals, improvement of conduct, disclosure of the secrets of creation, and manifestation of the hidden verities of the contin-

gent[1] world. Moreover, if interrogation of conscience, which is one of the private possessions of the heart and the soul, take place in this world, what further recompense remains for man in the court of divine justice at the day of general resurrection? Convictions and ideas are within the scope of the comprehension of the King of kings, not of kings; and soul and conscience are between the fingers of control of the Lord of hearts, not of [His] servants. So in the world of existence two persons unanimous in all grades [of thought] and all beliefs cannot be found. '*The ways unto God are as the number of the breaths of* [His] *creatures*[2]' is a mysterious truth, and '*To every* [people] *We have appointed a* [separate] *rite*[3]' is one of the subtleties of the Ḳur'án. If this vast energy and precious time which have been expended p. 205.
in persecuting other religions, and whereby no sort of result or effect has been obtained, had been spent in strengthening the basis of the monarchy, fortifying the imperial throne, making prosperous the realms of the sovereign, and quickening the subjects of the king, ere now the royal dominions would have become prosperous, the seed-plot of the people would have

[1] On the meaning of 'contingent' being, see note 1 on p. 115.

[2] This is a very well-known and often quoted tradition.

[3] Ḳur'án xxii. 35. The verse is inaccurately quoted here. It should be لكلّ امّة الخ '*to every people,*' *etc.*

been watered by the bounty of princely justice, and the splendour of the kingdom of Persia would be evident and apparent as the true dawn throughout the horizons of the world."

These questions and considerations, at all events, certain persons have reported. But let us return to our original subject. The Royal Personage was pleased to investigate the hidden secret in his own noble person. According to the account transmitted, it became clear and obvious before the [Royal]
p. 206. Presence that most of these suspicions arose from the intrigues of persons of influence who were continually engaged in fabricating matters behind the veil of fancy and casting suspicion upon the community, and who, to attain advantages for themselves and preserve their own positions, were wont to make motes appear as globes, and straws as mountains in the mirror of their imagination. For these suspicions there was absolutely no foundation or basis, nor had these assertions any proof or verisimilitude. What power and ability have the helpless people, or what boldness and strength have poor subjects that they should inflict injury or hurt on the sovereign might, or be able to oppose the military forces of the crown?

From that time till now disturbance and sedition have been on the wane in Persia, and clamour and
p. 207. strife have ceased; although [still] on rare occasions

certain of the official doctors do, for their own personal and private advantage, stir up the common folk, raise a hue and cry, and, by their importunity and pertinacity, molest one or two individuals of this sect, as happened ten or twelve years ago in Isfahán. For there were amongst the inhabitants of Isfahán two brothers, Seyyids of Ṭabáṭabá, Seyyid Ḥasan and Seyyid Ḥuseyn, celebrated in those parts for piety, trustworthiness, and nobility; men of wealth, engaged in commerce, behaving towards all men with perfect kindliness and courtesy. And to all outward appearance no one had observed in either of these two brothers any swerving from what was best, much less any conduct or behaviour which could deserve torment or punishment; for, as is related, they were p. 208.
admitted by all [pre-eminent] in all praiseworthy and laudable qualities, while their deeds and actions were like exhortations and admonitions. These had transacted business with Mír Muḥammed Ḥuseyn the Imám-Jum'a of Isfahán; and when they came to make up their accounts it appeared that the sum of eighteen thousand *tumáns*[1] was due to them. They [therefore] broke off [further] transactions, prepared a bond for this sum, and desired it to be sealed. This thing was grievous to the Imám-Jum'a, so that he came to the stage of anger and enmity. Finding

[1] About £5400.

himself in debt, and having no resource but to pay, he raised clamour and outcry saying "These two brothers are Bábís and deserve severe punishment from the king." A crowd at once attacked their house,
p. 209. plundered and pillaged all their goods, distressed and terrified their wives and children, and seized and despoiled all their possessions. Then, fearing that they might refer the punishment to the step of the king's throne and loose their tongues in demand of redress, he [i.e. the Imám-Jum'a] fell to thinking how to compass their death and destroy them. He therefore persuaded certain of the doctors to cooperate with him, and they pronounced sentence of death. Afterwards they arrested those two brothers, put them in chains, and brought them before the public assembly. Yet seek as they might to fix on them some accusation, find some fault, or discover some pretext, they were unable to do so. At length they said, "You must either renounce this faith, or else lay down your heads beneath the sword of
p. 210. punishment." Although some of those present urged them saying, "Say merely 'We are not of this sect,' and it is sufficient, and will be the means of your deliverance and protection," they would by no means consent, but rather confirmed and declared it with eloquent speech and affecting utterance, so that the rage and violence of the Imám-Jum'a boiled over, and, not satisfied with killing and destroying them,

they inflicted sundry indignities on their bodies after death to mention which is not fitting, and of which the details are beyond the power of speech. Indeed in such wise was the blood of these two brothers shed that even the Christian priest of Julfá cried out, lamented, and wept on that day; and this event befel after such sort that every one wept over the fate of those two brothers, for during the whole period of their life they had never distressed the feelings even of an ant, while by general report they had in the time of famine in Persia spent all their wealth in relieving the poor and distressed. Yet, notwithstanding this reputation, were they slain with such cruelty in the midst of the people!

p. 211.

But now for a long while the justice of the King has prevented and withheld, and none dares attempt such grievous molestations[1].

VALE.

[1] Unfortunately in face of the martyrdom of Áḳá Mírzá Ashraf of Ábádé at Isfahán in or about October 1888, and the still more recent persecutions at Si-dih near Isfahán, this statement can no longer be taken as true. For some remarks on these persecutions, and some further account of the martyrdom of Seyyid Ḥasan and Seyyid Ḥuseyn, with which our history concludes, see B. i. pp. 489–491, B. ii. pp. 998–999, and Note Y at end.

There ceased from the writing of this its poor writer

the Letter Zá

on the night of Friday the 18*th of*

Jamádí-ul-Úlá

A.H. 1307[1].

[1] January 10th, A.D. 1890. Concerning "the Letter Zá" (*Zeynu'l-Muḳarrabín*), and the colophons wherewith MSS. written by his hand conclude, see Note Z at end.

NOTES.

NOTE A.

Persian and European Accounts of the Báb and his Religion.

I. Persian Accounts.

Four works, besides the present, written in the Persian language treat more or less fully of the history of the Bábí movement. Two of these, the *Násikhu't-Tawáríkh* and the *Rawżatu'ṣ-Ṣafá*, are general histories compiled by Musulmán historians; one, the *Táríkh-i-Jadíd*, is a monograph on the said movement, whereof the author, if not actually a Bábí, at least sympathised warmly with the reformers; one, the *Ḳiṣaṣu'l-'Ulamá*, is a biography of Shi'ite divines, which deals incidentally at some length with the Bábí doctrines and the history of their originator and his precursors. Each of these works I shall now consider in detail.

1. The *Násikhu't-Tawáríkh*.

This is a general history of the world, intended, as its name implies, to supersede all preceding works of a similar character. Its author is Mírzá Taḳí *Mustawfí*, better known by his poetical *nom-de-guerre* of *Sipihr* and his official title of *Lisánu'l-Mulk* ('The Tongue of the Kingdom'). Gobineau, at p. 454 of his interesting work *Trois Ans en Asie* (Paris, 1859), gives a description of the social aspects of this historian (to whom he is indebted for the greater part of the facts relating to the Bábí movement so graphically pourtrayed in his *Religions et Philosophies dans l'Asie Centrale*), and of Riżá-Ḳulí Khán, the author of the work to be next mentioned. The *Násikhu't-Tawáríkh* consists of a series of large volumes, each of which deals with a particular period of history. The last volume is entirely devoted to the Kájár dynasty, and with it alone are we here concerned. It is divided into three parts, of which the *first* treats of the origin and rise of the Kájárs and the reigns of Áḳá Muhammad and Fatḥ-'Alí Sháh; the *second* of the reign of Muhammad Sháh; and the *third* of the reign of Náṣiru'd-Dín, the present Sháh, down to the year A. H. 1267 (A.D. 1850—1851). A further supplement published separately carries the history down to the year A.H. 1273 (A.D. 1856—1857). All that relates to the Bábís is contained in the *second* and *third* parts of the main volume and in the supplement, of the contents of which I shall immediately give a brief abstract. My intention was to have made this abstract a complete index of contents, but, having already written more than half of it, I perceived that it would occupy more space than could conveniently be spared, and I was therefore compelled to confine myself to a mere summary of the chief heads of the narrative, deferring a fuller presentation thereof till some future occasion. This is the less to be regretted, inasmuch as almost everything relating to the subject before us which is contained in this history has been embodied in the works of Gobineau and Kazem-Beg. The whole of the *Násikhu't-Tawáríkh* has been lithographed at Teherán, but unfortunately the pages are unnumbered and there is no index save occasional marginal references to the chief events narrated in the text. The numeration of the pages here given is supplied by myself. It is re-commenced for each part and for the supplement, but, inasmuch as my copy of the latter has no title-page and appears to be incomplete, it cannot in this case be regarded as having more than a relative value.

Contents of Part ii of the *Ḳájáriyya* volume in so far as they relate to the Bábís.

P. 130. Events of the year A. H. 1260 (A.D. 1844). Appearance of the Báb—His parentage, education, and character—Development of his claims—Peculiarities of his doctrines and ordinances—Reception accorded to him by different classes.

P. 131. Proofs advanced by the Báb—His innovations in matters of religion—Accusations against the chastity and temperance of his followers—The Báb's pilgrimage to Mecca and return to Bushire—Action taken against him and his missionaries by Ḥuseyn Khán *Ajudán-báshí* the governor of Fárs—The Báb confined to his house.

P. 132. The Báb is entrapped by a stratagem of Ḥuseyn Khán's into a too free enunciation of his doctrines—He is punished, and imprisoned with greater rigour for six months—Minúchihr Khán *Mu'tamadu'd-Dawla,* the governor of Isfahán, succeeds in effecting the Báb's release and bringing him to Isfahán, where he treats him with consideration and kindness.

P. 133. Ḥuseyn Khán expels Seyyid Yaḥyá and other prominent Bábís from Shíráz—Minúchihr Khán, anxious to test the Báb's knowledge, summons a number of learned men to confer and dispute with him. [See Note J, *infra.*]

P. 134 [first 7 lines]. Conclusion of this conference—Minúchihr Khán conceals the Báb in his house and sets afloat a rumour that he has sent him to Teherán.

* * * * *

P. 175 [last 3 lines]. Account of the Báb's first examination before the clergy of Tabríz in A.H. 1263 (A.D. 1847).

P. 176. } Continuation of the same. [See note M, *infra.*]
P. 177. }

P. 178 [first 9 lines]. Conclusion of the same—The Báb is bastinadoed until he recants.

Contents of Part iii of the *Ḳájáriyya* volume in so far as they relate to the Bábís.

P. 45. Events of the year A.H. 1264 (A.D. 1848). Ḳurratu'l-'Ayn, her parentage, education, beauty, learning and eloquence—She embraces the Bábí doctrines.

P. 46 [first 12 lines]. The devotion inspired by Ḳurratu'l-'Ayn in her followers—She discards the veil, and openly preaches the new doctrines—Anger of her uncle, Mullá Muḥammad Taḳí—He drives her from his house—He is assassinated by Bábís—Ḳurratu'l-'Ayn flies from

Ḳazvín, but continues her propaganda elsewhere. [See Note Q, *infra*.]

* * * * *

P. 53 [last line]. Mullá Ḥuseyn of Bushraweyh and the Bábí insurrection in Mázandarán.

P. 54. Mullá Ḥuseyn is converted to Bábíism—His missionary journey—His reception and adventures in Isfahán, Káshán, and Teherán.

P. 55. Mullá Ḥuseyn attempts to attach Muḥammad Sháh and Hájí Mírzá Áḳásí to the Báb's cause—He is compelled by threats to leave Teherán—He proceeds to Khurásán — Conversions to Bábíism — Measures adopted against the Bábís—Ḥamzé Mírzá imprisons Mullá Ḥuseyn in his camp at Rádagán—Escape of Mullá Ḥuseyn from custody—His journey westward, successes, and rebuffs.

P. 56. Continuation of Mullá Ḥuseyn's journey towards Mázandarán—Encounter with the populace at Miyámí and defeat of the Bábís—Altercation with Mullá Muḥammad Káẓim, the *mujtahid* of Sháhrúd—Death of Muḥammad Sháh—Account of Hájí Muḥammad 'Alí of Bárfurúsh—He falls in with the Báb on the pilgrimage to Mecca and embraces his doctrines—He returns to Bárfurúsh—He joins Mullá Ḥuseyn at Mash-had—Returns thence on the arrest of his colleague—At Badasht near Bisṭám meets Ḳurratu'l-'Ayn and her followers who have arrived from Ḳazvín.

P. 57. Ḳurratu'l-'Ayn's address—Its effect on the audience—She returns with Ḥájí Muḥammad 'Alí towards Mázandarán—Imputations on the conduct of Ḳurratu'l-'Ayn and Hájí Muḥammad 'Alí—They are attacked by the people of Hazár-Jaríb—They separate, he returning to Bárfurúsh, and she continuing to wander through Mázandarán preaching—Mullá Ḥuseyn joins his colleague at Bárfurúsh—Success of the Bábí propaganda—Enmity of the Sa'ídu'l-'Ulamá—Preparations for battle—Khánlar Mírzá's aid invoked by the orthodox party to put down the innovators.

P. 58. The Bábís retreat from, but return to, Bárfurúsh—'Abbás-Ḳulí Khán of Láriján interferes—Collision between the two parties in the city—Terms offered by the

Bábís and accepted by 'Abbás-Ḳulí Khán—The Bábís retire accompanied by an escort sent by 'Abbás-Ḳulí Khán —After the escort leaves them they are attacked by Khusraw of Ḳádí-Kalá at the head of a band of plunderers—Khusraw is killed and his followers routed—The Bábís take up their quarters at the Tomb of Sheykh Ṭabarsí.

P. 59. The Bábís fortify their position strongly without let or hindrance, most of the nobles and chiefs of the province having gone to assist at the Sháh's coronation at Teherán—Description of these fortifications—Garrison and commissariat of the Bábís—Mullá Ḥuseyn continues his propaganda—Extreme veneration paid to Hájí Muḥammad 'Alí by the Bábís—Mullá Ḥuseyn's encouragements and exhortations to his followers.

P. 60. A letter arrives from the Báb containing this passage :—

ينحدرون من جزيرة الخضراء الى سفح جبل الزّوراء

و يقتلون نحو اثنا عشر الفاً من الاتراك

'*They* [the Bábís] *shall descend from the Green Isle* [Mázandarán] *unto the foot of the mountain of Zawrá* [Teherán], *and shall slay about twelve thousand of the Turks*'—The Government, informed of the Bábís' proceedings, instructs the Mázandarání chiefs to take action against them—Áḳá 'Abdu'lláh marches against Sheykh Ṭabarsí with some Afghan, Kurdish, and Turkish tribesmen and volunteers from Ḳádí-Kalá—Mullá Ḥuseyn makes a night-attack on the besiegers.

P. 61. Áḳá 'Abdu'lláh is slain and his force routed with a loss of thirty killed—The fugitives flee to the village of Farrá, which is sacked, burned, and razed to the ground by the Bábís, and its inhabitants put to the sword—Rage of Náṣiru'd-Dín Sháh on hearing this news—Prince Mahdí-Ḳulí Mírzá is ordered to proceed against the Bábís with all speed and exterminate them—He quits Teherán at the end of Muḥarram [A.H. 1265 = Christmas, A.D. 1848] for Mázandarán—'Abbás-Ḳulí Khán marches by another route to join him—The Prince takes up his quarters at Vásaks near 'Alí-ábád—His negligence—Stormy weather and snow come on.

P. 62. Mullá Ḥuseyn makes a sortie with 300 resolute men before dawn on Ṣafar 15th [A.H. 1265 = January 10th A.D. 1849]—By means of a stratagem he enters Vásaks, surrounds and fires the Prince's quarters, and defeats and disperses the enemy, of whom many are killed, including two princes, Sulṭán Ḥuseyn Mírzá and Dá'úd Mírzá—Prince Mahdí-Ḳulí Mírzá escapes with difficulty—Hájí Muḥammad 'Alí is wounded in the mouth.

P. 63. Courageous stand made by the men of Ashraf against the Bábís—Cowardice of the other troops—Triumphant return of the Bábís to their fortress—The Prince is discovered and harboured by a peasant, and his troops gradually re-assembled—He declines to risk another encounter—Arrival of 'Abbás-Ḳulí Khán with his troops before Sheykh Ṭabarsí—His foolhardiness and negligence—Mullá Ḥuseyn at the head of 400 Bábís makes a sortie before dawn on Rabí'u'l-Avval 10th [A.H. 1265 = February 3rd A.D. 1849].

P. 64. Description of the engagement—Rout of the besiegers—Mullá Ḥuseyn is mortally wounded—The Bábís retire in good order to their stronghold—After their departure and the dawn of day some of the scattered besiegers return, bury their own dead, decapitate the Bábí corpses, and retire.

P. 65. How the news of the defeat is communicated to Prince Mahdí-Ḳulí Mírzá—Death of Mullá Ḥuseyn after re-entering Sheykh Ṭabarsí—His dying injunctions—His burial in the shrine—Thirty other Bábís die of their wounds—The Bábís go out to bury their dead, find them decapitated, and in retaliation exhume and decapitate the Musulmán corpses and fix their heads on posts round the gate of the fortress—How the news of the defeat is received by the Prince—After much hesitation he advances against the Bábís and encamps at Kiyá-Kalá.

P. 66. On reaching Sheykh Ṭabarsí the Prince's courage fails him—He retires to Kásht, and there meets 'Abbás-Ḳulí Khán—Preparations for the siege of Sheykh Ṭabarsí—Arrival of artillery—Discontent and insubordination amongst the besieging troops caused by the wilfulness and incapacity of Mahdí-Ḳulí Mírzá.

P. 67. Sortie of 200 Bábís—They capture one of the towers erected by the besiegers—Cruelty of Mahdí-Ḳulí Mírzá to one of his wounded officers—Renewed anger of the Sháh because the siege has lasted for four months without any decisive advantage having been gained—Threats and reproaches addressed by the Sháh to the besiegers.

P. 68. Suleymán Khán Afshár is sent from Teherán to superintend the siege—Revival of the courage of the besiegers—A breach is effected in the Bábí fortifications by means of a mine sprung under the western tower of the fortress—A vigorous attempt to storm the breach fails, once again through the incapacity of Mahdí-Ḳulí Mírzá—Desertions from the Bábí camp—Fate of Aḳá Rasúl and thirty other deserters.

P. 69. Desertion of Riẓá Khán and some others from the Bábís—They receive promises of pardon from the Prince—They are placed in the custody of Hádí Khán of Núr—The Bábís, having consumed all their provisions, are reduced to eating grass, leaves, boiled leather, and broth made from the bones of dead horses—They make another desperate sortie, and attempt, but fail, to capture the tower erected by the besiegers against the western gate—The Bábís capitulate on receiving a written promise, signed and sealed by the Prince, that their lives shall be spared.

P. 70. Evacuation of Sheykh Ṭabarsí and entry of the surviving Bábís (216 in number) into the royalist camp—They are reassured by the manner in which they are at first received, but on the following day are perfidiously massacred, except Hájí Muḥammad 'Alí and some of the other chiefs, who are reserved to grace the Prince's triumphal entry into Bárfurúsh—The Prince visits the deserted fortress, marvels at the skill displayed in its construction, and carries off the spoils accumulated by the Bábís—Execution of Hájí Muḥammad 'Alí and the other Bábí chiefs by command of the Musulmán clergy—During the whole war in Mázandarán 1500 Bábís and 500 soldiers perished.

* * * * *

P. 83 [last 12 lines]. Troubles at Zanján—Mullá Muḥammad 'Alí Zanjání—His character and previous career—His innovations, and disagreements with the other clergy.

P. 84. He is summoned to Teherán by Muḥammad Sháh and forbidden to return to Zanján—On the death of that king he escapes in disguise and returns home—He is received with acclamation by his admirers—He begins to preach the Bábí doctrines, and soon gains 15,000 adherents—Action is taken against him by the government—Collision between him and Aṣlán-Khán the governor of Zanján.

P. 85. The Bábís assume the offensive—Their organization and preparations—Fighting begins on Rajab 5th [A.H. 1266 = May 17th, A.D. 1850. In the *Násikhu't-Tawáríkh* these events are described under the year A.H. 1265, but this is an error, as proved by the accounts of Watson and Lady Sheil]—Names of some of the killed and wounded, who number about forty in all—Execution of a Bábí prisoner named Sheykhí remarkable for his valour—Attack on Aṣlán Khán's residence by a party of Bábís led by one Mír Ṣáliḥ—Repulse of the Bábís and death of their leader—Names of some of the killed and wounded.

P. 86. Arrival of Ṣadru'd-Dawla on Rajab 20th [June 3rd], and of Seyyid 'Alí Khán of Fírúzkúh, Shahbáz Khán of Marágha, Muḥammad 'Alí Khán Shahsívan, Káẓim Khán Afshár, and Maḥmúd Khán of Khúy with large reinforcements of cavalry and artilllery on Sha'bán 2nd—5th [June 13th—16th]—Capture of a Bábí position held by Mashhadí Pírí on Sha'bán 20th [July 1st]—Impatience of the Government—Muṣṭafá Khán Ḳájár, colonel of the 16th (Shaḳáḳí) regiment, is sent to join the besiegers—Capture of a Bábí position held by Mírzá Faraju'lláh after a desperate struggle on Ramaẓán 15th [July 25th]—Besiegers further reinforced by Náṣiriyya regiment and a corps of picked marksmen, and threatened with severe punishment unless they quickly bring the siege to a close—General attack on the Bábís on Ramaẓán 25th [August 4th].

P. 87. The day goes against the Bábís till Mullá Muḥammad 'Alí creates a diversion by setting fire to the bazaar—On Shawwál 8th [August 17th] the besiegers are further reinforced by Muḥammad Khán *Begler-begí* with 3000 troops, 6 cannons, and 2 mortars—On the same day the Náṣiriyya and Shaḳáḳí regiments are ordered to attack the Bábís—The stratagem whereby Mullá Muḥammad 'Alí throws the Náṣiriyya regiment into confusion—Description of the Bábí defences—The *Begler-begí* tries conciliatory measures, wherein he is seconded by 'Azíz Khán *Ajúdán-báshí* and Mírzá Ḥasan Khán the *Amír-Niẓám's* brother, both of whom happen to pass through Zanján at this time —Conciliation failing, a fresh attack is made.

P. 88. Failure of this attack—Punishment inflicted on certain officers—The *Ṣadru'd-Dawla* is replaced by Farrukh Khán (the son of Yaḥyá Khán of Tabríz and the brother of Suleymán Khán the Bábí), who reaches Zanján on Zi'l-Ḳa'da 4th [September 11th]—Arrival of fresh reinforcements—A way of escape is intentionally left open for the Bábís—The Bábís again turn to account the covetousness of the troops to inflict on them fresh losses—Extraordinary courage of the Bábí women—Letter from the *Amír-Niẓám* to Farrukh Khán—The stratagem whereby the Bábís decoy Farrukh Khán to his destruction.

P. 89. Capture of Farrukh Khán by the Bábís—He and two renegades are tortured to death and their heads cast into the camp of the besiegers—Anger of the King at this news—More artillery is sent against Zanján—Renewed attack on the Bábís—Capture of the Castle of 'Alí-Mardán Khán and other Bábí positions—Twenty Bábís taken prisoners.

P. 90. Execution of these prisoners—Desertion and capture of twenty-five Bábís—Their ultimate fate—Mullá Muḥammad 'Alí is wounded—He survives his wound for one week—His dying instructions—His death and burial—His followers capitulate on receiving promise of pardon—Entry of the royal troops into Zanján—Mullá Muḥammad 'Alí's body is exhumed and dishonoured—Bad faith of the royalist leaders—Plunder of the Bábí quarter—Massacre of the Bábí prisoners on the third day after the surrender.

P. 91 [first 7 lines]. Hájí Káẓim Ḳaltúḳí and Mashhadí Suleymán the cloth-maker are blown from the mouths of mortars—Approval of the Sháh—Some of the Bábí chiefs are brought to Teherán—Mírzá Riẓá, Hájí Muḥammad 'Alí, and Hájí Muḥsin are put to death at the command of the *Amír-Niẓám*, while the rest are cast into prison. * *

[Fourth and third lines from the bottom.] Suleymán

Khán Afshár arrives at Tabríz with the death-warrant of the Báb.

* * * * *

P. 93. Mírzá Taḳi Khán the *Amír-Niẓám* advises Náṣiru'd-Dín Sháh to order the Báb to be put to death—Discussion between the King and the Minister—The Báb's execution is finally decided on—Suleymán Khán Afshár is sent to Tabríz with the Báb's death-warrant and instructions to Ḥamzé Mírzá, the Prince-Governor of Ázarbaiján, as to the method of procedure—The Báb and his amanuensis, Áḳá Seyyid Ḥuseyn of Yezd, are brought from Chihríḳ to Tabríz—Áḳá [here called Mullá] Muḥammad 'Alí of Tabríz is also arrested—His brother, Áḳá 'Abdu'lláh, unsuccessfully attempts to induce him to recant—Ḥamzé Mírzá desires the clergy of Tabríz to dispute with and confute the Báb—They decline.

P. 94. The Báb is brought before Ḥamzé Mírzá, Mírzá Ḥasan, Hájí Mírzá 'Alí, and Suleymán Khán Afshár by night—Ḥamzé Mírzá asks him to recite verses concerning a crystal candlestick—The Báb complies, and these verses are writtten down—Ḥamzé Mírzá requests the Báb to repeat these verses—They are repeated differently—It is decided to kill the Báb with the utmost publicity—He is taken to the houses of three prominent members of the clergy, Hájí Mírzá Báḳir, Mullá Muḥammad Mámaḳání, and Áḳá Seyyid Zanvazí, who ratify the sentence of death—Áḳá Seyyid Ḥuseyn of Yezd recants—The steadfastness of Áḳá Muḥammad 'Alí—The execution takes place on Sha'bán 27th [A.H. 1266, *not* 1265 as stated by Sipihr and Kazem-Beg. See pp. 45 and 186—187]—The firing-party is formed of Christian soldiers—At the first volley Áḳá Muḥammad 'Alí is killed, but the Báb, released from his bonds by the bullets, falls uninjured to the ground—He takes refuge in the rooms of one of the soldiers.

P. 95 [first 9 lines]. Reflections on this strange occurrence—The Báb is dragged forth from his retreat by Ḳúch 'Alí Sulṭán, again bound, and once more fired on by the soldiers—This time he is killed—Indignities offered to his body.

* * * * *

P. 112 [last half]. The insurrection at Níríz—Áḳá Seyyid Yaḥyá of Dáráb—His character, and that of his father Áḳá Seyyid Ja'far-*i-Kashfí*—Seyyid Yaḥyá is converted to the Bábí doctrines—He goes to Teherán to preach the new faith—He goes to Yezd—The Yezd insurrection and its failure—Seyyid Yaḥyá goes to Fasá in Fárs—Bahrám Mírzá having been dismissed from the government of Fárs, and Fírúz Mírzá not having yet arrived to take his place, Mírzá Fazlu'lláh *Naṣíru'l-Mulk* is the supreme authority in the province—The nobles of Fasá request him to put a stop to Seyyid Yaḥyá's propaganda.

P. 113. The *Naṣíru'l-Mulk* writes a letter to Seyyid Yaḥyá—He receives a reassuring reply—Fresh complaints are made—Another message to Seyyid Yaḥyá proves equally ineffectual—Seyyid Yaḥyá goes to Níríz with the force which he has collected—Disaffection of Níríz, and unpopularity of its governor, Zeynu'l-'Ábidín Khán—Seyyid Yaḥyá, with 300 followers, occupies an old castle near Níríz—The *Naṣíru'l-Mulk* sends him a third message—His answer—He makes a night attack on Níríz, sacks the town, and puts Zeynu'l-'Ábidín Khán to flight—Hereupon many recruits join the Bábís, so that their forces amount to more than 2000 men.

P. 114. Fírúz Mírzá the new governor, when distant four stages from Shíráz, receives news of the success of the Níríz insurgents—He sends a messenger to Shíráz instructing Mihr 'Ali Khán Núrí *Shujá'ul-Mulk* and Muṣṭafá-Ḳulí Khán to proceed against Seyyid Yaḥyá with two Ḳáragúzlú regiments—The *Naṣíru'l-Mulk* writes to Zeynu'l-'Ábidin Khán the fugitive governor of Níríz ordering him to collect what forces he can and join the attacking force—The royalist forces combine and proceed to Níríz—Preliminary skirmish—Siege operations commenced—Failure of Muṣṭafá-Ḳulí Khán's attempts to bring about a peaceable settlement—Seyyid Yaḥyá supplies his followers with amulets—Sortie of 300 Bábís—Failure of the sortie after prolonged fighting, during which 150 Bábís and four soldiers are slain—Desertions amongst the Bábís—Second sortie of the Bábís.

P. 115 [first half]. Repulse of Bábí sortie—Valí Khán is sent with reinforcements from Shíráz—Seyyid Yaḥyá is induced to quit his fortress, and, accompanied by one attendant, to return to his house in Níríz—On his way thither he is met by the sons of 'Alí 'Askar Khán who kill him in revenge for their father's death—Seyyid Yaḥyá's two sons and thirty of his followers are brought to Shíráz—The former are spared in consideration of their being seyyids, but the latter are put to death by order of Fírúz Mírzá.

Contents of the Supplement to the *Kájáriyya* volume in so far as they relate to the Bábís.

P. 22. Events of the year A.H. 1268 [A.D. 1852]. Imám-Ḳuli Mírzá is appointed governor of Kirmánsháh—His energy in restoring order to his province—He arrests Mullá 'Alí Aṣghar, a Bábí missionary, and sends him in chains to Teherán—One Teymúr[1] of Ḳal'a-Zanjírí claims to be the vicegerent of the Absent Imám and draws to himself a great number of people—He is seized and put to death by Imám-Ḳulí Mírzá—Account of the attempt on the Sháh's life—Digression on the character and doctrines of Sheykh Aḥmad Aḥsá'í.

P. 23. Hájí Seyyid Káẓim of Resht succeeds Sheykh Aḥmad—Dissensions amongst his followers after his death—Mullá Ḥuseyn—Hájí Muḥammad Karím Khán—How Mullá Ḥuseyn persuades many of the Sheykhís to follow Mírzá 'Alí Muḥammad the Báb—His journey to Khurásán—Mullá Sheykh 'Alí [whom the Bábís entitle *Jenáb-i-'Aẓím*] becomes a Bábí and engages in active propaganda—He goes from Kerbelá to Káshán, where he sees and attempts to

[1] Ṣubḥ-i-Ezel informed me that this Teymúr was not a Bábí but advanced a claim on his own account. After his death, however, a youth calling himself Seyfúr, who *was* a Bábí, appeared, and used to declare that he was Teymúr returned again from the dead.

convert Mírzá Áḳá Khán of Núr, afterwards *Ṣadr-i-A'ẓam* (Prime Minister)—He goes to Teherán, where, under various names and in diverse disguises, he continues his attempts at proselytizing—During the ministry of the *Amír-Niẓám* he meditates a rising to be inaugurated by the slaughter of Mírzá Abú'l Ḳásim the *Imám Jum'a*—This plot is discovered by government spies and reported to the *Amír-Niẓám*—Mírzá 'Abdu'r-Raḥím, the brother of Mullá Muḥammad Taḳí of Herát, one of the disciples of Mullá Sheykh 'Alí, is arrested.

P. 24. Mírzá 'Abdu'r-Raḥím refuses to betray his confederates—Mírzá Ṭáhir, fellow-lodger of the above, is questioned—Hájí Seyyid Muḥammad of Isfahán is beguiled by a forged letter into revealing Mullá Sheykh 'Alí's abode —A servant of Mullá Sheykh 'Alí's is arrested and tortured, but discloses nothing—He is put to death, but Mírzá 'Abdu'r-Raḥím's life is spared—Mullá Sheykh 'Alí escapes and takes refuge in Sháh 'Abdu'l-'Aẓím, whence he presently flies to Ázarbaiján—On the fall of the *Amír-Niẓám*, Mullá Sheykh 'Alí returns to Teherán and begins to organize the conspiracy against the Sháh's life—The house of Hájí Suleymán Khán of Tabríz becomes the meeting-place of the conspirators, and there Mullá Sheykh 'Alí takes up his quarters—Seventy persons are involved in the conspiracy—Nature of the plot—Twelve Bábís volunteer for the attempt, amongst them being Muḥammad Ṣádiḳ [of Zanján], Mírzá 'Abdu'l-Wahháb of Shíráz, Mullá Fatḥ-u'lláh of Ḳum, and Muḥammad Báḳir of Najafábád.

P. 25. The attempt on the Sháh's life is made on Sunday, Shawwál 28th [A.H. 1268 = August 15th, 1852]—Account of the attempt and its failure. [See *infra*, Note T.]

P. 26. Fate of the assassins—Consternation of the ministers—Conjectures as to the originators of the plot—Firmness of the Prime Minister (*Ṣadr-i-A'ẓam*).

P. 27. Messengers despatched to all parts of the kingdom to announce the Sháh's safety—The search for the Bábís begins—Arrest of Hájí Suleymán Khán and twelve of his confederates—On information obtained from some of these prisoners 36 Bábís are captured, amongst whom is Mullá Sheykh 'Alí.

P. 28. The *Ḥájibu'd Dawla* cuts off Mullá Sheykh

'Alí's ear—Examination of the prisoners—Mírzá Ḥuseyn 'Alí Núrí [apparently Behá'u'lláh himself], Mírzá Suleymán-Ḳulí, Mírzá Maḥmúd, Áḳá 'Abdu'lláh, Mírzá Jawád of Khurásán, and Mírzá Ḥuseyn of Ḳum are imprisoned, there not being sufficient evidence to incriminate them in the plot: the other Bábí prisoners are apportioned amongst the different departments and classes each to be slain in such fashion as shall please those to whom he has been assigned—The slaughter takes place on the last day of Ẓi'l-Ḳa'da [A.H. 1268 = September 15th, A.D. 1852]—Account of the executions [see *infra*, Note T].

P. 29. Account of the executions continued, including that of Ḳurratu'l-'Ayn [see *infra*, Notes Q and T]—Public rejoicings.

Whoever carefully examines the arrangement of matter in the *Násikhu't-Tawáríkh* as indicated in the above table of contents will perceive that this arrangement is not strictly chronological, although ostensibly intended to be so. A desire not to interrupt the continuity of the narrative in relating an episode often induces the historian to include under the year in which the episode which he is describing first began, events properly belonging to subsequent years. Thus the first public appearance of the Báb was in the year A.H. 1260, but the narrative is carried on without interruption not only to the time of his return from Mécca to Bushire, which certainly did not occur till A.H. 1261, but to the period of his concealment by the *Mu-'tamadu'd-Dawla* in Isfahán, which belongs to the year A.H. 1262. So likewise the beginning of the insurrection in Mázandarán was in A.H. 1264, while its final suppression did not take place till A.H. 1265; yet the whole insurrection from its earliest beginning to its ultimate conclusion is described under the year A.H. 1264, the only indication of a change of year being afforded by the rotation of the months. Other instances might be adduced, but these are sufficient to prove a fact which it is most important to bear in mind. The erroneous dates given for the siege of Zanján and the Báb's martyrdom (of which events, according to all testimony, the latter took place during the former) cannot, however, be satisfactorily accounted for in this way; and I am forced to suppose that in this case the *Lisánu'l Mulk* has committed a positive error, which, as it has been copied and reproduced by Kazem-Beg and a number of writers who have followed him, it is necessary to expose in the clearest manner possible. This I strove to do in my first paper on the Bábís in the *Journal of the Royal Asiatic Society* for 1889 (pp. 511—513), where I attempted to prove that both of the events in question were to be assigned, *not*, as stated in the *Násikhu't-Tawáríkh* and repeated by those who have unreservedly followed it, to the year A.H. 1265 (A.D. 1849), but to the year A.H. 1266 (A.D. 1850). It is unnecessary for me to repeat in this place the arguments there adduced to support an opinion in which further study of the matter serves but to confirm me; I will only observe that further corroboration of that opinion is afforded not only by the present work (*supra*, pp. 44—45) and the *Rawżatu's-Ṣafá*, but also by Dr A. H. Wright's memoir contributed to the *Z. D. M. G.* in 1851, wherein the Báb's execution is described (p. 385) as having occurred "*last year*," and by Binning (*Journal of Two Years' Travel in Persia &c.*, London, 1857, vol. i, p. 407), who, in a passage written in 1850 or early in 1851, remarks, after describing the Báb's execution, that "a large number of them [i.e. the Bábís] are now up in arms in Zenjân."

Complete impartiality is a quality we could not reasonably expect to find in the court historian of a despot whose ears must hear what is pleasant rather than what is true, and whose actions must be not only justified but extolled as models of wisdom and virtue. When we consider that, apart from this, the *Lisánu'l-Mulk*, as a presumably orthodox Shi'ite Muhammadan, was bound to disparage and traduce in every way possible those whose object was nothing less than the complete overthrow of Islám and the abrogation of its ordinances, we cannot but admire the candour which he displays; for if, on the one hand, he brings against the Bábís many unfounded and absurd accusations, on the other hand he pourtrays with a fidelity scarcely surpassed by the witty and sarcastic Comte de Gobineau the cowardice, incapacity, and treachery of Mahdí-Ḳulí Mírzá, the courage of Mullá Ḥuseyn of Bushraweyh, the constancy of Áḳá Muḥammad ʻAlí of Tabríz, and the heroism of the Bábí women of Zanján.

Each page of the *Násikhu't-Tawáríkh* consists of 29 lines containing on an average 21 words each, so that a page is equivalent to about 600 words. That portion of the narrative which refers to the Bábís occupies in all not less than 46 pages, and cannot contain fewer than 27,000 words.

2. The *Rawżatu'ṣ-Ṣafá*.

The Teherán lithographed edition of this work, whereof the publication was completed in Rabíʻu'l-Avval A.H. 1274 (Oct.—Nov., A.D. 1857), consists of ten volumes bound in two. Of these ten volumes the first six composed by Mírkhwánd (d. A.D. 1498) and the seventh composed by his grandson Khwándamír (d. A.D. 1534) constitute the whole of what is generally understood by European writers when they speak of the *Rawżatu'ṣ-Ṣafá*. The three last (eighth, ninth, and tenth) volumes, which supplement the older work and bring the narrative down to our own days, were written by that most talented and learned scholar Riżá-Ḳulí Khán '*Lelé-Báshí*,' of whose life and works a most valuable account from the pen of Mr Sidney Churchill will be found in vol. xviii (New Series) of the *Journal of the Royal Asiatic Society*, pp. 196—206. All that relates to the Bábís is contained in the last (tenth) volume, with which alone, therefore, we are here concerned. The numeration of the pages in this volume is supplied by my hand, the pages in the original being unnumbered. As the narrative of the Bábí movement here given agrees very closely for the most part with that contained in the *Násikhu't-Tawáríkh*, I shall in the summary of its contents about to be given indicate very briefly that portion of it dealt with in each page, except in cases where some fact is added or differently stated.

Contents of vol. x of the *Rawżatu'ṣ-Ṣafá* in so far as they relate to the Bábís.

P. 69 [last 17 lines]. From the first appearance of the

Báb to the stratagem whereby Ḥuseyn Khán *Ajúdán-Báshí* induces him to expose his ideas without reserve.

P. 70 [first 18 lines]. From the Báb's disputation with the clergy of Shíráz to the death of Minúchihr Khán in Rabí'u'l-Avval A.H. 1263 and the Báb's removal to Chihríḳ. Reflections on the causes which led to the rapid spread of his doctrines. He is accused of holding and teaching the doctrine of metempsychosis.

* * * * *

P. 118 [last 26 lines]. From the beginning of Mullá Ḥuseyn's propaganda to his escape from Mash-had and advance on Mázandarán with 300 or 400 followers. It is stated that his original intention was to proceed to Chihríḳ and liberate the Báb. The last three lines of this page begin the account of the Báb's first examination (A.H. 1263 = A.D. 1847) by the clergy of Tabríz presided over by the present Sháh, at that time Crown-Prince. The account of the proceedings of this assembly is professedly copied "without favour or enmity" from the report written by Ḥájí Mullá Maḥmúd the *Niẓámu'l-'Ulamá*. Concerning this conference see *supra*, pp. 18—21, and *infra*, Note M.

P. 119. } P. 120. } Account of the conference continued.

P. 121. Conclusion of the conference, and punishment of the Báb, who is afterwards sent back to Chihríḳ—Exasperation of the Bábís on hearing what indignities have been offered to their master—Mullá Muḥammad 'Alí of Bárfurúsh—Ḳurratu'l-'Ayn—The meeting at Badasht—The attack on the Bábís at Hazár-Jaríb—The death of Muḥammad Sháh (Shawwál, A.H. 1264 = August 31st—September 28th, A.D. 1848[1])—Beginning of the Mázandarán insurrection.

P. 122. Recapitulation of Mullá Ḥuseyn's earlier adventures and behaviour—Narrative of events from the collision between Mullá Ḥuseyn's 700 or 800 white-robed, white-turbaned followers and the Musulmáns of Bárfurúsh to the occupation of Sheykh Ṭabarsí by the former—Description of the Bábí fortress.

[1] According to Watson (*History of Persia*, p. 354), the death of Muḥammad Sháh took place on September 4th, 1848.

P. 123. Continuation of narrative of the Mázandarán insurrection to the surprise and discomfiture of Mahdí-Ḳulí Mírzá by the Bábís at Vásaks.

P. 124. Continuation of narrative to the night attack of the Bábís led by Mullá Ḥuseyn on ʻAbbás-Ḳulí Khán's army. The date of this event is here stated as Rabíʻu'l-Avval 10th A.H. 1266 (January 24th, A.D. 1850), which is a mistake. The correct date, Rabíʻu'l-Avval (10th) A.H. 1265 (February 3rd, A.D. 1849) is given in the *Násikhu't-Tawáríkh.*

P. 125. From the death of Mullá Ḥuseyn to the second advance of Mahdí-Ḳulí Mírzá against Sheykh Ṭabarsí.

P. 126. Continuation of the narrative to the arrival of Jaʻfar-Ḳulí Khán and Ṭahmásp Ḳulí Khán with reinforcements for the besiegers.

P. 127. Continuation of the narrative to the Bábí sortie, which results directly in the death of Ṭahmásp-Ḳulí Khán, and indirectly in that of his uncle Jaʻfar-Ḳulí Khán through the wanton and inconsiderate cruelty of Mahdí-Ḳulí Mírzá.

P. 128. Conclusion of the narrative of the Mázandarán insurrection. Beginning of the narrative of the Zanján insurrection.

P. 129. Continuation of the narrative to Seyyid ʻAlí Khán's unsuccessful attempt at pacification.

P. 130. Continuation of the narrative to Farrukh Khán's capture and terrible fate.

P. 131. Continuation of the narrative to Ḥasan Khán's unsuccessful attempt at pacification. (According to the *Násikhu't-Tawáríkh* this event preceded the last, and this version is on the face of it more probable.)

P. 132. Conclusion of the narrative of the Zanján insurrection—Brief account of the execution of the Báb at Tabríz. (The date of this event is here correctly stated as A.H. 1266. The account itself is most meagre, amounting in substance merely to this: that the Báb was brought from Chihríḳ to Tabríz, condemned to death by the clergy of that city, and suspended and shot, together with *two* of his disciples, by the Christian regiment, his body being afterwards cast outside the city as food for wolves and dogs.

No mention is made of his miraculous escape from the first volley fired by the soldiers.)—Beginning of the narrative of the Níríz insurrection.

P. 133. Conclusion of the narrative of the Níríz insurrection. (According to this account, Aḳá Seyyid Yaḥyá of Dáráb the insurgent leader was brought to Shíráz and there put to death. Allusion is also made to the second Bábí rising at Níríz and the assassination of the governor Zeynu'l-'Ábidín Khán, which events occurred about two years later. See Note H, *infra.*)

* * * * *

P. 167 [last 21 lines]. The attempt on the Sháh's life (see Note T, *infra*). Preliminary recapitulation of similar attempts on the lives of kings and ministers made by members of heretical sects—Eulogies of Náṣiru'd-Dín Sháh.

P. 168. After the death of the Báb a new leader (whom the author of this history apparently believes to have been Mullá Sheykh 'Alí '*Jenáb-i-'Aẓím*') is chosen by his followers—The Bábí conspiracy—The assassination is planned by twelve Bábís, who arrange that the attempt shall take place on the morning of Sunday the 28th of Shawwál A.H. 1268 (August 15th, A.D. 1852) as the Sháh is riding out on a hunting expedition from his summer residence at Niyávarán—Description of the Royal Cavalcade and the approach of the conspirators in the guise of suppliants.

P. 169. Of the twelve assassins, six fail to arrive in time, while three lag behind—The three who are ready approach the Sháh as petitioners, surround him, and fire two shots at him—The Sháh's retainers come up and kill one of the conspirators—Another shot is fired wounding the Sháh in the shoulder—The two surviving conspirators are seized and retained for examination—The Sháh wishes to continue his expedition, but is dissuaded by the Prime Minister—Panic in Teherán—The Sháh holds a public reception on the following day.

P. 170. Messengers are despatched in all directions to announce the Sháh's safety—Certain malicious persons strive unsuccessfully to cast suspicion on the Prime Minister and Muḥammad Ḥasan Khán of Erivan—It is discovered that 70 Bábís are in the habit of resorting to the house of Hájí Suleymán Khán, on which accordingly a raid is made, resulting in the capture of Suleymán Khán and twelve others—Mullá Sheykh 'Alí and thirty-six other Bábís are also arrested—Account of the execution of these —The Sháh returns to Teherán from Niyávarán amidst general rejoicings on Friday, Ẓi'l-Ḳa'da 17th, A.H. 1268 (September 2nd, A.D. 1852).

Riẓá-Ḳulí Khán's narrative substantially agrees with that of the *Lisánu'l-Mulk*, but is on the whole less full, more bombastic, and more vituperative, execrations and curses on the Bábís severally and generally being freely introduced throughout. Some new dates are added, and some, such as that of the Zanján troubles, which are erroneously stated in the *Násikhu't-Tawáríkh*, are here correctly given; but, on the other hand, some fresh chronological errors, notably in the case of Mullá Ḥuseyn's last sortie and death, are introduced. The account given of the Báb's death is extremely meagre; and in other parts of the narrative we miss that abundance of detail and fulness of description which render the *Násikhu't-Tawáríkh* so readable and so graphic.

Each page of the *Rawzatu'ṣ-Ṣafá* contains 33 lines, and each line an average of 26 words, making about 858 words to the page. The number of pages devoted to the Bábís is in all twenty and a half, so that the whole narrative above summarized contains not fewer than 17,500 words, and is about two-thirds of the length of the account given in the *Násikhu't-Tawáríkh*.

3. The *Táríkh-i-Jadíd*.

Of this work, which exists only in manuscript, two copies only, so far as I know, have reached Europe[1]. One,

[1] Quite recently, as I have learned from Baron Rosen, another MS. of this work, obtained by M. Tumanski at Ishḳábád, has been added to the library of the Institut des Langues Orientales of St Petersburg.

obtained by Mr Sidney Churchill, is in the library of the British Museum, and is numbered Or. 2942. The other is in my own possession, and is briefly described at p. 496 of my first paper on the Bábís in the *J. R. A. S.* for 1889, and at pp. 1002—1003 of my second paper in the same volume. Of the manner in which I first became acquainted with this work, of the means whereby I obtained the MS. now in my possession, of my intention of publishing it, and of the causes which led me to lay aside (I trust but for a season) the text and translation on which I was engaged in favour of the present work, I have already spoken in the Introduction. As the *Táríkh-i-Jadíd* is not at present generally available to scholars, I shall confine myself to giving a brief statement of its contents based on my own MS. Before doing so, however, a few words must be said concerning the British Museum codex, which is superior alike in accuracy, neatness, and calligraphy to my own.

In the MS. catalogue of recent acquisitions the MS. in question is described thus:—

"Or. 2942. Táríkh-i-Jadid. A history of the Bábís. A.H. 1298 (1881). Persian."

On its cover it bears the following inscription:—

BRIT. MUS. OR. 2942	TARIKH JADID PERSIAN

Inside the cover is written:—

هذا التاريخ جديد (*sic*)

The blank leaf at the beginning bears the name of the work (تاريخ جديد) both in Arabic and English characters, the date July 1882, and Mr Sidney Churchill's signature, substituted for that of Mr Henry Churchill through which a pen has been drawn.

At the end of the text is the following colophon:—

فی شهر رجب المرجب سـ١٢٩٨ـه

(Rajab A.H. 1298 = May 30th—June 28th A.D. 1881).

A final note states that the MS. was bought of Mr S. Churchill on October 10th, 1885. It consists of 177 fol. (354 pp.). Quotations, headings, and the initial words of sentences are sometimes written in red. The paper is of a bluish colour. The text, so far as I have collated it, offers a good many variants from, and some additions to, my MS., and its readings are generally preferable.

My MS. consists of 374 pp., each of which contains 19 lines numbering on an average 10 words apiece. The whole history may be estimated to contain over 70,000 words.

As regards the authorship of the work, it is concealed for obvious reasons; and indeed the author goes out of his way to describe himself as a traveller who, having visited all parts of Europe and India, undertook a journey to Persia for scientific purposes and especially geographical research. He expresses thankfulness to God that he does not belong to the Persian nation, whose faults he exposes unsparingly. He pourtrays himself as a non-Muhammadan open to conviction on matters of religion and associating freely with all sects. And at the conclusion of his work he apologizes for his lack of literary style, advances as an excuse the statement that Persian is not his native tongue, and alludes to a "treatise written in his own language in French writing" wherein the matter in hand is more eloquently set forth. Now that any European should have been capable or desirous of composing such a work is on the face of it extremely improbable, and there can be little doubt that the author advanced the statements above alluded to merely as a blind. Of the Bábís whom I have questioned on the subject some attribute the authorship of the work to a certain well-known and widely-travelled resident in the Persian capital, whom, as he is still living, I do not feel myself justified in indicating more particularly; others to his *mírzá* or secretary, now dead. It appears not improbable that it was the joint product of these two. Whoever the author or authors may have been, the information set forth is so detailed and so minute that it must have been derived for the most part from persons who had conversed with actual eye-witnesses of the events described, if not from eye-witnesses themselves. The author, whether he had really embraced the Bábí faith or not, was, on his showing, a warm admirer of the Báb and his apostles and disciples, and was during the composition of his work in continual communication with certain prominent members of the sect. Yet the work when completed—perhaps because of the violence wherewith it denounces the Musulmán clergy and reproaches the Persian nation, perhaps because of the slight mention which it makes of Behá'u'lláh (of Ṣubḥ-i-Ezel it makes no mention at all) and the exaggerated veneration paid to the Báb—did not meet with the approval of the Bábí chiefs at Acre, and as early as the spring of 1888 I learned in Shíráz that instructions had been issued for the compilation of a new history more in accordance with the views entertained by those chiefs. Of these instructions the history now offered to the public is the outcome.

Summary of the contents of the
Táríkh-i-Jadíd.

Pp. 1—38[1]. Introduction.

,, 39—40. Hájí Seyyid Káẓim of Resht foretells the approaching 'manifestation' and dies.

Pp. 41—47. Conversion of Mullá Ḥuseyn of Bushraweyh.

Pp. 48—50. Conversions of Hájí Muḥammad 'Alí of Bárfurúsh ('*Jenáb-i-Ḳuddús*'), Mullá Muḥammad Ṣádiḳ of Khurásán ('*Muḳaddas*'), and others.

Pp. 51—55. From Mullá Ḥuseyn's journey to Khurásán to his entry into Bárfurúsh with Hájí Muḥammad 'Alí and their combined followers.

Pp. 56—114. From the first collision between the Bábís and the Musulmáns in Bárfurúsh to the fall of the Castle of Sheykh Ṭabarsí.

Pp. 115—132. Biographies of certain eminent Bábís who suffered martyrdom in Mázandarán, with some reflections on the heroism displayed by the besieged.

Pp. 133—155. The struggle at Níríz, and reflections thereon. (See Note H, *infra.*)

[1] The pagination refers to my own MS., not to the British Museum Codex.

Pp. 156—163. The siege of Zanján.

Pp. 164—166. Reflections thereon.

„ 167—176. Account of a disputation between a learned Bábí and an assembly of Musulmán divines.

Pp. 177—201. The decadence of the Persian empire and the deterioration of its people traced to the complete ascendency obtained by the clergy, whose ignorance, wickedness, and arrogance are unsparingly exposed.

Pp. 202—222. Personal history of the Báb from the beginning of his mission until his exile to Mákú.

Pp. 223—236. Sufficiency of the testimony given by a host of martyrs of every class to the truth of Bábíism. Objections answered.

Pp. 237—240. Personal history of the Báb continued until his removal from Mákú to Chihrík.

Pp. 241—243. History of the 'Indian believer' (مؤمن هندی)

Pp. 244—246. History of Seyyid Basír the Indian.

„ 247—249. Eulogy on the devotion and self-sacrifice of the Bábís.

Pp. 250—261. History of the 'Seven Martyrs.' (See Note B, *infra.*)

Pp. 262—264. Reflections thereon.

„ 265—277. History of Kurratu'l-'Ayn. (See Note Q, *infra.*)

Pp. 278—280. First examination of the Báb at Tabríz. (See Note M, *infra.*)

Pp. 281—286. Reflections on the unfairness of the proceedings.

Pp. 287—300. Personal history of the Báb until his martyrdom.

Pp. 301—305. Review of former prophetic dispensations and comparison of these with the present 'manifestation.'

Pp. 306—322. Discussion of the kind of proof necessary to establish the truth of a new revelation, and reflections on the hard-heartedness, obstinacy, and stiff-neckedness of the Musulmáns in general and their clergy in particular, together with further proofs of their want of fairness illustrated by additional details concerning the conference at Isfahán. (See Note J, *infra.*)

Pp. 323—331. The irrational beliefs, absurd traditions, and gross ignorance of the generality of Shí'ite divines.

Pp. 332—369. Account of a discussion which took place in the author's presence between a Bábí and a *mujtahid*, and discomfiture of the latter.

Pp. 370—372. Refutation of certain charges falsely alleged against the Bábís.

Pp. 373—374. Conclusion.

4. *The Ḳiṣaṣu'l-'Ulamá.*

This is a work of 350 pages containing biographical notices of 153 eminent Shí'ite divines, amongst whom the author, Mírzá Muḥammad ibn Suleymán-i-Tanakábuní, includes himself. It was published for the second time at Teherán in A.H. 1304 (A.D. 1886—7), together with two treatises composed by Seyyid Murtaẓá '*'Ilmu'l-Hudá*,' which are included in the same volume. The second biography in this volume, extending from p. 12 to p. 43, is devoted to Hájí Mullá Muḥammad Taḳí ibn Muḥammad al-Burghání al-Kazvíní, called by the Shí'ites *Shahíd-i-Thálith* ('the Third Martyr'), and treats incidentally at some length of the Bábís, with whom the subject of the memoir in question came into such fatal collision. Of the book under consideration we are here concerned with this section alone, and indeed only with a part of that.

Hájí Mullá Muḥammad Taḳí was the eldest of three brothers, of whom the second, Hájí Mullá Muḥammad Ṣáliḥ, was also a divine and jurisconsult, while the third, Hájí Mullá 'Alí, was first a disciple of Sheykh Aḥmad Aḥsá'í and afterwards a partisan of the Báb. Now Hájí Mullá Muḥammad Taḳí detested Sheykh Aḥmad and his doctrines, and was indeed the first amongst the Shí'ite clergy to denounce him as a dangerous heretic; but if his detestation of the Sheykhís was great, much bitterer and more violent was his hatred of the Bábís. The fact that not only his youngest brother Hájí Mullá 'Alí, but also his niece and daughter-in-law Zarrín-Táj (or, to give her the title whereby she has become for ever famous, Ḳurratu'l-

'Ayn), had embraced the doctrines which he so abhorred, must have greatly conduced to an intensification of this hatred, which rose to such a pitch that, as we learn from the present work, he was during the last year of his life chiefly engaged in violent public denunciation of the Báb and his religion. This cost him his life; for at length certain Bábís, stung by his words into uncontrollable anger, fell upon him early one morning as he was praying in the mosque, and with knives and daggers inflicted on him eight wounds, from the effects of which he expired two days later. He was buried at Ḳazvín in the precincts of Sháhzádé Ḥuseyn.

Contents of the *Ḳiṣaṣu'l-'Ulamá* in so far as they relate to the Bábís.

P. 20. Hájí Mullá Muḥammad Taḳí first denounces Sheykh Aḥmad Aḥsá'í as a heretic—Account of Sheykh Aḥmad.

Pp. 21—30. Account of Sheykh Aḥmad and Hájí Seyyid Káẓim—Exposition and refutation of their doctrines. (See Note E, *infra*, and B. ii, pp. 890—892.)

Pp. 30—35. Account of Hájí Muḥammad Karím Khán of Kírmán—Further remarks on the Sheykhí doctrines.

P. 36. Account of the assassination of Hájí Mullá Muḥammad Taḳí by certain Bábís in A.H. 1264 (A.D. 1848).

P. 37. Account of Mírzá 'Alí Muḥammad the Báb—His diligent attendance at Hájí Seyyid Káẓim's lectures. (See B. ii, p. 894.)

P. 38. How the attention of the author was first drawn to the Báb (see B. ii, pp. 894, 895)—The Báb returns to Bushire and begins to practise austerities—He composes a 'Ḳur'án'—The heresy of his doctrines exposed.

P. 39. Imprisonment of the Báb at Chihríḳ—His first examination before the clergy of Tabríz. (See Note M, *infra*.)

Pp. 40, 41. Account of the Báb's examination continued and concluded—He is bastinadoed—Further particulars concerning Hájí Muḥammad Karím Khán.

Pp. 42, 43. Disparagement of Hájí Muḥammad Karím Khán, and proofs of his lack of scholarship.

II. OTHER WRITINGS IN ORIENTAL LANGUAGES WHEREIN INCIDENTAL REFERENCE TO THE BÁBÍS IS MADE.

Besides the Persian works above noticed which bear directly on the history of the Bábí movement, we may observe that the Persian poet Ḳá'ání has two *ḳaṣídas* written to celebrate the Sháh's escape from the attempt on his life[1]. These, however, as one would naturally expect, throw very little new light on the facts of the case. It is said that Ḳá'ání was at first disposed to regard the Báb with favour, and that the *ḳaṣída* beginning:—

مقتدای انس و جان آمد پدید

پیشوای این و آن آمد پدید

"The ensample of men and *jinn* hath appeared,
The leader of these and those hath appeared,"

was written in his honour. If this be so, it is by no means the only instance of inconstancy wherewith this talented but fickle poet can be taxed.

In *Arabic* there is an article on Bábíism in the Encyclopaedia (دائرة المعارف) of Buṭrusu'l-Bustání (Beyrout, 1881) which contributes some important facts not previously published, but also contains one or two grave errors. It comprises about 1600 words, and is based on information communicated by Seyyid Jemálu'd-Dín al-Afghán. Of a portion of this I published a translation in my second paper on the Bábís (*J. R. A. S.* for 1889, pp. 942—943).

In *Turkish* a short article of about 240 words in vol. ii of Sámí Bey's *Dictionnaire Universel d'Histoire et de Géographie* (قاموس الاعلام, Constantinople, A.H. 1307) contains no new facts, but several new errors.

[1] See *infra*, Note T.

III. European Accounts.

Numerous accounts of the Báb and his religion have been published in Europe, and these, so far as they are known to me, I shall now enumerate in the order of their publication, noting as far as possible whence each work derives the information which it embodies. A mere casual remark of some traveller often sheds a fresh ray of light on the matter, or helps to decide some doubtful date, and therefore I shall include in my list several works wherein only a few paragraphs are devoted to the Bábís; while on the other hand I do not consider it necessary to refer to all of the numerous articles on the subject which have appeared in various encyclopædias and magazines, since these for the most part merely repeat more or less fully and eloquently the facts recorded by other writers.

[A.D. 1851.] *Báb und seine Secte in Persien*, by A. H. Wright of the American Mission at Urúmiyya, Persia, contributed by J. Perkins, also of the aforesaid Mission, to the German Oriental Society, and published in Vol. v of the *Z. D. M. G.* (Leipzig, 1851, pp. 384—385). From a note appended by the Editor we learn that the MS. of this article, dated March 31, 1851, was forwarded with a letter from Mr Perkins dated March 29, and that another copy of the same article was sent to the American Oriental Society. From the Journal of the last-named society it appears that this paper was read at one of their meetings, but, so far as I can discover, it was not published, so that we have it only in its German dress. This document is of capital importance, and I have more than once had occasion to refer to it in my notes.

[A.D. 1856.] *Glimpses of Life and Manners in Persia*, by Lady Sheil (London, 1856). The authoress of this work also was resident in Persia during the Bábí troubles, and much valuable information is supplied by her. That this information was derived for the most part, if not entirely, from bitter enemies of the new faith, or in other words from persons attached to the Persian Court, is sufficiently evident. Some of the statements advanced seem to be traceable to one or other of the Court historians whose works have been already noticed. Others—especially one to the effect that the Báb, while resident at Baghdad or Kerbelá, was arrested by the Turkish authorities, and only saved from execution at their hands by the intervention of the Persian consul (p. 177)—stand alone, and are unsupported by other testimony. What relates to the Bábís in this work is as follows:

P. 176. Origin of the sect.

P. 177. Personal history of the Báb until his death.

P. 178. Confessions of ex-Bábís.

P. 179. Bábí doctrines exposed.

P. 180. Bábís compared to Assassins and Mazdakites —Mázandarán and Yezd insurrections—Execution of the 'Seven Martyrs.'

P. 181. Rising at Zanján—Probability that the Bábí faith is spreading.

* * *

Pp. 273—282. Accounts of the attempt on the Sháh's life and of the Bábí executions which followed it, the latter translated from the 'Teheran Gazette' in which it appeared.

[A.D. 1857.] *Journal of Two Years' Travel in Persia, Ceylon, etc.*, by Robert B. M. Binning, Esq., of the Madras Civil Service (London, 1857, 2 vols.). Some few pages of the twentieth chapter of this work (vol. i, pp. 403—408) are devoted to the Bábís. Of all accounts which I have read, not excluding those given by the Musulmán historians, this is the most hostile, the most unfair—I had almost said the most libellous. The writer, not content with likening the Bábís to Mormons and Sadducees and describing their Founder as a kind of oriental Joe Smith, casts aspersions on the Báb's honesty, and almost accuses him of theft in so many words. This should not, perhaps, cause us much surprise in one who considers that the Gospel of Christ would be best commended to the people of Persia by the annexation of their country by some "Christian State," and who thinks that King Núshírván acted "very properly" in ordering the massacre of Mazdak and his adherents. In point of accuracy, too, this account leaves much to be desired. Thus the author, writing in 1850—1851, describes the Níríz insurrection and the death of Seyyid Yaḥyá as having occurred "about five years ago," and states that the Báb himself travelled into Mázandarán, evidently confusing him with Muḥammad 'Alí of Bárfurúsh. Yet, open to criticism as it is, Mr Binning's narrative has its value, and, as I have shown above (p. 187), helps to determine some doubtful points of chronology. Mr Binning appears to have left Persia by way of Bushire on February 7, 1852, having learned, almost at the moment of his departure, the tragic fate of Mírzá Taḳí Khán *Amír-Niẓám*, which befel in January of that year.

[A.D. 1864, 65.] In the *Bulletin de l'Académie Impériale de St Pétersbourg*, dated December 22, 1864 (vol. viii, pp. 247—248), is a most valuable article by Dorn on certain Bábí MSS. belonging to the St Petersburg collection. One of these—described as "the Koran of the Bábís"—derives special value from the fact that it was written by the Báb's own secretary, and by him placed in European hands. A portion of this text given by Dorn as a specimen was pronounced by Ṣubḥ-i-Ezel (to whom I submitted it) an extract from the *Book of Names* (كتاب الاسماء). The other MS. described is a history of the Mázandarán insurrection composed in the Mázandaráni dialect, and was obtained by Dorn during his sojourn in that province in 1860. From the abstract given of its contents it would appear to be of the highest interest, even though it be not in all respects worthy of credence. A short postscript referring to the authenticity of these two MSS. is added in the *Bulletin* for February 8, 1865. Concerning the occurrences in Mázandarán, Dorn also refers to a previous article of his at p. 353 of vol. iv of the *Bulletin* (*Mélanges Asiatiques*, vol. iv, p. 442), but this I have not seen.

[A.D. 1865.] *Les Religions et les Philosophies dans l'Asie Centrale*, by M. le Comte de Gobineau (Paris, 1865 and 1866). This most brilliant, most graphic, and most charming work is too well known to need any detailed description.

Though largely based on the *Lisánu'l-Mulk's* account of the Bábí movement, it embodies also many statements derived from Bábí sources; and not only are the facts thus obtained sifted with rare judgment and arranged with consummate skill, but the characters and scenes of this stirring drama are depicted in a manner so fresh, so vivid, and so lifelike that the work in question must ever remain a classic unsurpassed and indeed unapproached in the subject whereof it treats. The account of the Bábí books and doctrines (occupying 50 pages) is of the utmost value, being based on Bábí MSS. (now in the Bibliothèque Nationale at Paris) obtained by the author; and the translation of the *Book of Precepts* (كتاب احكام), which forms an Appendix of 82 pages, is still the only complete translation into any European language of a Bábí sacred book. Of the 543 pages composing this volume, 299 are devoted to the Bábís.

[A.D. 1865.] *Persien. Das Land und seine Bewohner*, by Dr Jakob Eduard Polak, formerly Physician to the Sháh of Persia and Professor at the Medical College of Teherán (Leipzig, 1865, 2 vols.). This work, embodying as it does researches into every phase of Persian life made by one whose position gave him rare opportunities of observing facts which his scientific training enabled him to describe with precision and accuracy, is also of the highest value. What relates to the Bábís occupies only four pages (pp. 350—353) of the first volume. Of these four pages the contents are briefly as follows:—

P. 350. The Báb and his teaching—Its rapid spread, especially amongst Seyyids, men of learning, and women of the most cultured class—Ḳurratu'l-'Ayn—Alleged use of narcotics such as *ḥashísh* by the Bábís—Determination of the *Amír-Niẓám* to put the Báb to death.

P. 351. Execution of the Báb—Insurrections in Mázandarán and Zanján. [Both of these risings are here described as having taken place *subsequently* to the Báb's death, whereas in fact the former had terminated and the latter was in progress when this event occurred.]—Attempt on the Sháh's life in 1852.

P. 352. Attempt on the Sháh's life—Persons suspected —"Macchiavellian means" adopted for the extirpation of the Bábís—Hájí 'Alí Khán the *Farrásh-Báshí*—His cruel disposition—Partition of the Bábí prisoners.

P. 353. Horrible cruelties perpetrated on the Bábís —Their extraordinary fortitude—The tortures inflicted on the beautiful Ḳurratu'l-'Ayn, and the "superhuman courage" wherewith she endured her lingering death. [Of this execution Dr Polak was himself a witness.]—Persecutions in the provinces—Activity of the Bábís continued, though concealed.

[A.D. 1865.] *Journey from London to Persepolis*, by John Ussher, F.R.G.S. (London, 1865). This work contains (pp. 627—629) some mention of the Bábís, and depicts in vivid colours the reign of terror which succeeded the attempt on the Sháh's life. A portion of this description is quoted in a footnote on p. 120, *supra*.

[A.D. 1866.] *Bab et les Babis*, an article—or rather a series of five articles—communicated to the *Journal Asiatique* for 1866 by Mirza Kazem-Beg. The *Journal Asiatique* for each year being divided into two volumes in the second of which the pagination is recommenced, I have, for the sake of brevity, denoted all that portion of Mirza Kazem-Beg's article which occurs in vol. vii (6th series) by the abbreviation 'Kazem-Beg i,' and that which occurs in vol. viii by 'Kazem-Beg ii,' whenever I have had occasion to refer to them. The whole article amounts to 251 pages distributed in the two volumes as follows:—

Vol. vii (sixième série), pp. 329—384. Preface, and biography of the Báb in 16 sections.

Pp. 457—522. The Sheykhí doctrines. History of the Bábís, until the final suppression of the Mázandarán insurrection.

Vol. viii (sixième série), pp. 196—252. History of the Bábís concluded. (Insurrections of Zanján and Níríz, attempt on the Sháh, persecution of A.D. 1852.)

Pp. 357—400. The doctrine of the Bábís, and its antecedents.

Pp. 473—507. Two letters from a Bábí Seyyid—

Changes in the original doctrine of the Báb wrought by his followers—Translations from a Bábí work of a devotional character. [This work, as I have attempted to show on pp. 897—899 of my second paper on the Bábís in the *J. R. A. S.*, is none other than the *Ziyárat-náma*—the so-called "Récit du Pèlerinage"—composed by the Báb.]—Conclusion.

The sources from which Mirza Kazem-Beg drew his information are, as stated by himself in a note on p. 332 (vol. vii), the following:—

(α) The *Násikhu't-Tawáríkh.*

(β) The MS. History in the Mázandarání dialect described by Dorn (see p. 202, *supra*). Its author calls himself *Sheykhu'l-'Ajam.* Kazem-Beg describes the work in question as "full of inexactitudes," "of no historic value," and "curious only because composed in the dialect of Mázandarán."

(γ) A memoir on the Bábís by M. Sévruguin, who resided for twenty years in Persia.

(δ) Another memoir by M. Mochenin, who was in Persia at the time of the Bábí troubles, and who (vol. vii, p. 371) was so fortunate as to be at Chihríḳ in June 1850, and even, as it would appear, to see the Báb addressing the multitudes who flocked thither.

Some of Kazem-Beg's dates and facts I have already had occasion to criticize (though in almost all such cases it is the *Násikhu't-Tawáríkh* which is ultimately responsible); neither can I concur in several of the views which he advances (especially his estimate of the characters of Áḳá Seyyid Ḥuseyn of Yezd and Áḳá Seyyid Yaḥyá of Dáráb and his theory of the passive part taken by the Báb in the formation of the new doctrines); but, whatever new light further research may throw on the subject treated of by Mirza Kazem-Beg, there is no doubt that his work will always remain one of the chief authorities thereon.

[A.D. 1866.] *History of Persia from the beginning of the Nineteenth Century to the Year* 1858, by Robert Grant Watson, formerly attached to Her Majesty's Legation at the Court of Persia (London, 1866). This work is also of the utmost value, since the author, from the position which he occupied, had at his disposal the best means for arriving at the truth of matters of historical fact (especially of chronology), and was, moreover, by no means disposed unreservedly to follow the Musulmán historians, of whose unreliability he was well aware. What refers to the Bábís in this work is as follows :—

Pp. 347—352. Origin of the movement—Early life of the Báb—The treatment experienced by him at the hands of Ḥuseyn Khán—Edicts against the Bábís.

* * *

Pp. 360—362. Rising at Yezd (not described in this passage as Bábí).

P. 385. Yezd rising described as a Bábí movement.

P. 386. Account of the 'Seven Martyrs.'

P. 387. Siege of Zanján.

Pp. 388—392. Execution of the Báb—Fall of Zanján.

* * *

Pp. 407—410. Attempt on Sháh's life—Executions of Bábís.

[A.D. 1867.] *Meine Wanderungen und Erlebnisse in Persien*, by Hermann Vámbéry (Pest, 1867). This well-known traveller, *à propos* of a conversation which he had during his passage through Mázandarán with some of the inhabitants of 'Alí-ábád, in whose minds the recollection of the siege of Sheykh Ṭabarsí was still fresh, gives a dissertation on the Bábís which extends from p. 286 to p. 303 of this work. This account seems to be based almost entirely on what be was able to learn from the Persians, though Gobineau's work is occasionally quoted. The details here given concerning Suleymán Khán's martyrdom (which differ somewhat from those embodied in other traditions) will be referred to in Note T, *infra*.

[A.D. 1868.] *Geschichte der herrschenden Ideen des Islams*, by Baron Alfred von Kremer (Leipzig, 1868). Twenty pages of this work (pp. 202—222) are devoted to *Báb und seine Lehre*, which article constitutes sect. vii of Book ii. One of the Bábí MSS. in the British Museum (Or. 3114) was, as appears from a note on the first page, bought from

Baron von Kremer, and contains a short note in pencil in his handwriting, but it does not seem that he made use of this in the compilation of the article in question.

[A.D. 1869.] *L'Année Philosophique* for this year contains an article by F. Pillon referred to with approbation in the last edition of the *Encyclopaedia Britannica* (vol. iii, s. v. *Bábi*).

[A.D. 1872.] *Essays und Studien*, by Dr Hermann Ethé (Berlin, 1872). Of this work 61 pages (pp. 301—362) are occupied by an essay on the Báb and his doctrine entitled *Ein moderner Prophet des Morgenlandes* and based on the works of Gobineau, Kazem-Beg, Vámbéry, and Perkins. This essay is written in a sympathetic spirit, and the Bábí doctrines are expounded in a very lucid and logical manner.

[A.D. 1873.] The *Journal Asiatique* for this year (7th series, vol. ii, pp. 393—395) contains an article "Sur les sectes dans le Kurdistan" by M. T. Gilbert wherein is included a short notice of the Bábís. After briefly describing the beliefs attributed to them by their neighbours, M. Gilbert estimates the number of those settled in Kurdistán at about five thousand.

[A.D. 1874.] *Persia—Ancient and Modern*, by John Piggot, F.S.A., F.G.S., F.R.G.S. (London, 1874). The account of the Bábí movement given in this work is full of inaccuracies. Thus, on p. 104, speaking of the Bábís up in arms at Yezd in May 1850, the writer says, "failing in this" (i.e. their attempt to capture the citadel) "they retired to Zinjan"; and he further describes the Báb as having been present in person amongst the besieged in that city, and as having been captured "in one of the assaults of the Shah's troops" and executed there.

[A.D. 1874.] *Gurret-ül-Eyn: Ein Bild aus Persiens Neuzeit*, by Marie von Najmájer (Vienna, 1874). This is a poem in six cantos in honour of the Bábí heroine Ḳurratu 'l-'Ayn, which, if not possessing much historic value, is at least a graceful and pleasing tribute to the memory of a noble woman.

[A.D. 1875.] *Journey in the Caucasus, Persia, and Turkey in Asia*, by Lieut. Baron Max von Thielmann, translated into English by Charles Henneage, F.R.G.S. (London, 1875, 2 vols.). The first volume of this work contains (at p. 262) a brief reference to the Bábís *à propos* of '*Muridism.*' The second volume contains (at p. 52) an allusion to the Báb's execution in the citadel *(arg)* of Tabríz, which event is wrongly described as having occurred in A.D. 1843; and (at pp. 90—91) an interesting account of a Bábí named Hájí Muḥammad Ja'far[1] who was the author's fellow-traveller from Tabríz to Mosul.

[A.D. 1877.] *Collections Scientifiques de l'Institut des Langues Orientales*, vol. i, *Manuscrits Arabes*, by Baron Victor Rosen (St Petersburg, 1886). To this most valuable contribution to our knowledge I have had occasion to refer frequently, both in my second paper on the Bábís (pp. 886, 905—909, 954—960, &c.), and in the present work. Of the two Bábí MSS. described, the first is conjectured by Baron Rosen (and there can hardly be a doubt that his conjecture is right) to be the *Commentary on the Súra of Joseph* (تفسیر سورهٔ یوسف) composed by the Báb at the beginning of his mission; the second, concerning which I was unable to arrive at a definite conclusion in my second paper on the Bábís (p. 954—958), has since been proved beyond all question to be a copy of Behá's *Súra-i-Heykal*, whereof the Epistles to the Kings (including the Epistle to the Sháh, a complete translation of which is given in the present work[2]) form a portion. Baron Rosen's convincing arguments (which he has kindly allowed me to see in proof) are prefixed to the text of the MS., which will be published *in*

[1] Baron von Thielmann's fellow-traveller is very probably identical with the Hájí Muḥammad Ja'far mentioned on p. 100, *supra*, and in note 1 on the same page.

[2] See pp. 108—151, *supra*, and Note X, *infra*. The latter contains a translation of that portion of the Arabic exordium which is not cited in the Persian text.

extenso in vol. vi of the *Collections Scientifiques &c.*, shortly to appear (p. 145 *et seq.*).

[A.D. 1879.] The *Deutsche Rundschau* (vol. xviii, pp. 284—291) contains an article entitled *Orientalischer Socialismus* by Professor T. Nöldeke, in which the tenets of the Bábís are briefly discussed, and compared with those of the Mazdakites.

[A.D. 1886.] *Collections Scientifiques &c.*, vol. iii, *Manuscrits Persans*, by Baron Rosen (St Petersburg, 1886). This volume, equally valuable with the other, contains descriptions of MSS. of the *Persian Beyán* (pp. 1—32) and the *Íḳán* (pp. 33—51).

[A.D. 1887.] The *Revue Critique d'Histoire et de Littérature* for April 18th of this year contains (pp. 297—298) a review of Baron Rosen's *Manuscrits Persans* by M. E. Fagnan. Special notice is taken of the Bábí MSS. described by Baron Rosen, and some valuable information is given concerning the five Bábí MSS. brought by Gobineau from Persia, which, on the death of their owner, were bought by the Bibliothèque Nationale.

[A.D. 1887.] *Haifa, or Life in Modern Palestine*, by Laurence Oliphant (Edinburgh and London, 1887). This work consists of a series of letters or essays on different subjects connected with the Holy Land, of which the twenty-first, entitled "*the Babs and their Prophet*" (pp. 103—107), gives an account of a visit paid by the writer to one of Behá's gardens in the vicinity of Acre, together with such information as to the history of the Báb and the Bábís and the personal character and claims of Behá as he was able to collect. This account is very noteworthy, since it is, so far as I know, the first published notice of Behá and the Bábí colony at Acre. Several erroneous statements are made, especially one to the effect that Behá "is visible only to women or men of the poorest class," and that "his own disciples who visit him are only allowed a glimpse of his august back." I myself, during the week which I spent at Acre (April 13th—20th, 1890), was admitted to the august presence four times, each interview lasting about 20 minutes; besides which on one occasion I saw Behá walking in his garden of Janayn surrounded by a dozen or so of his chief disciples. Not a day passes but numerous Bábís of all classes are permitted to wait upon him.

[A.D. 1887.] *Note sur trois ouvrages Bâbis* communicated by M. Clément Huart to the *Journal Asiatique* for 1887 (eighth series, vol. x, pp. 133—144). Of the first of the three MSS. described I submitted an extract to Ṣubḥ-i-Ezel, who pronounced it to be (as M. Huart had conjectured) from his own work the *Kitáb-i-Núr* ('Book of Light'), or rather from one of the two works which go by that name. The translation of Ṣubḥ-i-Ezel's words (contained in a letter written at the end of September 1889) will be found in Note U *infra*. The other two MSS. described by M. Huart appear to be from the same source. Baron Rosen alludes to another article about these MSS. by M. Huart in the *Revue de l'Histoire des Religions* (vol. xviii, p. 279—296), which I have not seen.

[A.D. 1889.] *La Religion de Bab*, a little volume of 64 pages, also by M. Huart, forming one of the series known as the *Bibliothèque Orientale Elzévirienne* (Paris, 1889). This contains some translations from the above MSS. The historical portion supplies us with no new facts.

[A.D. 1889.] The *Journal of the Royal Asiatic Society* [New Series] vol. XXI contains my two papers on the Bábís, whereof the first (throughout this work referred to as B. i) is entitled *The Bábís of Persia. I. Sketch of their History and Personal Experiences amongst them*, and the second (referred to as B. ii) *The Bábís of Persia. II. Their Literature and Doctrines.* These two papers embody the results of my investigations on this subject during the year which I spent in Persia (1887—1888).

[A.D. 1889.] Baron Rosen's *Zapiski* (vol. iv, parts 1 and 2, pp. 112—114) contains a short account of four Bábí works recently brought to St Petersburg. These four works are:—(1) A MS. of the ایقان; (2) A copy of the Bombay lithographed edition of the ایقان; (3) A MS. of the کتاب اقدس (which work I wrongly named لوح اقدس in my papers on the Bábís in the *J. R. A. S.*); (4) A MS. of the سورة الملوك (or سوره هيكل). A much fuller description of all these will be found in vol. vi of the *Collections Scientifiques* when it appears. See immediately below.

[To appear shortly.] *Collections Scientifiques*, vol. vi, by Baron Rosen. Although this volume is not yet published, the kindness of the learned author in sending me the proof-sheets as they were printed off has enabled me to make reference to it when occasion required. It will contain, amongst much other valuable matter, the complete text of the *Súra-i-Heykal.*

See also articles in the *Encyclopædia Britannica* s.v. *Bábi* (vol. iii, 1875, pp. 180—181), *Persia, Modern History* (vol. xviii, 1885, pp. 650—651), and *Sunnites and Shí'ites* (vol. xxii, 1887, p. 665); and articles in the following periodicals:—*Contemporary Review* (vol. xi, p. 581; vol. xii, p. 245), *Chambers' Journal* (vol. xxix, p. 45), *All the Year Round* (vol. xxii, p. 149), *Hours at Home* (vol. viii, p. 210), and *The Nation* (vol. ii, p. 793).

NOTE B.

THE MARTYRDOM OF MÍRZÁ SEYYID 'ALÍ THE BÁB'S MATERNAL UNCLE AMONGST THE 'SEVEN MARTYRS.'

"This year," says Lady Sheil writing in September 1850, "seven Bābees were executed at Tehran for an alleged conspiracy against the life of the Prime Minister. Their fate excited general sympathy, for every one knew that no criminal act had been committed, and suspected the accusation to be a pretence. Besides this Bābeeism had spread in Tehran too. They died with the utmost firmness. Previously to decapitation they received an offer of pardon, on the condition of reciting the Kelema, or creed, that Mahommed is the Prophet of God. It was rejected, and these visionaries died steadfast in their faith. The Persian minister was ignorant of the maxim that persecution was proselytism[1]". Amongst these seven—'the Seven Martyrs' as they are called by the Bábís—was the Báb's uncle Hájí Mírzá Seyyid 'Alí. The other sufferers were Hájí Mullá Isma'íl of Ḳum, Mírzá Ḳurbán 'Alí the dervish, Áḳá Seyyid Ḥuseyn of Turshíz the *mujtahid*, Hájí Mullá Naḳí of Kirmán, Mírzá Muḥammad Ḥuseyn of Tabríz, and Mullá Ṣádiḳ of Marágha. Of their martyrdom the *Táríkh-i-Jadíd* gives a long and touching account, of which I here append an abridgement.

What led to this tragic event was, as stated by Lady Sheil, a report conveyed to Mírzá Taḳí Khán the Prime Minister that the Bábís in Teherán meditated a rising. Thirty-eight persons suspected of belonging to the obnoxious sect were therefore arrested and cast into prison. After a few days it was decided that all of these who would consent to renounce or repudiate their connection with the Báb and his doctrines should be released, but that those who refused to do so should suffer death.

When this news was brought to the prisoners, Hájí Mullá Isma'íl of Ḳum, who was one of the earliest believers and who had been present at the conference at Badasht [see Gobineau, pp. 180—184], arose and addressed his fellow-captives, announcing his own intention of standing firm in the faith even unto death, and exhorting others like-minded with himself and not hindered by any impediment to follow his example, "for," said he, "if we do not show forth the religion of His Highness the *Ḳá'im*, who then will show it forth?" At the same time he declared that those whose faith was weak, or who were prevented by domestic ties from freely laying down their lives, must judge for themselves as to the duty incumbent upon them, and decide whether they were justified in making a formal renunciation of the Báb's doctrine.

[1] Lady Sheil's *Life and Manners in Persia*, pp. 180—181.

Accordingly of the thirty-eight prisoners seven (including Hájí Mullá Isma'íl) determined to adopt the more courageous course, while the others for various reasons were not prepared to forfeit their lives, and decided to recant. The latter were therefore released: the former were led out to die.

In spite of the wide-spread sympathy felt for the sufferers there were not lacking wretches to deride and mock them as they were led forth to the place of execution[1]. Some of these threw stones at them; others confined themselves to abuse and raillery, crying out, "These are Bábís and madmen." Thereupon Hájí Mullá Isma'íl turned towards them and said, "Yes, we are Bábís; but mad we are not. By God, O people, it is for your awakening and your enlightenment that we have foregone life, wealth, wife, and child, and have shut our eyes to the world and its citizens, that perchance ye may be warned and may escape from uncertainty and error, that ye may fall to making enquiry, that ye may recognize the Truth as is meet, and that ye may no longer be veiled therefrom."

Now when they were come to the place of execution, one came to Hájí Mullá Isma'íl and said, "Such an one of your friends will, on condition of your recanting, give a sum of money in order that they may not kill you. To save your life what harm is there in saying merely 'I am not a Bábí'?" To this, however, Hájí Mullá Isma'íl would by no means consent; and, when greatly importuned, he drew himself up and said,

ای صبا از من باسماعیل قربانی بگو
زنده بر گشتن ز کوی دوست شرط عشق نیست

"O zephyr! Say from me to Ismá'íl[2] destined for sacrifice,
'To return alive from the street of the Friend is not the condition of love.'"

[1] This, as I have heard, was the square called *Sabz-i-Meydán*, adjoining the northern limit of the bazaars, but according to the *Táríkh-i-Jadíd* the execution took place in the *Meydán-i-Sháh*.

[2] According to the Muhammadans it was Ishmael [Ismá'íl] not Isaac [Is-ḥáḳ] whom Abraham designed for a sacrifice to God.

Then he took off his turban and said to the executioner, "Go on with thy work;" and the latter, filled with amazement, struck the fatal blow.

The next victim was Mírzá Ḳurbán-'Alí the dervish, an old man highly respected and beloved of all, who had spent the last night in prison in exhorting and encouraging his comrades and reciting verses appropriate to their condition. So high was the consideration in which he was held that the Sháh's mother exerted her influence with her son to have him pardoned, declaring that it was impossible that he could be a Bábí. So, as he stood there awaiting death, messengers came from the palace to give him another chance of saving his life. "Thou art a dervish," said they, "and art a man of excellence and virtue: they have thrown suspicion upon thee, but thou art not of this misguided people." "I consider myself as one of the disciples and servants of His Highness [the Báb]," answered the old dervish, "though whether He hath accepted me into His service or not I know not." And when they continued to press him and urge him to save his life he cried, "This drop of blood—this poor life—is nought: were I possessed of the lordship of the world, and had I a thousand lives, I would freely cast them before the feet of His friends." So, when they perceived that their efforts were of no avail, they desisted therefrom, and signified to the executioner that he should proceed with his work. The first blow struck only wounded the old man's neck and cast his turban to the ground. He raised his head and exclaimed,

ای خوش آن عاشق سر مست که در پای حبیب
سر و دستار نداند که کدام اندازد

"O happy that intoxicated lover who at the feet of the Friend
Knoweth not whether it be his head or his turban which he casteth!"

Then the executioner quickly dealt him another blow which slew him.

After him was slain Áḳá Seyyid Ḥuseyn the *mujtahid* of Turshíz, who, returning homewards from Kerbelá to visit his friends and family, had been arrested in Teherán. He too died with the utmost firmness and alacrity.

Then came the turn of the Báb's uncle Hájí Mírzá Seyyid 'Alí. A merchant of his acquaintance wished to ransom him for the sum of three hundred *túmáns*, but he declared that to suffer martyrdom was his greatest desire. Then he took off his turban, and, raising his face towards heaven, exclaimed, "O God, Thou art witness of how they are slaying the son of Thy Most Honourable Prophet without fault on his part." Then he turned to the executioner and recited this verse:—

چند درد فرقتش بکشد مرا

سر بِبُر تا عشق سر بخشد مرا

"How long shall grief of separation from him slay me?
Cut off my head, that Love may bestow on me a head[1]."

When he had said this he too submitted himself to the executioner's hands.

After this the other three victims, each in his turn, met their death with like heroism. Of the martyrdom of one of these not specified by name but described as "a young Seyyid of pleasing countenance and attractive aspect"; of the attempt to save him made by Hájí 'Alí Khán the Ḥájibu'd-Dawla (see p. 52, note 1), who was superintending the execution and was moved to a compassion rare in him at the sight of so youthful and comely a sufferer; and of the refusal of the youthful Bábí to escape death and secure wealth, luxury, and a fair bride as the price of a simple recantation, the *Táríkh-i-Jadíd* gives a detailed account, which, notwithstanding its pathetic interest, lack of space compels me to omit in this place.

When the executioners had completed their bloody work, the rabble onlookers, awed for a while by the patient courage of the martyrs, again allowed their ferocious fanati-

[1] *Masnaví*, Book VI, p. 649, l. 2 (ed. 'Alá 'ud-Dawla).

cism to break out in insults to the mortal remains of those whose spirits had now passed beyond the power of their malice. They cast stones and filth at the motionless corpses, abusing them, and crying out, "This is the recompense of the people of affection and of such as pursue the Path of Wisdom and Truth!" Nor would they suffer their bodies to be interred in a burial-ground, but cast them into a pit outside the Gate of Sháh 'Abdu'l-'Aẓím, which they then filled up.

After detailing the occurrences briefly set forth above, the Bábí historian proceeds to point out the special value and unique character of the testimony given by the "Seven Martyrs." They were men representing all the more important classes in Persia—divines, dervishes, merchants, shop-keepers, and government officials; they were men who had enjoyed the respect and consideration of all; they died fearlessly, willingly, almost eagerly, declining to purchase life by that mere lip-denial, which, under the name of *ketmán* or *taḳiya*, is recognized by the Shi'ites as a perfectly justifiable subterfuge in case of peril; they were not driven to despair of mercy as were those who died at Sheykh Ṭabarsí and Zanján; and they sealed their faith with their blood in the public square of the Persian capital wherein is the abode of the foreign ambassadors accredited to the court of the Sháh. And herein the Bábí historian is right: even those who speak severely of the Bábí movement generally, characterizing it as a communism destructive of all order and all morality, express commiseration for these guiltless victims. To the day of their martyrdom we may well apply Gobineau's eloquent reflection on a similar tragedy enacted two years later:—"Cette journée donna au Bâb plus de partisans secrets que bien des prédications n'auraient pu faire. Je l'ai dit tout à l'heure, l'impression produite sur le peuple par l'effroyable impassibilité des martyrs fut profonde et durable. J'ai souvent entendu raconter les scènes de cette journée par des témoins oculaires, par des hommes tenant de près au gouvernement, quelques-uns occupant des fonctions éminentes. A les entendre, on eut pu croire aisément que tous étaient bâbys, tant ils se montraient pénétrés d'admiration pour des souvenirs où l'Islam ne jouait pas le plus beau rôle, et par la haute idée qu'ils avouaient des ressources, des espérances, et des moyens de succès de la secte[1]."

With regard to Hájí Mírzá Seyyid 'Alí the Báb's uncle, with whom we are more particularly concerned, the *Táríkh-i-Jádíd* gives the following additional particulars. Before leaving Shíráz (where, as it would appear, he had remained after the Báb departed to Isfahán) he set all his affairs in order and paid all his creditors in person, as though in anticipation of a speedy death. Then he took a tender farewell of all his friends and relatives, besought them to pardon any fault which he might have committed in regard to them, and set out for Teherán, apparently with the intention of proceeding thence to Chihríķ to visit the Báb. Perhaps on his arrival at the capital he was met with the news of his nephew's martyrdom at Tabríz on July 9th 1850: at all events it would appear that he continued there till, not two months later, he himself met with a similar fate.

As the Bábí historian does not omit to point out, no stronger evidence of the marvellous personal influence of the Báb over all with whom he came in contact can be found than the devoted attachment to him manifested by his aged uncle, who, knowing him from his childhood upwards, and being fully conversant with his daily life, was one of the first to embrace the faith for which he died. Of the extraordinary purity and piety of the Báb's life, indeed, we have ample evidence. His bitterest enemies cannot asperse his personal character. Hence those who knew him best loved and revered him most. I was fortunate enough to meet at Acre one who was the Báb's cousin, comrade, play-fellow, and brother-in-law. He was a gentle old man with light blue eyes and white beard. I begged him to give me some account of the Báb's personal character. "He was very dignified and gentle in his manner," replied he, "yet at times, when any attempt to treat him unfairly or discourteously was made, he could be very stern. Once I remember while we were engaged in business at Bushire a custom-house officer attempted to

[1] Gobineau, *Religions et Philosophies dans l'Asie Centrale*, 2nd ed. p. 303.

extort money from him wrongfully and treated him with disrespect. Thereupon the Báb, finding remonstrance unavailing, struck his assailant with his slipper once, accompanying the blow with a look of such majestic anger that the latter instantly became silent and took his departure."

NOTE C.

TEXTS FROM THE PERSIAN BEYÁN GIVING THE BÁB'S AGE AT THE COMMENCEMENT OF HIS MISSION, AND THE DATE THEREOF.

The Báb mentions his age in two passages in the Persian *Beyán*. The first of these occurs in *Váḥid* II, ch. 1 and runs as follows in my MS. The variants of the British Museum codex marked Or. 2819 are here and hereafter given at the foot of each page. This codex is denoted by the letter B.

و هرکاه کسی تصوّر[1] در ظهور این شجره نماید[2] بلا ریب تصدیق در علوّ امر اللّه می نماید زیرا که[3] نفسی که بیست و چهار سال از عمرش کذشته و از علومیکه کلّ بآنها متعلّم[4] کشته[5] متعرّی بوده و حال باین نوع تلاوت آیات مینماید بدون فکر و تأمّل در عرض پنج ساعت[6] هزار بیت در مناجات مینویسد بدون سکون قلم و تفاسیر[7]

[1] B inserts کند.
[2] B omits.
[3] B inserts از.
[4] B reads متکلّم.
[5] B reads میکشته.
[6] B adds دو.
[7] B adds و.

شئون علمیه در علوّ مقامات معرفت و توحید ظاهر مینماید[1] که[2] علماء و حکماء در آن موارد اعتراف بعجز از ادراك[3] نموده و[4] شبهه[5] نیست که کلّ ذلك[6] من عند الله هست و[7] علمائیکه از اوّل عمر تا آخر عمر[8] اجتهاد نموده چگونه در وقت نوشتن بطرز[9] عربی دقّت کرده[10] و آخر الامر کلماتی است که لائق ذکر نیست کلّ اینها از جهة حجّة خلق بوده و الّا امر الله اعزّ و اجلّ از این است که بتوان اورا شناخت بغیر[11] او بل غیر او شناخته میشود باو *

"And if anyone should reflect on the appearance of this Tree[12], he will without doubt admit the loftiness of God's religion. For in one from whose life [only] twenty-four years had passed, who was devoid of those sciences wherein all are learned, who now recites verses after such fashion without thought or hesitation, who in the course of five hours writes a thousand verses of supplications without pause of the pen, who produces commentaries and learned treatises of so high a degree of wisdom and understanding of the Divine Unity that doctors and philosophers confess their inability to comprehend those passages, there is no doubt that all this is from God. What pains do these doctors

[1] B reads میفرماید. [2] B inserts کلّ. [3] B inserts آنها. [4] B omits. [5] B inserts . [6] B inserts حق. [7] B omits. [8] B omits. [9] B reads بسطری. [10] B reads نموده. [11] B inserts از.

[12] i.e. the Báb, who repeatedly calls himself "the Tree of Truth."

take who study diligently from the beginning to the end of their lives when writing a single line in Arabic! Yet after all [the result] is but words which are unworthy of mention. All these things are for a proof unto the people; else is the religion of God too mighty and glorious for one to be able to understand it by aught other than itself; rather by it is all else understood."

The second passage occurs in *Váḥid* vi, ch. 11, which prohibits the cruel beating of children and defines the penalties incurred by schoolmasters and teachers who infringe this injunction. After stating these in full it continues as follows:—

ثمرهٔ این اوامر این است[1] لعلّ برآن نفسیکه[2] کلّ
از بحر جود او متوجّد میگردند حزنی وارد نیاید زیرا
که معلّم نمیشناسد معلّم خود و کلّ را چنانچه در
ظهور فرقان تا چهل سال[3] نگذشت کسی نشناخت[4]
شمس حقیقةرا[5] و در نقطهٔ بیان بیست و پنج سال*

"The fruit of these ordinances is this, that perchance no sorrow may befal that Soul from the ocean of whose bounty all are endowed with existence. For the teacher doth not recognize the Teacher of himself and of all, even as in the manifestation of the *Furḳán* [i.e. the *Ḳur'án*] none recognized that Sun of Truth till forty years had passed, and in the [case of the] Point of Revelation [i.e. the Báb] for twenty-five years."

In my first paper on the Bábís in the *J. R. A. S.* (B. i, pp. 509—511), I was disposed to believe that in each of these two passages the Báb referred to his actual age at

[1] B inserts که. [2] B reads آن نفس که. [3] B omits.
[4] B reads نشناخت کسی. [5] B reads حقیقت را.

the time of writing, and that this was why he described himself in one passage as being twenty-four years of age and in the other as twenty-five. Starting with this hypothesis, I attempted to fix as nearly as possible the date when the first of these passages was written, and decided that it must have been about the end of A.D. 1847 or the beginning of A.D. 1848. From this I concluded that the Báb must have been born not earlier than A.D. 1824, and that he was consequently only nineteen years old at the commencement of his mission, as alleged by Gobineau (pp. 142—143) and by some of the Bábís whom I saw in Kirmán. Further information as to the date of the Báb's birth, which reached me after the publication of my first paper, compelled me to abandon this view[1]. Indeed, had I not been unduly influenced by the idea that the Báb was nineteen years of age at the commencement of his mission, and had I more carefully considered the second of the two passages above quoted, I should have perceived that the Báb speaks of his own age and that of Muḥammad at the beginning of their respective missions when their prophetic office was first disclosed to mankind. In the دلائل سبعه *(Seven Proofs)* the Báb also describes himself as سنی که از خمسه و عشرین تجاوز نموده "*of an age which did not exceed five and twenty.*" When in Cyprus I one day enquired of Mírzá Yaḥyá *Ṣubḥ-i-Ezel* how old the Báb was at the time of the 'manifestation.' He replied without hesitation "twenty-four, and entering on his twenty-fifth year." Now the date of the 'manifestation' is given in the Persian *Beyán* (the passages will be quoted immediately) as Jamádí-ul-Úlá 5th A.H. 1260 (May 23rd A.D. 1844). It therefore follows that the Báb, being at that date, according to his own statement, over twenty-four and under twenty-five years of age, must have been born on Muḥarram 1st A.H. 1236 (October 9th, A.D. 1820) rather than on Muḥarram 1st A.H. 1235 (October 20th, A.D. 1819) as stated at p. 2 of the present work. The

[1] This information will be found at p. 993 of my second paper on the Bábís.

correctness of the former date is further corroborated by the enquiries kindly undertaken by a friend of mine at Shíráz who is himself connected with the Báb's family (see B. ii, p. 993), and I think there can be little doubt that it is the true one.

The first passage in the Persian *Beyán* where the date of the 'manifestation' is given occurs in *Váḥid* II, ch. 7, which treats of the real meaning of the Resurrection. It commences as follows:—

الباب السابع من الواحد الثانی فی بیان یوم القیامة ملخّص
این باب آنکه مراد از یوم قیامت[1] یوم ظهور شجرهٔ حقیقت
است و مشاهده نمیشود که احدی از شیعه یوم قیامت را[2]
فهمیده باشد بلکه موهوماً[3] امریرا توهّم نموده که عند الله
حقیقت ندارد [و آنچه عند الله حقیقت ندارد حقیقت ندارد][4] و
آنچه عند الله و عند عرفاء[5] اهل حقّه[6] مقصود از یوم قیامت
است[7] این است که از وقت ظهور[8] شجرهٔ حقیقت در هر
زمان بهر اسم [و رسم][9] الی حین غروب آن[10] یوم قیامت[11]
است مثلاً از یوم [بعث عیسی تا یوم][12] عروج آن قیامت

[1] B reads قیمة.
[2] B reads قیمةرا.
[3] B inserts همه.
[4] B omits.
[5] B reads عرف.
[6] B reads حقیقت.
[7] B omits.
[8] B omits.
[9] B omits.
[10] B omits.
[11] B reads قیمة.
[12] These four words, essential to the sense of the passage, are omitted in my MS. and supplied from B.

موسی بود که ظهور الله در آن زمان[1] ما شهد الله فی
الانجیل بود و بعد از آن[2] یوم بعثت رسول الله تا یوم
عروج آن قیامت[3] عیسی بود که شجرهٔ حقیقت ظاهر شد
در هیکل محمّدیه و جزا داده[4] هر کس که مؤمن بعیسی
بود[5] عذاب فرمود بقول خود هر کس که مؤمن باو[6]
نبود و از حین ظهور شجرهٔ بیان الی ما یغرب قیامت
رسول الله است که در قرآن خداوند وعده فرمود[7] که
اوّل آن بعد از دو ساعت [و پانزده][8] دقیقه از شب
[جمعه پنجم][9] جمادی الاولی[10] سنه ۱۲۶۰[11] که سنه ۱۲۷۰[12] بعثت
میشود اوّل یوم قیامت[13] قرآن بوده و[14] الی غروب شجرهٔ
حقیقت قیامت قرآن است زیرا که شیٔ تا بمقام کمال نرسد

[1] B here inserts the following passage :—

ظاهر بود بظهور آن حقیقت که جزا داد هر کس مومن بموسی بود بقول خود
و هر کس مؤمن نبود جزا داد بقول خود زیرا که ما شهد الله در آن زمان

[2] B omits. [3] B reads قیمة. [4] B reads داد.

[5] B inserts و. [6] B reads بان. [7] B reads فرموده.

[8] B reads پازده. [9] B omits. [10] B reads الاوّل.

[11] B reads سنه ۱۰۲۶. [12] B reads سنه ۱۲۷. [13] B reads قیمة.

[14] B reads بود and omits و.

قیامت او[1] نمیشود[2] کمال دین اسلام الی اوّل ظهور منتهی شد و از اوّل ظهور تا حین غروب اثمار شجره اسلام آنچه هست ظاهر میشود و قیامت بیان از[3] ظهور من یظهره الله است[4] زیرا که امروز بیان در مقام نطفه است و در اوّل ظهور من یظهره الله آخر کمال بیان[5] ظاهر میشود که ثمرات[6] اشجاریکه غرس کرده بچینند[7] *

"*The seventh chapter of the second Váḥid.* In explanation of the Day of Resurrection. The quintessence of this chapter is this, that what is intended by the Day of Resurrection is the day of the appearance of the Tree of Truth: but it is not seen that any one of the Shi'ites hath understood the Day of Resurrection; rather have they fancifully imagined a thing which with God hath no reality. [And that which hath no reality with God hath no reality.] But what is meant by God and by those who are wise amongst the people of truth by the Day of Resurrection is this, that from the time of the appearance of the Tree of Truth, at whatever period, and under whatever name [or form] (it be), until the moment of its disappearance is the Day of Resurrection. For example, from the (first) day of the mission of Jesus till the day of His ascension was the Resurrection of Moses, for during that period the manifestation of God [appeared in the form of that Truth, who rewarded by His word everyone who believed in Moses, and punished by His word everyone who did not believe. For what God regarded at that time] was what God beheld in the Gospel. And after the (first) day of the mission of the Prophet of God

[1] B reads آن. [2] B inserts و. [3] B reads در.

[4] B omits. [5] B inserts است. [6] B reads ثمر آن.

[7] B reads بچیند.

till the day of his ascension was the Resurrection of Jesus, wherein the Tree of Truth appeared in the form of Muḥammad, rewarding by his word every one who was a believer in Jesus, and tormenting by his word every one who was not a believer in Him. And from the moment when the Tree of the Beyán appeared until it disappeareth is the Resurrection of the Prophet of God which God hath promised in the Ḳur'án; of which appearance *the beginning was when two hours and fifteen minutes* (had passed) *from the eve of [Friday the fifth of] Jamádí-ul-Úlá* (A.H.) 1260, which is the year 1270 of the mission (of Muḥammad). (This) was the beginning of the Day of Resurrection of the Ḳur'án. And until the disappearance of the Tree of Truth[1] is the Resurrection of the Ḳur'án. For of no thing doth the Resurrection occur till it reacheth the stage of perfection. The perfection of the religion of Islám was consummated ere the beginning of this Manifestation, and from the beginning of this Manifestation till the moment of disappearance the fruits of the Tree of Islám, whatever they are, will become apparent. And the Resurrection of the Beyan is from the (first) appearance of Him whom God shall manifest; for to day the Beyán is in the stage of seed, but at the beginning of the manifestation of Him whom God shall manifest the ultimate perfection of the Beyán will become apparent, when He shall gather the fruits of the trees which have been planted."

The second passage giving the date of the 'manifestation' occurs in *Váḥid* vi, ch. 13 and runs as follows :—

و بعد از غرس شجرهٔ قرآن کمال آن در هزار و[2]
دویست و هفتاد سال[3] رسید[4] اکر بلوغ آن در دو ساعتی
که[5] در شب [پنجشنبهٔ][6] پنجم جمادی الاول میسود[7] پنج دقیقه
بعدتر[8] نمیشد *

1 See note 12 at the foot of p. 219.

2 B omits. 3 B omits. 4 B inserts كه. 5 B omits.

6 B omits. 7 B inserts به. 8 B inserts ظاهر.

"And after the planting of the Tree of the Ḳur'án the perfection thereof was attained in one thousand two hundred and seventy years. Had the maturity thereof been (attained) at two o'clock on the night of [Thursday] the fifth of Jamádí-ul-Úlá, it (i.e. the new manifestation) would not have appeared five minutes later."

The above quotations also illustrate what I have had occasion to notice in my first Paper on the Bábís (B. i, p. 507), *viz.* that the Báb prefers to date not from the *flight* of Muḥammad but from the *beginning* of his mission, which he places ten years earlier. Hence he usually states the beginning of his own mission as having occurred not in the year 1260 A.H., but "1270 *years after the mission of Muḥammad.*" Cf. Persian *Beyán*, *Váḥid* ii, ch. 7; iv, 14; iv. 16; iv, 18; vi, 7; vi, 8; vi, 13 (bis).

NOTE D.

The meaning of the title 'Báb.'

Every writer who has made mention of the Báb has pointed out that this title assumed by him at the beginning of his mission signifies in Arabic 'Gate' or 'Door,' but in specifying that whereunto he professed to be the 'Gate' they are no longer in accord. Kazem-Beg says (i, p. 343) that one day, falling into an ecstasy, Mírzá 'Alí Muḥammad "discovered that he was the *Báb*, the Gate of Truth," and a few lines lower he says, "Je ne sais si les paroles du Christ: 'Je suis la porte' lui étaient connues; mais il n'ignorait sans doute pas que Mahomet avait dit: 'Je suis la ville du savoir et Ali (son gendre) est la porte de cette ville'." Gobineau (pp. 149—150) says, "Il annonça qu'il était le Bâb, la Porte par laquelle seule on pouvait parvenir à la connaissance de Dieu." Lady Sheil says (p. 176), "this amiable sect is styled Bābee, from Bāb, a gate, in

Arabic, the name assumed by its founder, meaning, I suppose, the gate to heaven." Watson (p. 348) gives the clearest and most correct statement of the meaning of the title in question. He says, "He (Mírzá 'Alí Muḥammad) now gave out that as Ali had been the gate by which men had entered the city of the prophet's knowledge, even so he was the gate through which men might attain to the knowledge of the twelfth Imam. It was in accordance with this doctrine that he received the distinguishing appellation of Bāb, or gate; from which his followers were styled Bābis."

As regards the Muhammadan historians, the *Násikhu 't-Tawáríkh* of Sipihr, which gives the fullest account of the Bábí movement, and which has served as a basis of information to most European writers, says in speaking of the beginning of what it calls "the mischief (*fitna*) of Mírzá 'Alí Muḥammad the Báb":—

چون حاجی سیّد کاظم ازین جهان بسرای جاوید انتقال نمود چند تن از شاکردان اورا بر داشته برای ریاضت و عبادت بمسجد کوفه در رفت و چهل روز اقامت کرد و یکباره مزاجش از استقامت بکشت آنکاه در نهانی مردمانرا بزهادت و افادت خویش میفریفت و بارادت خود دعوت مینمود و از هر کس مطمئن خاطر میشد با او میکفت من باب اللّهم فادخلوا البیوت من ابوابها هیچ خانهرا جز از در بدرون نتوان شد هر که خواهد بخدای رسد و دین خدایرا باز داند تا مرا

دیدار نکند و اجازت نستاند نتواند ازین روی بمیرزا علی محمّد باب مشهور شد و چون روزی چند بگذشت مسمی بباب گشت و نام او کمتر بر زبانها رفت *

"When Hájí Seyyid Káẓim departed from this world to the Eternal Abode, he [Mírzá 'Alí Muḥammad] carried off several of his disciples and retired for vigils and worship to the mosque of Kúfa, where he abode forty days. All at once his disposition swerved aside from rectitude. Then he secretly seduced men to his own austerities and doctrine, inviting them to devote themselves to him. And in whomsoever he felt confidence, to him he would say, 'I am the Gate of God : *enter, then, houses by their gates :* one cannot enter any house otherwise than by the gate thereof. Whosoever desireth to come to God and to know the religion of God cannot do so until he seeth me and receiveth permission from me.' Therefore he became known as 'Mírzá 'Alí Muḥammad the Báb'; and when a few days had passed he was named 'the Báb,' and his own name rarely crossed men's tongues."

During the latter part of the reign of Muḥammad Sháh when the Báb, then in captivity at Chihríḳ, was brought to Tabríz, and examined concerning his doctrine by a council of divines and doctors presided over by the present Sháh of Persia, then Crown-Prince, he was required to explain the title which he had assumed and to state what meaning he attached to it. The account given of this examination in the present history (pp. 19—21, *supra*) is brief compared to the accounts contained in the supplement of the *Rawẓatu's-Ṣafá*, the *Táríkh-i-Jadíd*, and the *Ḳiṣaṣu'l-'Ulamá* (concerning which works see above, Note A). Of the proceedings of this council a fuller account compiled from the above sources will be found in Note M. For our present purpose it is sufficient to observe that when the Báb was asked by his inquisitors, "What is the meaning of [the name] *Báb*?" he answered, "The same as in the holy tradition, '*I am the City of Knowledge and 'Alí is the Gate thereof*'."

Von Kremer, in the account of the Báb which he gives in his *Herrschenden Ideen des Islams*, quotes this same tradition as the probable source whence Mírzá 'Alí Muḥammad derived his title, and further points out (p. 209) that he was not the first to adopt it, one Abú Ja'far Muḥammad ibn 'Alí ash-Shalmaghání, generally known as Ibn Abí Azáḳir, having suffered death under the Caliph Ar-Ráḍhí for assuming this same title of *Báb* and teaching new and heretical doctrines which included the tenet of metempsychosis. In his case also the title was explained by Ibn Abdús, one of his followers, as signifying "the door which led to the expected Imám." So likewise Abu'l-Ḳásim al-Ḥuseyn ibn Rúḥ[1], a contemporary of ash-Shalmagháni who died A.H. 326 (A.D. 937—938), was regarded by his disciples as one of the "doors leading to the Lord of the Age" (*Ṣáḥibu'z-Zamán*). Lack of space forbids further discussion on the history of this title and its employment. Those who desire fuller information may consult the authorities referred to by von Kremer, *viz.* Ibn Khallikán, ed. Wüst., p. 129, Vita 186; Baron MacGuckin de Slane's translation of Ibn Khallikán, vol. i, pp. 436—437, and notes on p. 439; Hammer-Purgstall, *Litt. Geschichte der Araber*, vol. v, p. 283; and Ibnu'l-Athír, vol. viii, p. 217.

It must be borne in mind that, as is clearly explained by Gobineau (pp. 150 and 156) and Watson (p. 348), the title of *Báb* was only provisionally and temporarily adopted by Mírzá 'Alí Muḥammad, nor is he now generally so styled by his followers, who call him حضرت اعلى ('*l'Altesse Sublime*' of Gobineau), حضرت نقطهٔ بیان ('His Highness the Point of Revelation'), حضرت نقطهٔ اولى ('His Highness the First Point'), or even حضرت ربى الاعلى ('His Highness my Lord the Supreme'). In the Persian *Beyán* he applies to himself other titles in addition to the

1 For further particulars concerning this personage, see Note O, *infra*.

second and third of those above enumerated, such as شجرهٔ حقیقت (the 'Tree of Truth'), ذات حروف سبعه (the 'Person' or 'Essence of the Seven Letters,' because his name, علی محمد, contains seven letters), and the like. But amongst the Behá'ís there is a tendency (very evident in the present work, where the term *Báb* is used throughout, and no mention is made of the fuller development of doctrine and exaltation of rank which marked the later period of Mírzá 'Alí Muḥammad's mission) to suppress the higher titles implying a supremacy which they would reserve for Behá, and to speak of the Báb as حضرت مبشّر ('His Highness the Evangelist'). In reading the present history, the fact that it represents throughout the view of the Behá'ís, not of the original Bábís or the Ezelís of to-day, must never be lost sight of. When, in the words of Gobineau (p. 156), Mírzá 'Alí Muḥammad "déclara qu'il n'était pas le Bâb, comme on l'avait cru jusqu'alors, comme il l'avait pensé lui-même, c'est-à-dire la Porte de la connaissance des vérités, mais qu'il était le *Point*, c'est-à-dire le générateur même de la vérité, une apparition divine, une manifestation toute-puissante," then, to continue the quotation, "le titre de Bâb, ainsi devenu libre, pouvait désormais récompenser le pieux dévouement de l'un des néophytes," and it was on Mullá Ḥuseyn of Bushraweyh that it was bestowed. Accordingly by Ṣubḥ-i-Ezel this illustrious champion of the new faith is always spoken of as جناب باب, while in the *Táríkh-i-Jadíd* he is called جناب باب الباب 'His Excellency the Gate of the Gate.'

In his earlier writings (e.g. the *Commentary on the Súra-i-Yúsuf*, for specimens of which see Rosen's *MSS. Arabes*, pp. 179—191) Mírzá 'Alí Muḥammad repeatedly uses the term *Báb* and apparently applies it to himself. In the Persian *Beyán*, which was composed during his imprisonment at Mákú and embodies his fully developed doctrine, he continues to use the term, but no longer limits it to himself, though still occasionally employing it as his own title, as, for instance, in the following passage in *Váḥid* ii, ch. 1:—

خداوند سوال فرمود بلسان خود که آیا قرآن کتاب
کیست[1] کلّ مؤمنین باو گفتند کتاب اللّه هست بعد
سؤال کرده شد که فرقی[2] در میان فرقان و بیان دیده
میشود اولو الافئده گفتند لا واللّه کلّ من عند ربّنا و
ما یذّکر الّا اولو الابصار بعد خداوند عالم نازل فرمود
که آن کلام[3] بلسان محمّد رسول اللّه است[4] و این[5]
کلام من بلسان ذات حروف السّبع باب اللّه است[6] *

"God demanded in His own speech, 'Whose book is the Ḳur'án?' All the believers said to Him, 'It is the Book of God.' Afterwards it was asked, 'Is any difference seen between the Furḳán [i.e. the Ḳur'án] and the Beyán?' The spiritually-minded answered, 'No, by God, all is from our Lord': and none are mentioned but those endowed with discernment. Then the Lord of the World [thus] revealed:—'That Word is by the tongue of Muḥammad the Apostle of God, and this is my Word by the tongue of the Person of the Seven Letters, the Gate of God'."

In other passages, however, the term is employed (often in the plural) in a more general sense. Thus the last four

1 B reads کتاب اللّه نیست.

2 B reads آیا فرق.

3 B reads که اوّل بود کلام من.

4 B omits.

5 B reads و اینست.

6 B omits.

chapters of the first *Váḥid*, consisting, as it would appear, of mere titles uncommentated and undeveloped, stand as follows :—

الباب السادس عشر من الواحد الاوّل در اینکه باب اوّل رجوع فرمودند بدنیا با هر کس که مؤمن باو بود من حقّ و دونه *

الباب السابع عشر من الواحد الاوّل در اینکه باب ثانی الخ

الباب الثامن عشر من الواحد الاوّل در اینکه باب ثالث الخ

الباب التاسع عشر من الواحد الاوّل در اینکه باب رابع الخ

"*The sixteenth chapter of the first Váḥid.* Concerning this, that the First Gate (*Báb*) hath returned to the world with everyone who believed in him truly or otherwise."

"*The seventeenth chapter...&c.* Concerning this, that the Second Gate..." &c.

"*The eighteenth chapter...&c.* Concerning this, that the Third Gate..." &c.

"*The nineteenth chapter...&c.* Concerning this, that the Fourth Gate..." &c.

In one of my interviews with Ṣubḥ-i-Ezel I asked him

who were intended by these '*Bábs*' or 'Gates,' and he answered that Sheykh Aḥmad Aḥsá'í and Hájí Seyyid Káẓim of Resht [see Note E, *infra*, and also B. ii, pp. 884—885 and 888—892] were two of them. But this would only signify that in them reappeared, or 'returned to the world,' two of the four original 'Gates.' And by these can only be meant those four persons who, during the period of seclusion of the twelfth Imám known as the "Lesser Occultation" (غيبت صغرا), acted as intermediaries between him and his followers. These four were, according to the عقائد الشيعة, (1) Abú 'Umar 'Othmán ibn Sa'íd; (2) Abú Ja'far Muḥammad ibn 'Othmán, son of the above; (3) Ḥuseyn ibn Rúḥ [see Note O, *infra*, and the beginning of this note, p. 229]; (4) Abú'l-Ḥasan 'Alí ibn Muḥammad Símarí.

So also in *Váḥid* ii, ch. iv, this sentence occurs:—

زيراكه خداوند مقرّن فرموده پناه بخودرا بپناه برسول خود و پناه برسول‌را بپساه[1] باوصياى خود و پناه [باوصياى خودرا بپناه][2] بابواب اوصياى خود[3] . . . . زيرا كه پناه برسول عين پناه بخداست و پناه بائمه[4] عين پناه برسول[5] و پناه بابواب عين پناه بائمه است *

"For God hath assimilated refuge in Himself to refuge in His Apostle, and refuge in His Apostle to refuge in His executors (i.e. the Imáms), and refuge [in His executors to refuge] in the Gates (*Abwáb* or *Bábs*) of His executors...... For refuge in the Apostle is identical with refuge in God,

[1] B reads پناه باوصياء او. [2] B omits. [3] B reads اوصياء او.

[4] B reads ائمّه. [5] B inserts است.

and refuge in the Imáms is identical with refuge in the Apostle, and refuge in the Gates is identical with refuge in the Imáms."

So likewise in other passages "Gates of the Fire" (ابواب النّار) are spoken of as identical with "Letters of Denial" (حروف نفی), both terms signifying such as vehemently oppose the Truth and lead men to hell.

NOTE E.

THE SHEYKHÍS, AND THEIR DOCTRINE CONCERNING THE 'FOURTH SUPPORT.'

The founder of the Sheykhí school, with which in its origin the Bábí movement is so closely connected, was Sheykh Aḥmad of Aḥsá (often, but apparently erroneously, written Laḥsá) in the province of Baḥreyn. The following is a brief account of his life, for which I am indebted to the kindness of one of my Persian friends in Teherán. The genealogy therein contained purports to be based on an account written by the Sheykh himself for his son Sheykh Muḥammad Taḳí.

Sheykh Aḥmad was the son of Sheykh Zeynu'd-Dín Aḥsá'í, son of Sheykh Ibrahím, son of Sheykh Ṣaḳr, son of Sheykh Ibrahím, son of Sheykh Dághir, son of Sheykh Ramaḍhán, son of Sheykh Ráshid, son of Sheykh Dihím, son of Sheykh Shamrúkh of the tribe of Ṣaḳr, one of the most important tribes of the Arabs. From Sheykh Shamrúkh to Sheykh Ramaḍhán the family were ostensibly not of the Imámite (Shi'ite) faith, but conformed outwardly to the practices of the Sunnites.

According to my correspondent's statement, the year of Sheykh Aḥmad's birth is represented by the chronogram

انفضّ المديفع (A.H. 1166 = A.D. 1752—53). I think, however, that it should be انفضّ المدافع, "*the water-courses overflowed.*" This sentence yields the date 1157 A.H., which agrees with the other particulars given, and also conveys an intelligible meaning, neither of which conditions, so far as I can see, are fulfilled by the first chronogram. The year of his death (A.H. 1242 = A.D. 1826—27) is contained in the following chronogram :—

فزت بالفردوس فوزاً يا بن زين الدين احمد

"*Thou hast victoriously attained unto Paradise, O Aḥmad son of Zeynu'd-Dín!*" Sheykh Aḥmad was eighty-five years old at the time of his death.

From his youth upwards Sheykh Aḥmad was pious, devout, and ascetic in his life. At the direction of his spiritual guides he quitted his native country and went to 'Iráḳ (Kerbelá and Nejef), where he took up his abode and occupied himself in teaching and diffusing religious knowledge. He soon acquired great fame, and many students gathered round him. His fame continuing to increase, he was invited by Fatḥ-'Alí Sháh, Prince Muḥammad 'Alí Mírzá *Ruknu'd-Dawla*, and other eminent personages, to visit Persia. He accordingly came to Teherán; thence he proceeded to Kirmánsháhán, and thence to Yezd, where he abode for twelve years. He performed the pilgrimage to Mecca several times, and on the last occasion of doing so died two stages from Medína, where he was buried in the cemetery called Baḳí' [-ul-Gharḳad. See Lane's *Arabic-English-Lexicon*, Book I. Part i, p. 235].

The account of Sheykh Aḥmad Aḥsá'í contained in the *Ḳiṣaṣu'l-'Ulamá*[1] differs somewhat from that above given. Thus it is asserted that he came direct from Baḥreyn to Yezd where he abode some time; that from Yezd he went to Kirmánsháhán, where he received yearly the sum of 700 *túmáns* from Fatḥ-'Alí Sháh's son Muḥammad 'Alí Mírzá

[1] See Note A, pp. 197—198, *supra*.

Ruknu'd-Dawla; and that thence he went to Kerbelá where he finally took up his abode. It would appear, however, that he again visited Persia towards the end of his life, and that on this occasion he passed through Ḳazvín, where he paid a visit to Hájí Mullá Muḥammad Taḳí[1]. The latter questioned him concerning his views on the resurrection, and, after a violent altercation, declared them to be heretical. In consequence of this many other divines, who had hitherto regarded Sheykh Aḥmad almost as a saint, began to look askance at him or even to display open hostility, so that he was compelled to leave Ḳazvín. He intended to proceed to Mecca, but died on his way thither at Baṣra.

The chief points wherein Sheykh Aḥmad's doctrine is regarded as heterodox are stated as follows. He believed that the body of man was compounded of parts derived from each of the nine heavens and the four elements; that the grosser elemental part perished irrevocably at death; and that only the more subtle celestial portion would appear at the resurrection. This subtle body he named جسم هورقليا (the word *Huwarḳilyá* being supposed to be of Greek origin) and believed to be similar in substance to the forms in the "World of Similitudes" (عالم مثال). Similarly he denied that the Prophet's material body had, on the occasion of his night-journey to heaven (معراج), moved from the spot where it lay in a trance or sleep. He was much given to fasts, vigils, and austerities, and believed himself to be under the special guidance of the Imáms, especially, as it would appear, the Imám Ja'far-i-Ṣádiḳ. He regarded the Imáms as creative forces, quoting in support of this view the expression الله احسن الخالقين "*God, the Best of Creators,*" occurring in Ḳur'án xxiii, 14; "for," said he, "if God be the *Best* of Creators He cannot be the *sole* Creator." He also adduced in support of this

[1] The maternal uncle and father-in-law of Ḳurratu'l-'Ayn, see Note Q, *infra*, and pp. 197—198, *supra*.

view the tradition wherein the following words are attributed to 'Alí:—

انا خالق السموات و الارض "I am the Creator of the heavens and the earth." He even went so far as to assert that in reciting the opening chapter of the Ḳur'án (سورة الفاتحة) the worshipper should fix his thoughts on 'Alí as he repeats the words اياك نعبد "Thee do we worship."

Sheykh Aḥmad composed a number of works, amongst which the following are enumerated by the author of the *Ḳiṣaṣu'l-'Ulamá*:—

شرح زيارت جامعه كبير *Commentary on the Ziyárat-i-Jámi'a*, in four vols. According to Ṣubḥ-i-Ezel's statement it is in this work that the doctrine of the subtle body (قالب مثالى or جسم هورقليا) which survives the dissolution of the material frame is elaborated.

اجوبة المسائل *Answers to questions.*

شرح عرشيه *Commentary on the 'Arshiyya of Mullá Ṣadrá*[1].

شرح مشاعر *Commentary on the Mashá'ir of Mullá Ṣadrá.*

شرح تبصره علامه *Commentary on the Tabṣira-i-'Allámа*[2].

[1] Concerning Mullá Ṣadrá and his doctrines see Note K, *infra.*

[2] Concerning *'Allámа* ('the Sage'), *i.e.* Jemálu'd-Dín Ḥasan ibn Yúsuf ibn 'Alí of Ḥilla, see a footnote on Note M, *infra.* The full title of the work here mentioned appears to be تبصرة المتعلمين فى احكام الدين ("The Enlightenment of students on the ordinances of Religion.")

فوائد و شرح فوائد *The Fawá'id and Commentary thereupon.*

Sheykh Aḥmad Aḥsá'í was succeeded at his death by his disciple Hájí Seyyid Káẓim of Resht, of whose life the following brief account was supplied to me by the same friend to whom I am indebted for the biography of Sheykh Aḥmad given at the beginning of this note. His family were merchants of repute. His father was named Áḳá Seyyid Ḳásim. When twelve years old he was living at Ardabíl near the tomb of Sheykh Ṣafí'ud-Dín Is-ḥáḳ, the descendant of the seventh Imám Músá Káẓim and the ancestor of the Ṣafaví kings. One night in a dream it was signified to him by one of the illustrious progenitors of the buried saint that he should put himself under the spiritual guidance of Sheykh Aḥmad Aḥsá'í, who was at this time residing at Yezd. He accordingly proceeded thither and enrolled himself amongst the disciples of Sheykh Aḥmad, in whose doctrine he attained such eminence that on the Sheykh's death he was unanimously recognized as the leader of the Sheykhí school. He died at Baghdad ere he had attained his fiftieth year A.H. 1259 (A.D. 1843—1844). The date of his death is contained in the following chronogram: غاب بدر الهدی, "The moon of guidance hath disappeared." His works are said to exceed 300 volumes.

Up to this point the Sheykhís were a united body, for the succession of Hájí Seyyid Káẓim would seem to have been approved and accepted by all. This unanimity was no longer to continue. Seyyid Káẓim had not explicitly nominated a successor; indeed according to the Bábí historian he had hinted that the transitional state of things under which he and his master Sheykh Aḥmad had assumed the guidance of the faithful was with his declining life drawing to a close, and that a brighter light was about to shine forth from the horizons of the spiritual world. Let the Bábí historian, the author of the *Táríkh-i-Jadíd*, take up the tale, and describe in the words of his informant the closing scenes of the life of Seyyid Káẓim.

"When Hájí Seyyid Káẓim had but recently departed

this life, I arrived at the Supreme Shrines [Kerbelá and Nejef] and heard from his disciples that the late Seyyid (may God exalt his station) had, during the last two or three years of his life, wholly restricted his discourse, both in lecture-room and pulpit, to discussing the promised Proof, the signs of his appearance, and their explanation, and enumerating the qualities of the Master of the Dispensation, repeatedly declaring that he would be a youth, that he would not be versed in the learning of men, and that he would, moreover, be of the race of Háshim. Sometimes, too, he would say, '*I see him as the rising sun.*' At length during the last journey which he made with the intention of visiting Káẓimeyn and Surra-man-ra'a, while he was returning from the latter place to Káẓimeyn and Baghdad, he was entertained by one of his friends and disciples, some dozen of his [other] disciples and pupils being [also] present in that garden. Suddenly an Arab entered, and, still standing, made representation thus:—'I have seen a vision touching your Reverence.' On receiving permission, he repeated the dream; whereupon Seyyid Kaẓim appeared somewhat troubled, and said, 'The interpretation of this dream is this, that my departure from this world is nigh at hand and I must go hence.' His companions who were present were much distressed and grieved at this intelligence, but he turned his face towards them and said, 'The time of my sojourn in the world has come to an end, and this is my last journey. Why are ye grieved and troubled because of my death? Do ye not then desire that I should go and the True One should appear?'

"This is as I have heard it from Hájí 'Abdu'l-Muṭṭalib of Isfahán, and Suleymán Khán Afshár[1] of Sá'ín Ḳal'a, who were present in that assembly. Indeed from the noble personage alluded to [apparently Suleymán Khán] I further

[1] This must be a mistake. Suleymán Khán Afshár was conspicuous as a persecutor of the Bábís, for he was not only chiefly instrumental in putting down the Mázandarán insurrection, but was also the bearer of the Báb's death-warrant from Teherán to Tabríz. Hájí Suleymán Khán the son of Yaḥyá Khán of Tabríz, one of the most ardent adherents and steadfast martyrs of the Bábí faith [see Note T, *infra*], is no doubt intended.

heard as follows :—'The late Seyyid specially promised me that I should myself apprehend the Manifestation, saying, "*Thou shalt be there and shalt apprehend.*" Now the utterance of these words and good tidings by him [Seyyid Káẓim] as here described is a matter of notoriety and a thing universally admitted amongst his intimates, being authenticated by several letters from well-known persons to others who accepted the new Manifestation also[1]. Indeed some of those [who were] present in that assembly are still alive, and confess to having heard that announcement from the late Seyyid. Mullá Ḥuseyn of Bushraweyh, one of the most distinguished of divines, who was moreover intimately acquainted with the late Seyyid, made urgent enquiry as to the manner in which the Manifestation should come to pass. The latter, however, only replied, '"Permission is not accorded unto me to say more than this[2]." But from whatever quarter the Sun of Truth shall arise it will irradiate all horizons and render the mirrors of believers' hearts capable of receiving the effulgences of the lights of wisdom.' At all events after his return from Surra-man-ra'a the revered Seyyid departed this life as he had foretold."

Whatever credence we may be disposed to attach to this narrative, there is no doubt that the Sheykhís were, in general, anxiously expecting the appearance of someone who should assume the leadership of their party. A number of the late Seyyid Káẓim's immediate disciples repaired directly after his death to the mosque at Kúfa, and there, with fasting, vigils and prayers, sought for God's guidance in the choice of a spiritual director. Having completed their religious exercises they dispersed each in his own way. Mullá Ḥuseyn of Bushraweyh proceeded to Shíráz, and on his arrival there paid a visit to Mírzá 'Alí Muḥammad, with whom he had become acquainted at Kerbelá. To him first of all did the young prophet announce his

[1] "The new Manifestation" (ظهور بديع) may mean only the dispensation inaugurated by the Báb, but the force of the "also" (هم) which follows leads me rather to conjecture that the dispensation of Behá is intended.

[2] This quotation is from the beginning of the first book of the *Masnaví*.

divine mission, adducing in proof thereof his *Commentary on the Súra of Joseph*, and showing other signs whereby Mullá Ḥuseyn, after a mental struggle which lasted several days, became firmly convinced that the Master so eagerly sought for and so earnestly desired had at length been found. No sooner was he himself convinced than, with that fiery energy which so pre-eminently distinguished him even amongst the eager active spirits who were soon to carry the new doctrine throughout the length and breadth of the Persian land, and cause the echo of its fame to reverberate through the civilized world, he hastened to apprise his friends and comrades of his discovery. Thus did he become the "Gate of the Gate" (باب الباب), the "First Letter" (حرف اوّل), the "First to believe" (اوّل من آمن). The rapidity with which the new doctrine spread was wonderful, representatives of all classes hastening to tender their allegiance to the young Seer of Shíráz, but it was from the old Sheykhí party that the most eminent supporters of the new faith were for the most part derived.

It must not be supposed, however, that *all* the followers of the late Seyyid Káẓim accepted the new doctrine. A considerable number, headed by Hájí Muḥammad Karím Khán of Kirmán, utterly declined to admit the Báb's pretensions (for so they regarded his claims), and these became the bitterest and most violent of his persecutors. Of those doctors who heaped insult on the Báb during his first examination at Tabríz, and those who two years later ratified his death-warrant in the name of religion, several were Sheykhís. Hence it is necessary to recognize clearly the difference between the relations of Bábíism to the old and the new Sheykhí school. From the bosom of the former it arose, and, in great measure, derived its strength; with the latter it was ever in fiercest conflict. Of Sheykh Aḥmad Aḥsá'í and Seyyid Káẓim of Resht both Bábís and Sheykhís speak with reverence and affection; but Hájí Muḥammad Karím Khán and his followers are as odious in the eyes of the Bábís as Mírzá 'Alí Muḥammad the Báb and his adherents are execrable in the opinion of the modern Sheykhís. The Báb stigmatized Hájí Muḥammad Karím Khán as "the Quintessence of Hell-fire" (جوهر جواهر کل نار) and "the [infernal] Tree of Zaḳḳum" (see B. ii, pp. 910—911), while Hájí Muḥammad Karím Khán wrote at least two treatises (one called "the crushing of Falsehood," (ازهاق الباطل) in refutation and denunciation of the Bábí doctrines. Of the bitter enmity which subsists between these two sects I had ample evidence during the two months which I spent at Kirmán in the summer of 1888, and on more than one occasion when representatives of both parties happened to visit me simultaneously their scarcely disguised animosity, which seemed ready at the slightest opportunity to burst forth into open conflict, caused me the liveliest disquietude.

I trust that I have succeeded in making clear the relations which exist between the Bábís on the one hand, and the old and new Sheykhís on the other; for a proper appreciation of these is essential to a clear understanding of the history of Bábíism. Indeed we cannot consider that we have thoroughly fathomed the drift and purport of the Bábí movement until the writings of Sheykh Aḥmad Aḥsá'í and Hájí Seyyid Káẓim of Resht shall have been submitted to careful and minute examination and study. This, however, is a labour still unaccomplished, and, with the exception of one point to be noticed immediately, I shall say no more about the Sheykhí doctrines in this place. Some further information concerning them will be found in Kazem-Beg's articles on the Bábís (*Journal Asiatique,* 1866, 6me série, tome vii, pp. 457—464); in von Kremer's *Herrschenden Ideen des Islams* (pp. 206—208); and in my second article on the Bábís in the *J. R. A. S.* for 1889 (pp. 884—885 and 888—892).

The point of doctrine above mentioned as demanding some explanation (for it is alluded to in the present text) is that of the "*Fourth Support*" (رکن رابع). What I shall say concerning it is derived from notes of a conversation which I had in June 1888 with a Sheykhí doctor of Kirmán named Mullá Ghulám Ḥuseyn. I asked him to explain to me wherein the doctrine of the Sheykhís chiefly differed from that of other Shí'ites. His answer was in substance as follows:—"The Bálásarís [i.e. non-Sheykhí Shí'ites] hold that the '*Supports*,' or essential principles of religion (اصول دين), are *five*, to wit (1) Belief in the Unity of God (توحيد); (2) Belief in the Justice of God (عدل); (3) Belief in Prophethood (نبوّت); (4) Belief in the Imámate (امامت); (5) Belief in the Resurrection (معاد). Now two of these (Nos. 2 and 5) we refuse to admit as separate principles, for why should we specify belief in the Justice of God as one of the essentials of faith and omit belief in the Mercifulness of God, the Wisdom of God, the Power of God, and all the other Attributes? These, moreover, as well as belief in the Resurrection, are really included in the third principle, for belief in Prophethood involves belief in the Prophet, and this again involves belief in his book, wherein these two so-called principles are set forth and whence only they are known. Of the five 'principles' of the Bálásarís, therefore, we only accept *three*, *viz.* (1) Belief in the Unity of God; (2) Belief in Prophethood; (3) Belief in the Imámate; but to these we add another, which we call the '*Fourth Support*' (رکن رابع), *viz.* (4) that there must always be amongst the Shí'ites some one perfect man (whom we call شيعهٔ كامل 'the perfect Shí'ite') capable of serving as a channel of grace (واسطهٔ فيض) between the Absent Imám and his church. Such is our doctrine of the '*Fourth Support*,' and it is evident that, whereas four supports are under all circumstances necessary for stability, a greater number than this is unnecessary."

As so explained, the '*Fourth Support*' is a term applicable rather to that article of faith which declares that there must always exist in the Church of the Imáms some visible head who enjoys their special spiritual guidance and serves to convey their wishes and their wisdom to all true Shí'ites, than to the actual personage who fulfils this function. Yet outside the Sheykhí circle, both amongst the Bálásarís and the Bábís, it certainly bears the second meaning as well; and it is commonly asserted that Hájí Muḥammad Karím Khán regarded himself, and was regarded by his followers, as being this '*Fourth Support*' or Channel of Grace from the Spiritual World. It is evidently this second meaning which the term bears in the present text, and if it bore it from the first it is evident that there was originally very little difference between the pretensions of Mírzá 'Alí Muḥammad the Báb and those of Hájí Muḥammad Karím Khán, since both, in the first instance, claimed to be neither more nor less than intermediaries between the absent Imám and his Church, exactly in the same sense as were the four original 'Gates' (*Abwáb*, or *Bábs*) who served as a connection between the Twelfth Imám and his followers during the period of the 'Lesser Occultation.' [See end of Note D, *supra.*]

As regards the actual condition of the Sheykhís at the present day, their head-quarters are still at Kirmán, near which city, in a little village called Langar, situated two or three miles from Máhán (the burial-place of the great dervish Sháh Ni'matu'lláh), several of the sons of Hájí Muḥammad Karím Khán still reside. During my stay at Kirmán I visited Langar and was permitted to sit for half an hour at the feet of 'the Masters' (*Áḳáyán*) as they are called by their followers. The elder brothers were at Kerbelá at that time (where, I believe, they were very coldly received, being, indeed, prevented from preaching in the mosque as they desired to do), but two younger brothers were engaged in expounding the doctrines of Sheykh Aḥmad to an appreciative audience of heavy-turbaned votaries. At the conclusion of the lecture I had some conversation with them, but, though I had no reason to complain of lack of courtesy on their part, I cannot say that I was greatly impressed with their wisdom. After Kirmán I believe that Tabríz contains more Sheykhís than any other city in Persia, but they are to be found in most of the large towns. They are generally regarded by orthodox Shí'ites with considerable dislike and suspicion.

NOTE F.

Additional Information concerning some of the Persons mentioned on p. 5.

Concerning several of the persons mentioned in the passage to which this note refers, the information at present at my disposal is deplorably scanty. Such as it is, however, I set it down, hoping that others may be able in the future to supplement these meagre notes with further details.

Mullá Ḥuseyn of Bushraweyh (‘The Gate of the Gate,’ جناب باب الباب). Concerning this illustrious personage we have the fullest information. The *Násikhu't-Tawáríkh* devotes some 10 pages (each containing about 600 words) to his history, and the *Rawẓatu'ṣ-Ṣafá* gives an almost equally detailed account of his career. Gobineau and Kazem-Beg both treat of his life, work, and gallant death at Sheykh Ṭabarsí very fully, and in the present work a sufficient summary thereof is contained. Some account of his conversion will be found in Note E above. Nothing further need be added here except that, so far as I can learn, his mortal remains still repose in the little inner room of the shrine of Sheykh Ṭabarsí where, at the direction of Mullá Muḥammad ‘Alí Bárfurúshí, they were reverently laid by the hands of his sorrowing comrades in the beginning of the year A.D. 1849.

Mírzá Aḥmad of Azghand is mentioned in the *Táríkh-i-Jadíd* in the following passage:—

خلاصه بعد از چندی جناب باب الباب عازم خراسان شدند و پس از آن از مصدر امر توقیعی بسر افرازئ اصحاب صادر [گشت] و در صورت امکان و استطاعت تکلیف

برفتن خراسان شده و در توقیع آقا میرزا احمد ازقندی که از اکابر شاگردان مرحوم سیّد بود واقعهٔ مازندرانرا اظهار نموده بودند *

"In short, after a while His Excellency 'the Gate of the Gate' [i.e. Mullá Ḥuseyn of Bushraweyh above mentioned] set out for Khurásán. And after that there emanated from the Source of Command [i.e. the Báb] an epistle to confer honour on the faithful, wherein it was made incumbent upon them to proceed to Khurásán in the case of this being possible and their being able. And in the epistle addressed to Áḳá Mírzá Aḥmad Azḳandí, who was one of the chief disciples of the late Seyyid [Káẓim of Resht], he [the Báb] foreshadowed the catastrophe of Mázandarán." In only one other passage in the *Táríkh-i-Jadíd* can I find any reference to Mírzá Aḥmad of Azghand, and this, consisting of a mere list of the names of learned and pious persons who believed in the Báb and "most of whom attained the lofty rank of martyrdom," throws no further light on the matter. I cannot find any other mention of this Mírzá Aḥmad in any of the documents at my disposal.

Mullá [*Muḥammad*] *Ṣádiḳ*, entitled "the Holy" (جناب مقدّس), or "the Holy one of Khurásán" (مقدّس خراسان), was, according to the *Táríkh-i-Jadíd*, one of the first converts gained by Mullá Ḥuseyn to the new faith. He was, previously to his conversion, a *mudarris*, or professor, at one of the colleges of Isfahán. On the arrival of Mullá Ḥuseyn in that city (the first visited by him on the missionary journey which at the command of his master he undertook) Mullá Ṣádiḳ sought and obtained an interview with him, listened to his arguments, examined the sacred books of the new creed, and, after a brief but severe mental struggle, wherein love of truth finally triumphed over fear and prudence, embraced the doctrines of the Báb. We next find him some months later (Sept. 23rd or 24th, A.D. 1845) at Shíráz, suffering the penalty of his zeal as described in the text. Expelled from Shíráz, he seems to have made his way to Mázandarán; at all events we find him amongst the number of the besieged at Sheykh Ṭabarsí, and after the capitulation he was one of those reserved from the general massacre to grace the triumphal entry of Prince Mahdí-Ḳulí Mírzá into Bárfurúsh. Here again fortune so far favoured him that he was saved by being sold into slavery[1] from the direr fate which overtook almost all of his companions. What befel him after this I know not, but from the manner in which he is referred to in the *Táríkh-i-Jadíd* it would appear that he was no longer alive at the time when that work was composed.

Sheykh Abú Turáb of Ashtahárd is only twice alluded to in the *Táríkh-i-Jadíd*, and I can find no further account of him elsewhere. In the second of these passages his name is merely mentioned in the list of eminent men converted to the new faith of which I have already spoken. In the first it is stated that he was married to the sister of Mullá Ḥuseyn of Bushraweyh, a woman of extraordinary virtue and piety, who, from association with the celebrated Ḳurratu'l-'Ayn [see Note Q, *infra*], had attained to the highest degree of excellence and learning. Although the Sheykh Abú Turáb here mentioned is described as *Ḳazvíní*, not as *Ashtahárdí*, I think that the same person is intended in both passages.

Mullá Yúsuf of Ardabíl. See Kazem-Beg (*Journal Asiatique*, sixième série, tome vii, pp. 357, 358, 467, 468, 473, 477, 486, and 522). Mullá Yúsuf was one of the Báb's most energetic missionaries, and was deputed to preach the doctrine in Ázarbaiján. Through his instrumentality the majority of the inhabitants of Mílán were converted. He afterwards attempted to join the Bábís at Sheykh Ṭabarsí, but on his way thither fell into the hands of Mahdí-Ḳulí Mírzá, who detained him as a prisoner till the conclusion of the siege, when, in company with several of the Bábí chiefs reserved from the general massacre to grace the Prince's triumph, he was led captive into Bár-

[1] See, however, note 2 at the foot of p. 129 *supra*.

furúsh. There, according to M. Sévruguin's account quoted by Kazem-Beg (*loc. cit.*, p. 522), he was blown from the mouth of a cannon. The remainder of Kazem-Beg's account differs from that given in the *Táríkh-i-Jadíd*, in that it represents him not only as reaching the Castle of Sheykh Ṭabarsí, but as taking a prominent part in the defence thereof.

Mullá Jalíl of Urúmiyya and *Mullá Mahdí of Kand* are merely mentioned in the list of illustrious martyrs contained in the *Táríkh-i-Jadíd.*

Of *Sheykh Sa'íd the Indian* I can find no other mention.

Mullá 'Alí of Bisṭám, according to the *Táríkh-i-Jádíd,* was one of those who, on the death of Hájí Seyyid Káẓim of Resht, assembled in the mosque at Kúfa to fast and pray for guidance. Ṣubḥ-i-Ezel in December 1889 wrote for me a short account of the history of the Bábí movement, which at some future date I hope to publish. In this occurs the following passage:—

جناب ملّا علی بسطامی که بقدس خویش معروف است
و مقدّس خراسانی او است بسمت روم تشریف برده در
بغداد گرفته حبس نموده پس از آن بفتوای مفتی بسمت
اسلامبول حرکت داده نزدیکی بغداد در مکانی که بد رائی
مذکور است مسموم گردانیدند و شهید نمودند *

"His Excellency Mullá 'Alí Bisṭámí, who was noted for his sanctity (for he is 'the Holy One of Khurásán'), set out towards Turkey, but in Baghdad they took him and imprisoned him. Then, at the decision of the *Muftí,* they sent him off towards Constantinople, but martyred him by poison at a place near Baghdad called Bad-rá'í." In one of the interviews which I had with Ṣubḥ-i-Ezel during my stay at Famagusta in March 1890 he communicated to me the following additional particulars:—"Mullá 'Alí of Bisṭám was the first martyr, and the only one who died by the hands of the Osmánlí Turks. His martyrdom occurred in the second or third year of the 'Manifestation' [A. H. 1262—3, A. D. 1846—7]. He was arrested at Baghdad and cast into prison. All the *muftís* of Baghdad, headed by Maḥmud Efendí and Sheykh Muḥammad Ḥasan[1], signed his death-warrant, save one, Muḥsin or Ḥasan by name, who refused, saying that he was doubtful as to the rightfulness of so doing. Subsequently the Báb addressed these words to the above-mentioned Muḥsin or Ḥasan in the *Book of Names* (كتاب اسما):—'Because you doubted and declined to take part in this murder, therefore hath God decreed that in the Day of Resurrection the fire shall not touch you.'"

NOTE G.

THE BÁB'S PILGRIMAGE TO MECCA AND RETURN TO SHÍRÁZ.

As the accounts hitherto published of the Báb's movements during the earlier period of his mission are somewhat contradictory, it has seemed to me advisable to embody in the present note all that I have been able to learn on this matter, together with the conclusions which may be fairly deduced from the facts at present available.

First of all let us enumerate briefly the facts which seem to be sufficiently established by good evidence.

(1) Mírzá 'Alí Muḥammad, afterwards the Báb, was born at Shíráz either on Muḥarram 1st A.H. 1236 (Oct. 9th, A.D. 1820), or on Muḥarram 1st 1235 (Oct. 20th, A.D. 1819), most probably (for the reasons advanced in Note C, p. 221, *supra*) the former.

[1] Probably the same Sheykh Muḥammad Ḥasan who is censured in the *Kitáb-i-Aḳdas* (see B. ii, p. 980).

(2) Whilst he was still of tender age he lost his father, Seyyid Muḥammad Riẓá, and was placed under the care of his maternal uncle, Mírzá Seyyid 'Alí (*supra*, p. 2).

(3) On attaining years of discretion (probably, as Kazem-Beg states at p. 335 of his first article, when about fourteen or fifteen years old) he was sent to Bushire to help in his uncle's business (*supra*, p. 2).

(4) Disinclined by nature to the calling for which he was destined, he proceeded at some time antecedent to the year A.H. 1259 (in which year Seyyid Káẓim died, see p. 238, *supra*) to Kerbelá, where he resided for some time (two months, according to the *Táríkh-i-Jadíd*), occasionally attending the lectures of Hájí Seyyid Káẓim of Resht.

(5) In A.H. 1258 (A.D. 1842) when in his twenty-third year he married (B. ii, p. 993). There is no positive evidence to show whether this marriage took place at Shíráz or Kerbelá, but the former hypothesis appears more probable. By this marriage he had (according to a statement made by Ṣubḥ-i-Ezel) one son named (if my memory serves me aright) Aḥmad, who died in infancy. The loss of this child is said to be alluded to in the *Commentary on the Súra of Joseph.*

(6) On Jamádí-ul-Úlá 5th, A.H. 1260 (May 23rd, A.D. 1844) Mírzá 'Alí Muḥammad—then "twenty-four years of age and entering on his twenty-fifth year" as Ṣubḥ-i-Ezel states, or, in his own words, "at an age which did not exceed five and twenty" (see p. 221, *supra*)—first became clearly conscious of the divine mission laid upon him, and (apparently without much delay) began to announce himself as the Báb. If by the 'manifestation' (ظهور) we are to understand that period at which the views of the young Seer first became definitely formulated rather than that at which they were first made known to others, it is of course possible that some little while elapsed between the 'manifestation' and its disclosure. This hypothesis is supported by the narrative of the *Táríkh-i-Jadíd*, according to which Mullá Ḥuseyn of Bushraweyh (who was, as is unanimously admitted, and as his titles 'the First Letter' and the 'First who believed' imply, the earliest convert) came to Shíráz shortly after the death of Seyyid Káẓim, visited Mírzá 'Alí

Muḥammad (with whom he had been previously acquainted at Ḳerbelá), and, during this first visit, was surprised by his former fellow-student demanding of him 'whether he saw in him the signs which must characterize Seyyid Kázim's successor?' (see B. ii, pp. 902—903). On the other hand it is clear that not more than a month or two can have elapsed between the time of the 'manifestation' and its disclosure, *firstly*, because the beginning of the Bábí propaganda is placed by both of the Musulmán historians in this same year of A.H. 1260; *secondly*, because seven months after the 'manifestation' (as will be shown immediately) the Báb, having laid the foundations of his religion at Shíráz, was away performing the pilgrimage to Mecca.

We have now reached the point to which this note specially refers—the Báb's pilgrimage to Mecca. Concerning this Gobineau says simply (pp. 144—145), "Il fit très-jeune le pèlerinage de la Mecque...Il est bien probable que ce fut dans la ville sainte elle-même qu'il se détacha absolument et définitivement de la foi du Prophète, et qu'il conçut la pensée de ruiner cette foi pour mettre à sa place tout autre chose." Kazem-Beg says (i, p. 344), "Après avoir semé bon gré mal gré quelques mauvais grains dans cette terre de Chiraz si fertile en préjugés et en superstitions, le Kerbèlaï Seïd Ali-Mohammed se rendit en pèlerinage à la Mecque." In this instance Kazem-Beg is undoubtedly right; it was *after*, not *before*, the manifestation that the Báb went to Mecca. The *Násikhu't-Tawárikh* is clear on this point. "To proceed with the narrative," it says, "when the Báb had laid the foundations of such an edifice, he, according to his promise, set out for Mecca the venerable." The promise alluded to in this passage is thus noticed on the preceding page: "Since tradition affirms that His Highness the Ḳá'im (i.e. the Imám Mahdí) shall come forth from Mecca the venerable, he (the Báb) used to tell his disciples that next year he would announce his claim in Mecca and come forth with the sword." A statement of Ṣubḥ-i-Ezel's to the effect that the manifestation was in Shíráz (not in Kerbelá, as stated in the *Násikhu't-Tawárikh*), that Mullá Ḥuseyn first believed, and that soon after this the Báb set out on the pilgrimage to Mecca, taken in conjunction with the above testimony, seems to prove conclusively that the pilgrimage-journey took place shortly after the 'manifestation.'

Now since, as we have seen, the 'manifestation' was on Jamádí-ul-Úlá 5th A.H. 1260, and since the pilgrimage must be performed in the month of Ẓi'l-Ḥijjé (the last month of the Muhammadan year), it follows that Kazem-Beg's statement (i, p. 346) that "at the end of the year 1260 (1844) he (i.e. the Báb) returned from Mecca to Bandar-Bushire, where he was arrested in the month of October, by order of the *Niẓámu'd-Dawla* Ḥuseyn Khán, governor of Shíráz," is erroneous. For, according to the *Násikhu't-Tawáríkh*, the horsemen sent to Bushire to arrest the Báb set out from Shíráz on Sha'bán 16th, and returned, bringing with them their prisoner, on Ramaẓán 19th. The latter of these dates is confirmed by the *Rawẓatu'ṣ-Ṣafá;* while the *Táríkh-i-Jadíd*, after mentioning that the Báb's return to Bushire occurred in A.H. 1261, says that he was brought before Ḥuseyn Khán on the eve of Ramaẓán 21st. Though neither of the Musulmán historians mentions the year[1], it is evident that A.H. 1261 is intended, for in Ramaẓán A.H. 1260 the Báb had not yet started for Mecca. We may therefore add to the facts previously stated about the Báb's earlier movements—

(7) That towards the end of the year A.H. 1260, and presumably in the month Ẓi'l-Ḳa'da of that year (November, A.D. 1844), he set out from Shíráz for Mecca.

(8) That he remained at Mecca at any rate till Ẓi'l-Ḥijjé 13th A.H. 1260 (December 24th, A.D. 1844) for the completion of the rites incumbent on pilgrims.

(9) That he returned by sea some time during the first half of the year A.H. 1261 (A.D. 1845) to Bushire, whence he sent missionaries to Shíráz, he himself remaining at the former place. (See *supra*, p. 5.)

(10) That on Sha'bán 2nd A.H. 1261 (August 6th, A.D. 1845) strong measures were adopted by Ḥuseyn Khán against these missionaries. (See *supra*, pp. 5—6.)

(11) That on Sha'bán 16th A.H. 1261 (August 20th, 1845) horsemen were sent from Shíráz to arrest the Báb at Bushire.

[1] Compare the remarks on pp. 186—187, *supra*.

(12) That these horsemen re-entered Shíráz with their prisoner on Ramaẓán 19th A.H. 1261 (September 21st, A.D. 1845), and that on that same day (according to the *Rawżatu'ṣ-Ṣafá*), or on the evening of the following day (according to the *Táríkh-i-Jadíd*), the Báb was brought before Ḥuseyn Khán.

There is not at present sufficient evidence to determine definitely the following points:—

(1) At what age the Báb lost his father.

(2) At what age he first left Shíráz and went to Bushire.

(3) How long he remained at Bushire engaged in commerce.

(4) When he went to Kerbelá, how long he remained there, and whether he married before, during, or after his sojourn there.

(5) Whether he returned directly to Bushire after performing the rites of the pilgrimage at Mecca and visiting Medína, or whether he remained some few months in Arabia.

The Báb was accompanied on the pilgrimage by Hájí Muḥammad 'Alí Bárfurúshí (Kazem-Beg, i, p. 344, note; confirmed by Ṣubḥ-i-Ezel), and was (according to Ṣubḥ-i-Ezel) joined later by Hájí Suleymán Khán.

NOTE H.

ÁḲÁ SEYYID YAḤYÁ OF DÁRÁB AND THE NÍRÍZ INSURRECTION.

Gobineau makes no mention of the Níríz insurrection. Kazem-Beg gives a long account of it, occupying fifteen pages (ii, pp. 224—239), which contains neither much more nor much less than the *Násikhu't-Tawáríkh*. His error as to the date of the Zanján siege (see *supra*, p. 187) has led him to give a wrong date for this event likewise. Áḳá Seyyid Yaḥyá's death—the closing catastrophe of the Níríz insurrection—occurred, not, as he implies, early in A.D. 1850, but on Sha'bán 28th A.H. 1266 (July 9th, A.D.

1850, see *supra*, p. 45, note 1). The *Rawẓatu'ṣ-Ṣafá* contains a much briefer account of the matter, which agrees in the main with those above alluded to. The *Táríkh-i-Jadíd*, on the other hand, differs considerably from the Musulmán histories, and supplies us with much new matter. As the versions embodied in the latter are rendered sufficiently accessible to the European reader by Kazem-Beg's narrative, I shall confine myself here to giving a brief presentation of the account according to the Bábí tradition.

Seyyid Yaḥyá's father Seyyid Ja'far, surnamed *Kashfí* or *Kashsháf* ('the Discloser') because of his skill in the exegesis of the Ḳur'án and the visions which he claimed to have, seems, according to all accounts, to have been universally respected and revered. Before the events with which we are concerned took place he left his native town of Dáráb and settled in Burújird. His son Seyyid Yaḥyá would seem to have resided at Teherán for some time previously to the Báb's appearance, but for how long does not appear. At all events, shortly after this took place he (at the command of Muḥammad Sháh as stated at p. 7 of the present work, at the request of his disciples and followers according to the *Táríkh-i-Jadíd*) proceeded to Shíráz with the express object of enquiring into the Báb's claims; and was present, according to the *Násikhu't-Tawáríkh*, at the Báb's examination before Ḥuseyn Khán on Ramaẓán 21st A.H. 1261 (Sept. 23rd, A.D. 1845). Although, if we are to give credence to the Musulmán historian's assertions, the Báb scarcely emerged from this ordeal with flying colours, Seyyid Yaḥyá was sufficiently impressed by what he saw of the young reformer to desire fuller opportunities of conversing with him. The usual result followed. After a brief period of hesitation and doubt, Seyyid Yaḥyá eagerly embraced the new faith. A long account of his conversion is given in the *Táríkh-i-Jadíd*, which, interesting as it is, lack of space compels me to omit.

Seyyid Yaḥyá does not seem to have remained in Shíráz long after his conversion. The present history (p. 8) states that he "hastened to Burújird to his father Seyyid Ja'far"; the *Táríkh-i-Jadíd* describes him as "setting out for Yezd";

while the *Násikhu't-Tawáríkh* asserts that after the Báb's flight to Isfahán he was informed by Ḥuseyn Khán that "his further sojourn in Fárs was undesirable," and that accordingly he betook himself to Yezd. Whatever his immediate movements on quitting Shíráz may have been (and it is not improbable that he may have visited many towns besides those mentioned to preach the new faith, being, as would appear, commissioned by the Báb so to do) he would seem to have again visited Teherán, and there to have remained for some considerable time. Ṣubḥ-i-Ezel, in reply to a question which I addressed to him as to the character of Áḳá Seyyid Yaḥyá and the truth or falsity of the charge of perfidy brought against him by a certain writer (Kazem-Beg, ii, p. 239), wrote thus:—"The virtue and perfections of His Excellency Áḳá Seyyid Yaḥyá were beyond all limits and bounds. He was not such as that historian has described. I bear witness by God and His Spirit that this [historian] has written downright falsehood. Most of the people of Persia admitted his virtue and perfections. I myself in the days of my youth met him several times at night in my own house and elsewhere, and witnessed the perfection of his virtues and endowments."

The information at our disposal is insufficient to enable us to trace Seyyid Yaḥyá's movements from the period of his conversion in the autumn of A.D. 1845 till we find him involved in the troubles at Yezd in May 1850. If the reiterated assertions of the *Táríkh-i-Jadíd* to the effect that he proceeded directly from Shíráz to Yezd, returned directly from Yezd to Shíráz and Níríz, and also visited Teherán, are to be credited, we must suppose that he visited Yezd twice at least during this period. At all events in May 1850 we find him in that city, busily engaged in preaching the Bábí doctrines, and surrounded by a considerable number of followers. The governor of Yezd, Áḳá Khán, at length considered it advisable to interfere, and sent men to arrest Seyyid Yaḥyá, who retired with some of his followers to the citadel and prepared to defend himself. An unsuccessful attack on the insurgents' position resulted in a loss of thirty lives to the besiegers and seven to the Bábís.

Seyyid Yaḥyá, however, does not seem to have been altogether satisfied with his position. One night he said, "If anyone could lead out my horse so that I could go forth to put an end to this matter and convey myself to some other place, it would not be a bad thing." A youth named Ḥasan, distinguished by a singular devotion to Seyyid Yaḥyá, at once volunteered to make the attempt, and persisted in his purpose in spite of his master's warning that he would be taken and slain. This actually befel. Ḥasan was captured by the enemy and brought before the governor, who ordered him to be blown from the mouth of a gun. So little did this terrible sentence affect the brave youth that he requested that he might be bound with his face towards the cannon so that he might see the match applied. In spite of this untoward event Seyyid Yaḥyá succeeded in effecting his escape from Yezd in company with one of his disciples. He first made his way to Shíráz, whence he proceeded to Níríz. After his departure, the Bábís at Yezd were soon subdued by the governor, who punished some with death, some with imprisonment, and some with fines.

No sooner had Seyyid Yaḥyá reached Níríz than he again began his propaganda, undeterred by the remonstrances and threats of the governor Zeynu'l-'Ábidín Khán. The latter finally called upon the people of Níríz to assist him in forcibly expelling the disturber. Seyyid Yaḥyá, being apprised of this, repaired to the mosque where his father had been wont to preach, and addressed to the people there assembled an affecting discourse, wherein he reminded them of their former love for himself, declared that his only object was to make them partakers in that faith which had been to him a source of such great happiness, and concluded by conjuring them by the veneration in which they held his father's memory not to suffer themselves to be made the instruments of the governor's malice. Having finished his discourse he left the town accompanied by seventeen of his followers, and took up his abode at an old ruined castle in the neighbourhood.

Seyyid Yaḥyá was not suffered to remain long undisturbed. His foes soon discovered his retreat and proceeded to lay siege to it. At first they were unsuccessful, Seyyid

Yaḥyá having apparently been joined by a large number of supporters (three hundred according to the Musulmán historian); and indeed the Bábís gained at least one decided victory over their foes. But in a short while the besiegers were re-inforced by troops sent from Shíráz at the command of Fírúz Mírzá, the new governor of Fárs, and commanded by Mihr 'Alí Khán *Shujá'u'l-Mulk* of Núr and Muṣṭafá-Ḳulí Khán Ḳára-gúzlú. The arrival of these troops greatly dispirited the besieged; many of the less ardent deserted, and in a short time the occupants of the castle were reduced to seventy.

In spite of the defections from their ranks, the Bábís (according to the *Táríkh-i-Jadíd*) continued to defend themselves with such vigour that the besiegers were fain to have recourse to treachery similar in character to that whereby Sheykh Ṭabarsí and Zanján were finally subdued. They sent a message to Seyyid Yaḥyá asking him to come to their camp and hold a peaceful consultation with the royalist leaders, and assuring him with oaths registered on the Ḳur'án that no harm should befal him at their hands. Seyyid Yaḥyá, in spite of the remonstrances and warnings of his followers, acquiesced in the proposed arrangement, and forthwith betook himself to the besiegers' camp. He was at first received with courtesy and treated with all respect, but when, on the following morning, he attempted to leave the tent which had been assigned to him, he was prevented by the sentinels from so doing. The Bábís, becoming aware in some way of the insult offered to their chief, made a sudden sortie and succeeded in greatly discomfiting their foes. Thereupon the officers of the besieging army hastened to Seyyid Yaḥyá's tent and remonstrated with him on the action of his followers, reminding him that he had agreed to co-operate with them in striving to bring about a peaceful settlement. Seyyid Yaḥyá in turn reproached them with wanton violation of good faith in confining him to his tent, which conduct on their part, he assured them, was the sole cause of what had now occurred. The royalist officers apologized for the insult offered, which, they declared, they had in no wise sanctioned, and finally prevailed on Seyyid Yaḥyá to write to his followers instructing them to lay down their arms, evacuate their fortress, and return to their homes. The Bábís faithfully obeyed the commands of their chief, but no sooner were they disbanded and scattered than they were seized by the soldiers and brought in chains to the camp, while their houses were given over to plunderers.

The besiegers, having now gained their object, readily forgot their oaths and plighted troth. Seyyid Yaḥyá was strangled with his own girdle by one whose two brothers had been killed during the siege, and the other Bábís likewise died by the hands of the executioner. The heads of the victims were stuffed with straw[1], and, bearing with them these grim trophies of their prowess, together with some forty or fifty Bábí women and one child of tender age as captives, the victorious army returned to Shíráz. Their entry into that city was made the occasion of general rejoicings; the captives were paraded through the streets and bazaars and finally brought before Prince Fírúz Mírzá, who was feasting in a summer-house called *Kuláh-i-Firangí*. In his presence Mihr 'Alí Khán, Mírzá Na'ím, and the other officers recounted the details of their victory, and received congratulations and marks of favour. The captive women were finally imprisoned in an old caravansaray outside the Isfahán gate. What treatment they experienced at the hands of their captors is left to our conjecture. Twelve Bábís who had escaped from Níríz to Isfahán were there captured and sent to Shíráz where they were executed. Thus ended the first Níríz insurrection.

The second insurrection occurred about two years later. A number of Bábís took refuge with their wives and children in the mountains about Níríz, and for a long while offered a vigorous and successful resistance to those who strove to dislodge them. They even attacked the town and killed the governor Zeynu'l-'Ábidín Khán—the chief author of their sufferings—while he was at the bath. Finally troops were sent from Shíráz by the governor Ṭahmásp Mírzá, and these, aided by the tribesmen of Dáráb and Ṣábúnát, succeeded at length in stamping out the insurrec-

[1] Concerning this disgusting practice compare Eastwick's *Diplomate's Residence in Persia*, vol. ii, pp. 55--56.

tion. The fate of the captives was in every respect similar to that which had befallen their predecessors.

The author of the *Táríkh-i-Jadíd* in concluding this narrative takes occasion to point out how literally was fulfilled in these events the prophecy contained in a tradition referring to the signs which shall mark the appearance of the Imám Mahdí :—

عليه كمال موسى و بهاء عيسى و صبر ايوب فيذل اولياؤه
فى زمانه و تتهادى رؤسهم كما تتهادى رؤس الترك و الديلم
فيقتلون و يحرقون و يكونون خائفين مرعوبين وجلين تصبغ
الارض من دمائهم و يفشو الويل و الرنّة فى نسائهم اولئك
اوليائى حقّاً *

"*In him* [shall be] *the perfection of Moses, the preciousness of Jesus, and the patience of Job; his saints shall be abased in his time, and their heads shall be exchanged as presents, even as the heads of the Turk and the Deylamite are exchanged as presents; they shall be slain and burned, and shall be afraid, fearful, and dismayed; the earth shall be dyed with their blood, and lamentation and wailing shall prevail amongst their women; these are my saints indeed.*"[1]

When I was at Yezd in the early summer of 1888, I became acquainted with a Bábí holding a position of some importance under government, two of whose ancestors had taken a prominent part in the suppression of the Níríz insurrection. Of what he told me concerning this the following is a summary taken from my diary for May 18th, 1888:—

"My maternal grandfather Mihr 'Alí Khán *Shujá'u'l-Mulk* and my great-uncle Mírzá Na'ím both took an active

[1] This tradition, called حديث جابر, is also quoted from the *Káfí* (one of the principal compilations of Shi'ite traditions) in the *Iḳán*.

part in the Níríz war—*but on the wrong side.* When orders came to Shíráz to quell the insurrection, my grandfather was instructed to take command of the expedition sent for that purpose. He did not like the task committed to him and communicated his reluctance to two of the *'Ulamá*, who, however, re-assured him, declaring that the war on which he was about to engage was a holy enterprise sanctioned by Religion, and that he would receive reward therefor in Paradise. So he went, and what happened happened. After they had killed 750 men, they took the women and children, stripped them almost naked, mounted them on donkeys, mules, and camels, and led them through rows of heads hewn from the lifeless bodies of their fathers, brothers, sons, and husbands towards Shíráz. On their arrival there, they were placed in a ruined caravansaray just outside the Isfahán gate and opposite to an *Imám-zádé*, their captors taking up their quarters under some trees hard by. Here they remained for a long while, subjected to many insults and hardships, and many of them died.

"Now see the judgement of God on the oppressors; for of those chiefly responsible for these cruelties not one but came to a bad end and died overwhelmed with calamity.

"My grandfather Mihr 'Alí Khán presently fell ill and was dumb till the day of his death. Just as he was about to expire, those who stood round him saw from the movement of his lips that he was whispering something. They leant down to catch his last words and heard him murmur faintly '*Bábí! Bábí! Bábí!*' three times. Then he fell back dead.

"My great-uncle Mírzá Na'ím fell into disgrace with the government and was twice fined, 10,000 *túmáns* the first time, 15,000 the second. But his punishment did not cease here, for he was made to suffer diverse tortures. His hands were put in the *el-chek*[1] and his feet in the *tang-i-Ḳájár*[2]; he was made to stand bare-headed in the sun

[1] The torture called *el-chek* consists in placing pieces of wood between the victim's fingers, binding them round tightly with cord. Cold water is then thrown over the cord to cause its further contraction.

[2] The *tang-i-Ḳájár* or 'Ḳájár squeeze' is an instrument of

with treacle smeared over his head to attract the flies; and, after suffering these and other torments yet more painful and humiliating, he was dismissed a disgraced and ruined man."[1]

Áḳá Seyyid Yaḥyá was, as Ṣubḥ-i-Ezel informed me, not more than forty years old at the time of his death. A certain Bábí named Biyúk Áḳá used to say jestingly, "I like a handsome 'Commander of the Faithful' like Seyyid Yaḥyá, not an ugly old man bent double with age like Mullá Sheykh 'Alí."

Major-General Sir Frederick Goldsmid was kind enough to call my attention to the following passage in Lovett's *Surveys on the road from Shíráz to Bam* (*Journal of the Royal Geographical Society*, 1872):—

"It (i.e. Níríz) is divided into three parishes or *maḥallas;* that to the South, termed the '*Maḥalla-i-Bábí*' is well known to be peopled almost entirely by Bábís, who, though they do not openly profess their faith in the teachings of Seyyid 'Alí Muḥammad the Báb, still practise the principles of communism he inculcated. It is certain, moreover, that the tolerance which was one of the precepts inculcated by the Báb is here shewed, for not only was I invited to make use of the public *ḥammám*, if I required it, but quarters were assigned to me in a *madrasa.*"

Is it in the least degree probable that, if Seyyid Yaḥyá's conduct had been such as Kazem-Beg describes it, Níríz should have continued so long one of the strongholds of that faith whereof he was the apostle?

torture resembling the 'boot' once used in England, for the introduction of which (as its name implies) Persia is indebted to the dynasty which at present occupies the throne.

[1] Another yet more striking instance of Divine vengeance was related to me in the same connection, but I omit it as not bearing on the present subject. The belief prevalent amongst the Bábís, that signal punishment befalls those who are most active in persecuting them, is strangely supported not only by the above instances but by the fates of the *Amír-Niẓám* (Gobineau, pp. 253—254), of Maḥmúd Khán the *Kalántar* (Gobineau, p. 295), of Sheykh Báḳir, and others (B. i, pp. 491—492).

NOTE I.

THE BÁB'S ESCAPE FROM SHÍRÁZ TO ISFAHÁN.

According to the *Táríkh-i-Jadíd* the Báb, after his examination before Ḥuseyn Khán on Ramaẓán 21st, A.H. 1261 (Sept. 23rd, A.D. 1845), was confined, not, as stated in this history (p. 6), in the house of his uncle Hájí Seyyid 'Alí, nor, as asserted by the Musulmán historians, in prison, but in the house of 'Abdu'l-Ḥamíd Khán the *Dárúghá* or chief constable of Shíráz. That for some portion of the six months which elapsed between his arrest and his escape to Isfahán the Báb was an inmate of the house of this official would appear certain, for Ṣubḥ-i-Ezel, whom I questioned on the subject, affirmed this to have been the case, adding, in answer to further questions as to how strict was the custody in which he was kept, that the *rawẓa-khwáns* or religious recitations, of which the constable's house was frequently the scene, afforded opportunities to the Bábís of seeing and conversing with their Master.

That some attack on the Báb's house such as that described at p. 10 of the present work did take place appears to be proved by the following passage from one of the Báb's works, for which I am also indebted to Ṣubḥ-i-Ezel:—

دخلوا حزبه لیلة القدر علی بیتی و اخذوا ما استطاعوا

ممّا ملّکنی ربّی بأمر مختار الفارس لعنة الله علیه *

"*His party entered in unto my house on the 'Night of Worth'*[1] *and took what they could of that which my Lord hath caused me to possess, at the command of the ruler of Fárs, upon whom be the curse of God!*"

[1] The *Leylatu'l-ḳadr* ("Night of Worth" or "Decrees") is generally supposed to be the night between the 23rd and 24th of Ramaẓán. (See Sale's translation of the Ḳur'án, note on *sura* xcvii.)

The account of the Báb's escape from Shíráz contained in the *Táríkh-i-Jadíd* differs somewhat from that here given, and is in substance as follows. When the plague broke out in Shíráz the son of 'Abdu'l-Ḥamíd Khán was amongst those stricken by that awful malady. 'Abdu'l-Ḥamíd Khán in his distress and anxiety appealed to the Báb, entreating him to pray for the youth's recovery. This shortly took place; whereat the grateful father sought out his illustrious guest, and, with profuse expressions of thankfulness, assured him that he might consider himself free to go where he pleased. According to the Musulmán accounts (which, together with a note containing a very pertinent criticism on their intrinsic improbability, will be found in Kazem-Beg's first paper, pp. 348—349) Minúchihr Khán *Mu'tamadu'd-Dawla*, the governor of Isfahán, sent horsemen to Shíráz expressly to deliver the Báb from his captivity and bring him to Isfahán. It is but fair to add that Ṣubḥ-i-Ezel also attributed the Báb's release directly to Minúchihr Khán's efforts.

Of the Báb's journey to Isfahán in company with Áḳá Ḥuseyn of Ardistán and Áḳa Seyyid Káẓim of Zanján (who died shortly after reaching Isfahán) the *Táríkh-i-Jadíd* gives a detailed account on the authority of Hájí Mírzá Jání of Káshán, who had heard it from the above-mentioned Áḳá Muḥammad Ḥuseyn himself. The most noteworthy feature of this account is its evident tendency to invest the Báb's slightest actions with a miraculous character.

The Báb probably reached Isfahán early in the summer of A.D. 1846, since, according to both the Musulmán historians, his captivity at Shíráz lasted six months, and since, according to the present history (p. 11), the hot weather (which seldom sets in till the beginning of May at the earliest) had already begun ere he left Shíráz. On approaching Isfahán he addressed a letter to the governor Minúchihr Khán asking permission to enter the city and craving protection. Of this letter Kazem-Beg (i. p. 352 and note) gives a translation, which, as it appears to be derived from authoritative sources, I here reproduce:—"Poursuivi par tous, persécuté, j'accours me placer sous votre égide ; j'attends votre réponse au seuil de la capitale, et n'y entrerai pas avant d'avoir obtenu l'assurance de votre protection."

During the first forty days of his sojourn in Isfahán the Báb was, as stated at p. 11 of the present work and also in the *Táríkh-i-Jadíd*, the guest of the Imám-Jum'a, who at first treated him with great respect, and at whose request he wrote the *Commentary on the Súratu'l-'Aṣr*. Of this work I have been fortunate enough to obtain a MS. quite recently. [See *infra* at the end of Note U].

NOTE J.

The conference at Isfahán.

Of the circumstances which led to the conference, and the considerations which induced the majority of the clergy invited to take part in it to absent themselves therefrom, the *Táríkh-i-Jadíd* gives the following account. Although the '*Ulamá* of Isfahán headed by the Imám-Jum'a had at first behaved towards the Báb with respect, and expressed themselves favourably with regard to him, they began after a while to be alarmed at his increasing influence over the governor Minúchihr Khán. Alarm presently passed into hatred: they began to speak ill of him whom they had professed to admire, and even destroyed certain books which he had composed at their request. Minúchihr Khán on hearing this was greatly incensed, and bitterly reproached these divines with the fickleness of their conduct. "At first," he said, "you praised and admired. What has happened now to cause you to become so hostile and envious and induce you to speak so ill? There is no sense in denunciation without investigation or enquiry. If you are in truth searchers and strivers in matters of faith and religion, then choose one of three places—the Imám-Jum'a's house, my house, or the Masjid-i-Sháh—and hold discussion with him [the Báb]. If he can establish and prove the truth of his claim so as to persuade and convince you, admit it, so that the clergy of Persia may not oppose and resist it without reason, or turn away from the truth without cause. If he cannot succeed in establishing his claim, then do you be the first to rebut it, so that this mischief may cease, and mankind may be set at ease. But it is a condition that I myself be present and that only one person at a time speak, for if once wrangling begins and clerical tricks are resorted to, the matter will not be understood."

The clergy agreed to this proposal, and selected the Masjid-i-Sháh as the scene of the conference. On the appointed day Mír Seyyid Ḥasan *Mudarris,* Hájí Mullá Ḥasan 'Alí of Túsirkán, Áḳá Muḥammad Mahdí Kalbásí, and other members of the clergy who were to take part in the discussion met at the house of Hájí Muḥammad Ja'far of Fárs, intending to proceed with him to the Masjid-i-Sháh. Hájí Muḥammad Ja'far, however, who was the oldest and most learned of those present, expressed a strong opinion to the effect that they would act most wisely in refusing to take any part in the projected discussion with the Báb, "for," said he, "if you prevail over him you will add but little to your reputation, seeing that he is confessedly unlearned and untrained in science; while if he prevail over you, you will be for ever shamed and disgraced. Under these circumstances it is best that we should sign a declaration stating that we are convinced of the heretical character of his doctrines, and refuse to have any further dealings with him." This expedient was, after some discussion, unanimously adopted, and the declaration was sent to Minúchihr Khán, who was greatly incensed thereat.

That some of the clergy who had been invited to take part in the discussion refused to attend is a fact vouched for by both of the Bábí historians, though as to the names of the absentees they are not in complete accord, Áḳá Muḥammad Mahdí, for instance, being specially designated in the present work (p. 12) as having been present at the conference. The *Násikhu 't-Tawáríkh* gives a totally different account of the matter, including a report of the discussion. This account is in substance as follows.

Minúchihr Khán, anxious to test the Báb's wisdom, one

night invited to his house several eminent members of the clergy of Isfahán, amongst these being Mírzá Seyyid Muḥammad *Imám-Jum'a,* Áḳá Muḥammad Mahdí Kalbásí, and Mírzá Muḥammad Ḥasan of Núr. Shortly after these had arrived the Báb entered and was placed in a seat of honour. The following colloquy then took place:—

Áḳá Muḥammad Mahdí.—"Persons who follow the path of Religion belong to one of two classes: either they themselves deduce and determine religious questions from history and tradition, or else they follow some competent authority (*mujtahid*)".[1]

Báb:—"I follow no one, and moreover I regard it as unlawful for each one to act after his own fancy."

Á. M. M.—"To-day the Gate of Knowledge (*Báb-i-'ilm*) is shut, and the Proof of God[2] absent. Unless you hold converse with the Imám of the Age and hear the explanation of questions of truth from his tongue, how can you attain certainty and be assured? Tell me, whence have you acquired this knowledge, and from whom did you gain this assurance?"

Báb.—"You are educated in tradition and are as a child learning the alphabet. The 'Station of Praise and of the Spirit' is mine. You cannot speak with me of what you know not."

Mírzá Ḥasan (*the Platonist and follower of Mullá Ṣadrá*).—"Stop at this statement which you have made! We in our terminology have assigned a station to 'Praise and the Spirit,' whereunto whosoever attaineth is conversant with all things; from him nothing remains concealed, and there is nothing which he knoweth not. Do you recognize the 'Station of Praise and of the Spirit' as such, and does your nature thus comprehend all things?"

Báb (*without hesitation*).—"It is even so. Ask what you please."

M. Ḥ.—"One of the miracles of the Prophets and Saints was, as it appears, the [instant] traversing of the

[1] He who follows is called *muḳallid*, and he who leads, *mujtahid*. Everyone belonging to the former class is at liberty to select his own guide from the latter.

[2] i.e. the Twelfth Imám.

earth. Tell me now, that I may know, how the earth can be thus traversed. For instance, His Holiness Jawád[1] (upon him be peace) lifted up his foot in Medína and put it down in Ṭús. Whither went the space which was between Medína and Ṭús? Did the ground between these two cities sink down, so that Medína became contiguous to Ṭús? And when the Imám (upon him be peace) reached Ṭús, did the earth again rise up? This cannot have been, for how many cities are there between Medína and Ṭús, all of which must in that case have been swallowed up and every living thing therein destroyed! And if you say that the lands [between them] were agglomerated so that they became amalgamated, this too is impossible, for in that case how many cities would have been obliterated or would have passed beyond Medína or Ṭús, whereas [in fact] no part of the earth was altered or moved from its place. And if you say, 'The Imám flew, and leapt with his mortal body from Medína to Ṭús,' this likewise agreeth not with sound reasonings. Say also how 'Alí the Prince of Believers (upon him be peace) was in one night—nay, in one moment—a guest in forty [different] houses. If you say, 'It was not 'Alí, but a simulacrum [of him] appeared,' we admit it not, for God and the Prophet lie not, neither was 'Alí a juggler. And if it was in truth he, how was it so? So likewise it is [stated] in tradition that the heavens moved swiftly in the time of Sulṭán Jábir, but had a slow motion in the time of the Imáms. Now *firstly* how can there be two sorts of motion for the heavens? And *secondly* the Omeyyad and 'Abbásid Kings were contemporary with our Imáms (upon them be peace), so that the heavens must at one time have had both a slow and a swift motion. Discover this mystery also."

Báb.—"If you wish, I will explain these difficulties verbally; if not, I will write [their solutions] with fingers and pen on paper."

M. Ḥ.—"The choice is yours. Do whichever you please."

Then the Báb took pen and paper and began to write.

[1] *Jawád* ("the Generous") is one of the titles assigned to the ninth Imám, Muḥammad Taḳí.

At this moment supper was brought in. Mírzá Ḥasan picked up the paper on which the Báb had written a few lines, and, after glancing at it, said, "It appears that you have begun a homily, and have only written an exordium of praise to God and a few words of prayer, without acquainting us with that which we desired to know." Here the discussion dropped, and after partaking of supper each one returned to his own home.

Whatever may be the truth about this conference and the behaviour of the clergy of Isfahán towards the Báb, one fact is clearly proved by all accounts, namely, that from first to last Minúchihr Khán shewed himself a sincere and faithful friend to the Báb. Whether, as stated by Ṣubḥ-i-Ezel, he wrote to Muḥammad Sháh telling him that "it was unseemly for the Government to engage in a quarrel with a private individual," and offered all the money at his disposal and even the rings on his hand to the Báb; or whether, as asserted by the *Táríkh-i-Jadíd*, he even went so far as to offer to place 50,000 troops at the Báb's disposal, march on Teherán, and compel the King to accept the new faith and bestow the hand of one of his daughters on its founder, must remain doubtful; but this much at least is certain, that almost the only period of comparative peace and comfort enjoyed by the Báb from the beginning of his mission till his martyrdom was the year which he passed in Isfahán under the protection of the wise and powerful Georgian eunuch.

NOTE K.

Mullá Ṣadrá and His Philosophy.

Gobineau in his *Religions et Philosophies dans l'Asie Centrale* (pp. 81—91) has given so admirable an account of the life of this great philosopher and of the part played by him in the revival of metaphysical learning in Persia that any very detailed notice of his career on my part would be superfluous. I shall therefore confine myself to reproducing a brief sketch of his biography as it was related to me by a most learned and amiable scholar—himself a pupil of Hájí Mullá Hádí of Sabzawár, whose fame as a metaphysician has almost eclipsed that of the illustrious Mullá Ṣadrá—with whom it was my privilege to study for some time in Teherán. This account agrees in the main with Gobineau's, but differs in some few points.

Mullá Ṣadrá's father was a rich merchant of Shíráż, but though he had reached an advanced age he had no child to whom he might bequeath his wealth. This caused him much sorrow, and he prayed earnestly to God that a son might be vouchsafed to him, making a vow that if his prayer were granted he would bestow a *túmán* a day in alms on the poor. Shortly after this, that which he so earnestly desired came to pass, and a son—afterwards the great Mullá Ṣadrá—was born to him. From an early age the boy gave indications of extraordinary talent and virtue. When his father died, he decided, after consulting his mother, to give the greater portion of the wealth which he had inherited to the poor, reserving only what was sufficient for his modest needs. He then left Shíráz and took up his residence in Isfahán, which was at that time unrivalled in Persia as a seat of learning. On his arrival there he enquired who were the best teachers of philosophy, and was answered that they were three—Mír Dámád, Mír Fandariskí, and Sheykh Behá. To the first of these he forthwith presented himself, and asked advice as to the course of study which he should pursue. "If you want sheer ideas," replied Mír Dámád, "go to Mír Fandariskí; if you want merely eloquence, go to Sheykh Behá; if you want both, come to me." Mullá Ṣadrá accordingly attended with diligence the lectures of all three, but chiefly those of Mír Dámád. After a while Mír Dámád, wishing to make the pilgrimage to Mecca, bade a temporary farewell to his students, and instructed each of them to compose during his absence a treatise on some branch of Philosophy. On his return he asked to see the results of their labours. These he glanced over in private, and all of them he laid aside after a cursory inspection save the treatise composed by Mullá Ṣadrá under the name of *Shawáhid-i-Rubúbiyya* ('Evidences of Divinity')—a treatise to this day most highly esteemed in Persia. A few days after, as he was riding through the streets attended by his disciples, he called Mullá Ṣadrá to him and said:—"*Ṣadrá ján! Kitáb-i-mará az meyán burdí!*" ("My dear Sadrá, you have done away with my book!"), meaning to signify that the pupil had superseded the teacher. Shortly after this Mullá Ṣadrá, having completed his studies, went to Káshán, and thence, after a while, to Ḳum, in the mountains around which city he long lived a secluded and studious life, troubled occasionally by the malice and hostility of the *mullás*.

Gobineau says (*loc. cit.*, p. 89) that Mullá Ṣadrá's philosophy was simply a revival of Avicenna's and contained nothing new; but this, as he himself remarks, is not the general opinion in Persia. The following three points, as I was informed, constitute the chief original features of Mullá Ṣadrá's system:—

(1) The aphorism

بسيط الحقيقة كلّ الاشياء و ليس بشیء منها

"The elementary Reality is all things, yet is no one of them."

(2) The doctrine of "the Union of the Intellect with the Intelligible" (اتحاد عاقل با معقول), according to which the clear apprehension of an idea implies and involves the establishment of a kind of identity between it and the mind which apprehends it.

(3) The doctrine of "the Incorporeality of Imagination" (تجرد خيال)—a doctrine involving the important consequence that Reason (or the development of that principle which stands above Imagination in the evolution of the spiritual faculties) is not a necessary condition of immortality, and hence that not infants only but even animals possess a spiritual part which survives the death of the body.

Mullá Ṣadrá composed a great number of works, whereof the *Asfár* ('Treatises'), in two large volumes, and the *Sha-*

wáhid-i-Rubúbiyya ('Evidences of Divinity') mentioned above, are the most important. His influence on Persian thought has been great; and his relations with the later developments thereof—especially with the Sheykhí school (concerning which see Note E *supra*)—merit a much more careful study than they have yet received.

NOTE L.

The Báb at Mákú and Chihrík.

The Báb was accompanied on his journey to Mákú by his amanuensis Áḳá Seyyid Ḥuseyn of Yezd, Mullá Sheykh 'Alí *'Jenáb-i-'Aẓím'*, Mullá Muḥammad *'Mu'allim-i-Núrí'* (afterwards killed at Sheykh Ṭabarsí)[1], and an escort of twelve horsemen under the command of Muḥammad Beg *Chápárjí*. A full account of this journey, on the authority of Hájí Mírzá Jání of Káshán, who had it directly from the aforesaid Muḥammad Beg, is contained in the *Táríkh-i-Jadíd*. The substance of this account is as follows:—

When Muḥammad Beg was ordered to conduct the Báb to Tabríz and there deliver him over to Bahman Mírzá the governor, he was so averse to undertaking this charge that he feigned illness in hopes of being excused so thankless a task. His orders, however, were peremptorily repeated, and he was obliged to set out. He had been instructed not to take the Báb into the towns which they must pass on the road, and accordingly on approaching Zanján he called a halt at a stone caravansaray situated outside and at some distance from the city. In spite of this, no sooner did their arrival become known than numbers of the inhabitants came out in the hopes of being able to get a

[1] This is according to Ṣubḥ-i-Ezel's statement. According to the *Táríkh-i-Jadíd* his companions were, besides the escort, Áḳá Mírzá 'Abdu'l-Wahháb, Mullá Muḥammad, Áḳá Seyyid Ḥuseyn the amanuensis, his brother Áḳá Seyyid Ḥasan of Yezd, and Seyyid Murtaẓá.

glimpse of the Báb. Muḥammad Beg, being occupied with other business, took no heed of what was passing, while the other men who composed the escort only offered such opposition to the entry of each group of eager visitors as sufficed to procure for themselves a gift of money. Presently an urgent message was brought from Ashraf Khán the governor of Zanján (who was greatly alarmed at the popular excitement caused by the Báb's proximity to the town) ordering Muḥammad Beg at once to start again and proceed to some spot further distant. Muḥammad Beg accordingly informed the Báb, with many apologies and expressions of regret, that he must prepare to resume his journey without delay, to which, with a single expression of surprise and regret at the governor's harshness, he submitted, and they pushed on to a brick caravansaray two *farsakhs* beyond Zanján. At Mílán the Báb's arrival was the signal for a similar demonstration of enthusiasm on the part of the populace, and some two hundred persons who had come out of mere curiosity were converted to the new faith.

Before Tabríz was reached Muḥammad Beg too began to experience that marvellous fascination which the Báb exerted over almost everyone with whom he came in contact, and ere the journey was completed he had become an avowed believer in the divine mission of the captive whom he was conducting into exile. Of those disciples who accompanied the Báb on this journey two only—Áḳá Seyyid Ḥuseyn and Seyyid Murtaza—allowed it to appear that they were his companions. The others used to follow at some distance behind, and only on halting for the night did they seek to find some pretext for approaching their beloved Master. In spite of these precautions, Muḥammad Beg, whose faculties were perhaps quickened by his own recent conversion, did not fail in time to discover what they wished to keep secret from him, for of the change which had been wrought in his opinions and feelings they were not yet aware. One day, however, he opened his heart to them, declaring that when he reflected on the service in which he was engaged he felt himself to be worse than Shimr and Yazíd, and expressing the warmest admiration for the patience, sweetness, gentleness, and holiness of the Báb, "for," said he, "had he chosen to give the slightest hint to the people of Zanján or Mílán that they should effect his deliverance, they would not have given us time to draw our breath ere they had effected their object."

Muḥammad Beg was in hopes that he might be appointed to accompany the Báb to Mákú—his ultimate destination—and this hope he communicated to the Báb, who, however, replied that this was by no means a thing which he desired, for that in *that* journey there would be harshness and cruelty shewn wherein he would not that Muḥammad Beg should bear any part. When they had come within a stage of Tabríz the Báb requested Muḥammad Beg to go on in advance and announce his approach to Bahman Mírzá, to whom he also sent a message praying that he might not be sent to Mákú but might be allowed to remain in Tabríz. To this message the Prince merely replied that it had nothing to do with him, and that the instructions given at the capital must be complied with. Much distressed at being the bearer of such unwelcome tidings, Muḥammad Beg returned to meet the Báb, whom he brought in to his own house at Tabríz. There the Báb remained for several days until the fresh escort which was to conduct him to Mákú arrived. Then the Báb sent Muḥammad Beg with a second message to the Prince, again renewing his request for permission to remain at Tabríz. To this message also Bahman Mírzá turned a deaf ear; and such was Muḥammad Beg's chagrin, and so great the sorrow which he experienced on parting from the Báb (whose new escort would suffer no further delay in starting), that he fell ill of a fever which did not quit him for two months.

No sooner had Muḥammad Beg recovered his health than he set out for Mákú to visit the Báb. On his arrival there he fell at the Báb's feet, entreating him to overlook and condone any fault of which he might have been guilty. The Báb answered that he was not willing that even his enemies should suffer, much less his friends, and that he freely forgave all who had wittingly or unwittingly trespassed against him. He then enquired concerning the details of the disgrace which had befallen two of those who had slighted him—Ashraf Khán and Bahman Mírzá—with which Muḥammad Beg forthwith proceeded to acquaint him; and, on hearing the indignities to which Ashraf Khán had been subjected by the relatives of a woman whom he had seduced, he expressed sorrow that so severe a punishment should have overtaken him.

The confinement to which the Báb was subjected at Mákú was by no means an excessively rigorous one. Not only his amanuensis Áḳá Seyyid Ḥuseyn, but also (according to Ṣubḥ-i-Ezel) Mullá Sheykh 'Alí, and apparently others amongst the most earnest and devoted of his followers, were constantly with him, while many others flocked to Mákú from all parts of Persia and were permitted to hold almost unrestricted converse with their Master. Besides this, continual correspondence was carried on between the Báb and his most active apostles, in spite of the instructions given to 'Alí Khán the warden of Mákú Castle by the Prime Minister Hájí Mírzá Áḳásí to the effect that no such correspondence was to be permitted. Whether 'Alí Khán found himself unable to prevent this correspondence (at any rate without risking a popular tumult), or whether he simply connived at it either from indolence, indifference, or partiality for the Báb, does not very clearly appear. It would at any rate seem that he always treated his prisoner with the utmost respect and deference, toiled daily up the steep road from the village to the Castle (which stood on the summit of a neighbouring hill), and, when questioned by his friends as to the opinion which he had formed of the Báb, would reply that, although he was not clever enough to understand his sayings, he was convinced of his greatness and holiness.

During his sojourn at Mákú the Báb composed a great number of works, amongst the more important of which may be especially mentioned the Persian *Beyán* and the 'Seven Proofs' (*Dalá'il-i-Sab'a*), both of which contain ample internal evidence of having been written at this period (B. ii, pp. 912—913). Indeed, if we may credit a statement made in the *Táríkh-i-Jadíd* on the authority of Mírzá 'Abdu'l-Wahháb, the various writings of the Báb current in Tabríz alone amounted in all to not less than a million verses! The Prime Minister himself, Hájí Mírzá Áḳásí, was made the object of a homily entitled "The Sermon of Wrath" (خطبهٔ قهریه) "which," says the author of the *Táríkh-i-Jadíd*, "if anyone will peruse, he shall understand the true meaning of inward Strength and Power." Whether this document reached the eyes of him for whom it was intended and roused him to take further steps for the more effectual isolation of its author is uncertain; but at all events fresh instructions of a more peremptory character were despatched by the Prime Minister to the Warden of Mákú commanding him at once to put a stop to the interchange of letters between the Báb and his followers. 'Alí Khán replied that he was absolutely unable to do this; whereupon orders were issued by the Prime Minister for the removal of the Báb from Mákú to Chihríḳ. 'Alí Khán, though his own action had brought about this transference, communicated the announcement thereof to the Báb with every expression of distress and concern, but the latter sternly cut short his apologies saying, "Why dost thou lie? Thou didst thyself write, and dost thou excuse thyself?" So the Báb was taken to Chihríḳ and placed in the custody of Yaḥyá Khán.

The *Táríkh-i-Jadíd*, ever disposed towards the marvellous if not the miraculous, relates that Yaḥyá Khán saw the Báb in a dream a short time before his actual arrival at Chihríḳ, and that this dream he related to *Jenáb-i-'Aẓím* (Mullá Sheykh 'Alí), declaring at the same time that should the Báb's appearance prove to be such as he had seen in his vision he would know for a surety that this was indeed the promised Imám Mahdí. On the Báb's arrival Yaḥyá Khán went out to meet him and beheld his face even as the face in the dream. Thereupon, being greatly moved, he bowed himself in reverence before the Báb, and brought him in with all honour into his own house, neither would he sit down in his presence without permission. In consequence of the impression thus produced on Yaḥyá Khán, the Báb, in spite of Hájí Mírzá Áḳásí's stringent orders, was not much more isolated from his followers at Chihríḳ than he had been at Mákú.

Ṣubḥ-i-Ezel's version is quite different, and is not only much more probable in itself, but also rests on much better authority, since through his hands passed the greater part of the correspondence which was carried on with the Báb. According to this version, the Báb's confinement at Chihríḳ was of the most rigorous kind, and it was only with the greatest difficulty that letters could be conveyed to or from him. Some of the expedients resorted to for this purpose were described by Mullá Sheykh 'Alí to Ṣubḥ-i-Ezel and by him to me. Sometimes the letter to be conveyed to the Báb was carefully wrapped up in a waterproof covering, weighted, and sunk in a vessel filled with *mást* (curdled milk), which vessel the Bábí messenger would pray the guards to convey as a trifling present to the captive. Sometimes the letter was enclosed in a candied walnut of the kind called *juzghand*. The bearer, on his arrival at Chihríḳ, would enter into conversation with the sentries, offer them a share of his *juzghands*, and finally, having sufficiently ingratiated himself with them, request them to carry a handful of sweetmeats to their prisoner. If they consented to do this, the walnut containing the letter was dexterously slipped into the handful destined for the Báb.

A passage from M. Mochenin's memoir quoted by Kazem-Beg (i. p. 371) would seem, however, to imply that even at Chihríḳ the Báb was permitted to address those who came to hear and see him. "The concourse of people," he says, "was so great that, the court not being spacious enough to contain all the audience, the greater number remained in the street listening attentively to the verses of the new Ḳur'án." But at all events the Báb was subjected to a closer and more rigorous confinement at Chihríḳ than he had been at Mákú. Hence he used to call the former "*the Grievous Mountain*" (جبل شدید)[1], and the latter "*the Open Mountain*" (جبل باسط). His gaoler at Chihríḳ was moreover a coarse and unsympathetic creature, to whom Áḳá Seyyid Ḥuseyn of Yezd gave the name of "*Fierce and Terrible*" (غلاظ شداد)[2].

The last point which requires discussion is this:—of the three and a half years which elapsed between the death

[1] It will be noticed that the numerical value of the word شدید (318) is the same as that of the name Chihríḳ (چهریق) for which it stands.

[2] Ḳur'án, lxvi. 6.

of Minúchihr Khán (Rabí'ul-Avval A. H. 1263 = Feb.—March A. D. 1847) and the execution of the Báb (Sha'bán 27th A.H. 1266 = July 8th A.D. 1850) what portion was passed by the Báb at Mákú and Chihríḳ respectively? As the Báb did not leave Isfahán till after Minúchihr Khán's death, we may, allowing for the time consumed in travelling and probable delays, assume that he did not reach Mákú much before June A.D. 1847. Kazem-Beg says that he remained there six months ere he was transferred to Chihríḳ, where, if this statement be correct, he must have arrived about the beginning of A.D. 1848. From Chihríḳ he was brought to Tabríz to undergo his first examination (see subsequent note) during the life of Muḥammad Sháh, who died on Sept. 4th, A.D. 1848; and from Chihríḳ he was again brought to Tabríz in July A.D. 1850 to suffer martyrdom. It would therefore seem that of the last three years of the Báb's life six months (from June to December, A.D. 1847) were spent at Mákú, and two years and a half (January A.D. 1848—July A.D. 1850) at Chihríḳ.

NOTE M.

The first examination of the Báb at Tabríz.

Of what took place in this assembly we have four accounts besides that which is contained in the present work, whereof two—those contained in the *Rawżatu 's-Safá* and the *Ḳiṣaṣu 'l-'Ulamá*—are almost identical. The version contained in the *Násikhu 't-Tawáríkh* is substantially a mere condensation of these, and contains little new matter, though the order of the proceedings is somewhat differently given. The account contained in the *Táríkh-i-Jadíd* is relatively very brief, and in the main agrees with what is stated in the present work. Bábí tradition, in short, supplies us with no detailed narrative of this event, the reason for this being apparently that the assembly in question was held with closed doors, and that the Báb (so far as we can tell) was unsupported by the presence of a single friend.

As to the credibility of the Muhammadan version, Kazem-Beg has some very pertinent remarks in his first article (pp. 360—363). While fully sharing the doubts which he expresses as to the historical value of this version, I have nevertheless thought it worth reproducing in this place, believing that, whether it be true or false, it will not be found altogether uninteresting as a specimen of the method of judicial enquiry adopted by an Ecclesiastical Court in Persia. I have in the main followed the account given in the *Rawẓatu 'ṣ-Ṣafá* and the *Kiṣaṣu 'l-'Ulamá*, except in a few cases where a question or answer seemed to be more clearly put in the *Násikhu 't-Tawáríkh.*

In the *Násikhu 't-Tawáríkh* this conference is described as having taken place in the year A.H. 1263. If this were so[1], it must have been at the close of that year (which ended on December 8th, A.D. 1847), inasmuch as the Báb was, according to all authorities (including Dr A. H. Wright of Urúmiyya), brought to Tabríz *from Chihríḳ*, whither (as I have attempted to shew in the previous note) he was not transferred much before the beginning of A.D. 1848.

The chief persons who took part in this examination of the Báb were :—

Náṣiru 'd-Dín Mírzá, now King, then Crown-Prince, of Persia, who was at this time about sixteen years old, and on whom the government of Ázarbaiján had only recently been bestowed; *Hájí Mullá Maḥmúd* entitled *Niẓámu 'l-'Ulamá*, the young Prince's tutor; *Mullá Muḥammad Mámaḳání* entitled *Ḥujjatu 'l-Islám*, an eminent Sheykhí divine; *Hájí Murtaẓá-Ḳulí Marandí* entitled *'Ilmu 'l-Hudá; Háji Mírzá 'Alí Aṣghar* the *Sheykhu 'l-Islám;* and (according to the present work) *Mírzá Aḥmad* the *Imám-Jum'a.* Shortly after these had assembled the Báb was brought in, and (according to the Musulmán, but not the Bábí, accounts) was motioned to a seat of honour. The following dialogue then ensued :—

Hájí Mullá Maḥmúd.—"The command of His Imperial Majesty the King is that you should set forth your

[1] But see remarks on pp. 186—187 *supra.*

claims in the presence of the doctors of Islám, so that the truth or falsehood thereof may be established. Although I myself am not one of the learned and only occupy the position of an attendant, I am free from prejudice, and my conversion will not be without importance. Now I have three questions to ask of you. *Firstly*, are these books composed in the fashion and style of the Ḳur'án, of Epistles, and of Prayers, and disseminated through all parts and regions of Persia yours, and did you compose them, or do men [wrongly] attribute them to you?"

Báb.—"They are from God."

H. M. M.—"I am no great scholar: if they are yours, say so; and if not, don't."

Báb.—"They are mine."

H. M. M. "The meaning of your saying 'They are from God' is that your tongue is like the Tree on Sinai[1]—

[2]روا باشد انا الحق از درختی *
* چرا نبود روا از نیك بختی

[3]این همه آوازها از شه بود *
* گرچه از حلقوم عبد الله بود"

Báb.—"Mercy be upon you!"

H. M. M.—"They call you '*Báb*.' Who gave you this name, and where did they give it? What is the meaning of '*Báb*'? And are you content with this name or not?"

Báb.—"God gave me this name."

H. M. M.—"Where? In the House of the Ka'ba, or in the 'Holy House,'[4] or in the 'Frequented House'?"[5]

1 i.e. The Burning Bush. Cf. Ḳur'án xxvii, 7—9; and xxviii, 29—30.

2 "If [to say] 'I am the Truth' (i.e. God) be right in a tree,
Why should it not be right in some favoured man?"

3 See note 1 at the foot of p. 23 *supra*.

4 Jerusalem.

5 See Ḳur'án lii, v. 4, and explanations in the commentaries.

Báb.—"Wherever it was, it is a divine name."

H. M. M.—"In that case of course you are content with a 'divine name.' What is the meaning of '*Báb*'?"

Báb.—"The same as the word '*Báb*' in [the tradition]—

"انا مدينة العلم و على بابها"[1] *

H. M. M.—"Then you are the 'Gate of the City of Knowledge'?"

Báb.—"Yes."

H. M. M.—"Praise be to God! For forty years have I journeyed seeking to meet with one of the 'Gates,' and it was not granted to me. Now, praise be to God, you have come to me in my own country, even to my very pillow! If it be so, and I can but assure myself that you are the 'Gate,' give me, I pray, the office of shoe-keeper!"

Báb.—"Surely you are Hájí Mullá Maḥmúd?"

H. M. M.—"Yes."

Báb.—"Your dignity is great; great offices should be bestowed upon you."

H. M. M.—"I only want that office, and it is sufficient for me."

The Prince.—"We too will leave and deliver over this throne to you who are the 'Gate.'"

H. M. M.—"As the Prophet or some other wise man hath said—

[2]العلم علمان علم الابدان و علم الاديان *

I ask, then, in Medicine, what occurs in the stomach when a person suffers from indigestion? Why are some cases amenable to treatment? And why do some go on to permanent dyspepsia or syncope,[3] or terminate in hypochondriasis?"

[1] "I am the City of Knowledge and 'Alí is its Gate (*Báb*)."

[2] "Knowledge is twofold—knowledge of bodies, and knowledge of religions;" i.e. Medicine and Theology are the only two branches of science which are really worthy of attention.

[3] غشيان, swooning or syncope. For fainting-fits in connection with dyspepsia, see Avicenna's *Ḳánún* (Rome, A.D. 1593), vol. i, p. 440.

Báb.—"I have not studied Medicine."

The Prince.—"If so be that you are the 'Gate of Knowledges,' yet say 'I have not studied Medicine,' this is quite incompatible with your claim!"

H. M. M.—(*To the Prince*) "It is of no consequence, for this is but the art of the veterinarian and is not included amongst sciences; so that herein is no incompatibility with Báb-hood." (*To the Báb*) "Theology consists of the sciences of 'Principles' (اصول) and 'Applications' (فروع). The science of 'Principles' has a beginning (مبدأ) and a conclusion (معاد). Say then: are [the Divine Attributes of] Knowledge, Hearing, Seeing, and Power identical with the [Divine] Essence, or otherwise?"

Báb.—"Identical with the Essence."

H. M. M.—"Then God is multiple and composite; the [Divine] Essence and the [Divine] Knowledge are two things like vinegar and syrup which have yet become identical; [God is] compounded of [the Divine] Essence *plus* Knowledge, of [the Divine] Essence *plus* Power, and so on. Besides this, the [Divine] Essence is 'without Opposite, without Antithesis.' But Knowledge, which is identical with the [Divine] Essence, has an opposite, which is Ignorance. Besides these two objections, God knows, the Prophet knows, and I know: we [therefore] partake in Knowledge. We also have a 'ground of distinction'; for the Knowledge of God is from Himself, while our knowledge is from Him. Therefore God is compounded of a 'ground of distinction' and a 'ground of identity.' But God is not composite."

Báb.—" I have not studied Philosophy." (*The Prince smiles, but preserves silence.*)

H. M. M.—"The science of 'Applications' is elucidated from the Book and the Code[1], and the understanding of the Book and the Code depends on many sciences, such as Grammar, Rhetoric, and Logic. Do you who are the Báb conjugate *Ḳála*?"

Báb.—"What *Ḳála*?"

[1] i.e. the Ḳur'án and the Traditions.

H. M. M.—"*Ḳála, yaḳúlu, ḳawlan.*" (*Begins to say the past tense after the fashion of a school-boy*—"*Ḳála, ḳálá, ḳálú; ḳálat, ḳálatá, ḳulná.*" *Then, addressing the Báb*) "Do you say the rest."

Báb.—"I learned it in childhood, but I have forgotten it."

H. M. M.—"Give the derivatives of *Ḳála.*"

Báb.—"How give the derivatives?"

H. M. M. (*after giving some of the derivatives*)—"Now give the rest."

Báb.—"I told you, I have forgotten."

H. M. M.—"Explain this verse of the Glorious Ḳur'án :—

[1] هُوَ ٱلَّذِي يُرِيكُمُ ٱلْبَرْقَ خَوْفًا وَ طَمَعًا *

and tell me also what is the construction of خَوْفًا وَ طَمَعًا ?"

Báb.—"I don't remember."

H. M. M.—"What is the meaning of this tradition :—

لعن الله العيون فانّها ظلمت العين الواحدة * ?"[2]

Báb.—"I don't know."

H. M. M.—"Explain the meaning of this tradition of what passed between Ma'mún the Caliph and His Highness Riẓá the eighth Imám :—

[1] "*It is He who maketh you to behold the lightning, a fear and a hope.*" Ḳur'án, xiii, 13.

[2] "*May God curse the eyes, for verily they have acted unjustly towards the one eye.*" I regret to say that I have failed to ascertain by whom and on what occasion these words were uttered or to what they allude.

[1] قال مأمون ما الدليل على خلافة جدك على بن ابيطالب

قال اية انفسنا قال لولا نسائنا قال لولا ابنائنا فسكت مأمون *

What was the nature of the argument employed by Riẓá (on him be peace), and what the point of Ma'mún's objection and of Riẓá's reply thereto?"

Báb.—"Is it a tradition?"

H. M. M.—"Yes." (*Cites authorities.*) "The circumstances under which the *Súratu 'l-Kawthar* was revealed were, as is well known, the following:—His Highness the Prophet was passing by. 'Ás said, 'This is the childless man!' Shortly afterwards he died, leaving no children. His Highness the Prophet was grieved, and so this Súra was revealed for his consolation. Tell me now, what was the nature of the consolation which it contained?"[2]

Báb.—"Were these indeed the circumstances under which it was revealed?"

[1] "*Ma'mún said, 'What is the proof for* [the right to] *the Caliphate of thine ancestor 'Alí ibn Abí Ṭálib?' He* [i.e. Riẓá] *said, 'The sign of ourselves.' He* [i.e. Ma'mún] *said, 'If it were not for our wives!' He* [i.e. Riẓá] *said, 'If it were not for our sons!' Then Ma'mún was silent.*" By his first answer the Imám Riẓá means that the right of 'Alí and his descendants to the Caliphate is sufficiently proved by their being what they are and connected as they are with the Prophet. Ma'mún objects, 'Yes, that is all very well, but we too are related to the Prophet on the female side;' to which objection the Imám Riẓá replies, 'But *our* connection is in the male line;' for connection in the male line is a much closer tie, as expressed in the following verse from an old Arab poet for which I am indebted to my friend Mr Khalíl Khayyáṭ of Beyrout:—

بنونا بنو ابنائنا و بناتنا * بنوهن ابناء الرجال الاباعد *

"Our sons' sons are our sons, but as for our daughters
Their sons are the sons of strange men."

This, at least, appears to me to be the explanation of the tradition.

[2] Concerning the circumstances under which the *Súratu 'l-Kawthar* was revealed see Ibn Hishám's *Life of Muḥammad*, ed. Wüstenfeld, p. 261.

H. M. M.—"Yes." (*Cites authorities.*)

(*The Báb asks for time to think.*)

H. M. M.—"In the days of our youth we used, according to the dictates of our age, jestingly to repeat this sentence of '*Allúma*[1], whereof I desire you now to explain to me the meaning :—

[2] اذا دخل الرّجل على الخنثى و الخنثى على الانثى وجب
الغسل على الخنثى دون الرّجل و الانثى *

Why should this be so?"

Báb.—(*after reflecting for a while*) "Is this sentence from '*Allúma*?"

The audience (*unanimously*).—"Yes!"

H. M. M.—"Suppose it is not '*Allúma's* but mine, do you nevertheless explain its meaning. After all you are the 'Gate of Knowledge'!"

Báb.—"I cannot think of anything."

H. M. M.—"One of the miracles of the Arabian Prophet is the Ḳur'án, and the miraculous character thereof is derived from its *faṣáḥat* and its *balághat.* What is the definition of *faṣáḥat* and *balághat*? Is the relation which subsists between them *tabáyun, tasáwí, 'umúm wa khuṣúṣ min wajh,* or '*umúm wa khuṣúṣ-i-muṭlaḳ*?"[3]

[1] The title of '*Allúma* ("the very erudite") is used by the Shí'ites to designate one of their great theologians named Ḥasan ibn Yúsuf ibn 'Alí of Ḥilla. According to the *Ḳiṣaṣu'l-'Ulamá* he was born on Ramaẓán 19th, A.H. 648 (December 15th, A.D. 1250), and died on Muḥarram 11th, A.H. 726 (December 18th, A.D. 1325). No less than seventy-five of his works are enumerated.

[2] "*Si vir cum hermaphrodito, hermaphroditus cum muliere rem habet, ab hermaphrodito requiritur ut aquâ se purget, non vero a viro et muliere.*"

[3] *Faṣáḥat* and *balághat* both signify in general "eloquence," but the former especially denotes *correctness of diction* and *chasteness of style*, the latter *moving and affecting language* which *reaches* the hearts of the hearers or causes the speaker to *reach* his object. (See Lane's *Arabic-English Lexicon*, s.v. بلغ and فصح.)

Báb.—"I don't know." (*The audience manifest signs of anger and impatience.*)

H. M. M.—"If you were in doubt between two and three [inclinations in prayer] what would you do?"[1]

Báb. "I would assume two."

Mullá Muḥammad Mámáḳání:—"O impious one! You do not even know what to do in cases of doubt in prayer, and yet you claim to be the Báb!"

Báb.—"I would assume three."

The "four relations" recognized by Muhammadan logicians and here enumerated are in detail as follows:—(1) *Tasáwí* ("Equivalence" or "Co-extensiveness"), as "man" and "endowed with articulate speech." (2) *Tabáyun* ("Diversity"), as "man" and "stone." (3) *'Umúm wa khuṣúṣ i-mutlaḳ* ("Relation of genus and species absolutely"), as "animal" and "man." (4) *'Umúm wa khuṣúṣ min wajh* ("Relation of genus and species under one aspect"), as "animal" and "white."

[1] This question, with what immediately follows it, refers to the duty incumbent on a Musulmán who, while engaged in the performance of one of the prescribed prayers, becomes conscious of a doubt as to whether he has duly fulfilled some one or more of its essential elements, *e.g.* as to whether he has performed two or three inclinations (*rak'a*). Every possible case of doubt is provided for in that section of Muhammadan jurisprudence which is entitled الشّكّ في الصلوة concerning which see Querry's *Droit Musulman* (Paris, 1871) vol. i, pp. 107—109. The general rule is thus stated at p. 21 of the catechism called *Su'ál ú Jawáb* ("Questions and answers") composed by Hájí Seyyid Muḥammad Báḳir of Isfahán and printed at Teherán in A.H. 1247 (A.D. 1831—2):—"He who is doubtful assumes the [performance of the] act concerning which he doubts, whether it relates to the number of inclinations (*rak'a*) or not; except in cases where [the performance of] the act concerning which he doubts would cause nullity [of the prayer], when he assumes its omission. If, then, he be doubtful whether it is two or three inclinations [which he has performed], he assumes three; if he be doubtful whether he has performed the inclination or the prostration or not, he assumes that he has performed them; and if he be doubtful whether he has performed the recitation (*ḳará'at*), he assumes that he has performed it. But [on the other hand] if he be doubtful whether he has inclined twice or once he assumes that he has inclined [only] once; and if he be doubtful whether he has performed four inclinations of prayer or five, he assumes that it is four."

M. M. M. "Evidently if it is not two you must say three."

H. M. M. "Three is also wrong. Why did you not ask whether it was in the morning or evening prayer that I was in doubt, and whether it was after the inclination or before the inclination, or after the completion of two prostrations?"

M. M. M.—"You ought to give thanks, for had he said 'I would assume two' (inasmuch as engaging in an indubitable duty demands fulfilment of that indubitable duty) what would you have done then[1]?" (*To the Báb*)

"Did you write:—اول من امن بی نور محمّد و علی?[2]

Is this expression yours or not?"

Báb. "Yes, it is mine."

M. M. M.—"Then in that case you were the leader and they were followers, and you must be superior to them?"

Hájí Murtazá-Kulí Marandí.—"The Lord of the Universe has said:—

[3]و اعلموا انّما غنمتم من شیٔ فانّ للّه خمسه و للرّسول

[1] If I have rightly understood this rather obscure expression (شغل ذمّه یقینی برائت ذمّه یقینی میخواهد) it means that the undertaking of an obligation such as prayer necessitates and requires the due discharge of all that is properly involved therein, without which it is null and void. Hence if it were necessary in a case of doubt such as is indicated above to assume that only two inclinations had been performed (or, in other words, to assume the minimum instead of the maximum), then all persons who had followed the rule ordinarily received would have been guilty of numerous sins of omission for which they would be held responsible.

[2] "*The first to believe in me was the Light of Muḥammad and* [the Light of] '*Alí.*"

[3] "*And know that whenever ye seize anything as a spoil, to God belongs a fifth thereof, and to His Apostle......*" Ḳur'án, viii, 42.

while you in your Ḳur'án say ثُلُثُه[1]. On what authority, and why?"

Báb.—"A third is the half of a fifth. What difference does it make?"

(*The audience laugh*).

H. M.-Ḳ. M.— "In how many ways is nine divisible?"

(*The Báb gives no answer*).

H. M. M.

"چند ازین الفاظ و اضمار و مجاز

سوز خواهم سوز و با ان سوز ساز"[2]

I am not tied down to words; shew me a miracle suitable to your claims, so that I may become your follower, and on my submission many will set their footsteps within the circle of devotion to you, for I am well known as learned, and the learned man will never follow the ignorant."

Báb.—"What miracle do you desire?"

H. M. M.—"His Majesty the King Muḥammad Sháh is sick. Restore him to health."

The Prince.—"Why go so far? Are not you present? Let him exert an influence over your being and restore you

[1] "*A third thereof.*" As a matter of fact the ordinances contained in the Persian *Beyán* relative to the disposal of spoils taken from infidels do not accord with the statement here made, which is probably quite fictitious. They will be found in *Váhid* v, *ch.* vi, and are in substance as follows:—(1) One-fifth of the spoils, together with whatever is incomparable in value or beauty, belongs to the Báb. If he be no longer alive it is to be held in trust for "Him whom God shall manifest." (2) Of what remains the warriors who have won it take what suffices for their needs. (3) The residue is given to the poor, all of whom, so far as possible, are to be made partakers in the bounty. Should anything still remain over, it may be expended on building or repairing shrines etc.

[2] "*How long these words and this concealment and metaphor? I would burn, burn, and acquiesce in that burning.*"

Masnaví (ed. 'Alá'u'd-Dawla, p. 143, line 8).

to youthfulness, so that you may ever continue in attendance on our stirrup. We too, on witnessing the accomplishment of this miracle, will resign this throne to him."[1]

Báb.—"It is not in my power."

H. M. M.—"Then honour is not rendered without some reason. O dumb in the realms of words and dumb in the realms of ideas, what virtue then do you possess?"

Báb.—"I can utter eloquent words" (*Recites*)

"الحمد لله الّذى خلق السّمواتَ"[2]

(*pronouncing the last word with final fat-ḥa*).

Prince (*smiling*).—

"و ما بتا و الف قد جمّعا *[3]

يكسرفى النصب و فى الجرّ معا * "

Báb.—"My name 'Alí Muḥammad corresponds with *Rabb*" (Lord).[4]

H. M. M.—"Every 'Alí Muḥammad and Muḥammad 'Alí corresponds with *Rabb.* Besides in that case you should claim to be the Lord rather than the Báb."

Báb.—"I am that person for whose appearance ye have waited a thousand years."

H. M. M.—"That is to say you are the Mahdí, the Lord of Religion?"[5]

[1] There is something almost ludicrous in the eagerness wherewith the Crown-Prince interposes to check the miracle designed to restore his dying father to health.

[2] "*Praise be to God who created the heavens.*"

[3] "That which forms its plural in *alif* and *tá* is pointed with *kesra* alike in the objective and in the dependent cases." This sentence is from the well-known versified Arabic Grammar called the *Alfiyya*, and will be found on p. 19 of Dieterici's edition of that work (Leipsic, 1851).

[4] The sum of the letters in *'Alí Muḥammad* is 202, which is also the numerical equivalent of *Rabb*.

[5] i.e. the Twelfth Imám. See Note O *infra*.

Báb.—"Yes."

H. M. M.—"The same in person, or generically?"

Báb.—"In person."

H. M. M.—"What is your name, and what are the names of your father and mother? Where is your birth-place? And how old are you?"

Báb.—"My name is 'Alí Muḥammad; my mother was named Khadíja and my father Mírzá Riẓá the cloth-seller; my birth-place is Shíráz; and of my life, behold, thirty-five years have elapsed."[1]

H. M. M.—"The name of the Lord of Religion is Muḥammad; his father was named Ḥasan and his mother Narjis; his birth-place was Surra-man-Ra'a; and his age is more than a thousand years. There is the most complete variance. And besides I did not send you."

Báb.—"Do you claim to be God?"

H. M. M.—"Such an Imám is worthy of such a God."

Báb.—"I can in one day write two thousand verses. Who else can do this?"

H. M. M.—"When I resided at the Supreme Shrines I had a secretary who used to write two thousand verses a day. Eventually he became blind. You must certainly give up this occupation, or else you too will go blind."

The conference then broke up, and the Báb was taken back to the house of Muḥammad Káẓim Khán the *Farrásh-báshí*. Next day he was again brought before the Prince and the doctors, who sentenced him to the bastinado. The Muhammadan historians admit that the *farráshes* were still, in spite of what had taken place at the examination on the previous day, so strongly inclined to sympathize with the Báb that they positively refused to take part in administering the punishment decreed, the execution of which therefore devolved on the servants of Hájí Mullá Maḥmúd and the Sheyku 'l-Islám. It is of course asserted

[1] Kazem-Beg (i, p. 334, note 4) bases the calculation whereby he arrives at the date of the Báb's birth on this passage, which, as a matter of fact, affords a strong proof of the falsity of the whole narrative wherein it occurs, since the Báb's age certainly did not exceed 29 years at this time (see Note C *supra*).

by the Musulmán historians that the Báb again recanted and revoked all his claims under the chastisement inflicted upon him, whereupon he was released and sent back to Chihríḳ.

It is difficult to decide to what measure of credence the above narrative is entitled. Very probably such questions as are there recorded—and assuredly some of them are sufficiently frivolous and even indecent—were asked; but, even though the Báb may have been unable to answer them, it is far more likely that, as stated in the *Táríkh-i-Jadíd*, he preserved a dignified silence than that he gave utterance to the absurdities attributed to him by the Muhammadan writers. These, indeed, spoil their own case; for, desiring to prove that the Báb was not endowed with superhuman wisdom, they represent him as displaying an ignorance which we can scarcely credit. That the whole examination was a farce throughout, that the sentence was a foregone conclusion, that no serious attempt to apprehend the nature and evidence of the Báb's claim and doctrine was made, and that from first to last a systematic course of brow-beating, irony, and mockery was pursued appear to me to be facts proved no less by the Muhammadan than by the Bábí accounts of these inquisitorial proceedings.

NOTE N.

THE BÁB'S CLAIM TO BE THE IMÁM MAHDÍ.

The Báb's original claim was, as has been already explained in Note D, that he was the 'Gate' whereby men could communicate with the Ḳá'im, Imám-Mahdí, or Twelfth Imám. At a later period of his mission, however, he declared himself to be none other than the Imám himself, and, as has been set forth in the previous Note (p. 288 *supra*), it was this claim which he boldly advanced before his inquisitors at Tabríz. The advancement of this claim certainly marks a very important point in the development of the Báb's doctrine, but as Gobineau (p. 159) very acutely observes in speaking of Mullá Ḥuseyn's announcement thereof to Minúchihr Khán, "il faut dire ici, pour prévenir toute erreur, qu'en assimilant le Bâb au douzième Imam, le missionnaire cherchait à se faire comprendre de la foule et à gagner ses sympathies, absolument comme saint Paul lorsqu'il révélait aux Athéniens que le Dieu qu'il leur annonçait était ce Dieu inconnu auquel ils avaient déjà élevé un autel. C'était des deux parts une façon de parler, et on verra plus tard qu'il n'y a aucun rapport entre l'idée que les Bâbys se font du *Point,* et ce que les musulmans pensent au sujet de l'Imam Mehdy."

From the present history (pp. 20 and 24) it would appear that this new claim was publicly advanced by the Báb for the first time during his examination before the 'Ulamá of Tabríz at the end of A.D. 1847 or the beginning of A.D. 1848. The following passage in the *Táríkh-i-Jadíd* affords corroborative evidence of this :—

بعد از آنکه آن حضرت بقلعهٔ چهریق تشریف بردند با وجود شدّت نهی حاجیٔ مرحوم بنحو حکمت اصحاب واحباب مراوده مینمودند و در آن نواحی جمعی بشرف ایمان فائز شدند و تصدیق نمودند و تا زمانیکه یحیی خان حکومت داشتند نهایت احترام را نسبت بآن حضرت بعمل می آوردند و آن حضرت نظر باقتضای زمان و مقتضیات مصلحت و حکمت و استعداد عباد اظهار قائمیّت خودرا در چهریق فرمودند اگرچه بعضی در اواخر زمان توقّف ماکو میدانند *

"After His Highness [the Báb] had removed to the

Castle of Chihríķ, his companions and friends, notwithstanding the rigorous prohibition of the late Hájí [Mírzá Áķásí], still continued to hold intercourse with him in a cautious manner, and a number of persons in that neighbourhood attained the dignity of belief and were converted. And so long as Yaḥyá Khán held the office of governor he used to observe the utmost respect towards His Highness [the Báb]. And His Highness [the Báb], having regard to the exigencies of the time, the requirements of expediency and caution, and the capacity of men, [first] made himself known as the Ķá'im in Chihríķ; though some believe that [he did so] during the latter part of the period of his sojourn at Mákú."

In the Persian Beyán (of which the greater part, if not the whole, was composed at Mákú) I have found two passages wherein the Báb identifies himself more or less clearly with the Imám Mahdí. The first of these passages occurs in *Váḥid* viii, *ch.* 17, and runs as follows:—

چنانچه در ظهور [نقطهٔ][1] فرقان شنیدی کلّ مؤمنین
بانجیل منتظر بودند احمد موعودرا و شنیدی [که][2] بر آن
شمس حقیقت در بیست و سه سال [ظهور خود][3] چه
گذشت حتّی آنکه فرمود ما اوذی نبیٌّ مثل ما اوذیت با
آنکه کلّ از برای ظهور او تضرّع و ابتهال مینمودند و[4]
بقول عیسی در حقّ او عمل میکردند[5] ولی حمد خدایرا[6] که
در آن روز نبودی ولی در ظهور [نقطهٔ][7] بیان بودی که

[1] B omits. [2] B omits. [3] B omits. [4] B reads که.
[5] B reads کنند. [6] B reads خدارا. [7] B omits.

کلّ مؤمنین برسول الله[1] منتظرند[2] ظهور مهدیٔ موعودرا
زیرا که این حدیث از رسول اللّه هست و عامّه و خاصّه[3]
بر آن متّفق اند[4] و شبههٔ نیست که جوهر ایمان منحصر
بود باثنی[5] عشریّه [و][6] قطع اسلام همین [قطع][7] ظاهر
است که [اهل آن][8] خودرا اثنی[9] عشریه میگویند و بظاهر
فارس‌را [اهل][10] دار العلم میگویند با وجود آنکه شجرهٔ
حقیقت طالع واحدی[11] از اهل آن نشناخت اورا[12] بعد از
شناختن ظاهر [است][13] حدّ [بعد][14] ایشان که همان کافی
است[15] در ذلّ ایشان و حال آنکه شب و روز العجل العجل
میگویند *

"As thou hast heard, at the manifestation of the *Nuḳṭa-i-Furḳán* [i.e. Muḥammad, who was in his time the 'Point of Revelation'] all those who were believers in the Gospel were expecting the promised Aḥmad,[16] and thou hast

[1] B inserts ع.   [2] B reads منتظر بودند.   [3] B reads خواصّه.
[4] B reads معتقدند.   [5] B reads اثنا.   [6] B omits.
[7] B omits.   [8] B omits.   [9] B reads اثنا.   [10] B omits.
[11] B reads احدی.   [12] B inserts و.   [13] B omits.
[14] B omits.   [15] B reads کافیست.

[16] In Muhammadan tradition Christ is said to have foretold the coming of Muḥammad in the words يأتى من بعدى احدٌ اسمه احمد "One shall come after me whose name is Aḥmad". This tra-

heard what befel that Sun of Truth during the twenty-three years of his mission, so that he said, 'No prophet hath been afflicted as I have been afflicted.' Yet all were entreating and craving his appearance, and, in the words of Jesus, working for him. Praise be to God that in that day thou wast not! But thou wast in the manifestation of the *Nuḳṭa-i-Beyán* [i.e. the Báb, the 'Point of Revelation'] when all believers in the Apostle of God were expecting the appearance of the promised Mahdí; for this tradition is from the Apostle of God, and all, simple and gentle, are agreed therein. Now there is no doubt that the substance of Faith was confined to the Shí'ites, and that the sect of Islám is this same outward sect whereof the adherents call themselves Shí'ites; while men avowedly call Fárs the 'Abode of Knowledge':[1] Yet, although the Tree of Truth arose, not one of the people recognized it [even] after perceiving it. The degree of their remoteness is evident, for this sufficeth unto their abasement; yet night and day they exclaim 'speed! speed!'[2]

The second passage occurs in *Váḥid* ix, *ch.* 3, and runs as follows:—

و ملتفت باش حق التفات که امر بسیار دقیق است در
حینیکه[3] اوسع [است][4] از سموات و ارض و ما بینهما مثلاً
اگر [کلّ][5] منتظرین بقول عیسی یقین نموده بودند ظهور

dition is based on the prophecies relating to the coming of the Παράκλητος, for which word the Muhammadans would substitute Περικλυτός, whereof the signification is nearly the same as Aḥmad or Muḥammad. (See Ibn Hishám's *Life of Muḥammad*, ed. Wüstenfeld, pp. 149—150.)

[1] The official title of Shíráz is دار العلم "The Abode of Knowledge".

[2] The Shí'ites, whenever they mention the Imám Mahdí, add the formula عجّل الله فرجه "May God hasten his joy!"

[3] B reads زمینی که. [4] B omits. [5] B omits.

احمدی را[1] یك نفر منحرف نمیشد از قول عیسی و همچنین در ظهور نقطهٔ بیان[2] اگر [کلّ][3] یقین کنند باینکه همان مهدیٔ موعود است که رسول خدا خبر داده یك نفر از مؤمنین بقرآن منحرف نمیشد[4] از قول رسول اللّه[5] و همچنین در ظهور من یظهره اللّه همین مطلب[6] مشاهده کن [که][7] اگر کلّ یقین کنند [که این][8] همان من یظهره اللّه است که نقطهٔ بیان خبر[9] داده احدی منحرف نمیشود *

"Consider with due attention, for the matter is very strait, even while it is more spacious than the heavens and the earth and what is between them. For instance, if all those who were expecting [the fulfilment] of the saying of Jesus had been assured of the manifestation of Aḥmad [i.e. Muḥammad], not one would have turned aside from the saying of Jesus. So likewise in the manifestation of the *Nuḳṭa-i-Beyán* [i.e. the Báb] if all should be assured that this is that same Mahdí [whose coming was] promised, whom the Apostle of God foretold, not one of the believers in the Ḳur'án would have turned aside from the saying of the Apostle of God. So likewise in the manifestation of Him whom God shall manifest behold the same thing, for should all be assured that he is that same 'He whom God shall manifest' whom the *Nuḳṭa-i-Beyán* foretold, not one would turn aside."

[1] B reads احمد رسول الله. [2] B inserts که. [3] B omits.
[4] B reads نمیشدند. [5] B reads خدا. [6] B adds را.
[7] B omits. [8] B omits. [9] B reads خبری.

NOTE O.

On certain points of Shi'ite doctrine referred to in the text.

1. *The Occultation of the Twelfth Imám.* The cardinal point wherein the Shi'ites (as well as the other sects included under the more general term of Imámites) differ from the Sunnites is the doctrine of the Imámate. According to the belief of the latter, the vicegerency (خلافت) of the Prophet is a matter to be determined by the choice and election of his followers, and the visible head of the Musulmán world is qualified for the lofty position which he holds less by any special divine grace than by a combination of orthodoxy and administrative capacity. According to the Imámite view, on the other hand, the vicegerency is a matter altogether spiritual; an office conferred by God alone, first by His Prophet, and afterwards by those who so succeeded him, and having nothing to do with the popular choice or approval. In a word, the Caliph (خليفه) of the Sunnís is merely the outward and visible Defender of the Faith: the Imám of the Shi'ites is the divinely-ordained successor of the Prophet, one endowed with all perfections and spiritual gifts, one whom all the faithful must obey, whose decision is absolute and final, whose wisdom is superhuman, and whose words are authoritative. The general term *Imámite* is applicable to all who hold this latter view without reference to the way in which they trace the succession, and therefore includes such sects as the *Báķirís* and *Isma'ílís* as well as the Shi'ites or "*Church of the Twelve*" (مذهب اثنى عشريه), as they are more specifically termed, with whom alone we are here concerned. According to these, twelve persons successively held the office of Imám. These twelve are as follows:—

1. *'Alí ibn Abí Ṭálib*, the cousin and first disciple of the Prophet, assassinated by Ibn Muljam at Kúfa, A.H. 40 (A.D. 661).

2. *Ḥasan*, son of 'Alí and Fáṭima, born A.H. 2, poisoned by order of Mu'áwiya I. A.H. 50 (A.D. 670).

3. *Ḥuseyn*, son of 'Alí and Fáṭima, born A.H. 4, killed at Kerbelá on Muḥarram 10th, A.H. 61 (Oct. 10th, A.D. 680).

4. *'Alí*, son of Ḥuseyn and Shahrbánú (daughter of Yezdigird the last Sásánian king), generally called *Imám Zeynu'l-'Ábidín*, poisoned by Walíd. [See also note 3 on p. 139.]

5. *Muḥammad Báḳir*, son of the above-mentioned Zeynu'l-'Ábidín and his cousin Umm 'Abdi 'lláh the daughter of Imám Ḥasan, poisoned by Ibrahím ibn Walíd.

6. *Ja'far-i-Ṣádiḳ*, son of Imám Muḥammad Báḳir, poisoned by order of Manṣúr the 'Abbáside Caliph. [See note 3 at foot of p. 24.]

7. *Músá Káẓim*, son of Imám Ja'far-i-Ṣádiḳ, born A.H. 129, poisoned by order of Hárúnu 'r-Rashíd A.H. 183.

8. *'Alí ibn Músá er-Riẓá*, generally called Imám Riẓá, born A.H. 153, poisoned near Ṭús in Khurásán by order of the Caliph Ma'mún, A.H. 203, and buried at Mesh-hed, which derives its name and its sanctity from him.

9. *Muḥammad Taḳí*, son of Imám Riẓá, born A.H. 195, poisoned by the Caliph Mu'taṣim at Baghdad A.H. 220.

10. *'Alí Naḳí*, son of Imám Muḥammad Taḳí, born A.H. 213, poisoned at Surra-man-Ra'a A.H. 254.

11. *Ḥasan 'Askarí*, son of Imám 'Alí Naḳí, born A.H. 232, poisoned A.H. 260.

12. *Muḥammad*, son of Imám Ḥasan 'Askarí and Narjis Khátún, called by the Shi'ites "*Imám Mahdí*", "*Ḥujjatu 'lláh*" ("the Proof of God"), "*Baḳiyyatu 'llah*" ("the Remnant of God"), and "*Ḳá'im-i-ál-i-Muḥammad*" ("He who shall arise of the family of Muḥammad"). He bore not only the same name but the same *kunya*—Abu'l-Ḳásim—as the Prophet, and according to the Shi'ites it is not lawful for any other to bear this name and this *kunya* together. He was born at Surra-man-Ra'a, A.H. 255, and succeeded his father in the Imámate A.H. 260[1]. The Shi'ites hold that he did not die, but disappeared in

[1] It is worthy of note that the 'Manifestation' of Mírzá 'Alí Muḥammad the Báb took place exactly one thousand years after this date.

an underground passage in Surra-man-Ra'a, A.H. 329; that he still lives, surrounded by a chosen band of his followers, in one of those mysterious cities, Jábulḳá and Jábulsá; and that when the fulness of time is come, when the earth is filled with injustice, and the faithful are plunged in despair, he will come forth, heralded by Jesus Christ, overthrow the infidels, establish universal peace and justice, and inaugurate a millennium of blessedness. During the whole period of his Imámate, *i.e.* from A.H. 260 till the present day, the Imám Mahdí has been invisible and inaccessible to the mass of his followers, and this is what is signified by the term "*Occultation*" (غيبت). After assuming the functions of Imám and presiding at the burial of his father and predecessor, the Imám Ḥasan 'Askarí, he disappeared from the sight of all save a chosen few, who, one after the other, continued to act as channels of communication between him and his followers. These persons were known as "*Gates*" (ابواب See Note D, pp. 229 and 233 *supra*). The first of them was Abú 'Umar 'Othmán ibn Sa'íd 'Umarí; the second Abú Ja'far Muḥammad ibn 'Othmán, son of the above; the third Ḥuseyn ibn Rúḥ Naw-bakhtí (concerning whom somewhat will be said directly); the fourth Abú 'l-Ḥasan 'Alí ibn Muḥammad Símarí. Of these "Gates" the first was appointed by the Imám Ḥasan 'Askarí, the others by the then-acting "Gate" with the sanction and approval of the Imám Mahdí. This period—extending over sixty-nine years—during which the Imám was still accessible by means of the "Gates" is known as the "*Lesser*" or "*Minor Occultation*" (غيبت صغرى). This was succeeded by the "*Greater*" or "*Major Occultation*" (غيبت كبرى). When Abú 'l-Ḥasan 'Alí, the last of the "Gates", drew near to his latter end, he was urged by the faithful (who contemplated with despair the prospect of complete severance from the Imám) to nominate a successor. This, however, he refused to do, saying لله امرٌ هو بالغه "*God hath a purpose which He will accomplish.*" So on his death all communication between the

Imám and his Church ceased, and the "*Major Occultation*" began and shall continue until the Return of the Imám take place in the fulness of time. Besides these two Occultations mentioned in the text, another, called the "*Least Occultation*" (غيبت اصغر), is recognized by Shi'ite theologians. This last, however, refers to the future, and indicates a period extending from noon on Friday to the morning of Saturday the 10th of Muḥarram, during which the Imám will temporarily disappear after his Return.

2. *The mystical cities of Jábulḳá and Jábulṣá.* Concerning these I will confine myself to citing two passages illustrating the light in which they are regarded by Muḥammadan cosmographers. The first passage is from M. Reinaud's introduction to his translation of Abu'l-fedá's *Geography* (Paris, 1848), and occurs at p. cclvii of that work. It runs as follows:—"Thabary, se plaçant sous un autre point de vue, reproduit la légende sur la montagne de Caf, qui entoure la disque de la terre, et il place deux villes aux points est et ouest: Djaboulka à l'orient, et Djaboulsa à l'occident." The second passage which I wish to quote occurs in al-Ḳazvíní's celebrated work on cosmography. The text thereof will be found on pp. 17—18 of Wüstenfeld's edition. The translation is as follows:—

"JÁBARSÁ. A city in the remotest regions of the East. On the authority of Ibn 'Abbás (may God be satisfied with him):—he says, 'In the remotest East is a city whereof the name is Jábars, and its inhabitants are of the children of Thamúd. And in the remotest West is a city whereof the name is Jábalḳ, and its inhabitants are of the children of 'Ád. And in each one are remnants of these two peoples.' The Jews say that the children of Moses (upon him be peace) fled in the fight with Bukht-Naṣṣar [Nebuchadnezzar], and God (Exalted is He) caused them to journey towards Jábars and to alight therein. And in that place they dwell; none can come unto them nor reckon their number. Again [it is related] on the authority of Ibn 'Abbás (may God be satisfied with him) that the Prophet (may God look favourably upon him and grant him peace) on the night wherein he made the night-journey said to Gabriel (upon him be peace), 'I wish to see the people concerning whom God (exalted is He) hath said, "*Of the people of Moses there is a party who are guided in truth, and act justly according to the same.*"' [Ḳur'án vii, 159]. 'Between thee and them,' said Gabriel (upon him be peace), 'is a journey of six years to go and six years to return; and between thee and them is a river of sand which runs swiftly as the flight of an arrow and ceaseth not save on the Sabbath day; but ask of thy Lord.' So the Prophet prayed, and Gabriel said 'Amen'[1]; and God revealed unto Gabriel, 'Grant him what he hath asked.' So he mounted Buráḳ, who took a few steps, and behold he was in the midst of the people. Then he saluted them, and they asked him 'Who art thou?' He said, 'I am the unlettered Prophet.' They said, 'Yea, thou art he concerning whom Moses was given good tidings, and verily the angels would take thy people by the hand, were it not for their faults.' 'I saw their tombs,' saith the Apostle of God, 'at the doors of their abodes, and I said unto them, "Wherefore this?" They answered, "That we may remember death morning and evening; for did we not do thus, we should only remember it from time to time."' Then he said, 'How is it that I see your buildings equal [in height]?' They answered, 'That none of us may overlook another, and that none may shut out the air from another.' Then he said, 'How is it that I see no King or judge amongst you?' They said, 'We are just one to another and give what is due of ourselves, wherefore we need not any to deal out justice in our midst.' Then he said, 'Wherefore are your streets empty?' They answered, 'We all sow and all reap, and every man amongst us taketh what sufficeth him and leaveth what remaineth for his brother.' Then he said, 'Wherefore do I see these people laughing?' They replied, 'One amongst them hath died.' He said, 'Why then do they laugh?' They answered, 'For joy, because he hath been taken away in

[1] At the suggestion of my friend Mr A. A. Bevan of Trinity College I have ventured to read آمّن for امّن.

the belief of the Unity.' He said, 'What aileth these that they weep?' They answered, 'A child hath been born unto them, and they know not in what faith he will be taken away.' He said, 'When a male child is born unto you, tell me what you do?' They said, 'We fast for a month in thankfulness to God.' He said, 'And if a girl be born unto you?' They answered, 'We fast two months in thankfulness to God, because Moses hath told us that resignation on account of a female child hath a greater reward than resignation on account of a male child.' He said, 'Do ye commit adultery?' They said, 'Doth any one do this thing whom the heaven stoneth not with pebbles from above, and whom the earth swalloweth not from beneath?' He said, 'Do ye take usury?' They answered, 'He alone taketh usury who believeth not in the provision of God.' He said, 'Do ye sicken?' They said, 'We sin not, neither do we sicken; thy people are afflicted with sickness only as an atonement for their sins.' He said, 'Have ye wild beasts and reptiles?' They answered, 'Yes; they pass us by and we pass them by, and they hurt us not.' Then the Prophet proposed unto them his Law; and they asked, 'How shall we do as regards the Pilgrimage, for between us and it is a great distance?' Then the Prophet prayed, 'and,' saith Ibn 'Abbás, 'the earth was rolled up for them so that those of them who would perform the Pilgrimage might do so with [the rest of] mankind. And when' (saith he) 'it was morning, the Prophet told this [to] such as were present of his people, amongst whom was Abú Bekr (may God be satisfied with him). And he said, "Verily it is well with the people of Moses, and God (Exalted is He) knew what was in their hearts, and revealed '*Of those whom We have created is a nation who are guided in truth and thereby act with equity.*'" [Ḳur'án vii, 180.] And Abú Bekr fasted for a month and set at liberty a slave, because God had not preferred the Church of Moses to the Church of Muḥammad (may God look favourably upon him and grant him peace).'" Such are the cities of Jábulḳá and Jábulsá—the Muslim 'Land of Cocagne'—wherein, according to the Shí'ite belief, the Imám Mahdí dwells.

3. *Ḥuseyn ibn Rúḥ* has been already mentioned in

this note as one of the vicars or 'Gates' of the Imám Mahdí. The following note concerning him occurs on p. 439 of Baron Mac Guckin de Slane's translation of Ibn Khallikán's *Biographical Dictionary* (London, 1842):—"Abû'l-Kâsim al-Husain Ibn Ruh was a holy shaikh and one of the *doors* leading to the *Sâhib az Zamân* (*the lord of the time*, or last grand Imâm, according to the Shiite doctrine; see *Druzes*, introd. p. 65). He was chosen by Abû Jaafar Muhammad Ibn Othmân al-Omari as his lieutenant, and when the latter classed the Shiites according to their degrees (*of initiation*), Abû'l-Kâsim was authorized to enter into his presence the first of them all.—He then went to see Ibn as-Shalmaghâni" [see *supra*, Note D, p. 229], "and gained over so many proselytes, that the vizirs, ex-vizirs, and other persons of high rank rode (*publicly*) to visit him. He continued to be treated with the greatest deference till Hâmid Ibn Abbâs became vizir (*to al-Muktadir*) and ordered him to be arrested. He remained in prison for five years, but was liberated immediately after the deposition of al-Muktadir, A.H. 317 (A.D. 929). From that time till his death, which took place A.H. 326 (A.D. 937—8), he never ceased to be highly respected, but at the moment in which his influence had attained its utmost pitch, and his plans were ripe for execution, God preserved (*the Khalifat*) from his evil designs. He had been accused of inviting the Karmats by letter to lay siege to Baghdad, but he defended himself with great ability, presence of mind, and learning. He was a benefactor to the Shiites, and held a very high rank among them.—(Ad-Dahabi's *Târîkh-al-Islâm*, No. 646, *in anno.*)"

4. *Ibn Mihriyár*. Of this person I can find mention only in two works of Shi'ite theology, *viz.* the '*Tenets of the Shi'ites*' (عقائد الشيعة), and the '*Garden of the Shi'ites*' (حديقة الشيعة), in each of which his name is written differently. In the first he is called محمد بن ابرهيم مهرزيار, and in the second محمد بن ابرهيم ابن قهريار. In both works

he is mentioned amongst those who, during the period of the "*Minor Occultation*," obtained access to, or corresponded with, the Imám; and in both he is described as a native of Ahwáz. What "tradition" of his is specially referred to in the text, I am unable to say.

5. *The Guardians and the Helpers.* These constitute two grades of a spiritual hierarchy whereof the members are called generically "*Men of the Unseen World*" (رجال الغيب), and at the head of which is the "*Pole*" (قطب). Al-Jorjání in his *Definitiones* (ed. Flügel, p. 266) describes the "*Guardians*" or "*Overseers*" (نقباء) as follows:—"They are those who have discovered the Inward Name so that they look into the hearts of men and discern secret thoughts, because for them veils are withdrawn from the faces of mysteries. And they are of three kinds:—Superior Souls, which are embodiments of [Divine] commands; Inferior Souls, which are mundane; and Intermediate Souls, which are human essences. And in each one of them God (Exalted is He) hath a trust deposited which compriseth mysteries divine and mundane. And they are [in number] three hundred." Concerning the "*Helpers*" (نجباء) he says (p. 259):—"They are forty, and they are engaged in bearing the burdens of creatures, generally such accidents as human strength cannot cope with. And this [they do] by reason of their abundant natural pity and mercy, neither do they desist [therefrom] save for the sake of another, for no increase of advancement is [possible] to them save by this channel." What is meant by the "flight" of these is, as I suppose, described in a passage of the *'Aḳá'idu'sh-Shí'a* of which this is a translation:—"And amongst them" [i.e. the signs of the Return of the Imám] "are the *Men of the Unseen*, who are thirty or forty persons who in a week traverse the whole surface of the earth, spending each day in a different region. Every Friday they appear before His Holiness [the Imám Mahdí] for the Friday prayers......Then, when it is morning,

they traverse the earth in the twinkling of an eye and appear before His Holiness, or else come riding upon a cloud and stand in attendance on Him."

6. *The Conquest of the East and West* which will be effected by the Imám Mahdí on his appearance, of which it is one of the signs, needs no detailed notice.

7. *The Ass of Antichrist.* Concerning Antichrist (*Dajjál*), and the ass on which he is mounted, the *'Aká'idu'sh-Shí'a* has the following passage:—"The *forty-sixth* of the signs of the appearance [of the Imám Mahdí] is the coming forth of Antichrist. And the name of that accursed one is Ṣá'id ibn Ṣayd. The traditions concerning him are various. Some imply that he has existed from the time of Adam until now, as it is related in a tradition that the Apostle of God went to one of the houses in Medína wherein was a babbling madman with his mother. The Prophet pointed him out to his companions and said, 'O people, God hath not sent any prophet without filling his church with the fear of Antichrist, whom he has respited and left until your time. And this man shall come forth with a mountain of bread and a river of water; and he will appear in a time of famine. Most of his followers will be Jews, women, Arabs, and nomads. He will enter into all quarters and regions of the earth save Mecca and its two mountains, and Medína and its two mountains. And whenever he comes forth he will claim to be God, although he is one-eyed and God is not one-eyed.' And in some traditions it hath come down that he was born in the time of His Highness [the Prophet]; that he had a beard and spoke when he was born; that the Prophet went to his house; that he claimed the rank of a prophet and said 'I am one sent of God'; that then His Highness [the Prophet] commanded an angel which was in the form of a great bird to carry him away and cast him into a well situated in one of the Jewish villages near Sajistán or Isfahán; and that he is chained [there] till such time as he shall receive permission to come forth. And he has an ass whereof each step covers a mile (three miles being equal to one parasang), and on the body of his ass are white spots

like a leopard. Now the characteristics of Antichrist are these:—his right eye is crushed; his left eye is in his forehead, and glitters as though it were the morning star, and in it is a piece of blood, so that it seems to be pervaded with blood; between his two eyes it is written that he is a misbeliever, so that everyone, whether learned or unlearned, can read it; he is a skilled magician, who, by his magic, descends into the oceans; with him travels the sun; before his face is a mountain of smoke, and behind his back is a white mountain, and through [his] magic it seemeth in men's eyes that they are two mountains of water and bread, though in truth it is not so, but a mere juggle; he traverseth all oceans, and over whatsoever ocean or water he passeth it sinketh down and cometh forth no more till the Day of Judgement; before him Satan dances, and the devils cause him and his ass to appear pleasing in men's eyes, and this is a mischief for the proving of mankind. And he crieth out so that the dwellers in the East and in the West, whether of *jinn* or of mankind, hear his voice, and he saith, 'O my friends, I am that God who created and fashioned the members and parts of the world; I am that God who predestined the affairs of [His] servants and guided and directed mankind; I am your Supreme Lord.' And most of his followers are women, Jews, bastards, and musicians. But when he cometh to *'Akaba-i-Afík*, which is a mountain in Syria, His Highness the Ḳá'im shall slay him at the third hour on Friday, and shall cleanse the world of the filth and foulness of that Accursed One." Many other wonderful qualities are attributed to the ass of Antichrist, as, for instance, that the distance between its ears is a full mile, that each of its hairs gives forth ravishing strains of music, and the like, of which things the further enumeration appears to be unprofitable and unnecessary.

8. *The appearance of Sofyán.* In enumerating the signs which shall usher in the return of the Imám Mahdí, the *'Aká'idu'sh-Shí'a* first mentions the appearance of Sofyán in these words:—"His name is 'Othmán the son of 'Ataba of the children of Yazíd ibn Mu'áwiya ibn Abí Sofyán. He is a thick-set man with an ill countenance, a face

pitted with small-pox, a large head, and blue eyes. He has never rendered service to God, nor seen Mecca or Medína, and his eyes seem to squint. He will appear during the month of Rajab from the direction of Mecca in a desert devoid of water and grass, and will send his army, which will cause much ruin and act right foully, westward and towards Baghdad. He will destroy the region of Najaf the Most Noble, and will plunder Medína for three days. He will sojourn in Kúfa, and will proclaim, 'Whosoever shall bring the head of one of 'Alí's sectaries, to him will I give a thousand gold pieces.' Then men will yield one another into the hand of that Accursed One, for all the chiefs of that time are base-born. And the time of his empire shall be eight months, and in his hands are five cities:—Damascus, Ḥomṣ, Falasṭín, Ardín, and Falzín. The decline of his dominion corresponds with the appearance of the triumph of the Truth, and a great number of his army shall sink down in Beydá, which is the name of a place near Medína." A few pages further on in the same work the following passage occurs:—"At that time [i.e. at the time when the bearded woman Sa'ída and the crusader Mazíd shall appear] a man shall come forth from the direction of Mecca whose name is Sofyán ibn Ḥarb. Perhaps he may be that same Sofyán who has been previously mentioned, whose dominion endureth eight months and continueth until the empire of the Ḳá'im of the race of Muḥammad doth appear. And perhaps Ḥarb may be his father and 'Ataba his grandfather."

NOTE P.

THE EXECUTION OF MULLÁ MUḤAMMAD 'ALÍ OF BÁRFURÚSH.

When, in the summer of A.D. 1849, the remnant of the brave defenders of Sheykh Ṭabarsí, beguiled by the treacherous promises of Prince Mahdi-Ḳulí Mirzá, evacuated the fortress which they had held so long and so gallantly, and yielded themselves up to the besiegers, they were at first received with an apparent friendliness and even respect which served to lull them into a false security and to render easy the perfidious massacre wherein all but a few of them perished on the morrow of their surrender.

From this massacre some of the Bábí chiefs were reserved to grace the Prince's triumphal entry into Bárfurúsh. Amongst these the *Táríkh-i-Jadíd* mentions the following:—Mullá Muḥammad 'Alí of Bárfurúsh, called by the Bábís "His Excellency the Most Holy" (*Jenáb-i-Ḳuddús*); Áḳá Mírzá Muḥammad Ḥasan, the brother of Mullá Ḥuseyn of Bushraweyh; Mullá Muḥammad Ṣádiḳ of Khurásán; Hájí Mírzá Muḥammad Ḥasan of Khurásán; Sheykh Ni'matu 'lláh of Ámul; Hájí Naṣír of Ḳazvín; Mullá Yúsuf of Ardabíl; and Áḳá Seyyid 'Abdu'l-'Aẓím of Khúy.

Jenáb-i-Ḳuddús (for the sake of brevity I shall make use of the title in preference to the name of him who is the subject of this note) requested the Prince to send him to Teherán there to undergo judgement before the Sháh. The Prince was at first disposed to grant this request, thinking, perhaps, that to bring so notable a captive into the Royal Presence might serve to obliterate in some measure the record of those repeated failures to which his unparalleled incapacity had given rise. But when the Sa'ídu'l-'Ulamá heard of this plan, and saw a possibility of his hated foe escaping from his clutches, he went at once to the Prince, and strongly represented to him the danger of allowing one so eloquent and so plausible to plead his cause before the King. These arguments were, according to the *Táríkh-i-Jadíd* (from which these particulars are taken), backed up by an offer to pay the Prince a sum of 400 (or, as others say, of 1000) *túmáns* on condition that Jenáb-i-Ḳuddús should be surrendered unconditionally into his hands. To this arrangement the Prince, whether moved by the arguments or the *túmáns* of the Sa'ídu'l-'Ulamá, eventually consented, and Jenáb-i-Ḳuddús was delivered over to his inveterate enemy.

The execution took place in the *meydán*, or public square, of Bárfurúsh. The Sa'ídu'l-'Ulamá first cut off the ears of Jenáb-i-Ḳuddús and tortured him in other ways, and then killed him with the blow of an axe. One of the

Sa'ídu'l-'Ulamá's disciples then severed the head from the lifeless body, and others poured naphtha over the corpse and set fire to it. The fire, however, as the Bábís relate (for Ṣubḥ-i-Ezel corroborates the *Táríkh-i-Jadíd* in this particular), refused to burn the holy remains; and so the Sa'ídu'l-'Ulamá gave orders that the body should be cut in pieces, and these pieces cast far and wide. This was done, but, as Hájí Mírzá Jání relates, certain Bábís not known as such to their fellow-townsmen came at night, collected the scattered fragments, and buried them in an old ruined *madrasa* or college hard by. By this *madrasa*, as the Bábí historian relates, had Jenáb-i-Ḳuddús once passed in the company of a friend with whom he was conversing on the transitoriness of this world, and to it he had pointed to illustrate his words, saying, "This college, for instance, was once frequented, and is now deserted and neglected; a little while hence they will bury here some great man, and many will come to visit his grave, and again it will be frequented and thronged with people."

Jenáb-i-Ḳuddús is said to have foretold his death and the manner thereof to several other persons, including his wife and her mother; and Ṣubḥ-i-Ezel told me that he had seen at Teherán a letter in his handwriting, taken from his pocket when he was buried, wherein the date and manner of his death were clearly set forth; also that he had previously to the siege of Sheykh Ṭabarsí written a letter to Mullá Ḥuseyn of Bushraweyh wherein the following sentence occurred:—

كانّى دفنت نفسى فى التراب مع سبعين من الصّالحين *

"It is as though I had buried myself in the earth with seventy righteous men." This letter Ṣubḥ-i-Ezel had copied at Baghdad.

As for the Sa'ídu'l-'Ulamá, he did not escape the Divine vengeance; for, as the *Táríkh-i-Jadíd* relates, all the vital heat seemed to be withdrawn from his body, and even in the midst of summer he used to suffer so severely from cold that when he went to the mosque two chafing-dishes full of burning charcoal were carried with him and placed on either side of him. Yet, in spite of these and the thick skin cloak which he wore, he could hardly remain long enough to perform his prayers, and used to hasten back as soon as he was able to his house, where, enveloped in wraps and covered with quilts, he would sit shivering over his *kursí*[1].

Concerning the writings of Jenáb-i-Ḳuddús, see note 1 at the foot of p. 30 *supra*.

NOTE Q.

ḲURRATU'L-'AYN.

The appearance of such a woman as Ḳurratu'l-'Ayn is in any country and any age a rare phenomenon, but in such a country as Persia it is a prodigy—nay, almost a miracle. Alike in virtue of her marvellous beauty, her rare intellectual gifts, her fervid eloquence, her fearless devotion, and her glorious martyrdom, she stands forth incomparable and immortal amidst her countrywomen. Had the Bábí religion no other claim to greatness, this were sufficient—that it produced a heroine like Ḳurratu'l-'Ayn.

In this note I do not propose to repeat facts with which everyone who has studied the subject is acquainted, neither shall I attempt to re-tell a tale which has been already set forth by Gobineau in language far more eloquent than I can command. My purpose is merely to add such new particulars as I have been able to glean from the *Táríkh-i-Jadíd* and from oral tradition. Before proceeding to do this, I wish once more to call attention to the graceful poem by Marie von Najmájer whereof Ḳurratu'l-'Ayn is the heroine (see *supra* p. 207).

[1] The *kursí*—much used by the Persians during winter—is, roughly speaking, like a large table with very short legs. A chafing-dish containing ignited charcoal is placed beneath it, as are also the legs of those who sit round it. With a good supply of quilts, pillows, and amusing books, it affords the means of passing a cold winter's day very comfortably.

The following table, taken in conjunction with the remarks on pp. 197—198 *supra*, will sufficiently serve to indicate Ḳurratu'l-'Ayn's family relationships:—

Muḥammad el-Burgháni el-Ḳazviní.

Hájí Mullá Muḥammad Taḳí, called by the Shí'ites *Shahíd-i-Tháliṭh* ('The Third Martyr').

Hájí Mullá Muḥammad Ṣáliḥ.

Hájí Mullá 'Alí, who embraced the Bábí doctrines.

Mullá Muḥammad. = Ḳurratu'l-'Ayn.

The following particulars are derived from the *Táríkh-i-Jadíd*. During the life of Hájí Seyyid Káẓim of Resht Ḳurratu'l-'Ayn visited Kerbelá, where she became acquainted not only with Seyyid Káẓim himself, but with many of his chief followers, including Mullá Ḥuseyn of Bushraweyh. When, on the death of Seyyid Káẓim, Mullá Ḥuseyn set out for Shíráz, Ḳurratu'l-'Ayn wrote a letter to him begging that should he succeed in finding the spiritual guide whom they were expecting (see pp. 239—240 *supra*) he would at once inform her. This letter Mullá Ḥuseyn on his conversion placed in the hands of the Báb, who, recognizing the rare qualities and attainments of which it gave evidence, included its writer amongst the eighteen "Letters of the Living" (حروفات حی) who composed the "First Unity" of the Bábí hierarchy.

Ḳurratu'l-'Ayn continued for some time at Kerbelá, where, seated behind a curtain, she used to lecture and preach to the disciples of the late Seyyid Káẓim. The governor, becoming aware of this, wished to arrest her, but she hastily quitted Kerbelá without a passport and went to Baghdad, where she proceeded directly to the house of the chief *Muftí*, before whom she defended her creed and her conduct with great ability. The question whether she should be allowed to continue her teaching was submitted first to the Páshá of Baghdad and then to the central government, the result being that she was ordered to leave

Turkish territory. During her journey from Baghdad to Kirmánsháh and Hamadán she continued to preach, and made several converts to the Bábí faith, amongst these being Sheykh Ṣáliḥ the Arab, Sheykh Ṭáhir, Mullá Ibrahím of Maḥallát, and Sheykh Sulṭán the Arab. Certain of the Bábís, however, were at first disposed to regard her efforts with disapproval, and some of these even wrote to the Báb asking whether it was seemly for a woman to preach publicly to men. In reply the Báb not only sanctioned her preaching and applauded her zeal, but bestowed on her the title of *Jenáb-i-Ṭáhira* ("Her Excellency the Pure"), whereupon those who had been disposed to censure her expressed contrition and penitence, and her high position in the Bábí church became uncontested.

From Hamadán Ḳurratu'l-'Ayn intended to go to Teherán, hoping, it is said, to be able to convert Muḥammad Sháh himself; but her father Hájí Mullá Muḥammad Ṣáliḥ, being apprized of this plan, sent servants to intercept her and bring her home to Ḳazvín. Perhaps it was on her return thither that she was married to her cousin Mullá Muḥammad the son of Hájí Mullá Muḥammad Taḳí, but of the date when this marriage was contracted I can find no indication. At all events the marriage must have been a most unhappy one, for Mullá Muḥammad seems fully to have shared his father's hatred of the Sheykhís and Bábís, and finally Ḳurratu'l-'Ayn refused to live with him any longer.

The position of Ḳurratu'l-'Ayn, sufficiently irksome and even precarious already, was rendered perilous in the highest degree by the death of her uncle at the hands of certain Bábís (see p. 198 *supra*). Some have hinted that Ḳurratu'l-'Ayn was privy to this assassination, but of this there is absolutely no proof, and we may be sure that, had there been any evidence of her complicity, the Musulmáns would not have failed to make use of it to rid themselves of one who was well known to be amongst the most zealous supporters of the Báb. As it was, she was brought before the governor of Ḳazvín, charged by her husband with complicity in the murder of his father, and acquitted. Several of the Bábís were arrested and tortured, until finally one—Mírzá Ṣáliḥ of Shíráz, according to the

Táríkh-i-Jadíd, Ṣáliḥ Ṭáhir according to Ṣubḥ-i-Ezel—confessed that he, alone and unabetted, had compassed the death of the murdered *mujtahid*, in proof of which he described in detail how the murder had been committed, and where the blood-stained knife with which the deed was done might be found. This Ṣáliḥ was sent to Teherán with several others suspected of complicity, but he succeeded in making his escape, fettered as he was, to Mázandarán, where he was subsequently killed at Sheykh Ṭabarsí. As to the others arrested, the *Táríkh-i-Jadíd* and Ṣubḥ-i-Ezel are not completely in accord. Both agree, however, that Sheykh Ṣáliḥ the Arab and Mullá Ibrahím of Maḥallát (who, as we have already seen were amongst the first proselytes gained by Ḳurratu'l-'Ayn) were of their number. The first of these was killed at Teherán; the second was taken back to Ḳazvín, where, in company with another (Sheykh Ṭáhir according to the *Táríkh-i-Jadíd*, Hájí Muḥammad 'Alí according to Ṣubḥ-i-Ezel), he was cruelly done to death by the populace. These were the first Bábís who were put to death in Persia. The *Táríkh-i-Jadíd* adds the name of another—an old man called Hájí Asadu'lláh—who died of cold and fatigue during his conveyance to Teherán.

Although Ḳurratu'l-'Ayn had been acquitted of all share in her uncle's death, it was clearly impossible for her to remain in Ḳazvín any longer, even had she desired to do so, which scarcely seems probable. She accordingly set out by way of Teherán for Khurásán, and was present at the celebrated meeting of the Bábí chiefs at Badasht (see Gobineau, pp. 180—184). From Badasht she turned back with Mullá Muḥammad 'Alí of Bárfurúsh and his party towards Mázandarán. At this point the narrative of the *Táríkh-i-Jadíd* breaks off, neither is it, in spite of the author's promise, again renewed; while all other written histories are equally silent as to what befel Ḳurratu'l-'Ayn from the time that she separated from Mullá Muḥammad 'Alí and his followers to the time when she was brought captive to Teherán and placed in the custody of Maḥmúd Khán the *Kalántar*. From Ṣubḥ-i-Ezel, however, I learned the following particulars. After separating from the Bábís who went to form the garrison of Sheykh Ṭabarsí, Ḳurratu'l-

'Ayn went to Núr, where she remained unmolested till the final suppression of the Mázandarán insurrection. She was then delivered up to the government authorities by the people of Núr and sent to Teherán. On her arrival there she was brought before Náṣiru'd-Dín Sháh, who, on seeing her, said:—

از هیئتش خوشم می آید بگذار باشد

"I like her looks: leave her, and let her be."

She was accordingly placed under the custody of Maḥmúd Khán the *Kalántar*, and in his house she remained till her execution in August A.D. 1852. Her imprisonment was not very rigorous, and she was occasionally seen by different Bábís under various pretexts. Her life, indeed, was in no jeopardy till the disastrous attempt on the Sháh's life by certain Bábís (see Note T *infra* and pp. 49—50 *supra*) made the mere profession of the Bábí faith a crime deserving not death only, but the most horrible tortures, and gave rise to that reign of terror which has been so vividly described by Gobineau (pp. 301—303), Lady Sheil (pp. 273—282), Polak (pp. 352—353), and Ussher (pp. 627—629). Even then Ḳurratu'l-'Ayn might, by abjuring her faith, have escaped death, and exchanged glorious martyrdom and immortal fame for a few brief years of life; but this her noble spirit scorned to do. That she met the cruel fate reserved for her with "superhuman fortitude" is a fact to which Dr Polak, who actually witnessed her execution, testifies in the following words:—"*Ich war Zeuge von der Hinrichtung der Kurret el ayn, die vom Kriegsminister und seinen Adjutanten vollzogen wurde; die schöne Frau erduldete den langsamen Tod mit übermenschlicher Stärke.*" In what manner death was inflicted I have not been able to learn. Gobineau says that she was burned, but that the executioner first strangled her; Ṣubḥ-i-Ezel says that the accounts of her death are various, one being that she was strangled with the bowstring in the Bágh-i-Íl-Khání; some with whom I conversed in Persia stated that she was killed in the Bágh-i-Lálé-zár; others that she was cast into a dry well in the garden of the palace called Nigáristán, which well was then filled up with stones. However this may be, we have it on Polak's authority that her death was painful and lingering, and that she met it as a heroine should do.

I was anxious to discover from Ṣubḥ-i-Ezel whether it was true, as has often been alleged, that Ḳurratu'l-'Ayn discarded the veil. His reply, so far as I can remember, was as follows:—"It is not true that she laid aside the veil. Sometimes, when carried away by her eloquence, she would allow it to slip down off her face, but she would always replace it after a few moments."

Ḳurratu'l-'Ayn's fame as a poetess is great, but during my sojourn in Persia I only succeeded in obtaining three of the poems attributed to her, *viz.* two short but very beautiful *ghazals* and a long *masnaví*. Of one of these *ghazals* I published the Persian text with a translation into English verse in my second paper on the Bábís in the *J. R. A. S.* for 1889 (pp. 936—937 and 991). I now give the second, which, though its authorship is more disputed, certainly savours strongly of Bábí doctrines and modes of expression.

ط

هو المحبوب

لمعات وجهك اشرقت و شعاع طلعتك اعتلا

زچه رو اُلَسَت بریکم نزنی بزن که بَلَی بَلَی

بجواب طبل الستِ تو ز ولا چه کوس بلی زدند

همه خیمه زد بدر دلم سپه غم و حشم بلا

من و عشق آن مه خوبرو که چو زد صلای بلا برو

نشـاط و قهقهه شد فرو که انا الشهید بکربلا

چو شنید نالهٔ مرك من پیٔ ساز من شد و برك من

فمشی الیٰ مهرولاً و بکی علی مجلجلا

چه شود که آتش حیرتی زنیم بقلهٔ طور دل

فسککته و دککته متدکدکاً متزلزلاً

پیٔ خوان دعوت عشق او همه شب ز خیل کروبیان

رسد این صفیر مهیمنی که گروه غمزده الصلا

تو چه فاس ماهیٔ حیرتی چه زنی ز بحر وجود دم

نشین چو طاهره دم بدم بشنو خروش نهنگ لا

(TRANSLATION.)

"The effulgence of thy face flashed forth and the rays of thy visage arose on high;
Why lags the word '*Am I not your Lord?*' '*Yea, that thou art*' let us make reply[1].
'*Am I not's*' appeal from thy drum to greet what '*Yeas*' do the drums of devotion beat;
At the gate of my heart I behold the feet and the tents of the host of calamity[2].

[1] *i.e.* "Why do you hesitate to lay claim to a divine nature? Were you to do so, all of us would admit your claim." See Ḳur'án vii. 171, and B. ii., pp. 917—918 and note.

[2] The following lines from a poem attributed to Nabíl express a similar idea:—

چو کسی طریق مرا رود   کنمش ندا که خبر شود

که هر انکه عاشق من شود   نرهد ز محنت و ابتلا

"If one should choose my path to go I will cry to him that he well may know
That none shall escape from grief and woe who is once afflicted with love for me."

That fair moon's love for me, I trow, is enough, for he laughed at the hail of woe,
And exulting cried as he sank below, 'The Martyr of Kerbelá am I.'[1]
When he heard my death-wail drear, for me he prepared, and arranged my gear for me,
He advanced to lament at my bier for me, and o'er me wept right bitterly.
What harm if thou with the fire of amaze should'st set my Sinai-heart ablaze
Which thou first mad'st fast in a hundred ways but to shake and shatter so ruthlessly?[2]
To convene the guests to his feast of love all night from the angel-host above
Peals forth this summons ineffable 'Hail, sorrow-stricken community!'
Can a scale of the fish of amaze like thee aspire to sing of Being's Sea?
Sit still like Ṭáhira, hearkening to what the monster of 'No' doth cry[3]."

[1] *i.e.* Imám Ḥuseyn, with whom the Báb repeatedly declares himself to be identical in essence.

[2] *i.e.* "You first strengthened my heart with knowledge, and inspired it with zeal and enthusiasm; then you crushed and subdued it with love. Were it not well if you would now kindle on it, as on Mount Sinai, that fire whence comes the cry انّی انا الله 'Verily I am God'?" Cf. Ḳur'án xxviii. 30, and vii. 139.

[3] *i.e.* "How can you, who are but as a scale on some little fish which swims wonderingly in the vast expanses of the sea, speak fittingly of the Ocean of Being? Sit still then, as I, Ḳurratu'l-'Ayn (*Jenáb-i-Ṭáhira*), do, and listen to the roar of the monster, whale, crocodile, or Leviathan which continually cries لا اله الّا انا 'There is no God but me'." Some versions of this poem have بنشین چو طوطی و دم بدم "Sit still like a parrot" &c. at the beginning of the second hemistich of this couplet.

NOTE R.

On the Bábí system of forming derivatives.

One of the peculiarities of style especially affected by the Báb is the employment of all theoretically possible derivatives of roots, whether sanctioned by usage or not. The number of these derivative forms in Arabic is great, but of course no single root is susceptible to all the modifications which they represent. Custom and authority, as well as the intrinsic meaning of each root, limit the number of actual derivates employed in any given case to a fractional part of those theoretically possible. It would appear that the Báb believed some special talismanic virtue to reside in each possible form of every Attribute of God. Thus in the Persian Beyán (*Váḥid*, viii., *ch.* 2), he says:—

ملخّص این باب آنکه از آنجائیکه مراتب توحید بر[1] هفت حرف تامّ میگردد که حروف[2] اثبات باشد از اینجهة حکم شده که ارث نبرد از میّت بسرّ حقیقة الّا هفت نفس چنانچه [از][3] هر صفتی بهفت[4] رتبه توان خدارا [خواند بان صفت][5] مثل اوحد و وحّاد و وحید و واحد[6] و متوحّد و موحِد[7] و موحَّد *

[1] B reads در.

[2] My MS. reads حرف.

[3] B substitutes در رتبه.

[4] B reads هفت.

[5] B reads بان صفت خواند.

[6] B transposes واحد and وحید.

[7] B reads موحد.

"The quintessence of this chapter is this, that inasmuch as the degrees of Unity are fulfilled in seven letters, which are the Letters of Affirmation, therefore it hath been ordained that, according to the Mystery of the Truth, none shall inherit from the dead save seven persons, even as one can invoke God by every Attribute in seven degrees of that Attribute, as *Unissimus, Unator, Unicus, Unus, Unatus, Unificiens, Unificatus*[1]."

The '*Book of Names*' (كتاب اسما), of which, according to Ṣubḥ-i-Ezel's assertion, the extracts from a Bábí MS. published by Dorn in the *Bulletin de l'Académie Impériale de St Pétersbourg* for December 22nd, 1864, form part, appears to consist in great measure of these permutations[2].

With regard to the derivatives formed as described in the text from the root *Behá* (بهآء), the following passage, occurring in a MS. presented to me by Ṣubḥ-i-Ezel and called by him شئون خمسه "*the Five States*" or "*Grades*" (because it contains specimens of each of the five styles into which the Báb divides his writings, concerning which see *infra*, Note U) may serve to give us some idea of what the letter in question must have been like. No attempt has been made to translate what is hardly capable of translation.

كتاب الفآء يا طاهر

بالله الله البهى البهى

بسم الله الابهى الابهى الله لا اله الا هو الابهى الابهى

الله لا اله الا هو البهى البهى الله لا اله الا هو المبتهى

[1] I trust that I may be pardoned the use of such words. Only in this way can one convey some idea of the original to the European reader unacquainted with Arabic.

[2] See p. 202 *supra*.

المبتهی الله لا اله الّا هو المبهی المبهی الله لا اله
الّا هو الواحد البهیان و لله بهی بهیان بهآء السّموات
و الارض و ما بینهما و الله بهآء باهی بهی و لله بهی
بهیان بهیئة السّموات و الارض و ما بینهما و الله بهیان
مبتهی متباه قل الله ابهی فوق کلّ ذی ابهآء لن یقدر
ان یمتنع عن ملیك سلطان ابهآئه من احد لا فی السّموات
و لا فی الارض و لا ما بینهما انّه کان بهآء باهیا بهیا *

This short extract, containing over a dozen derivatives of the root in question, not more than half of which, if so many, could be supported by previous authority, will suffice to give an idea of this style of composition.

NOTE S.

THE BÁB'S LAST NIGHT ON EARTH.

The account of the Báb's condemnation and execution contained in the *Táríkh-i-Jadíd* agrees in the main with the narratives of Gobineau and Kazem-Beg, but adds some curious particulars concerning what passed in the prison on the eve of the martyrdom. Of this passage I here give a translation.

"They imprisoned him who was athirst for the draught of martyrdom [i.e. the Báb] for three days [after sentence of death was passed], along with Áḳá Seyyid Ḥuseyn [of Yezd] the amanuensis, and Áḳá Seyyid Ḥasan, which twain were brothers wont to pass their time for the most part in the Báb's presence.

"Now before this event the Báb had, for the completion of the proof, graciously sent by means of Áḳá Seyyid Aḥmad of Tabríz known as 'the scribe'[1], Mírzá Muḥammad 'Alí of Tabríz, and two other persons, sundry epistles containing exhortations, admonitions, and declarations of his truth to the doctors of Tabríz. At the time when these epistles were delivered one of the doctors had desired to show contempt and disrespect towards the blessed epistle. These forerunners of the field of courage put forward the foot of bravery to prevent this, and, their dispute ending in strife, were incarcerated in the prison of His Highness Prince Ḥamzé Mírzá; where, as is currently reported, two of them would seem to have been poisoned, though, according to one account, the Prince released them unknown to the doctors. But Mírzá Muḥammad 'Alí was incarcerated till such time as the Báb was brought to the prison, and there obtained the honour of meeting him.

"On the very eve of the day whereon they martyred that gem of created essences [i.e. the Báb] he said to his companions, 'Tomorrow they will martyr me with boundless shame and dishonour. Let one of you now arise and slay me, so that I may not have to suffer all this dishonour and humiliation from the adversaries; for it is far pleasanter for me to be slain by the hand of friends than by the hands of enemies.' His companions, with expressions of sorrow and grief, sought to excuse themselves, save Mírzá Muḥammad 'Alí, who at once made as though he would obey the command. His comrades, however, anxiously seized his hand, crying, 'Such boldness and rashness is not the characteristic of true service.' 'This act of mine,' replied

[1] The author appears to have confounded this Áḳá Seyyid Aḥmad of Tabríz (who, according to Ṣubḥ-i-Ezel's statement, disappeared altogether and broke off all communications with the Bábís after his escape from Tabríz) with Mullá 'Abdu'l-Karím of Ḳazvín, who was commonly known amongst the Bábís by the name of Mírzá Aḥmad-i-*Kátib* ('the Scribe'). There seems to be no doubt that they were quite distinct persons, and that the title *Kátib* is wrongly applied to the Aḥmad here spoken of. Cf. note 2 on p. 41 *supra*.

he, 'is not due to boldness, but rather to an excessive obedience, being [undertaken] in conformity with his command. After carrying out the order of His Highness [the Báb], I will assuredly pour out my own life also at his feet.' His Highness [the Báb] smiled, and, applauding his faithful devotion and sincere belief, said, 'Tomorrow, when they ask of you, renounce [me] and conceal your belief, for thus is the command of God now laid upon you, especially on Áḳá Seyyid Ḥuseyn, with whom are the gems of knowledge[1], which he must convey to the people of God and the seekers after the way of true guidance.' The [Báb's other] companions agreed, but Mírzá Muḥammad 'Alí fell at the feet of His Highness [the Báb] and began to entreat and implore, thus praying with utmost self-abasement:—'Deprive not this thy faithful servant of the blessing of thy presence, and graciously grant to this worthless dust and mote permission to lay down his life.' How much soever His Highness [the Báb] would have prevented him, he continued to pray, crave, and entreat, until [the Báb], through the exceeding kindness of his disposition, consented.

"Now when a little while had elapsed after the rising of the sun, they brought them without cloak [*'abá*] or coat [*kabá*], and having [only] their vests on their breasts and their nightcaps on their heads, to the governor's palace, where it was decreed that they should be shot. Áḳá Seyyid Ḥuseyn the amanuensis and Áḳá Seyyid Ḥasan his brother renounced [the Báb] as they had been commanded, and were released, and Áḳá Seyyid Ḥuseyn bestowed the gems of knowledge treasured in his bosom upon such as sought for them and were worthy of them, and, according to his instructions, conveyed and carried certain secrets of the religion to those who were entitled to receive them. He [subsequently] attained to the rank of martyrdom in Ṭeherán." (Here follows the account of the execution of the Báb and Mírzá Muḥammad 'Alí, which, as it agrees substantially with that given in the present work and in other published accounts, I omit.)

[1] *i.e.* the Bab's last words, behests, and directions.

According to Ṣubḥ-i-Ezel, the Báb signified his acceptance of Mírzá Muḥammad 'Alí's request that he might share in the glorious martyrdom of his Master in these words:—

ان محمد على معنا فى الجنة

"Verily Muḥammad 'Alí [shall be] with us in Paradise."

If these words be authentic (and there is no reason for doubting that they are) they offer a most striking analogy to one of the last utterances of Jesus Christ (Luke xxiii. 43).

Whether the narrative of the *Táríkh-i-Jadíd* be altogether worthy of credence or not, there seems no reason to doubt that Seyyid Ḥuseyn recanted, not, as Kazem-Beg asserts (i. pp. 375—377), from a craven dread of death, but in accordance with the command of his master, the object of this command being the preservation of the last words and writings of the Báb. When we consider how rare was the fear of death and torture amongst the Bábís, and how readily Seyyid Ḥuseyn himself met his fate two years later (cf. Gobineau, pp. 300—301), it seems most improbable that he of all the Bábís, he, the chosen companion, amanuensis, and intimate friend of the Báb, should exhibit so craven a fear. Amongst the Bábís, at least, no stigma of even a temporary and bitterly repented failure of courage, such as is supposed by Gobineau, lies on the memory of Seyyid Ḥuseyn. It is at least certain that he continued to correspond with Suleymán Khán and the other Bábí chiefs after the Báb's execution. Some of these letters, wherein he alludes to Tabríz as محلّ ضرب ('the Place of the Blow') and مشهد ('the Place of Martyrdom'), were shewn to me by Ṣubḥ-i-Ezel. From these letters and Ṣubḥ-i-Ezel's statements it would appear that Seyyid Ḥuseyn was kept in custody for at any rate some considerable portion of the two years by which he survived his master.

Of the touching and beautiful letter written by Mírzá Muḥammad 'Alí from his prison to his elder brother the text will be found at p. 992 and the translation at p. 938 of my second paper on the Bábís in the *J. R. A. S.* for 1889.

NOTE T.

THE ATTEMPT ON THE SHÁH'S LIFE AND THE MASSACRE OF TEHERÁN.

The attempted assassination of Náṣiru'd-Dín Sháh on Sunday August 15th, 1852, though very lightly touched on in the present work, is so fully described by the two Musulmán historians, Lady Sheil, Gobineau, Polak, Kazem-Beg and others, that I shall confine myself here to reproducing the substance of what was told me about this event by the nephew of one of the three Bábís actually engaged in the plot. This account naturally exhibits the Sháh's behaviour in a less heroic light than do the Musulmán chroniclers Sipihr and Riẓá-Ḳulí Khán. I give it only for what it is worth, thinking that here, as elsewhere, the truth may lie between the two extremes.

According to this account, then, the Bábí conspirators were originally seven in number, but four of them drew back at the last moment from the projected enterprise. The three who actually made the attempt were Mullá Fatḥu'lláh of Ḳum, Ṣádiḳ of Zanján, and Mírzá Muḥammad of Níríz[1]. These three approached the Sháh as he was riding out to the chase somewhat in advance of his retinue from the Palace of Niyávarán. The Sháh, supposing that they had some petition to prefer, allowed them to draw near without suspicion. When within a short distance of him one of the three Bábís (apparently the Nírízí) drew a pistol from his pocket and fired at the Sháh. Mullá

[1] According to the *Násikhu't-Tawáríkh* the conspirators were originally *twelve* in number. Of these, the names of four only—Ṣádiḳ of Zanján, Mírzá 'Abdu'l-Wahháb of Shíráz, Mullá Fatḥu'-lláh of Ḳum, and Muḥammad Báḳir of Najafábád—are given. It is subsequently stated that all save three drew back at the last, and that of these three one was "a man of Níríz" (presumably the same Mírzá Muḥammad mentioned above). Lady Sheil (*op. cit.*, p. 274) says that four Bábís took part in the attack.

Fatḥu'lláh of Ḳum then threw himself upon the King and dragged him from his horse on to the ground, meaning to cut his throat[1]. The Sháh, having almost fainted with terror, was already incapable of offering any further resistance, when a *farrásh* (still living, and, thanks to the service rendered by him on that day, in the enjoyment of a good pension) came up, struck the would-be assassin in the mouth, and cut down one of the other two conspirators. A moment after, one of the *mustawfís* arrived on the spot and threw himself as a shield on the Sháh's body. The Sháh, imagining that it was another assassin, cried out, "Why do you wish to kill me? What harm have I done?" "It is I," answered the *mustawfí*, "all danger is past. Fear not." All danger was in fact over. As soon as it was evident that the attempt had failed and that the Sháh still lived, other retainers, who had at first hung back[2], hastened forward to bear a part in the seizure of the two surviving assassins (for Ṣádiḳ of Zanján had already been killed). The two captives, on being interrogated, declared that they were Bábís, and that they had made the attempt with a view to avenging the blood of their Master. In spite of their frank confession, it was at first believed that the object of the attempt was political, and that it had been instigated by some rival claimant to the throne. Ṣádiḳ of Zanján, who was killed on the spot, was described by Ṣubḥ-i-Ezel as a youth of short stature with very small eyes. He was the servant of Mullá Sheykh 'Alí (*'Jenáb-i-'Aẓím'*) from whom he is said to have received the pistol with which he was armed. According to Ṣubḥ-i-Ezel he alone fired at and wounded the Sháh, but the *Násikhu't-Tawáríkh* states that each of the three assassins discharged his pistol.

With regard to the Sháh's behaviour, it may not be altogether uninstructive to compare with the above account the following passage from the *Násikhu't-Tawáríkh:*— "The dust of perturbation settled not on the skirt of the

[1] According to Gobineau (p. 282) the conspirators did not succeed in unhorsing the King. See also p. 289 of the same work. Lady Sheil, however, (*op. cit.*, p. 274) says that the Sháh was dragged to the ground.

[2] Cf. Polak's *Persien*, vol. i. p. 352.

patience and self-control of the King, whose elemental material God the Creator had leavened with the liver of the lion, the heart of Ardashír, the ardour of Shápúr, and the majesty of Tímúr; nor did the pellucid stream of his mind become troubled by the foulness and filth of these events. Neither did he urge his horse to leap aside, nor did he utter a word indicative of alarm or consternation. He kept his place on his poplar-wood saddle like some mountain of massive rocks, and, notwithstanding that wound, turned not aside in any direction, and carried not his hand to his hurt, so that those present in his escort knew not that any hurt had befallen the king or that he had suffered any wound."

Ḳá'ání of Shíráz, the most famous and the most talented of modern Persian poets, has two *kaṣídas* in celebration of the Sháh's escape from this danger. These will be found respectively at p. 26 and p. 254 of the edition of his works published at Teherán in A.H. 1302 (A.D. 1884). Although they add no new facts to the sum of our knowledge, they agree with the authorities already cited in stating that the attempt took place at the end of the month of Shawwál, and that those actually concerned therein were three in number. Thus in the first *ḳaṣída* Ḳá'ání says:—

آخر شوال خسرو شد سوار از بهر صید

آسمانش در عنان و آفتابش در رکاب

کز کمین ناگه سه تن جنبید و افکندند زود

تیرهای آتشین زی خسرو مالك رقاب

"At the end of Shawwál the King rode forth to hunt,
Heaven by his reins and the sun beside his stirrup,
When suddenly three persons sprang forth from ambush,
and swiftly hurled
Fiery darts towards the King, the Lord of [men's] necks."

So in the second *kaṣída* he says:—

آخر شوال‌را هر سال زین پس عید کن

چاکران شاهرا دعوت نما از هر کران

هی بگو شاهد بیا زاهد برو خازن ببخش

هی بگو ساقی بده چنگی بزن مطرب بخوان

عید قربان شهش کن نام و همچون گوسفند

دشمنان‌را سر ببّر در راه شاه کامران

"Henceforth keep the end of Shawwál as a festival every year;
Invite the servants of the King from every quarter.
Ho, say, 'Come, O beloved! Go, O anchorite! Give, O treasurer!'
Ho, say, 'Give, O cup-bearer! Play, O harper! Sing, O minstrel!'
Name it 'the Feast of Sacrifice of the King,' and, like sheep[1],
Cut off the heads of enemies in the path of the victorious King."

Between the attempt on the Sháh's life and the fearful vengeance wherewith it was visited on the Bábís a whole month appears to have elapsed, for the executions are stated by the *Násikhu't-Tawáríkh* to have taken place on Wednesday the *salkh* (*i.e.* the last day) of *Ẓi'l-Ḳa'da* A.H. 1268 (September 15th, A.D. 1852). It must not be supposed, however, that this month was idly spent by the government officials. Messengers were at once despatched

[1] The custom of shewing honour to a great man returning home from a journey by decapitating a sheep and throwing the bleeding head across his path is still maintained in Persia.

to all parts of the kingdom to publish the failure of the plot and the safety of the Sháh. The police of Teherán, instructed to make a diligent search for members of the obnoxious sect[1], succeeded in surprising a gathering of a dozen Bábís in the house of Hájí Suleymán Khán[2] the son of Yaḥyá Khán of Tabríz, and other arrests soon raised the total number of captives to nearly forty. Some few of these were able to prove their innocence in a manner which satisfied even their judges, little disposed as they were towards acquittals. Amongst these the *Násikhu't-Tawáríkh* mentions five, to wit:—Mírzá Ḥuseyn 'Alí of Núr [Behá'u'lláh]; Mírzá Suleymán-Ḳulí; Mírzá Maḥmúd, nephew of the above; Áḳá 'Abdu'lláh, the son of Áḳá Muḥammad Ja'far; and Mírzá Jawád of Khurásán; all of whom were committed to prison pending further investigations.

The majority of those arrested, however, were condemned to death; and, according to the list given in the *Násikhu't-Tawáríkh*, twenty-eight of them expiated their faith with their lives. I say 'their faith' advisedly, for some of those doomed to death, such as Ḳurratu'l-'Ayn and Áḳá Seyyid Ḥuseyn of Yezd, had long been in strict confinement, and could not by any possibility have been concerned in the conspiracy. Others, such as Mullá Ḥuseyn of Khurásán, were convicted solely on the evidence of Bábí writings found on their persons or in their houses. When a verdict of 'Not Guilty' bids fair to jeopardize the judge's reputation for loyalty, if not to place him in actual peril, acquittals in such a country as Persia are hard to win.

Weak as the evidence of criminality was in many cases, there could be little hope of averting the impending butchery; for so audacious an attempt demanded a commensurate revenge calculated to strike terror into the hearts of all. Efforts were nevertheless made by some of the European representatives at the Persian court to induce the Sháh to content himself with the execution of the condemned without subjecting them to the tortures which there was but too much reason to apprehend would be

[1] Cf. Gobineau, p. 284 *et seq.*
[2] *Násikhu't-Tawáríkh.*

superadded to the death-penalty[1]. These efforts were fruitless. The Sháh's alarm and anger, far from diminishing, were constantly stimulated by the representations of his ministers, who succeeded in convincing him of the existence of a wide-spread disaffection which could only be checked by the most stringent measures[2]. Nor was this sense of dread confined to the King: it reacted on those who had inspired it, until, in Gobineau's words, "On ne savait plus sur quel terrain on se trouvait, et, faute de réalités qu'on ne saisissait pas, qui fuyaient devant toutes les recherches, on voyait errer autour de soi une multitude de fantômes. L'épouvante devint générale au camp du roi....En face, on avait une quarantaine de captifs muets; mais par derrière, savait-on ce qui s'agitait?"[3]

Then, because of this great fear, was devised that devilish scheme whereby all classes of society should be made to share in the bloodshed of that fatal day. It was suggested that if the responsibility for the doom of the captives rested solely on the Sháh, the Prime Minister, or the ordinary administrators of the law, these would become thereafter targets for the vengeance of the Bábís. If, on the other hand, a partition of the prisoners were made amongst the different classes; if a representative body of each of these classes were made responsible for the execution of one or more Bábís; and if it were further signified to the persons thus forced to act the part of executioners that the Sháh would be able to estimate their loyalty to himself by the manner in which they disposed of their victims[4], then all classes, being equally partakers in the blood of the slain, would be equally exposed to the retaliation of the survivors, from whom they would be therefore effectually and permanently alienated, while at the same time the Sháh himself would avoid incurring the odium of the massacre. Such were the "Machiavellian means"[5] adopted for the extirpation of the supposed conspirators.

Of the victims of that day the *Násikhu't-Tawáríkh*

[1] Lady Sheil's *Glimpses of Life and Manners in Persia*, p. 276.
[2] Polak's *Persien*, vol. I. p. 352.
[3] Gobineau, p. 290.
[4] Gobineau, p. 292.
[5] Polak's *Persien*, vol. I. p. 352.

gives a complete list, which I here append. This list I read over to Ṣubḥ-i-Ezel. The comments thereon made by him are added in square brackets.

(1) Mullá Sheykh 'Alí ("*Jenáb-i-'Aẓím*") was killed by the *'Ulamá.*

(2) Seyyid Ḥasan Khurásání was hacked in pieces by the Princes.

(3) Mullá Zeynu'l-'Ábidín of Yezd was killed by the *Mustawfís.* [The *Mustawfí'ul-memálik* (Secretary of State), unwilling to shed blood, shut his eyes and fired his gun in the air, while another *Mustawfí* named Ibrahím of Núr only touched the prisoner with his penknife, leaving the bloody work to others less scrupulous. Mullá Zeynu'l-'Ábidín had succeeded once in escaping from his pursuers at Ḳum by throwing a handful of dust in their eyes.]

(4) Mullá Ḥuseyn of Khurásán was killed by the *Niẓámu'l-Mulk,* Mírzá Sa'íd Khán, and the employés of the Foreign Office. [He had held no communication with Hájí Suleymán Khán or the other chief Bábís at Teherán, where he had but recently rented a house. A fragment of Bábí writing found in his house was the sole ground whereon he was convicted.]

(5) Mírzá 'Abdu 'l-Wahháb of Shíráz ['a youth of good understanding'] was killed by Ja'far-Ḳuli Khán the Prime Minister's brother, and his sons Mírzá 'Alí Khán, Músá Khán, and Ẓú'l-Fiḳár Khán.

(6) Mullá Fatḥu'lláh of Ḳum, the son of Mullá 'Alí *Ṣaḥḥáf,* who had fired the shot which wounded the King, was killed by Hájí 'Alí Khán the *Ḥájibu'd-Dawla* and his *farráshes.* Several incisions were made in his body, and in these lighted candles were inserted. After he had been tortured in this fashion for some time, the Ḥájibu'd-Dawla shot him in the back, and he was then hacked in pieces by the *farráshes* with knives. His execution took place at Niyávarán. [Ṣubḥ-i-Ezel confirmed the fact that he suffered torture by lighted candles inserted in wounds inflicted on his body, but asserted that he, together with Hájí Suleymán Khán, was sawn in two.]

(7) Sheykh 'Abba of Teherán was killed by the Kháns and nobles. [According to Ṣubḥ-i-Ezel, however, he was suffered to escape privily.]

(8) Muḥammad Báḳir of Najafábád (near Isfahán), who had, on his own confession, taken an active part in the insurrections of Mázandarán and Zanján, was killed by the *písh-khidmats* (pages in waiting).

(9) Muḥammad Taḳí of Shíráz was delivered over to the *Mír-ákhúr* (Master of the Horse) and the attendants of the Royal Stables. These first nailed iron horse-shoes on his feet, and then, in the words of the Musulmán historian, "broke up his head and body with clubs and nails."

(10) Muḥammad of Najafábád was killed by the *Eshik-áḳásí-báshí*, the *Járchí-báshí*, the *Nasaḳchí-báshí*, and their attendants.

(11) Mírzá Muḥammad of Níríz, who had fought for the Bábí cause at Níríz, Sheykh Ṭabarsí, and Zanján[1], was killed by Mírzá Muḥammad Khán the *Sar-kishík* (captain of the guard) and the *Yúz-báshís* (centurions).

(12) Muḥammad 'Alí of Najafábád was delivered over to the artillerymen. They first plucked out his eyes, and then blew him from the mouth of a gun.

(13) Aḳá Seyyid Ḥuseyn of Yezd (see preceding note, pp. 319—322) was killed by 'Azíz Khán *Ajúdán-báshí*, and the brigadier-generals, colonels, captains, and other officers.

(14) Aḳá Mahdí of Káshán (see note 1 on p. 46 *supra*) was slain by the *farráshes*.

(15) Mírzá Nabí of Damávand [a youth about twenty-one years of age] was sent to the College (*Dáru'l-funún*) of Teherán, by the professors and students of which he was torn in pieces.

(16) Mírzá Rafí' of Núr [a relation of Ṣubḥ-i-Ezel's, aged about fifty years, and noted for his skill in calligraphy] was killed by the cavalry.

(17) Mírzá Maḥmúd of Ḳazvín was hewn in pieces with daggers and knives by the men of the camel-artillery (*zambúrakchíyán*).

(18) Ḥuseyn of Mílán, called by the Bábís "Abú 'Abdi 'lláh," was slain by the soldiers with spears. [According

[1] As the risings at Zanján and Níríz were almost simultaneous, though the former was not suppressed for two months after the termination of the latter, it would appear very improbable that any one person could have taken an active part in both.

to Ṣubḥ-i-Ezel, Ḥuseyn of Mílán acted most discreditably, being at once the most turbulent and eager for mischief and the most pusillanimous of those who professed to follow the Báb. When he came to Teherán from Tabríz, he took up his abode in the house of Hájí Suleymán Khán. While resident there, he began to advance various claims to spiritual authority, first declaring himself to be a re-incarnation of the Imám Ḥuseyn, and then "He whom God shall manifest," whose coming the Báb had foretold. A considerable number of persons became his disciples, and, encouraged by this success, he seems to have meditated some act of violence, which was, however, discovered and frustrated by Ṣubḥ-i-Ezel. He had a brother named Ja'far, who gave himself out as "King of Baghdad." Ḥuseyn of Mílán, when arrested, would have saved himself by recanting and disclaiming all fellowship with the Bábís, but, while he was under examination, a child came in, and mockingly greeted him with the words "*Es-selámu 'aley-kum, yá Imám Ḥuseyn*" ("Peace be upon you, O Imám Ḥuseyn!"). This sufficed to secure his conviction. It is worth noting that three other persons[1] besides Ḥuseyn of Mílán advanced vain claims to supreme authority in the Bábí church, to wit, Mírzá Asadu'lláh of Tabríz surnamed *Deyyán* (see Gobineau, pp. 277—278); Seyyid Ḥuseyn of Hindiyan near Muḥammara, who gathered round him about forty disciples, and who, though not recognized or accredited by the Bábí chiefs, continued to send greetings to them while they were in exile at Baghdad; and Sheykh Isma'íl, believed to be still alive, who subsequently with-drew the claim which he had advanced.]

(19) Mullá 'Abdu'l-Karím of Ḳazvín (called by the Bábís "Mírzá Aḥmad-i-*Kátib*"; see note 2 on p. 41 *supra*) was killed by the artillerymen.

(20) Luṭf-'Alí of Shíráz was put to death by the royal footmen.

(21) Najaf of Khamsa was delivered over to the people of the city, who "with sticks and stones crimsoned the earth with his blood."

[1] But see Note W *infra*, where, on the authority of the Ezelí controversial work called *Hasht Bihisht*, other pretenders are mentioned.

(22) Hájí Mírzá Jání of Káshán, the merchant, was delivered over to Áḳá Mahdí the chief of the merchants (*Maliku't-tujjár*), and the other merchants and shop-keepers of the city, "each of whom inflicted a wound on him until he perished." [According to Ṣubḥ-i-Ezel, Hájí Mírzá Jání took refuge in the sanctuary of Sháh 'Abdu'l-'Aẓím, which is situated about four miles south of Teherán. The sanctuary was, however, not respected in his case, and he was dragged forth. In compensation for this violation of the holy place the Sháh plated or replated the roof of the shrine with gold. Of Hájí Mírzá Jání's death Ṣubḥ-i-Ezel gave a different version, according to which he was strangled with the bowstring. After he was let down, being supposed to be dead, he half raised himself, opened his eyes, gazed at his executioners, and then fell back dead. He had three brothers, two of whom were also Bábís. Of these two, one, Hájí Mírzá Ismá'íl, died in Teherán. The other, Hájí Mírzá Aḥmad, was killed in Baghdad by certain Behá'ís[1], he being one of those who refused to transfer their allegiance from Ṣubḥ-i-Ezel to Behá. The *Táríkh-i-Jadíd* makes frequent mention of Hájí Mírzá Jání, and repeatedly quotes from a history of the Bábí movement which he wrote.]

(23) Ḥasan of Khamsa was slain by Naṣru'lláh Khán the superintendent of the royal kitchen and his myrmidons.

(24) Muḥammad Báḳir of Ḳuhpáyé was slain by the Ḳájár chiefs with their swords.

(25) The body of Ṣádiḳ of Zanján, who was slain, as above narrated, while attacking the Sháh, was cut into several pieces, which were suspended from the different gates of Teherán.

(26) Hájí Suleymán Khán, the son of Yaḥyá Khán of Tabríz, and—

(27) Ḳásim of Níríz, who regarded himself as the successor of Seyyid Yaḥyá of Dáráb, were, by command of Áḳá Ḥasan the deputy-chief of the *farráshes*, wounded in many parts of their bodies, and in these wounds lighted candles were inserted. The two unfortunate men were thus paraded through the streets and bazaars of the city to

[1] See Note W *infra*.

the sound of minstrelsy, while dust and ashes were hurled upon them by the spectators. After being made to traverse a great distance in this fashion, they were led out of the city, and sawn asunder into four quarters outside the Sháh 'Abdu'l-'Aẓím gate by the *farráshes* of the gaol. Their mangled remains were then attached to the city gates. [Vámbéry (*Wanderungen und Erlebnisse in Persien*, Pest, 1867, p. 299) gives a quite different account of Suleymán Khán's martyrdom, which runs as follows:—"Suleiman Chan, ein wohl-beleibter Mann, hatte zuerst vier Schnitte in die Brust bekommen, in welche brennende Kerzen gesteckt wurden und man führte ihn so lange im Bazar herum, bis das Wachs der Kerzen von den Flammen verzehrt war und der Docht sich später am herausfliessenden Fett des Delinquenten nähren musste. Darauf wurde ihm glühende schwere Hufeisen auf die nackten Fusssohlen angeschlagen und aufs Neue wurde er herum geführt, bis man ihm endlich alle Zähne vom Munde herausriss und in der Form eines Halbmondes auf den Schädel einschlug. Da starb er erst." The extraordinary heroism with which Suleymán Khán bore these frightful tortures is notorious, and I have repeatedly heard it related how he ceased not during the long agony which he endured to testify his joy that he should be accounted worthy to suffer martyrdom for his Master's cause. He even sang and recited verses of poetry, amongst them the following:—

باز آمدم باز آمدم از راه شیراز آمدم

با عشوه و ناز آمدم هذا جنون العاشقِ

"I have returned! I have returned! I have come by the way of Shíráz!
I have come with winsome airs and graces! Such is the lover's madness!"

"Why do you not dance," asked the executioners mockingly, "since you find death so pleasant?" "Dance!" cried Suleymán Khán—

یك دست جام باده و یك دست زلف یار

رقصی چنین میانهٔ میدانم ارزوست

"'In one hand the wine-cup, in one hand the tresses of the Friend--
Such a dance in the midst of the market-place is my desire!'"]

(28) Last but not least amongst the victims of that fatal day was the beautiful and accomplished Ḳurratu'l-'Ayn, who had been imprisoned for two or three years previously in the house of Maḥmúd Khán the *Kalántar*. Concerning her life and death, see Note Q, *supra*.

Gobineau (pp. 301—302) and Vámbéry (*op. cit.*, pp. 299—300) both assert that amongst the martyrs of that day were women and children, who rivalled the men in the fortitude wherewith they met death; but of this assertion (except as regards Ḳurratu'l-'Ayn) I have been unable to obtain any corroborative evidence from Musulmán or Bábí tradition. The crimes and cruelties which that day beheld are black enough without going beyond even the Muhammadan chronicles, and one would be reluctant to add to them, unless compelled to do so by convincing evidence. The wife of Hájí Suleymán Khán would appear from Ṣubḥ-i-Ezel's account to have been in imminent peril, but by eating flies she induced so violent an attack of vomiting that her gaolers, believing her to be stricken with a mortal sickness, released her. Two women related to Ṣubḥ-i-Ezel were arrested and imprisoned for a while in the house of Maḥmúd Khán the Kalántar, but were subsequently sent back to their homes at Núr. A large reward was offered for the apprehension of Ṣubḥ-i-Ezel (then residing at Núr), who actually conversed for some time with one of those sent out to arrest him without being recognized.

NOTE U.

WRITINGS OF THE BÁB AND ṢUBḤ-I-EZEL.

On October 11th, 1889, I received a letter from Captain Young (dated September 30th) enclosing a letter and sundry other documents from Ṣubḥ-i-Ezel. Amongst these documents was a list of some of the writings of the Báb and Ṣubḥ-i-Ezel written out by the latter. Although this list does not profess to be complete, comprising only such works as were carried by the Bábí exiles to Baghdad, and although, in the absence of detailed information about the works enumerated therein, it is incapable of affording much help in the identification of Bábí MSS., I here append a translation of it, in the hope that it may serve in some measure to throw light on the very imperfectly explored bibliography of the sect. Explanatory notes of my own are added in square brackets.

[WRITINGS OF THE BÁB.]

"*What was collected of the books of the Beyán of the remnant left from Persia, which was taken away in Baghdad, carried off by the relations of this humble one* [i.e. Ṣubḥ-i-Ezel].

[1] *Commentary on the Ḳur'án* in the style of the Ḳur'án, complete, 1 vol.

[2] *Answers and Commentaries* (اجوبه و تفاسير), 1 vol.

[3] *Commentary on the Ḳur'án* in the fashion of the verses of the Ḳur'án, complete, 1 vol.

[4] *The Five Grades* (شئون خمسه), 1 vol. [A MS. of this work was forwarded to me by Ṣubḥ-i-Ezel with the letter above referred to. It comprises 395 pages of 14 lines each, and contains selections of pieces in each of the "five

grades" or "styles" employed by the Báb, the nature of which will be briefly discussed at the end of this note.]

[5] *Verses* (ايات), 2 vols.

[6] *The Book of Recompense* (كتاب جزا), 2 vols. [A small fragment of this work, transcribed by Ṣubḥ-i-Ezel, is in my possession. One peculiarity thereof is the occurrence of groups of verses differing from one another only in one or two words. By combining the first letters of the divergent words or clauses proper names are formed, so that the book would appear to be in part a cabbalistic register of the names of believers. In the following specimen, which will render the nature of this procedure more clear, the catch-words are indicated by a line drawn over them:—

و لله الحمد فى ملكوت السّموات و الارض و ما بينهما
و كان الله حميداً مجيداً * و لله الامر من قبل و من بعد
يبدع الله ما يشآء بامره انّه كان على كلّ شىء وكيلاً *
و لله جبروت السموات و الارض و ما بينهما و كان الله
ذا جبروت حقّ عظيماً * و لله يمين السّموات و الارض
و ما بينهما ينفق كيف يشآء بفضله و كان الله واسعاً
عليماً * و لله العظمة فى ملكوت السموات و الارض و
ما بينهما و كان الله علياً عظيماً * و لله بر السموات
و الارض و ما بينهما و كان الله ذا بر قريباً * و لله
دوام الذكر فى ملكوت السموات و الارض و ما بينهما و

كان الله دائماً قديماً * قل الله ربّى و انّه هو حسبى لينصرننى فى كلّ حين بامره انّه كان ذا نصر عزيزاً * و لله لطائف السموات و الارض و ما بينهما و كان الله ذا لطف عظيماً * و لله ملك السموات و الارض و ما بينهما و كان الله ذا ملك كبيراً * و لله طهر السموات و الارض و ما بينهما و كان الله طاهراً لطيفاً * و لله لطائف السموات و الارض و ما بينهما و كان الله ذا لطف عظيماً * و لله بهاء السموات و الارض و ما بينهما و كان الله ذا بهاء عز عظيماً *

By combining the first letters of the catch-words in the above extract (after discarding the definite article, in cases where this is prefixed) we get the name حاجى عبد المطلب Ḥájí 'Abdu'l-Muṭṭalib. Similarly the verses immediately succeeding these give the name حاجى محمد مهدى Ḥájí Muḥammad Mahdí.]

[7] *Supplications and Visitations* (مناجات و زيارات), 1 vol. [In my second article on the Bábís in the *J.R.A.S.* for 1889, I described one of these "Visitations" under the name *Ziyárat-námé* (pp. 894—902, 1000), and attempted to prove its identity with Gobineau's "Journal du Pèlerinage" and with a Bábí MS. described by Mirza Kazem-Beg (ii, pp. 498—502). At that time I was not aware that the Báb had composed more than one work

of this character. I subsequently enquired of Ṣubḥ-i-Ezel as to the authenticity of this work. In reply he wrote as follows:—"The 'Book of Visitation' (*Kitáb-i-ziyárat*) which you alluded to is from His Highness the Point (i.e. the Báb), and was after the 'Manifestation,' as its contents testify. He wrote many 'Visitations': it is not limited to one. But there is also a 'Book of Visitations' by myself. That is in another style, but there is in this land but a small portion thereof." Some of these 'Visitations' are included in the MS. of the 'Five Grades' mentioned above, amongst them being one designed for the use of pilgrims visiting the graves of the martyrs who fell at Sheykh Ṭabarsí. This, according to Ṣubḥ-i-Ezel, was also composed by the Báb.]

[8] *Prayers* (دعوات), 1 vol.

[9] *Various Grades* (شئون مختلفه), unbound, 1 [vol.].

[10] *Writings of the Scribe* [probably Áḳá Seyyid Ḥuseyn of Yezd or Mullá 'Abdu'l-Karím of Ḳazvín] *comprising what was revealed at Shíráz and Iṣfahán and during the journey of the Pilgrimage* [to Mecca], 3 vols.

[11] *The Best of Stories* (احسن القصص), 1 vol. [This work, better known as the 'Commentary on the Súra of Joseph,' is so called in allusion to Ḳur'án xii, 3, where the history of Joseph is thus characterized. Specimens of it have been published by Baron Rosen in vol. i of the *Collections Scientifiques de l'Institut des Langues Orientales* (St Petersburg, 1877), pp. 179—191. Some description of it, based on the extracts published by Baron Rosen, is given at pp. 904—909 of my second article on the Bábís. See also p. 3 *supra*, and note 3 thereon.]

[12] *The Book of Names* (کتاب اسما), comprising 361 Names, amongst which is the Name '*Musakkin*' ('the Calmer'), incomplete, 2 vols. [The extracts from a Bábí MS. in the St Petersburg collection published by Dorn in the *Bulletin de l'Académie Impériale de St Pétersbourg* of Dec. 22nd, 1864, were pronounced by Ṣubḥ-i-Ezel, to whose inspection I submitted them, to belong to this work.]

[13] *Writings of the deceased Áḳá Seyyid Ḥuseyn* [of Yezd], original copy, 2 vols.

[14] *Various Grades* (شئون مختلفه), 1 vol.

[15] *The Book of Figures* (کتاب هیاکل), 1 vol. [See note 1 on p. 42 *supra*, Mirza Kazem-Beg, ii, p. 498, and Gobineau, p. 498, note 1.]

[16] *Sundry* (متفرقه), 1 vol.

[17] *Things appertaining to Jenáb-i-Sheykh-i-'Aẓím* [Mullá Sheykh 'Alí, see Note T, p. 329 *supra*], 3 vols., together with his effects.

[18] *Copies and originals of writings* (فرع و اصل نوشتها), tied up together in four bundles.

[19] *Beyán*, 1 vol. [Concerning the application of this name see below.]

[20] *Prayers* (دعوات), 1 vol.

[21] *Prayers and Visitations* (دعوات و زیارات), 1 vol.

[22] *The Best of Stories* [see No. 11 *supra*], *and another Beyán which is missing* (بیان دیگر که خارج شده است), 2 [vols.].

[23] *The Five Grades* [see No. 4 *supra*], 1 vol.

[24] *Sundry* (متفرقه).

[25] *Another Book*, 1 vol.

"Besides what was destroyed in Persia, some of which never reached [my] hand, and what went to foreign lands and was therefore ignored in [making out the catalogue of] the trust. What was promulgated [by the Báb] at first in Shíráz and other places [included] the *Book of seven hundred Súras* (کتاب هفتصد سوره); the *Book of the Proof* (صحیفهٔ حجتیه, *sic*); the *Book of the two Sanctu-*

aries (صحيفهٔ حرمين); the [Book of] *Justice* (عدليه); the *Prayer of the two alifs* (or, *of the two thousand*, كتاب الفين); *Epistles of the earlier period of the dispensation* (الواح اول امر), each of which was sent to a different destination; the *Commentary on the 'Bismi'lláh'* (شرح بسمله); and the *Commentary on* [Súra ciii of the Ḳur'án beginning] '*Wa'l-'aṣr*' (see *supra*, p. 11).

"As to what appertained to [i.e. was composed by] the 'Name of the Last' (اسم اخر) [by which title, as Ṣubḥ-i-Ezel explained elsewhere, Mullá Muḥammad 'Alí of Bárfurúsh, called by the Bábís *Jenáb-i-Ḳuddús*, is intended], but little remained in [my] hands. All the rest passed into the hands of strangers. Amongst other things the *Commentary on* [the opening chapter of the Ḳur'án entitled '*Al-*]*Ḥamd,*' [the eloquence of] which was beyond the power of man, was entirely destroyed, and no copy remained in [my] possession."

[Writings of Ṣubḥ-i-Ezel.]

"*What appertaineth to this humble one* [i.e. Ṣubḥ-i-Ezel], *apart from that whereof the existence in Persia is unknown* [i.e. besides what may exist in Persia unknown to me].

[1] *The Book of Light* (كتاب نور), 1 vol. [See Gobineau, pp. 312—313; B. ii, pp. 939—942; and M. C. Huart's *Note sur trois ouvrages Bâbis* in the *Journal Asiatique* for 1887 (série viii, tome x, pp. 133—144). M. Huart identified the first of the three works which he described with the *Book of Light* mentioned by Gobineau, but did not fail to observe the discrepancy in size between the "assez gros in-folio" of the latter writer and the small volume which was the subject of his own description. The solution of the difficulty appears to be that there are two separate works bearing the same name, both composed by

Ṣubḥ-i-Ezel. I forwarded an abstract of M. Huart's description of the supposed *Book of Light* to Ṣubḥ-i-Ezel, who replied as follows:—"The *Book of Light* is by this humble one [i.e. by myself], but there are two *Lights*, a first and a second. If it be the second, it will be worthy of attentive perusal, and will be a voluminous work. Some of the names of the *súras* which you wrote are from the *Book of Light*, provided that there be not therein interpolations of enemies, such as my relatives have effected in some cases, inserting their own calumnies in certain epistles; though to him who hath knowledge of God this will be apparent." The *Book of Light* mentioned in this list is, as I ascertained during my sojourn at Famagusta, the larger of the two works bearing this name.]

[2] *The Highest Heaven* (علیین), 1 vol. [Of this work Ṣubḥ-i-Ezel mentioned two copies, one in Persia, and one (the same here mentioned) in the hands of the Behá'ís at Acre.]

[3] *Miscellaneous* (مختلفه), 1 vol.

[4] *The Wakeful, &c.* (مستیقظ), 1 vol. [A copy extant in Persia.]

[5] *Writings of the Scribe* (خطوط کاتب), 2 vols. [By "the Scribe," as subsequently explained by Ṣubḥ-i-Ezel, Mullá 'Abdu'l-Karím of Ḳazvín is intended. See note 2 on p. 41 *supra*.]

[6] *Tracts, &c., of* [the nature of] *Visitations* (صحیفه و غیرها از زیارات), 1 large vol.

[7] *Another book, miscellaneous*, 1 vol.

[8] *Commentary on the Ḳaṣída, and other miscellaneous writings* (شرح قصیده و مختلفه), unbound, 1 vol.

[9] [Book of] *Light*, unbound, 1 vol. [The same as No. 1 *supra*.]

[10] *Verses* (آیات), 1 vol.

"Besides what may exist unknown [to me] in other

lands, and entirely apart from [what exists in] the prison of this land. All these books and epistles have disappeared, save what have remained in other countries and the few which remain in this land."

In the letter accompanying this list Ṣubḥ-i-Ezel wrote as follows concerning the fate of the Báb's works generally and of those above enumerated in particular:—

"As to what you asked concerning the existence of certain epistles, it is even as you have heard, leaving out of account that which from first to last passed into the hands of strangers, whereof no copy was preserved. At the time of the martyrdom [of the Báb] at Tabríz, as they wrote from thence, many of the original writings passed into the hands of persons belonging to the country of your Excellency or to Russia, amongst these being even autograph writings of His Highness the Point [i.e. the Báb]. Search is necessary, for to read the originals is difficult. If this humble one be applied to, copies thereof will be sent. What I myself arranged and copied out while at Baghdad, and what was commanded to be collected of previous and subsequent [writings] until the Day of Martyrdom [of the Báb], was nigh upon thirty volumes of bound books. I myself wrote them with my own hand, and up to the present time I have written many. The originals and copies of these, together with what was in the writing of others, sundry other [books] written in proof of this religion by certain learned friends[1], and what I myself wrote and compiled, amounted to numerous volumes, as [recorded in] the list thereof [which] I have sent. For some years all of these were in a certain place in the hands of a friend as a trust. Afterwards they were deposited in another place[2].

[1] In answer to a question as to the nature and authorship of the works here alluded to, Ṣubḥ-i-Ezel informed me that the Báb declared it to be a meritorious action for each of his followers who was competent thereunto to compose a treatise in defence of the Faith. Many such treatises were accordingly composed by the more learned Bábís, amongst them being one by *Jenáb-i-'Aẓím* (Mullá Sheykh 'Alí), and one called سبعمائه (*'The seven hundred'*) by *Jenáb-i-Ṭáhira* (Ḳurratu'l-'Ayn).

[2] One of these depositaries, as I subsequently learned from

Eventually I entrusted them to my own relatives[1], [in whose keeping] they were preserved for a while; for, inasmuch as the friends of this recluse [i.e. myself] had attained unto martyrdom through the *equity* and *justice* of the oppressors of the age, who consider themselves as seekers after truth and just men, there was no resource but that this humble one [i.e. myself] should make his relatives his trustees. So did this humble one; and whatever [was mine] of books and epistles was [deposited] in their house. The vicissitudes of the world so fell out that these also unsheathed the sword of hatred and wrought what they would. They cruelly put to the sword the remnant of [my] friends who stood firm[2], and, making strenuous efforts, got into their hands such of the books of His Highness the Point as were obtainable, with the idea of destroying them, and [thereby] rendering their own works more attractive. They also carried off my trust [i.e. the books above referred to committed to their care], and fell not short in anything which can be effected by foes."

As to the meaning of the word *Beyán*, Ṣubḥ-i-Ezel writes in another passage of the same letter as follows:—"But in the *Beyán* different grades (شئون مختلفه) are observed. The *first grade* is like [i.e. in the style of] previous [sacred] books; the *second* [is] of the nature of supplications and prayers (مناجات و دعوات); the *third* [is] the grade of homilies (خطب), wherein he had regard to clearness and eloquence; the *fourth* [comprises] scientific treatises (شئون علميه), commentaries, and answers to en-

Ṣubḥ-i-Ezel, was Áḳá Seyyid Jawád, who died lately at Kirmán. The other was a certain merchant of great wealth whom I cannot more particularly designate.

[1] By his 'relatives' Ṣubḥ-i-Ezel means his half-brother Behá'u'llah and those of his kindred who followed him. I never heard Ṣubḥ-i-Ezel allude to Behá'u'llah and his followers by name. When he spoke of them at all (which he did but rarely) it was as his 'relatives,' the 'people at Acre,' or the 'Mírzá'ís.'

[2] See Note W *infra*.

quirers; the *fifth* [comprises what is written] in the Persian language, which is [in substance] identical with the afore-mentioned grades, '*for that all this is watered with one water*'."

This statement of what is meant by the term *Beyán* is (with the exception of some slight differences in the arrangement of the 'grades') fully corroborated by the Persian Beyán, which, at the beginning of Váḥid iii, ch. 17, has the following passage:—

ملخّص این باب آنکه کلّ آثار نقطه مسمی به بیان
است ولی این اسم بحقیقة اوّلیه مختّص بآیات است و بعد
در مقام مناجات بحقیقة ثانویه ذکر میشود و بعد در مقام
تفاسیر بحقیقة ثالثیه و بعد در مقام صور علمیه بحقیقة رابعیه
و بعد در مقام کلمات فارسیه بحقیقة خامسیه اطلاق میشود
ولی این اسم مختّص آیات است نه غیر او باستحقاق *

"The substance of this chapter is this, that all the writings of the Point [i.e. the Báb] are named *Beyán*. But this name is, in its primary nature, peculiar to *verses* [i.e. verses written in Arabic in the style of the Ḳur'án]; then it is uttered in its secondary nature in regard to *supplications;* then in its tertiary nature in regard to *commentaries;* then in its quaternary nature in regard to *scientific treatises;* then in its quinary nature it is used in regard to *Persian words* [i.e. writings and discourses]. But properly speaking this name [of Beyán] is peculiar to *verses*, and [is applicable] to nought else."

Again in Váḥid vi, ch. 1, the following passage occurs:—

اسم بیان بحقیقة اوّلیه اطلاق بر آیات وحده میگردد زیرا

که اوست حجّة عظمی و بیّنهٔ کبری که دلالت نمیکند الاّ
علی الله وحده و در حقیقة ثانویّه اطلاق بمناجات
و در ثالث بتفاسیر و در رابع بکلمات علمیّه و در خامس
بکلمات فارسیّه میگردد ولی کلّ در ظلّ آیات ذکر
میگردد اگرچه آن سرّ فصاحتی که در اوّل ظاهر
است در آخر هم منظور[1] است ولی چون کلّ نتواند
درك نمود ذکر نشده *

"The name *Beyán* is, in its primary nature, applied to *verses* alone, for they are the chiefest proof and greatest argument, which point not save unto God alone. But in its secondary nature it is applied to *supplications;* in its tertiary [nature] to *commentaries;* in its quaternary [nature] to *scientific treatises;* and in its quinary [nature] to *Persian words.* But all [these] are mentioned in the shadow of [i.e. as subsidiary or subordinate to] *verses*, for, although that mysterious eloquence which is apparent in the first [grade] is also observable [or, if we adopt B's reading, *latent*] in the last, yet, since all cannot understand, they [i.e. the lower grades] are not mentioned [as a proof]."

From all this it follows that, although the book generally known as the *Persian Beyán* is a definite work of limited extent, we can no longer employ the term *Arabic Beyán* in an equally definite sense. As Ṣubḥ-i-Ezel states in another letter, as a rule only those books which were composed by the Báb during the earlier part of his mission received special names, while at a later date all that he 'uttered' or 'revealed' was named collectively *Beyán* ('Utterance' or 'Revelation'). Some of these 'utterances' (such as the

[1] B reads مستور.

'verses' recited by the Báb before his judges at Tabríz, concerning which see Gobineau, pp. 261—262) can hardly have been preserved at all, much less were all ever collected into a single work, though, according to Ṣubḥ-i-Ezel, a selection in nineteen volumes was compiled, or ordered to be compiled, during the Báb's lifetime. Gobineau, with his usual acumen, appears to have clearly apprehended this peculiar and elastic use of the term Beyán, for he says (p. 311):—"Le mot *Biyyan*, une fois employé par le Bâb, lui parut convenir très-bien pour désigner la sphère d'idées dans laquelle sa pensée se mouvait, et il le donna dès lors pour titre à tout ce qu'il composa." When, therefore, he speaks of "a Beyán written in Persian, which is not the commentary on the first Beyán written in Arabic," and of "a third Beyán, likewise composed by the first Báb," he apparently intends merely to signalize certain specially noteworthy parts of that almost limitless mass of religious literature emanating from the Báb which is known collectively as the Beyán.

From what has been said it is evident that the short list of the Báb's works which I gave at the end of my second article on the Bábís in the *J. R. A. S.* for 1889 (pp. 1000—1002) requires much alteration both in the way of correction and extension. The sum total of the Báb's writings would appear, both from the Persian Beyán and from the *Táríkh-i-Jadíd*, to have been enormous; and, though much of this mass of literature perished, much is still preserved in Persia and elsewhere in the East. Quite recently I received from Ṣubḥ-i-Ezel MSS. of the *Commentary on the Súratu'l-'aṣr* (see *supra*, p. 11, and B. ii, p. 912) and the *Commentary on the Súratu'l-Baḳara* (see B. ii, pp. 902—903, 912), which had been brought from Persia to Cyprus during the present year (1890). Of the genuineness of these MSS. I entertain no doubt. Four other MSS. of different works composed by the Báb (amongst which are included the Commentaries on the Súras called *Kawthar* and *Yúsuf*) were brought to Cyprus at the same time, but of these I have not yet obtained copies[1]. Of the *Súra-i-*

[1] Since writing the above I have received two of these four MSS. One of them is the commentary on the *Súratu'l-Kawthar*

Yúsuf at least two copies are preserved in Europe, one (numbered Or. 3539) in the British Museum, and one (fully described by Baron Rosen at pp. 179—191 of vol. i of the *Collections Scientifiques &c.*) at St. Petersburg.

NOTE V.

TEXTS FROM THE PERSIAN BEYÁN ILLUSTRATING THE BÁB'S VIEW OF HIS RELATION TO 'HIM WHOM GOD SHALL MANIFEST.'

(i) The whole Beyán revolves round the saying of 'Him whom God shall manifest.'
[*Váḥid iii, ch.* 3.]

الباب الثالث من الواحد الثالث فی ان البیان و من فیه
طائف[1] فی حول قول من یظهره الله بمثل ما کان الالف
و من فیه طائف فی حول[2] قول محمد رسول الله و ما
نزل الله [علیه][3] فی اولاه[4] و من فیه طائف فی حول قوله
حین ظهور اخریه ملخص این باب آنکه مد نظر بیان
نیست الا بسوی من یظهره الله زیرا که غیر او رافع[5] او

above mentioned. It contains 227 pages, and is dated Ẕi'l-Ḥijjé 4th, A.H. 1296 (Nov. 19, A.D. 1879). The other, a much larger work, is named by Ṣubḥ-i-Ezel "*Commentary on the Names*" (تفسیر الاسماء).

1 B omits.
2 B omits.
3 Omitted in my own MS. and B, but supplied from the portion of the text published by Baron Rosen (*MSS. Persans*, p. 14).
4 B reads ادلاه.
5 B reads واقع.

نبوده و نیست چنانچه منزل[1] او[2] غیر او نبوده و نیست و بیان و مومنین به بیان مشتاقترند بسوی او از اشتیاق هر حبیبی بمحبوب خود ❁

"*The third chapter of the third Váḥid. Concerning this, that the Beyán and whosoever is therein revolve round the saying of Him whom God shall manifest, even as the Alif* [i.e. the Gospel, *Injíl*] *and whosoever was therein revolved round the saying of Muḥammad the Apostle of God, and as that which God revealed unto him at first and whosoever was therein revolved round that which he said at the period of his later manifestation.* The quintessence of this chapter is this, that the gaze of the Beyán is not extended save towards Him whom God shall manifest, for none but He hath raised or doth raise it up, even as none but He hath sent or doth send it down. And the Beyán and such as are believers therein yearn more after Him than the yearning of any lover after his beloved."

(ii) A thousand perusals of the Beyán are not equal to the perusal of one verse of what shall be revealed by 'Him whom God shall manifest.'
[*Váḥid* v, *ch.* 8.]

قسم بذات اقدس الهی عزّ و جلّ[3] که در یوم ظهور من یظهره الله اگر کسی یك آیه‌را[4] از او شنود و تلاوت کند بهتر است از آنکه هزار مرتبه بیان‌را تلاوت کند ❁

[1] B reads منزّل. [2] B omits.

[3] B reads جلّ و عزّ. [4] B reads آیه.

"I swear by the Most Holy Essence of God (Glorious and Splendid is He !) that in the day of the manifestation of Him whom God shall manifest if one should hear a single verse from Him and recite it, it is better than that he should recite the Beyán a thousand times."

[The same assertion is repeated in slightly different words in *Váḥid vi, ch.* 6.]

(iii) The Beyán is to day in the stage of seed, but in the day of 'Him whom God shall manifest' it will arrive at the degree of fruition.

[*Váḥid ii, ch.* 7. The passage referred to will be found in Note C at pp. 224—225].

(iv) All the splendour of the Beyán is 'He whom God shall manifest.'
[*Váḥid iii, ch.* 14.]

كلّ بهاء بيان من يظهره الله است كلّ رحمت از
راى كسيكه ايمان[1] اورد و كلّ نقمت از براى كسيكه
ايمان باو نياورد ۞

"All the splendour [*Behá*] of the Beyán is He whom God shall manifest. All mercy be on him who believeth, and all chastisement on him who believeth not in Him."

NOTE W.

MÍRZÁ YAḤYÁ "ṢUBḤ-I-EZEL."

After the Báb himself, Behá'u'lláh and Ṣubḥ-i-Ezel are without doubt the most important figures in the history of Bábíism. To the words and deeds of the former a large

[1] B inserts باو.

portion of the present work is devoted, while the latter, when mentioned, is spoken of slightingly as a mere "man of straw." One whose knowledge of Bábí history should be limited to the account given in this *Traveller's Narrative* would, therefore, by no means properly apprehend the importance of the part actually played by Ṣubḥ-i-Ezel. In my opinion it is proved beyond all doubt that the Báb ere his death chose him as his successor, duly appointing him as such by the form of words which I published at pp. 996—997 of my second paper on the Bábís in the *J.R.A.S.* for 1889, and that during the period which elapsed from the Báb's death till the advancement of Behá'u'lláh's claim to be "He whom God shall manifest" (i.e. from 1850 to 1864 at any rate) he was recognized by all the Bábís as their spiritual chief. Even now the number of his followers, though small in comparison to that of the Behá'ís, is considerable; and since, in addition to all this, the old Bábí doctrines and traditions, which have undergone considerable modification at the hands of Behá'u'lláh, are preserved intact by Ṣubḥ-i-Ezel, I have considered it incumbent on me to embody in a separate note all the more important facts relating to him which I have been able to ascertain, together with a complete account of the Bábís exiled to Cyprus based on the most authentic documents.

The sources from which my information is derived are, broadly speaking, four in number, as follows:—

(1) Letters received from Ṣubḥ-i-Ezel himself between August 1889 and the present time, the correspondence still continuing. In only one or two of these letters, however, does he speak of his own adventures and circumstances with any approach to freedom.

(2) Conversations between Captain Young or myself on the one hand and Ṣubḥ-i-Ezel or his sons on the other. In the numerous and protracted interviews which I had with Ṣubḥ-i-Ezel between March 22nd and April 4th, 1890, I was able to recur for my own satisfaction to almost every point which the preliminary enquiries kindly undertaken by Captain Young had first elicited.

(3) Official documents relative to the exiles preserved in the archives of the Cyprus government. Sir Henry Bulwer, with a kindness and courtesy for which I cannot

sufficiently express my gratitude, permitted me freely to inspect and copy all the more important of these documents, and, with one exception, to make use of the information therein contained, as has been set forth in detail in the Introduction.

(4) A bulky MS. of a hitherto unknown Ezelí controversial work entitled *Hasht Bihisht* ("The Eight Paradises"), which I was fortunate enough to obtain a few days ago (February 2nd, 1891) from a learned Ezelí resident in Constantinople. The whole of this work is not at present in my possession, 10 fasciculi (160 pp.) out of the middle having unfortunately fallen into the hands of the Philistines after they had been written out by the scribe. The original MS. is, however, in safe keeping, and in the course of a month or two I hope to receive a fresh transcript of the missing portion, which extends from p. 128 to p. 329 inclusive[1]. The whole work contains nearly 450 pp., and deals chiefly with the philosophical basis of Bábíism, its superiority to other religions, and the proofs of its divine origin; but a great deal of information is also given about the history, especially the later history, of the movement. The account given of the schism which separated the Behá'ís from the Ezelís is, especially when taken in conjunction with the version given in this present work, extremely instructive; and the polemical portion, wherein the claims of Behá are attacked, and those of Ṣubḥ-i-Ezel defended, is full of interest. At some future date I hope to give a fuller notice of this valuable work, but for the present I must needs content myself with extracting from it the chief facts recorded concerning the life of Ṣubḥ-i-Ezel.

How best to deal with the information scattered through these numerous documents, notes, and letters in a manner which shall combine reasonable brevity with sufficient fullness is a matter which has cost me considerable thought. The plan which I have finally decided to follow is to give *firstly*, a full and literal translation of a short section of the *Hasht Bihisht* entitled *Sharḥ-i-ḥál-i-Ḥazrat-i-Thamara-i-*

[1] The fresh transcript of the missing portion reached me on March 23rd, 1891.

Beyán ("Elucidation of the circumstances of His Highness the Fruit of the Beyán"); *secondly*, a brief abstract of the account given in the same work of the origin and progress of the schism; *thirdly*, an epitome of the information derived directly from Ṣubḥ-i-Ezel, either by letter or in conversation; and *lastly*, a *resumé* of the official documents preserved in the archives of the Cyprus government.

I. *Translation from Hasht-Bihisht.*

"Now during the two last years [of the Báb's mission], when the five years' cycle[1] of the 'Minor Resurrection' had come to an end, the manifestation of His Highness the Eternal (*Ḥaẓrat-i-Ezel*) took place. And he, being then nineteen years of age, appeared in the hamlet of Takúr in [the district of] Núr of Mázandarán, and began with untaught tongue (*lisán-i-ummí*) to utter the Innate Word (*kalima-i-ẓátí*) and spontaneous verses (*áyát-i-fiṭrí*). When the first letter from him was conveyed by means of Mírzá 'Alí Sayyáḥ to His Highness the Point [i.e. the Báb], the latter instantly prostrated himself to the earth in thankfulness, saying, 'Blessed be God for this mighty Luminary which hath dawned and this noble Spathe which hath arisen in the night[2],' testifying of him that he spoke spontaneously and by the Self-Shining Light, which is the Innate Word, the Natural Reason (*'akl-i-fiṭrí*), the Holy Spirit, the Immediate Knowledge (*'ilm-i-laduní*), the Suffi-

[1] A passage in the *Dalá'il-i-sab'a* ("Seven Proofs"), to which I referred at p. 913 of my second paper on the Bábís in the *J. R. A. S.* for 1889, affords confirmatory evidence of what is here alleged concerning the date of Ṣubḥ-i-Ezel's first appearance. This passage runs as follows : یقین منمائی بر اینکه ظهور موعود منتظر همان ظهور حقیقت مسئول عنه است که در حدیث کمیل دیده در سنهٔ اول کشف سبحات الجلال من غیر اشاره در ثانی محو الموهوم و صحو المعلوم و در ثالث هتك السرّ لغلبة السرّ و در رابع جذب الاحديّة بصفة التوحيد ببين و در خامس نور اشرق من صبح الازل را خواهی دید اگر خود هارب نشوی و مضطرب نکردی *

[2] .تبارك الله من ذلك الشرق المتشارق العظيم و الطلع المتطالع الكريم

cing Light (*núr-i-mustakfí*), or, after another manner of speech, by Inspiration (*waḥy*), Revelation (*tanzíl*), and Illumination (*fardáb ú fartáb*).

"At this time His Highness the Point was imprisoned on the mountain of Mákú, and he therefore sent the writings of His Highness the Eternal for each of the Letters of the Living and the chief believers, testifying to his [i.e. *Ḥazrat* or *Ṣubḥ-i-Ezel's*] innate capacity (*fiṭrat*), and calling him by the names of 'Fruit of the Beyán' (*Thamara-i-Beyán*), 'Morning of Eternity' (*Subḥ-i-Ezel*), 'Countenance' (*Wajh*), 'Splendour of God' (*Behá'u'lláh*), 'Mirror' (*Mir'at*), 'Crystal' (*Bellúr*), 'Essence of Sweet Perfume' (*Jawhar-i-Káfúr*)[1], 'Sun of Eternity' (*Shams-i-Ezel*), 'Second Point' (*Nuḳṭa-i-thání*), 'One' (*Waḥíd*)[2], 'the Living, the Speaking' (*Ḥayy*[3]*-i-Náṭiḳ*), and sundry other titles. Having designated *Ḥazrat-i-Ezel* as his successor, he made over to him generally and particularly all the affairs of the *Beyán*, even transferring to him the [right of] disclosing the eight 'paths' (*manhaj*) of the Beyánic ordinances[4] which had [hitherto] remained con-

[1] Cf. Lane's *Arabic-English Lexicon*, Book i, part vii, p. 2622, col. 3, *s. v.* كافور, and Ḳur'án, lxxvi, 5. For an instance of the employment of this expression (which occurs repeatedly in the Báb's writings), see Mirza Kazem-Beg's last article on the Bábís in the *Journal Asiatique* for 1866 (sixième série, vol. viii) p. 501, last line.

[2] The numerical equivalent of *Waḥíd* (28) is the same as that of *Yaḥyá*. [See my second paper on the Bábís in the *J. R. A. S.* for 1889, pp. 996—997.]

[3] Concerning the sacred nature of the word حیّ, see Gobineau, p. 320. Ṣubḥ-i-Ezel's name *Yaḥyá* not only contains the root *ḥayy* (indeed by merely altering the vowel-points it becomes *Yuḥyí*, "he quickens," or "gives life"), but is also, as has just been pointed out, numerically equivalent to *Waḥíd* "One," another word of singular virtue.

[4] By these 'eight paths' of the *Beyán* are evidently intended the unrevealed *Váḥids*. Gobineau, whose penetration suffered nothing to escape him, has not failed to notice that the *Beyán*—or rather *Beyáns*, for, as has been pointed out, there are several—are purposely left incomplete. I cannot do better than quote his own words (p. 332):—"Le Biyyan étant le livre divin par excellence, doit nécessairement être constitué sur le nombre divin,

cealed within the Divine Volition (whereon their disclosure depended), in case the time should demand this.

"In short, during the two last years [of the Báb's life and mission] all that emanated from the Supreme Pen bore reference to His Highness the Fruit [of the Beyán], whom he [i.e. the Báb] recommended to all the people of the Beyán, saying that should they bring sorrow, even to the extent of the mention of aught, on his holy heart, all their good works and devotions would become as scattered dust. Of the words of His Highness the Point [i.e. the Báb] still extant at the present day, what bears reference to the Fruit [of the Beyán, i.e. Ṣubḥ-i-Ezel] exceeds 20,000 verses, not counting what has disappeared. And for ten years after [the death of] His Highness the Point all the people of the Beyán were unanimous and agreed as to the bestowal of the successorship on His Highness the Eternal [i.e. Ṣubḥ-i-Ezel]. And he abode for more than two years in Teherán and Shimírán, whence he departed into Mázandarán, whence again (because men had been stirred up on behalf of the government to seek him out) he set out disguised in the garb of a dervish for Hamadán and Kirmánsháhán[1]. Thence he proceeded to the Abode of Peace of Baghdad[2], and in reference to this the 'Tongue of the Unseen' [i.e. the poet Ḥáfiẓ] says:—

c'est-à-dire sur le nombre 19. Il est donc composé, en principe, de 19 unités ou divisions principales, qui, à leur tour, se subdivisent chacune en 19 paragraphes. Mais le Bâb n'a écrit que onze de ces unités, et il a laissé les huit autres au véritable et grand Révélateur, à celui qui complétera la doctrine, et à l'égard duquel le Bâb n'est autre chose que ce qu'était saint Jean-Baptiste devant Notre-Seigneur."

[1] Cf. pp. 51—52 *supra*.

[2] *Dáru's-salám* ("the Abode of Peace") is the official title of Baghdad, just as Teherán is called *Dáru'l-khiláfat* ("the Abode of the Caliphate"), Isfahán *Dáru 's-salṭanat* ("the Abode of the Sovereignty"), Shíráz *Dáru 'l-'ilm* ("the Abode of Knowledge"), Yezd *Dáru 'l-'ibádat* ("the Abode of Worship"), Kirmán *Dáru 'l-amán* ("the Abode of Security"), and the like. The Bábís, so prone to regard such coincidences, attach great importance to this title of Baghdad (which for eleven or twelve years was their head-quarters and rallying-point and the home of their chiefs), and quote as prophetic Ḳur'án vi, 127:— و لهم دار السلام عند ربهم و هو

(*Couplet*)

'Baghdad shall be filled with tumult; one with lips like sugar shall appear;
I fear lest the disturbance of his lips may cast Shíráz into confusion[1].'

"At this juncture Mírzá Ḥuseyn 'Alí [i.e. Behá'u'lláh], the elder brother of His Highness [Ṣubḥ-i-Ezel], came to Baghdad with two other brothers and several of the believers, and these gathered round that Most Mighty Light, who, in accordance with instructions which His Highness the Point of Revelation [i.e. the Báb] had given him, passed his nights and days behind the curtains of seclusion apart from believers and others—

(*Couplet*)

'Behind a veil sits that moon-browed beauty;
He has rent asunder the veils of the world, yet sits behind a veil'—

and none approached him save his brothers and certain favoured followers. But from behind that veil issued forth letters, epistles (*alwáḥ*), and books [written] in reply to men's questions and petitions."

Here ends that section of the *Hasht Bihisht* which I deemed it desirable to translate in full. It is followed by a section entitled *Sharḥ-i-ḥál-i-'ijl ú Sámirí* ("Elucidation of the circumstances of the Calf and Sámirí")[2], which in

وليهم بما كانوا يعملون ("Theirs is an Abode of Peace beside their Lord, and He is their Protector by reason of that which they have done").

[1] This verse I have generally heard somewhat differently quoted; see B. ii, pp. 993—994 and note 2 at foot of former page. My MS. of the *Hasht Bihisht* puts "*Ahwáz*" in the margin as an alternative reading for "*Shíráz*." The couplet is not to be found in the Díván of Ḥáfiẓ—at least in any of the copies which I have seen.

[2] Allusion is made to the Golden Calf which the Children of Israel were misled by Sámirí into worshipping. (See Ḳur'án, vii, 146; xx, 87, *et seq.;* and numerous other passages.) By "*the Calf*" the Ezelí controversialist, of course, means Behá'u'lláh (or,

turn is succeeded by another entitled *Sharḥ-i-ḥál-i-fitné-i-ṣaylam* ("Elucidation of the Direful Mischief"), by which is meant the secession (according to the Ezelí view) of Behá and his followers. These sections occupy many pages, are of a violently polemical character, and contain grave charges against the Behá'ís and vehement attacks on their position and doctrines. The gist of their contents is given in the following abstract.

II. *Abstract from Hasht Bihisht.*

Ṣubḥ-i-Ezel having retired into a seclusion inviolable save to a chosen few, his elder brother Mírzá Ḥuseyn 'Alí [Behá'u'lláh] found the practical direction of affairs in his own hands. Now he was a man who from his youth upwards had associated and mixed with men of every class, whereby he had acquired a certain "breadth of disposition" (*wus'at-i-mashrab*) and "religious pliability" (*rakháwat-i-maẓ-hab*) which attracted round him men of like mind, to whom some slackening of the severer code of the Beyán was not unwelcome. Certain of the old school of Bábís, such as Mullá Muḥammad Ja'far of Nirák, Mullá Rajab 'Alí "*Kahír*," Hájí Seyyid Muḥammad of Isfahán[1], Hájí Seyyid Jawád of Kerbelá, Hájí Mírzá Aḥmad-*i-Kátib*[2], the *Mutawallí-báshí* (Chief Custodian of the Shrine) of Ḳum, Hájí Mírzá Muḥammad Riẓá, and others, perceiving this tendency to innovation and relaxation, remonstrated so vigorously with Mírzá Ḥuseyn 'Alí that he left Baghdad in

as he calls him throughout, Mírzá Ḥuseyn 'Alí), and by '*Sámirí*,' Áḳá Mírzá Áḳá Ján (abusively designated as the "scald-headed soap-seller of Káshán"), to whom he attributes a *rôle* similar to that wherewith Seyyid Muḥammad of Isfahán is credited by the Behá'ís at pp. 93—98 of the present work. Concerning Áḳá Mírzá Áḳá Ján (called by the Behá'ís *Jenáb-i-Khádimu 'lláh*, "His Excellency the Servant of God") see Introduction, and also B. i, p. 519.

[1] See pp. 93—98 *supra*.

[2] Mullá 'Abdu'l-Karím of Ḳazvín is generally designated by this title (see *supra*, pp. 41—42, and footnote to former), but, as he was killed at Teherán in 1852, either this must be a mistake, or some other person bearing the same name must be intended.

wrath and went towards Suleymániyyé, in the neighbourhood of which he abode amongst the Kurds for nearly two years[1]. During all this period his whereabouts was unknown to the Bábís at Baghdad. When at length it became known, Ṣubḥ-i-Ezel wrote a letter to him inviting him to return.

About this time Mírzá Asadu'lláh entitled "*Deyyán*[2]" (one of the second group of "Letters of the Living" or "Second Unity"), called by the author of the *Hasht Bihisht* "the Judas Iscariot of this people," who had been appointed by the Báb amanuensis to Ṣubḥ-i-Ezel, and who was learned in the Hebrew and Syriac languages, declared himself to be "He whom God shall manifest"; and one Mírzá Ibráhím forthwith believed in him. Mírzá Ḥuseyn 'Alí [Behá'u'lláh], after a protracted discussion with him, instructed his servant Mírzá Muḥammad of Mázandarán to slay him, which was accordingly done. Shortly after this, Mírzá 'Abdu'lláh called *Ghawghá* ["Conflict"] advanced the very same claim; and he in turn was followed by Ḥuseyn of Mílán, commonly known as "Ḥuseyn Ján," who made the same pretension in Teherán[3]. The matter did not end even here, for these pretenders were followed by Seyyid Ḥuseyn of Isfahán[4], and Mírzá Muḥammad "*Nabíl*" of Zarand, called "the tongue-tied" (*akhras*)[5];

[1] Cf. pp. 64—65 *supra*, and verse 6 of Nabíl's chronological poem at pp. 983 and 987 of my second paper on the Bábís in the *J. R. A. S.* for 1889. Ṣubḥ-i-Ezel also mentioned that Behá'u'lláh withdrew for some while from Baghdad because he "got angry" (*ḳahr kard*).

[2] See Gobineau, pp. 277—278. The passage is quoted in full on p. 365 *infra*.

[3] See *supra*, pp. 330—331. If Ḥuseyn of Mílán was killed at Teherán in 1852, it is evident that whatever claim he advanced was long anterior to this period, for, according to Nabíl's chronological poem (B. ii, pp. 983—984 and 987, verses 6 and 7), Behá'u'lláh was 40 years old when he returned from Kurdistán to Baghdad, which, as he was born in A.H. 1233, must have been in A.H. 1273 (= A.D. 1856—7).

[4] Or of Hindiyán. See p. 331 *supra*, and cf. Gobineau, p. 278.

[5] The same Nabíl who is now at Acre, and who wrote the chronological poem referred to in the last footnote but one. Some poems attributed to him and written apparently during the

until, to quote *verbatim* from the *Hasht Bihisht*, "the matter came to such a pass that everyone on awakening from his first sleep in the morning adorned his body with this pretension."

Now when Mírzá Ḥuseyn 'Alí beheld matters in this disordered state, he bethought himself of advancing the same claim himself (considering that from the prominent position which he had long held as practical director of affairs, he stood a better chance of success than any previous claimant), and in this idea he was greatly encouraged by Áḳá Mírzá Áḳá Ján of Káshán. Little by little his resolution took more definite shape, and he fell to thinking how he might compass the destruction of such of the Bábís as were likely to oppose his contemplated action.

About this time the Muhammadan clergy of Baghdad, Kerbelá, and Nejef began to complain loudly because of the large number of Bábís who continued to flock thither from Persia, and the Persian Government accordingly instructed Mírzá Ḥuseyn Khán *Mushíru'd-dawla*, its representative at the court of the Ottoman Sultan, to petition the Turkish authorities for the removal of the Bábís to some part of their dominions remote from the Persian frontier[1]. To this request the Turkish authorities, anxious to put a stop to the quarrels which were continually arising between the Bábís and Muhammadans, acceded. The Bábís were summoned to Constantinople; whence, four months after their arrival, they were sent to Adrianople. On their arrival in that city, Mírzá Ḥuseyn 'Alí, still instigated and

period of his claim are in my possession. In one of them the following verse occurs :—

شبحر مرفّع جان منم ثمر نهان و عیان منم

ملك الملوك بیان منم و بی البیان فقد علا

"I am the uplifted Tree of Life; I am the hidden and apparent Fruit;
I am the King of Kings of the Beyán, and by me is the Beyán exalted."

[1] Cf. pp. 82—89 *supra*.

encouraged by Áḳá Mírzá Áḳá Ján, gradually made public his claim to be, not only "He whom God shall manifest," but an Incarnation of the Deity Himself, and began to send letters and epistles in all directions. And now, according to the Ezelí historian, began a series of assassinations on the part of the Behá'ís. All prominent supporters of Ṣubḥ-i-Ezel who withstood Mírzá Ḥuseyn 'Alí's claim were marked out for death, and in Baghdad Mullá Rajab 'Alí "*Ḳahír*" and his brother, Ḥájí Mírzá Aḥmad, Ḥájí Mírzá Muḥammad Riẓá, and several others fell one by one by the knife or bullet of the assassin[1]. But the author of the *Hasht Bihisht* brings a yet graver charge against Mírzá Ḥuseyn 'Alí, and asserts that he caused poison to be placed in one side of a dish of food which was to be set before himself and Ṣubḥ-i-Ezel, giving instructions that the poisoned side was to be turned towards his brother. As it happened, however, the food had been flavoured with onions, and Ṣubḥ-i-Ezel, disliking this flavour, refused to partake of the dish. Mírzá Ḥuseyn 'Alí, fancying that his brother suspected his design, ate some of the food from his side of the plate; but, the poison having diffused itself to some extent through the whole mass, he was presently attacked with vomiting and other symptoms of poisoning. Thereupon he assembled his own followers and intimates, and declared that Ṣubḥ-i-Ezel had attempted to poison him[2].

Shortly after this, according to the Ezelí writer, another plot was laid against Ṣubḥ-i-Ezel's life, and it was arranged that Muḥammad 'Alí the barber should cut his throat while shaving him in the bath. On the approach of the barber, however, Ṣubḥ-i-Ezel divined his design, refused to allow him to come near, and, on leaving the bath, instantly

[1] Cf. B. i, p. 517, and B. ii, pp. 995--6.

[2] The Behá'ís reverse this story as well as the following in every particular, declaring that Mírzá Yaḥyá *Ṣubḥ-i-Ezel* attempted to poison Mírza Ḥuseyn 'Alí *Behá'u'lláh*, and after his failure spread abroad the report that the attempt had been made on himself. Behá'u'lláh's version will be found in the *Súra-i-Heykal* at pp. 154—155 of Baron V. Rosen's forthcoming work. The text and translation of this passage, which Baron Rosen has most kindly permitted me to copy from the proof-sheets of his still unpublished work, will be found a few pages further on.

took another lodging in Adrianople and separated himself entirely from Mírzá Ḥuseyn 'Alí and his followers.

Some while after this, says the author of the *Hasht Bihisht*, Mírzá Ḥuseyn 'Alí devised a new stratagem. A number of letters were written in different handwritings by Áḳá Mírzá Áḳá Ján, Mushkín Ḳalam, 'Abbás Efendí, and other partisans of Mírzá Ḥuseyn 'Alí to sundry Turkish statesmen and officials to the following effect:—"About thirty thousand of us Bábís are concealed in disguise in and around Constantinople, and in a short while we shall rise. We shall first capture Constantinople, and, if Sulṭán 'Abdu'l-'Azíz and his ministers do not believe [in our religion], we shall depose and dismiss them from their rule and administration. And our King is Mírzá Yaḥyá *Ṣubḥ-i-Ezel*." These letters were left by night at the Sulṭán's palace and the houses of the different ministers by Mushkín Ḳalam and other partisans of Mírzá Ḥuseyn 'Alí resident in Constantinople. When next day these letters were discovered, the Turkish Government, which had treated the Bábís with kindness, and afforded them shelter and hospitality, was naturally greatly incensed. The letters were forthwith laid before the Persian Ambassador, and, at a joint assembly of Turkish and Persian officials, it was decided to exile the Bábí chiefs to some remote island or fortress on the coast[1].

Meanwhile Hájí Seyyid Muḥammad of Isfahán, a philosopher of note, and Áḳá Ján Bey, nicknamed *Kaj-kuláh* ("Skew-cap")[2], who held the rank of lieutenant-colonel (*ḳá'im-maḳám*) in the Turkish army, discovered how matters stood, and made known to the Ottoman authorities the hostility which existed between the two brothers at Adrianople. The only good result which followed from their intervention was that it was decided by the Turkish government to exile Mírzá Yaḥyá *Ṣubḥ-i-Ezel* and Mírzá Ḥuseyn 'Alí *Behá'u'lláh* not to the same but to two different places; the former was ordered to be sent with his

[1] Cf. the Behá'í account of the events which led to the removal of the Bábí chiefs from Adrianople at pp. 98—99 *supra*, and Ṣubḥ-i-Ezel's account in note 1 at the foot of the latter page.

[2] See B. i, p. 517, and note 1 at foot of p. 99 *supra*.

family and four of Behá'u'lláh's followers, to wit Mushkín-Ḳalam[1], Mírzá 'Alí Sayyáḥ, [Muḥammad] Báḳir, and 'Abdu'l-Ghaffár, to Famagusta [*Mághúsá*] in Cyprus; the latter, with his family, about 80 of his adherents, and four of Ṣubḥ-i-Ezel's followers, to wit Hájí Seyyid Muḥammad of Isfahán, Áḳá Ján Bey, Mírzá Riẓá-Ḳulí of Tafrísh, and his brother Áḳá Mírzá Naṣru'lláh, to Acre ['*Akká*] in Syria. Before the transfer was actually effected, however, Mírzá Naṣru'lláh was poisoned by Mírzá Ḥuseyn 'Alí at Adrianople. The other three Ezelís were assassinated shortly after their arrival at Acre in a house which they occupied near the barracks, the assassins being 'Abdu'l-Karím, Muḥammad 'Alí the barber, Ḥuseyn the water-carrier, and Muḥammad Jawád of Ḳazvín.

After remarking that Adrianople is called "the Land of the Mystery" (ارض سرّ)[2] because therein took place the separation between the Light and the Fire, the People of the Right Hand and the People of the Left Hand, the Good and the Evil, the True and the False, the Ezelí historian proceeds to describe, with much censure and animadversion, the propaganda by letters and missionaries set on foot throughout Persia by Mírzá Ḥuseyn 'Alí, the extravagant claims advanced by him, and the high-sounding titles conferred on his wives, sons, and chief followers. Amongst the titles so conferred are enumerated the following:—(on his wives) *Mahd-i-'Ulyá* ("the Supreme Cradle"—a title reserved for the Queen-mother in Persia); *Waraḳa-i 'Ulyá* ("the Supreme Leaf"); (on his sons) *Ghuṣn-i-A'ẓam* ("the Most Mighty Branch"); *Ghuṣn-i-Akbar*[3] ("the Most Great Branch"); *Ghuṣn-i-Aṭ-har* ("the Most Pure Branch"); (on Áḳá Mírzá Áḳá Ján of Káshán) *Avvalu man ámana* ("the First to believe") and *Jenáb-*

[1] See B. i, p. 516, and B. ii, p. 994. Fuller particulars concerning all of these will be found at the end of this Note.

[2] Moreover the sum of the letters in the word سرّ (Mystery) is the same as in the word ادرنه (Adrianople), *viz.* 260.

[3] See B. i, p. 518.

i-Khádimu'lláh ("His Excellency the Servant of God")[1]; (on others of his followers) *Mushkín-i-Iláhí* ("Divinely Fragrant"); *Zeynu'l-Muḳarrabín*[2] ("the Ornament of the Favoured"); *Ghulámu'l-Khuld* ("the Servant of Paradise"); *Jabrá'íl-i-Amín* ("Gabriel the Trusty"); *Ḳannádu'ṣ-Ṣamadániyyat* ("the Confectioner of the Divine Eternity"); *Khabbázu'l-Wáḥidiyyat* ("the Baker of the Divine Unity"); *Dalláku'l-Ḥaḳíḳat* ("the Barber of the Truth"); *Malláḥu'l-Ḳuds* ("the Sailor of Sanctity"); and the like.

The author of the *Hasht Bihisht,* after indulging in a good deal of strong invective, garnished with many allusions to Pharaoh, the Golden Calf, and Sámirí, brings forward further charges against the Behá'ís. Certain persons, he says, who had at first been inclined to follow Mírzá Ḥuseyn 'Alí, subsequently withdrew and separated themselves from him. Some of these, such as Áḳá 'Abdu'l-Aḥad, Áḳá Muḥammad 'Alí of Isfahán, Hájí Áḳá of Tabríz, and the son of Hájí Fattáḥ, fled from Acre; but the *Khayyáṭ-báshí* (chief tailor) and Hájí Ibrahím were assassinated in the Caravansaray of the corn-sellers (*Khán-i-gandum-firúshán*) and buried in quick-lime under the platform, which was duly mortared up over their bodies. After a while, however, the smell of the decomposing corpses became so offensive that the other inhabitants of the caravansaray complained to the local authorities, who instituted a search and discovered the bodies. Without mentioning what further action was taken by the Turkish government in the matter (a point certainly demanding elucidation, for we cannot suppose that, if what the Ezelí historian relates be true, they took no action at all to punish the murderers) the author proceeds with his indictment. Hájí Ja'far, says he, had a claim of 1200 pounds against Mírzá Ḥuseyn 'Alí, and demanded the payment of this debt with some violence and importunity. Mírzá Áḳá Ján of Káshán thereupon instructed one 'Alí of Ḳazvín to slay the old man and throw his body out of the window of the upper room which

[1] See Introduction, and B. i, p. 519.

[2] The writer of the MS. from which the fac-simile forming vol. i of the present work is taken. See Note Z, *infra*.

he occupied into the courtyard of the caravansaray. It was then put about that he had "cast himself out and died, yielding up his life to the Beloved." Another disappointed creditor, a native of Khurásán, is said to have gone mad in Acre from chagrin and deferred hope. Other assassinations in other places are alleged, the following being specially notified:—Áḳá Seyyid 'Alí the Arab, one of the original "Letters of the Living," was killed in Tabríz by Mírzá Muṣṭafá of Niráḳ and Sheykh [name omitted] of Khurásán; Mullá Rajab 'Alí *Ḳahír*, also one of the "Letters," was killed at Kerbelá by Náṣir the Arab; his brother Áḳá 'Alí Muḥammad was killed in Baghdad by 'Abdu'l-Karím; and, in short, if we are to believe the Ezelí writer, most of the more prominent Bábís who withstood Mírzá Ḥuseyn 'Alí's pretensions were sought out and slain wherever they chanced to be, amongst these being Hájí Áḳá of Tabríz.

The indictment does not stop here. Amongst those who had at first inclined to follow Mírzá Ḥuseyn 'Alí was, according to the *Hasht Bihisht*, a merchant named Áḳá Muḥammad 'Alí of Isfahán, who at this time resided in Constantinople. Owing to certain discoveries which he had made, however, his faith had undergone considerable abatement, and signs of coolness had been observed in him. Mírzá Abú'l Ḳásim the Bakhtiyárí robber was consequently despatched from Acre with instructions to "bleed that block of heedlessness whose blood is in excess." On his arrival in Constantinople he took up his lodging with the unsuspecting merchant in the *Khán-i-Sharḳí*. Here he remained till one day he found opportunity to break open his host's private safe and abstract therefrom £350. A part of this sum he retained for himself; with the remainder he bought clothes, stuffs, and other goods which he sent to Acre. In return for this service he received the following epistle:—"*O phlebotomist of the Divine Unity! Throb like the artery in the body of the Contingent World, and drink of the blood of the 'Block of Heedlessness' for that he turned aside from the aspect of thy Lord the Merciful*[1]!" Here

[1] The original text of this epistle stands as follows in the *Hasht Bihisht*:—

ends the list of charges alleged against the Behá'ís by the Ezelís, and what follows is of a purely controversial nature, consisting of refutations of the claims advanced by Mírzá Ḥuseyn 'Alí *Behá'u'lláh*, and arguments to prove the rights of Mírzá Yaḥyá *Ṣubḥ-i-Ezel.* This controversial portion, interesting as it is, I am forced to omit here for lack of space.

It is with great reluctance that I have set down the grave accusations brought by the author of the *Hasht Bihisht* against the Behá'ís. It seemed to me a kind of ingratitude even to repeat such charges against those from whom I myself have experienced nothing but kindness, and in most of whom the outward signs of virtue and disinterested benevolence were apparent in a high degree. Yet no feeling of personal gratitude or friendship can justify the historian (whose sole desire should be to sift and assort all statements with a view to eliciting the truth) in the suppression of any important document which may throw light on the object of his study. Such an action would be worse than ingratitude; it would be treason to Truth. These charges are either true or false. If they be true (which I ardently hope is not the case) our whole view of the tendencies and probable influences of Behá's teaching must necessarily be greatly modified, for of what use are the noblest and most humane utterances if they be associated with deeds such as are here alleged? If, on the other hand, they be false, further investigation will without doubt conclusively prove their falsity, and make it impossible that their shadow should hereafter darken the page of Bábí history. In either case it is of the utmost importance that they should be confronted, and, to this end, that they should be fully stated. Inasmuch as the *Hasht Bihisht* only fell into my hands as I was beginning to write this note, and as several of the charges alleged in it against the Behá'ís are new to me, I regret that I cannot at present offer any important evidence either for their support or

ان يا فصّاد الاحديّة كنّ نبّاضاً كالشّريان فى بدن الامكان و اشرب من دم جرثوم الغفلة لانّه اعرض عن طلعة ربّك الرّحمن *

their refutation. Certain points, however, which are connected with the narrative of the Ezelí controversialist and can be checked by other testimony are as follows :—

(1) For the claim advanced by Mírzá Asadu'lláh "*Deyyán*" of Tabríz, and the fate which it brought down upon him, we have Gobineau's testimony, given (at pp. 277—278 of his work) in the following words :—"L'élection [c-à-d. de *Hezret-è-Ezel*] avait été toute spontanée et elle fut reconnue immédiatement par les bâbys. Cependant, un des membres de l'Unité, qui n'était pas à Téhéran au moment où elle eut lieu, et qui se nommait Mirza-Asad-Oullah, de Tebriz, surnommé *Deyyân*, ou 'le Juge suprême,' personnage très-important et membre de l'Unité prophétique, entreprit de se faire reconnaître lui-même pour le nouveau Bâb. Il courut dans l'Arabistan et chercha à y réunir un parti. Mais les religionnaires se mettant sur ses traces, l'atteignirent près de la frontière turke, et lui attachant des pierres au cou, le noyèrent dans le Shât-el-Arâb. Cette tentative malheureuse n'encouragea pas les dissidents." From Gobineau's account we are led to infer that this episode occurred very soon after the death of the Báb and the election of Mírzá Yaḥyá *Ṣubḥ-i-Ezel*, that is to say some time before the Baghdad period.

(2) For the claim advanced by Ḥuseyn of Mílán we have Ṣubḥ-i-Ezel's evidence (see Note T, p. 331 *supra*), but since, as has been already pointed out, this Ḥuseyn was amongst the Bábís killed at Teherán in 1852, this event has no more connection than the last with the Baghdad period.

(3) That Nabíl advanced a similar claim which he subsequently withdrew is a statement which I have heard made once if not oftener by Bábís (of the Behá'í sect) in Persia. Some of the poems attributed to him, if really his, afford confirmatory evidence, as has been already observed (p. 357, note 5, *supra*).

(4) The assertion that Behá'u'lláh alleges against Ṣubḥ-i-Ezel an attempted fratricide, of which, according to the Ezelí writer, he was in reality himself the author, is fully borne out by the following passage in the earlier part of the *Súra-i-Heykal*, which Baron Rosen has most kindly permitted me to quote from his still unpublished work :—

ثمّ اذكرى لهم بانّا اصطفينا من اخواننا احداً و رشّحنا
عليه من طمطام بحر العلم رشحاً ثمّ البسناه قميص اسم
من الاسماء و رفعناه الى لمقام الذى قام الكلّ على ثناء
نفسه و حفظناه عن ضرّ كلّ ذى ضرّ على شأن يعجز
عنه القادرون * و كنّا وحده فى مقابلة اهل السماوات و
الارض فى ايّام كلّ العباد قاموا على قتلى و كنّا بينهم
ناطقاً بذكر الله و ثنائه و قائماً على امره الى ان حقّقت
كلمة الله بين خلقه و اشتهرت آثاره و علت قدرته و لاحت
سلطنته و يشهد بذلك عباد مكرمون * انّ اخى لمّا رأى
الامر ارتفع وجد فى نفسه كبراً و غروراً اذاً خرج خلف
الاستار و حارب بنفسى و جادل باياتى و كذّب برهانى و
جحد آثارى و ما شبع بطن الحريص الى ان اراد اكل
لحمى و شرب دمى و يشهد بذلك عباد الّذين هم هاجروا
مع الله و عن ورائهم عباد مقرّبون * و شاور فى ذلك
مع احد خدّامى و اغواه على ذلك اذاً نصرنى الله بجنود
الغيب و الشهادة و حفظنى بالحقّ و انزل علىّ ما منعه

عمّا اراد و بطل مكر الّذينهم كفروا بايات الرحمن الّا انّهم قوم منكرون فلّما شيّع ما سوّلت له نفسه و اطّلع به الّذينهم هاجروا ارتفع الضجيج من هولاء و بلغ الى مقام كاد ان يشتهر بين المدينة اذاً منعناهم و القينا عليهم كلمة الصبر ليكوننّ من الّذينهم يصبرون فوالله الذى لا اله الّا هو انّا صبرنا فى ذلك و امرنا العباد بالصبر و الاصطبار و خرجنا من بين هؤلاء و سكنّا فى بيت آخر لتسكن نار البغضاء فى صدره و يكون من الذينهم مهتدون و ما تعرّضنا به و ما رأيناه من بعد و جلسنا فى البيت وحده مرتقباً فضل الله المهيمن القيّوم انّه لمّا اطّلع بانّ الامر اشتهر اخذ قلم الكذب و كتب الى العباد و نسب كلّ ما فعل بجمالى الفريد المظلوم ابتغاء فتنة فى نفسه و ادخال البغضاء فى صدور الّذينهم آمنوا بالله العزيز الودود فوالذى نفسى بيده تحيّرنا من مكره بل تحيّر منه كلّ الوجود من الغيب و الشهود مع ذلك ما سكن فى نفسه الى ان ارتكب ما لا يجرى القلم عليه و به ضيّع حرمتى و حرمة الله المقتدر العزيز المحمود لو اذكر ما فعل بى لن تتمه بحور

الارض لو يجعلها الله مداداً و لن تنفده الاشياء و لو
يقلّبها الله اقلاماً كذلك نلقى ما ورد على نفسى ان انتم
تعلمون *

"Then tell them that we chose out one from amongst our brethren, and sprinkled upon him drops from the depths of the Ocean of Knowledge; then we arrayed him in the raiment of one of the [Divine] Names[1], and upraised him unto [such] a station that all arose to praise him; and we preserved him from the hurt of every hurtful thing in such wise as [even] the powerful cannot do. We were alone against the dwellers in the heavens and the earth in the days when all men arose to slay me, and we were in their midst, speaking in commemoration of God and His praise, and steadfast in His affair, until the Word of God was realized amongst His creatures, and its tokens became public, and its power waxed high, and its dominion shone forth; whereunto testify favoured servants. Verily my brother, when he saw that the matter had waxed high, discovered in himself pride and error; then he came forth [from] behind the veils, and warred with me, and contended with my signs, and denied my proof, and repudiated my tokens; neither was the belly of the glutton sated till that he desired to eat my flesh and drink my blood, whereunto bear witness those servants who fled into exile with God, and beyond them those brought nigh. And herein he took counsel with one of my attendants, tempting him unto this. Then God helped me with the hosts of the Invisible and the Visible, and preserved me by the truth, and revealed unto me that which withheld him from what he purposed, and brought to naught the device of those who denied the signs of the Merciful [God]: are they not a people unbelieving? And when that whereunto his passion [had] seduced him was divulged, and those who [had] fled into exile became aware thereof, outcry arose from these,

[1] Cf. pp. 95—96 *supra*, and footnotes thereon.

and attained such a pitch that it was within a little of being published throughout the city. Then we restrained them, and revealed unto them the word of patience, that they might be of those who are patient; and by God, than whom there is none other god, we were assuredly patient in this, and enjoined patience and self-restraint on [God's] servants, and went out from amongst these, and dwelt in another house, that the fire of hatred might be quenched in his bosom and he might become of those rightly directed. Neither did we interfere with him nor see him afterwards; we sat alone in the house watching for the Grace of God, the Protector, the Self-subsistent. But he, when he became aware that the matter had become publicly known, took the pen of falsehood, and wrote unto the people, and attributed all that he had done to my peerless and wronged Beauty, seeking mischief in himself, and the introduction of hatred into the breasts of those who [had] believed in God the Mighty, the Loving. By Him in whose hand is my soul, we are amazed at his device, nay rather all being, invisible and visible, is amazed! Yet withal he rested not in himself till he committed that which the pen cannot set down, that whereby he dishonoured me, and God, the Potent, the Mighty, the Praised. Should I describe that which he did unto me, the seas of the earth would not complete it were God to make them ink, neither would all things exhaust it were God to turn them into pens. Thus do we reveal that which hath befallen us, if ye [will] know it."

I never heard Ṣubḥ-i-Ezel himself allude to the events in question, for he is little addicted to complaints, and reticent as to all that concerns his brother Behá'u'lláh, but his son 'Abdu'l-'Alí gave me the same account as is set forth in the *Hasht Bihisht*.

(5) The account of the forged letters circulated by the Behá'ís is improbable in itself (for the catastrophe which they were intended to produce was bound to involve all the Bábís at Adrianople), and is at variance with the versions given by Behá'u'lláh (*supra*, pp. 98—99) and Ṣubḥ-i-Ezel (*supra*, p. 99, note 1).

(6) The names of the Behá'ís exiled with Ṣubḥ-i-Ezel to Famagusta are stated correctly, as proved by the documents of the Cyprus Government shortly to be cited.

(7) As to the assassination of the three Ezelís, Áḳá Ján Bey, Hájí Seyyid Muḥammad of Isfahán, and Mírzá Riẓá-Ḳulí of Tafrísh, by some of Behá's followers at Acre, there can, I fear, be but little doubt; for the account of this event which I published at p. 517 of my first paper on the Bábís in the *J. R. A. S.* for 1889 was given to me by a Behá'í who had during his visit to Acre seen, and, I think, conversed with some of the perpetrators of this deed. It is curious that he, so far from attempting to minimize the matter, raised the number of the victims and assassins from three and four to seven and twelve respectively. Ṣubḥ-i-Ezel's account (B. ii, pp. 995—6) agrees with that contained in the *Hasht Bihisht.* There is, however, no evidence to prove that the assassins acted under orders, though the passage in the *Kitáb-i-Aḳdas* alluding (apparently) to Hájí Seyyid Muḥammad's death, which is quoted at the foot of p. 93 *supra*, proves that Behá'u'lláh regarded this event with some complaisance. His son 'Abbás Efendí would also seem to have interceded for the murderers (B. i, p. 517). Mr Oliphant in his work entitled *Haifa* (see *supra*, pp. 209—210), after speaking of the mystery which surrounds Behá'u'lláh and the difficulty of seeing him, says, in a passage which appears to bear reference to these assassinations (*op. cit.*, p. 107):—

"Not long ago, however, public curiosity was gratified, for one of his [i.e. Behá'u'lláh's] Persian followers stabbed another for having been unworthy of some religious trust, and the great man himself was summoned as a witness.

"'Will you tell the court who and what you are?' was the first question put.

"'I will begin,' he replied, 'by telling you who I am not. I am not a camel-driver'—this was an allusion to the Prophet Mohammed—'nor am I the son of a carpenter'—this in allusion to Christ. 'This is as much as I can tell you to-day. If you will now let me retire, I will tell you tomorrow who I am.'

"Upon this promise he was let go; but the morrow never came. With an enormous bribe he had in the interval purchased an exemption from all further attendance at court."

Since these assassinations took place within the last

23 years, it is not too much to hope that further investigation may serve to throw fuller light on the matter. The examination of Turkish official records (should this be possible) would probably do more than anything else to elicit the truth.

Of the other assassinations alleged by the author of the *Hasht Bihisht,* those of the following persons were independently mentioned by Ṣubḥ-i-Ezel:—Mullá Rajab 'Alí *Ḳahír;* Áḳá 'Alí Muḥammad of Isfahán, brother of the above; Mírzá Naṣru'lláh; Hájí Mírzá Aḥmad, brother of Mírzá Jání (see Note T, p. 332 *supra*); and Hájí Ibrahím. The last was stated to have been at first a fanatical Behá'í, and to have cruelly beaten Hájí Seyyid Muḥammad of Isfahán the Ezelí on board the ship which bore the exiles to Acre, of which action he subsequently repented sincerely. The following three persons, not mentioned in the *Hasht Bihisht,* were also stated by Ṣubḥ-i-Ezel to have been assassinated:—Ḥuseyn 'Alí and Áḳá 'Abdu'l-Ḳásim of Káshán; Mírzá Buzurg of Kirmánsháh. This raises the total number of alleged assassinations of Ezelís to sixteen (unless, as appears probable, one of the last three be identical with the "*Khayyáṭ-báshí*" mentioned in the *Hasht Bihisht*), which agrees pretty well with Ṣubḥ-i-Ezel's statement to Captain Young (B. ii, p. 996) that about twenty of his followers were killed by the Behá'ís[1].

It should be borne in mind, however, that the removal of persons inimical to a religious movement by violent means, or in other words religious assassination, is a thing far less repugnant to the Eastern than to the Western mind. Since the first beginning of Islám (not to go further back) it has been freely practised; and the Prophet Muḥammad gave to it the sanction of his example on numerous occasions. Nothing can illustrate in a more striking manner the difference between the Oriental and the Occidental attitude of mind than a narrative given by

[1] The words "at Acre" added to this statement are clearly due to a misapprehension of the interpreter, and should read "of Acre," for Ṣubḥ-i-Ezel distinctly and repeatedly alluded to the majority of these assassinations as having taken place at Baghdad and elsewhere.

Ibn Hishám in his *Life of Muḥammad* (ed. Wüstenfeld, pp. 553—555) to which my attention was first called by my friend Mr A. A. Bevan. This narrative is briefly as follows. There were in the time of Muḥammad two brothers, of whom the younger, named Muḥayyiṣa, had embraced Islám, while Ḥuwayyiṣa, the elder, still remained a pagan. Muḥayyiṣa, at the command of the Prophet, assassinated a Jewish merchant named Suneyna (or Subeyna) with whom Ḥuwayyisa was on terms of friendship. Ḥuwayyísa, on hearing of this, fell upon his younger brother with blows and reproaches, saying, "O enemy of God, hast thou slain him? By God, many a fat morsel of his wealth has gone into thy maw!" To this the other replied, "By God, I was ordered to kill him by one at whose command I would smite off thy head were he so to direct me!" "Would'st thou indeed slay me if Muḥammad should order it?" asked Ḥuwayyiṣa. "Yes," answered the other, "by Alláh, were he to command me to cut off thy head I would assuredly do so." "By Alláh," said the elder brother, "a religion which hath brought thee to this is assuredly a marvellous thing!" and he thereupon adopted the Muhammadan faith. The legend of Khiẓr and Moses in the Ḳur'án (*súra* xviii, v. 64—81), and the first story in the *Masnaví* of Jalálu'd-Dín Rúmí (well styled by Jámí "the Ḳur'án in the Persian language"), which describes with the utmost *nonchalance* how a poor goldsmith is slowly poisoned by a saintly personage to gratify the ignoble passions of a king, afford further illustration of this attitude of mind, which also revealed itself to me very clearly in a conversation which I had with a Bábí Seyyid of Shíráz with whom I was disputing about the divine origin of Islám. In the course of the discussion I animadverted on the bloodshed and violence resorted to by Muḥammad and his followers for the propagation of their religion. "Surely," replied the Seyyid, with a look of extreme surprise, "you cannot pretend to deny that a prophet, who is an incarnation of the Universal Intelligence, has as much right to remove anyone whom he perceives to be an enemy to religion and a danger to the welfare of mankind as a surgeon has to amputate a gangrened limb?"

I have insisted thus strongly on this point because we

cannot properly estimate the probability or improbability of an action alleged but not proved to have been committed by a given body of men unless we are in a position to form a just judgment on their opinions as well as their character. The idea of secret assassination is so repugnant to us, and so incompatible with our notions of virtue and moral rectitude, that we naturally shrink from imputing it without the clearest evidence to a man or body of men of whose character and qualities we have otherwise formed a high opinion. But in Asia, where human life is held cheap, and religious fervour runs high, a different standard of morality prevails in this matter; and we must beware of being unduly influenced in our judgment by our own sentiments.

III. *Additional information derived directly from Ṣubḥ-i-Ezel.*

Mírzá Yaḥyá *Ṣubḥ-i-Ezel* is the son of Mírzá 'Abbás (better known as Mírzá Buzurg) of the district of Núr in Mázandarán, and the half-brother of Mírzá Ḥuseyn 'Alí *Behá'u'lláh* (see note 2 on p. 56 *supra*), to whom he is junior by 13 years[1]. He was born in Teherán about the year A.D. 1830[2]. His father died when he was 7 years old.

[1] This is according to the first statement made to Captain Young, but on another occasion the difference was stated as 11 or 12 years. Since, however, Behá'u'lláh was, according to Nabíl (see B. i, p. 521, and B. ii, pp. 983 and 986), born in the year A.D. 1817, and since Ṣubḥ-i-Ezel would seem to have been born in A.D. 1830 or 1831, thirteen years is the probable difference between their ages.

[2] The Persians are, as a rule, very careless about dates, and even well-educated men are often unable to state their exact age. To this rule Ṣubḥ-i-Ezel is no exception. Thus in November 1884 (according to official documents) he gave his age as 56, while in October 1889 he informed Captain Young that he was 58 or 59 years old. Perhaps, however, the former figure may be due to a misunderstanding on the part of the official engaged in drawing up the report on the exiles, for several remarks which Ṣubḥ-i-Ezel made to me point to the correctness of the latter. Thus on one occasion he said, pointing to his son 'Abdu'l-Waḥíd (a youth of apparently about 17 years of age), "I was quite young

When and how he was brought to embrace the Bábí doctrines I have not been able to ascertain, but he was appointed by the Báb as his successor after the deaths of Mullá Ḥuseyn of Bushraweyh and Mullá Muḥammad 'Alí of Bárfurúsh (who was killed in the summer of A.D. 1849), the appointment (for text and translation of which see B. ii, pp. 996—997) being written from Chihríḳ. From that time until A.D. 1852 he generally resided during the summer at Teherán or Shimrán, and during the winter in the district of Núr in Mázandarán, being continually occupied in teaching and diffusing the Bábí doctrines. At the time of the Báb's martyrdom (July 1850) he was residing at the village of Zargandé near Teherán. Mírzá Áḳá Khán of Núr, who succeeded Mírzá Taḳí Khán as Prime Minister at the end of A.D. 1851 under the title of *Ṣadr-i-A'ẓam*, was related to Ṣubḥ-i-Ezel. Although formerly, when living in retirement at Káshán, he had pretended to be favourably disposed towards the Bábís, and had even had several interviews with Mullá Sheykh 'Alí *Jenáb-i-'Aẓím*, he now shewed the utmost hostility towards them, especially towards Ṣubḥ-i-Ezel. Indeed his brother, Ja'far-Ḳulí Khán, who was on extremely bad terms with him, strongly advised Ṣubḥ-i-Ezel to keep out of his power, and, if possible, to avoid both Teherán and Núr.

When the attempt on the Sháh's life was made in August 1852, Ṣubḥ-i-Ezel was at Núr, and so escaped arrest, though the Sháh offered a reward of 1000 *túmáns*

like him when I left Persia" (in A.D. 1852). "About seventeen?" I enquired. "No," he answered, "more than that; about 20 or 21." A Turkish dervish who, impelled by curiosity to see so celebrated a heresiarch, visited him soon after his arrival in Cyprus, remarked with surprise دها چوجق در "He is still but a child!" Gobineau (p. 277) makes his age only 16 at the time of the Báb's death (A.D. 1850), but it is more probable that this was his age when he was designated by the Báb as his successor, in which case he would be about 19 when he actually succeeded. Bearing in mind the extraordinary virtue attributed by the Bábís to this mystical number, we may well believe that such a coincidence would strongly influence the choice of the faithful in his favour.

for his capture, and though on one occasion he actually met and conversed with an Arab who had been sent to apprehend him but failed to recognize him. It was probably immediately after this that he set out, disguised as a dervish (pp. 51—52 and p. 354 *supra*), for Baghdad, where he arrived, according to his own statement, "in the year A.H. 1268, a few days after the arrival of Behá'u'lláh." Since, however, Behá'u'lláh was imprisoned in Teherán for four months after the attempt on the Sháh's life, i.e. till December 1852, and since the year A.H. 1268 ended on October 14th, 1852, this date would appear to be erroneous.

Forty days after the attack on the Sháh, after Ṣubḥ-i-Ezel had fled in disguise as above described, a raid was made on Núr by two regiments of soldiers under the command of Mírzá Abú Ṭálib Khán. It appears that the Sháh was induced to sanction this raid by representations made by Mírzá Áḳá Khán the *Sadr-i-A'ẓam* to the effect that Ṣubḥ-i-Ezel had "arrived there, declared himself to be the Imám-Mahdí, and collected about a thousand followers." Mírzá Abú Ṭálib Khán, though related to Ṣubḥ-i-Ezel by marriage (his sister being wedded to Ṣubḥ-i-Ezel's eldest brother), shewed no compunction in carrying out the designs of his uncle the *Ṣadr-i-A'ẓam* with the utmost rigour, and, indeed, totally disregarded the remonstrances and pleas for mercy which some of his subordinate officers ventured to advance on its appearing that, so far from there being any rising, such of the inhabitants of the doomed village as had not fled into the mountains were unarmed and entirely unprepared for resistance. The village (containing some sixty houses) was sacked and plundered; two of its inhabitants, who were Bábís, were killed; Ṣubḥ-i-Ezel's house was occupied by the principal officers; and his female relatives were confined to the upper rooms. A day or two after this a pursuit of the fugitives was organized; a shepherd betrayed their retreat; and the soldiers, falling upon them unawares, killed some (including Mírzá Muhammad Taḳi Khán), wounded others (including Mullá Fattáḥ, who subsequently died in prison), and carried off 26 or 27 (amongst whom were two women) to Teherán as captives. These captives, except the two women, were compelled to perform the journey on foot and in chains. On their arrival at Teherán they happened to meet the Russian Ambassador, who was moved with compassion at the sight of their misfortunes, and addressed a remonstrance to the Sháh. He, finding on enquiry that there had been no insurrection at all, ordered them to be set at liberty; but the *Ṣadr-i-A'ẓam* contrived to detain them in prison on various pretexts, and there most of them died of erysipelas, gaol-fever, and other diseases which rage in Persian prisons, or were secretly made away with. The ravaged district of Núr was made over to the *Ṣadr-i-A'ẓam*, and one of the two houses possessed by Ṣubḥ-i-Ezel in Teherán was confiscated by the Sháh, the other being sold by Behá'u'lláh.

As I have embodied in previous footnotes all the more important particulars which I learned from Ṣubḥ-i-Ezel relative to the expulsion of the Bábís from Baghdad (p. 84, note 2 *supra*), the journey from Baghdad to Constantinople (p. 90, note 1 *supra*), and the expulsion of the Bábís from Adrianople (p. 99, note 1 *supra*); and as the Ezelí version of the state of things which prevailed in the Bábí community at Baghdad and Adrianople is sufficiently set forth in the earlier portion of this note, I may now pass on to consider the evidence afforded by the state archives preserved in Cyprus.

IV. *State papers preserved by the Cyprus Government.*

These documents, to which, as explained in the Introduction, the kindness and courtesy of Sir Henry Bulwer allowed me so free an access during my stay in Cyprus, are very numerous, and range from August 1878 (the year of the English occupation) to June 1889. The majority of them are written in English, and to those written in Turkish English translations are always appended. All the papers of importance bearing on the subject, with the exception of certain despatches, were placed at my disposal, and during the four days for which they remained in my hands I was able to make a complete transcript of them. This transcript occupies 32 pages of foolscap.

With these documents a desire to avoid undue prolixity compels me to deal as briefly as may be. Many of them, indeed, would not be worth reproducing in full in any case, while others are abrogated by fuller and later reports, and there are naturally a good many repetitions, besides discussions of the basis whereon the pensions of the exiles are to be calculated, which may well be omitted or abbreviated; but, were space of no object, there are several which I would fain have inserted in full. As it is, I can only give the substance and not the form of the papers; while, to save explanations and prevent confusion, I have normalized the spelling of names in accordance with the system adopted throughout this work, besides correcting obvious errors. With these preliminary observations I proceed to the examination of the documents in question.

When the Turks evacuated Cyprus in 1878 they left behind them certain prisoners who had been interned in the fortress of Famagusta. In August of that year the Chief Secretary requested the Commissioner of that town to report on the number of these prisoners, their terms of imprisonment, their offences, and the like. The Commissioner of Famagusta stated in a brief reply (dated August 8th, 1878) that the prisoners in question were five in number, to wit (1) a Greek named Ḳáṭirjí Yání, sentenced for life for robberies committed in Syria; (2) a Bosnian named Musṭafá, (3) a Turk named Yúsuf, sentenced for life for "speaking against the Turkish religion," and two Persians, (4) Ṣubḥ-i-Ezel, and (5) Mushkín Ḳalam, whose crime and punishment are described as follows:—"They wished to invent some new religion, and, when pressed, fled from Persia and settled in Turkey. After a time they again tried to carry out their madness, and were consequently condemned by the Turkish authorities to imprisonment for life."

Nearly three months after this date further information concerning the prisoners was demanded by the Chief Secretary, with the especial object of determining the amounts of the pensions or allowances which they were drawing. In his reply (dated November 5th, 1878) the Commissioner of Famagusta states that he "cannot get any official information about them. The *Ḳáẓí* says if there were any papers about them the late *Ḳá'im-maḳám* destroyed them, or his secretary lost them, for there are none forthcoming now." He then proceeds to speak of the two Persian prisoners as follows, premising that all the information which he has been able to obtain was "gathered from the men themselves":—

"1st, *Ṣubḥ-i-Ezel.* Handsome, well-bred looking man, apparently about 50. In receipt of pias. 1193 per month (the *Ḳáẓí* only gets pias. 1020). States that he was for a long time at the Persian Court, where his brother[1] was next officer in rank to the vizier. He afterwards went to Stamboul and then to Adrianople, where he was accused of plotting against the Porte and the religion of Islám. Sentence—for life. Been here 11 years.

"2nd, *Mushkín Ḳalam.* From Khurásán. Allowed pias. 660 per month. Sentence—for life. Been here 11 years. Came here at same time as Ṣubḥ-i-Ezel. Sentenced for religious offence against Porte. Is 53 years old. Has two families, one here, and one in Persia. In appearance is a dried-up, shrivelled old man, with long hair almost to the waist." Similar accounts of the other prisoners follow, and the report concludes with the statement that the late *Ḳá'im-maḳám* had left some old books, which, being alleged to contain only accounts for past years, were used in the office as Account and Military Police books, but that some old books still left would be searched for further particulars.

The next document of interest is a petition from Mushkín-Ḳalam addressed to "His Excellency the High Commissioner of Cyprus" and dated August 15th, 1879. The original of this petition (apparently written by Mushkín Ḳalam himself) is in Turkish, but an English translation is appended. In it Mushkín Ḳalam states that he is a native of Khurásán; that, having proceeded to Mecca by way of Diyár Bekr, he had extended his journey to Adrianople to see his "Sheykh" Mírzá Ḥuseyn 'Alí [*Behá'u'lláh*]; that, after accomplishing this object, he was arrested in A.H. 1284 ("A.D. 1867")[2] and exiled to Famagusta, where he had now

[1] Probably this is a mistake for "father," as Ṣubḥ-i-Ezel repeatedly described the position of his father Mírzá Buzurg in these very words.

[2] A report from the *Muḥásébéjí's* (Accountant's) Office dated December 10th, 1884, states that, although the original *fermán* of

resided for 12 years; and that he has suffered much grief by reason of his long banishment and separation from his family. In conclusion, he begs the High Commissioner "to pity his position, deprived so long of his family, and to deliver him from such a hard punishment." The immediate effect of this petition was to call forth another demand for fuller information from the Chief Secretary, who desired especially to be informed on what authority Mushkín Ḳalam had been permitted to reside outside Famagusta (his petition having been sent in from Nicosia). The Commissioner of Famagusta replied that the permission in question had been granted by a letter from the Chief Secretary dated June 20th, 1879, and that, in the absence of any official Turkish register, a report based on the statements of the prisoners themselves and information supplied by the Turkish *Ḳá'im-maḳám* had been compiled by the Local Commandant of Military Police. This report discusses the cases of seven "prisoners," to wit those five previously mentioned, a woman named Khadíja charged with incendiarism, and an old blind man named Khudáverdí, formerly in the Turkish artillery, who proved not to be a prisoner at all but a pensioner! That portion of the report which deals with the cases of Ṣubḥ-i-Ezel and Mushkín Ḳalam is as follows:—

"No. 3. Ṣubḥ-i-Ezel of Írán. *Trade?* Nil. *Crime?* Falsely accused of preaching against the Turkish religion. *Where?* Adrianople. *Who was charge made by?* A man of Írán. *By whom tried?* Came from Baghdad and went to Adrianople where charge was made. Válí of Adrianople ordered him to Constantinople, where he was examined by Kámil Páshá (Prime Minister). *When?* Twelve years ago. *Previous imprisonment before coming here?* Five months in Constantinople, before coming here under arrest, five years at Adrianople. *Undergone here?* Twelve years.

banishment cannot be found, an unofficial copy of it, received at the time, gives the date of their banishment as *Rabí'ul-Ákhir* 5th A.H. 1285 (July 26th, A.D. 1868), and there is no doubt that this is the correct date. The reckoning called *Rúmí* (Turkish), which is more than a year behind the *hijra*, was probably used by Mushkín Ḳalam, and misapprehended by the translator.

Pension? 38½ piastres a day current. *Do. before?* 38½ piastres a day Government exchange. Has a family of 17. His father was Chief Secretary of State to the present Sháh of Persia (Náṣiru'd-Dín Sháh).

"No. 4. Mushkín Ḳalam Efendí. *Trade?* Writer. *Crime?* Being in company with a preacher against Mahometanism who came from Persia and Acre in Syria. *Where?* Constantinople. *Punishment?* Transported for life, and to be imprisoned in Famagusta fortress. *By whom?* Authority of Sulṭán 'Azíz. *Date?* November A.H. 1284 (A.D. 1868)[1]. [In the original document the corresponding Christian year is erroneously given as "A.D. 1876"]. *Previous Imprisonment?* Six months in Constantinople. *Has undergone?* Twelve years. *Any lodging?* The *fermán* ordering banishment stated that he was to get free lodging, but he has not had any [*sc.* free] lodging. This man has sent a petition to government about a week ago. 23/6/'79."

A document based on records of the Temyíz Court and dated March 8th, 1880, first mentions Bábíism ("i.e." it explains, "communism") as the crime with which Ṣubḥ-i-Ezel and Mushkín Ḳalam were charged. It is further stated that they were deported under Imperial Fermán, and not sentenced by a judicial tribunal. The next document (undated), embodying the results of further enquiries at Famagusta, gives the date of their arrival in the Island as August 24th, A.H. 1284. [As the month and year are seemingly given according to the Turkish style, this would correspond to September 5th, A.D. 1868.] In this document mention is first made of Sheykh 'Alí Sayyáḥ, who arrived as an exile at Famagusta, accompanied by his wife and five children, in A.H. 1285 (A.D. 1869—70)[1]. He died[2] on July

[1] See preceding footnote.

[2] According to a statement made to me by Ṣubḥ-i-Ezel, Sheykh 'Alí Sayyáḥ (who was only about 35 years old) died very suddenly as though from poison, scarcely having time to summon his wife to his side ere he expired. He was arrested in company with 'Abdu'l-Ghaffár and Muḥammad Báḳir (immediately to be mentioned), and banished with them to Famagusta. He continued till his death to profess friendship towards Ṣubḥ-i-Ezel, declaring that his only object in keeping on good terms with the

22nd, A.H. 1287 ("August 4th, A.D. 1871[1]"), and an allowance of $2\frac{1}{2}$ piastres a day to his widow and each of his children was made by the government. Mushkín Ḳalam subsequently married the widow, and drew her pension in addition to his own. At the end of this document it is mentioned that "a note in the Register of Orders in the *Muḥásebéjí's* [Accountant's] office states that an allowance of 4 piastres a day for 14 persons in all, and 2 servants at 5 piastres the two" was granted to Ṣubḥ-i-Ezel, Sheykh 'Alí Sayyaḥ, Mushkín Ḳalam, and their respective families.

The next document of importance is a report in Turkish, dated March 11th, 1880, from the *Muḥásebéjí's* office, to which an English translation is appended. From this it appears that the original number of Bábí exiles sent to Famagusta was 14; that these were accompanied by 2 servants; that to each of the former 4 piastres a day and to each of the latter $2\frac{1}{2}$ piastres a day (making a total of 61 piastres a day) were allowed; that 'Abdu'l-Ghaffár succeeded in effecting his escape from the Island on September 17th, A.H. 1286[1] ("Sept. 29th, A.D. 1870"); that [Sheykh] 'Alí Sayyáḥ of Ḳára-Bágh died on July 22nd, A.H. 1287 (see preceding paragraph); that Fáṭima, one of Ṣubḥ-i-Ezel's daughters, died on August 17th, A.H. 1287 ("Aug. 29th, A.D. 1871"); and that Muḥammad Báḳir died on November 10th, A.H. 1288 ("Nov. 22nd, A.D. 1872"); that in consequence of this diminution in the number of the exiles a deduction of 16 piastres a day was made, thus reducing the daily allowance to 45 piastres; but that subsequently, by an order dated September 25th, A.H. 1289 (? Oct. 7th, A.D. 1873), $2\frac{1}{2}$ piastres a day were allowed to

Behá'ís was to endeavour to bring about a reconciliation and heal the schism. Ṣubḥ-i-Ezel, however, held aloof from him, and disregarded his overtures. From the *Hasht Bihisht* (see p. 352, *supra*) it would appear that the first communications between the Báb and Ṣubḥ-i-Ezel passed through him.

[1] In this and the succeeding dates wherein Christian months are combined with Muhammadan years the Turkish reckoning (which, as already noted, is more than a year behind the normal Muhammadan reckoning) seems to be employed. The Christian dates here given in inverted commas are derived from another document dated October 13th, 1884.

the widow and each of the five children of Sheykh 'Alí Sayyáḥ, thus raising the daily allowance of the exiles again to 60 piastres[1].

The following document in Mr Cobham's handwriting, dated March 11th, 1880, gives some additional statements made by Mushkín Ḳalam about himself:—

"It appears that in 1867 Mushkín Ḳalam Efendí came from Mesh-hed in Khurásán to Constantinople. His fame as a scribe had preceded him, and Fu'ád and 'Álí Páshás asked him to remain in Constantinople. He refused both pension and presents offered him by [Sulṭán] 'Abdu'l-'Azíz, for whom he executed some illuminations.

"Presently he was accused by one Ṣubḥ-i-Ezel, a Persian then at Adrianople, himself a member of some schismatic sect, of heresy. He had lived six months at Constantinople, where he was imprisoned, without question or trial, for another six months, and then sent to Famagusta.

"Ṣubḥ-i-Ezel was exiled at the same time on a similar charge of heresy."

The next document of importance is a petition in Turkish addressed by Ṣubḥ-i-Ezel to the Commissioner of Famagusta, bearing the date April 27th, A.D. 1881. From this it appears that on the 24th of the preceding month Ṣubḥ-i-Ezel had been informed that he might consider himself free to go where he pleased. For this permission he expresses the warmest gratitude, and further prays that, if it be possible, he may become an English subject, or be taken under English protection, so that he may with safety return to his own country or to Turkey. To this request, however, the Government did not see fit to accede.

The next group of documents belong to the latter part of the year 1884, when a fresh attempt was made to

[1] It appears that Sheykh 'Alí Sayyáḥ's wife and five children (or such of them as were then born) joined him in Cyprus some time subsequently to his banishment, and hence were not included in the enumeration of the original exiles, and were not entitled to a pension. But in any case the rule appears to be that, unless specially continued by the Government, pensions to the families of exiles cease on the death of their head.

establish the amount of the pension paid to the exiles on a definite basis. To this end it became important to discover (1) who were the original exiles; (2) which of them had died or quitted the island, and when; (3) which of their children had been born previously to and which subsequently to their banishment. For the elucidation of these points several lengthy reports were compiled in the *Muḥasebéjí's* (Accountant's) office. As it was also decided that any one of the exiles entitled to a pension lost that pension on quitting the island, but might recover it on returning thither, their subsequent movements were carefully recorded. The details of apportionment of these pensions are of little historic interest, and I therefore omit them; but it is a most fortunate circumstance that they were apportioned in this way, inasmuch as the full record of facts embodied in these documents is entirely due to this circumstance. These various reports and tables I have striven to combine in the following tabular form, wherein is incorporated also information derived from Captain Young and Mr Houston independently of the reports. The names of the original exiles (described as 14 "masters" and 2 servants) are printed in italics, and after each of these is placed in heavier type the number which they bear on the pension-roll. The names of those who subsequently settled or were born in the island are printed in ordinary type. To the names of all alike ordinal numbers are prefixed.

Order.	Name.	Original number.	Relation to head of family.	Age in 1884.	Remarks.
1.	*Ṣubḥ-i-Ezel.*	**1.**	Head.	56	
2.	*Fáṭima.*	**9.**	Wife.	—	Died, apparently soon after arrival.
3.	*Rukayya.*	**10.**	"	48	Appears also to bear the name of *Badr-i-Jihán*, since a petition written in Greek to the Commissioner of Famagusta on September 13th, 1886, is signed "Πέδρι Τζιχάν." In this petition the writer asks leave for herself and her two daughters *Ṭal'at* and *Ṣafiyya* to go to Constantinople. In reply she is informed that only her husband [Subḥ-i-Ezel] is a State prisoner, and that she is free to go where she pleases.
4.	Núru'lláh.	—	Son.	—	Was residing in Persia in 1889, and seems never to have been included amongst the exiles (probably because he parted from Ṣubḥ-i-Ezel previously to 1868), as his name nowhere appears. It is only from information given to Captain Young by Ṣubḥ-i-Ezel that his existence is known to me. He has thrice visited his father in Cyprus, once before, and twice since the English occupation. The last time is said to have been in 1878.

5.	Hádí.	—	„	—	Also lives in Persia. The first portion of the preceding remarks applies to him also.
6.	*Aḥmad.*	2.	Son.	31	Left for Constantinople on May 3rd 1884. Seems to have visited his father since then.
7.	*'Abdu'l-'Alí.*	3.	„	27	Resident in Famagusta. See Introduction.
8.	*Ṣafiyya.*	5.	Daughter.	23	Named in some of the documents "Rekié" (رقيه) and "Refié" (رفيه), but, as it would seem, incorrectly. She went to Constantinople on September 21st 1886, married a man named Hasan 'Abdu'r-Raḥmán Efendí, and returned without her husband to Cyprus on December 12th 1888.
9.	*Bahjat Raf'at.*	6.	„	22	Also called in some documents "*Bákir*," on which the following comment is made by the Local Commandant of Police:—"*Bákir* means in Turkish a virgin or girl. Ṣubḥ-i-Ezel has no daughter called Bákir."
10.	*Riẓván 'Alí.*	4.	Son.	21	Resident in Famagusta. See Introduction.
11.	*Ṭal'at.*	7.	Daughter.	20	Accompanied her sister Ṣafiyya to Constantinople, and returned thence with her (see above). Described as "either a widow, or left by her husband."

Order.	Name.	Original number.	Relation to head of family.	Age in 1884.	Remarks.
12.	*Fáṭima.*	**8.**	Daughter.	—	Died on August 29th 1871.
13.	Muhammad.	—	Son.	17	Though the names of these occur on nearly all the lists, I could discover no other trace of their existence.
14.	Fu'ád.	—	"	15	
15.	'Abdu'l-Waḥíd.	—	"	13	Called in some of the documents '*Abdu'r-Rashíd.*
16.	Maryam.	—	Daughter.	11	
17.	Taḳiyyu'd-Dín.	—	Son.	8	Called in some of the documents *Ẓiyá'u'd-Dín.* From an undated Turkish document preserved at Famagusta it appears that the last three are the children of *Badr-i-Jihán* (see No. 3 *supra*). From this document the following particulars are also derived.
18.	Fáṭima.	—	Daughter-in-law.	21	Wife of Aḥmad (see No. 6 *supra*).
19.	'Ádila.	—	Grand-daughter.	4	Daughter of Aḥmad and Fáṭima.
20.	*Sheykh 'Alí Sayyáḥ,* of Ḳára-Bágh.	**11.**	Head.	See p. 380 *supra.*	Died August 4th 1871. See pp. 380—381 *supra*, and note 2 on former.

21.	Fáṭima.	—	Wife.	47	After the death of Sheykh 'Alí Sayyáḥ married Mushkín Ḳalam, and was with him at Nicosia in 1884. It does not appear that she accompanied him to Acre in 1886.
22.	Jalálu'd-Dín.	—	Son.	25	Was employed as Land Registry clerk at Kyrenia in 1889.
23.	Jamálu'd-Dín.	—	"	23	Was employed as a trooper in the Cyprus Military Police in 1889.
24.	Kamálu'd-Dín.	—	"	21	Sheykh 'Alí Sayyáḥ's family are described as having arrived "from Babylon" in a state of destitution. No allowance seems to have been made to them till two years after his death, i. e. in October 1873. This allowance was stopped in the case of the sons on April 1st 1884, but the allowance to the widow and daughter was continued, and thus went to increase Mushkín Ḳalam's pension, which, in 1884–5, amounted to £58. 17. 0. As the estimates for 1889–90 still shew a sum of £20. 13. 0 payable to Mushkín Ḳalam's family, and as he lost his pension on leaving Cyprus for Acre in September 1886, while his sons' pensions ceased in 1884, it would appear certain that Fáṭima, Jamáliyya, and the servant Ruḳayya remained in Cyprus.
25.	Jamáliyya.	—	Daughter.	16	
26.	Ruḳayya.	—	Servant.	47	

Order.	Name.	Original number.	Relation to head of family.	Age in 1884.	Remarks.
27.	*Mushkín-Ḳalam*, of Khurásán.	12.	Head.	—	From the colophon of a MS. transcribed by Mushkín Ḳalam and presented by him to Mr Cobham on his departure for Acre, it appears that in the year [A.H. 12]91 (=A.D. 1874) he was still, to use his own phrase, "imprisoned for the love of God" (مسجوناً لحبّ الله) at Famagusta. He subsequently went to Nicosia, and thence to Larnaca, where he was in 1884. His final departure from Cyprus is notified by Mr Cobham in a letter dated September 18th 1886:—"The Persian heresiarch and calligraphist Mushkín Ḳalam left Cyprus for St. Jean d'Acre on the night of Tuesday September 14–15, renouncing his pittances and the protection of the Island Government. He found an unwonted opportunity in a Syrian vessel going direct to Acre, the head quarters of the Báb [sc. Behá'u'lláh]...I am extremely sorry to lose him as a Persian *munshí*." He was still in April 1890 at Acre, where I met him (see Introduction).
28.	(Name not given).	—	Servant.		After his marriage with Sheykh 'Alí Sayyáḥ's widow, Mushkín Ḳalam obtained

					possession of both the servants allotted to the exiles. "It is not clear," observes the Receiver General, "why Mushkín Ḳalam should have both the servants, but Government need not, I think, object to the arrangement if Ṣubḥ-i-Ezel consents, which I doubt his doing."
29.	*'Abdu'l-Ghaffár.*	**13.**	Head.	—	Escaped from Cyprus on September 29th 1870, during the fair held at Famagusta, in company with two other prisoners. According to Ṣubḥ-i-Ezel he went to Acre, but, though a Behá'í, was somewhat coldly received. He subsequently settled in Beyrout and changed his name.
30.	*Muḥammad Báḳir,* of Isfahán.	**14.**	Head.	—	Died at an advanced age on November 22nd 1872.

NOTE X.

Translation of the superscription and exordium of the Epistle to the King of Persia.

My original purpose was to give in this note nothing more than a translation of that portion of the "Epistle to the King of Persia" which is omitted in the text, but the permission so generously accorded to me by Baron Rosen to make full and free use of the proof-sheets of his still unpublished work enables me to add the text and translation of the instructions given to the bearer of the missive. [See p. 102 *supra,* and footnote.] The text of these instructions is as follows:—

هذه صورة ما كتب على ظهر كتاب السلطان .

هو الله تعالى

نسئل الله بان يبعث احداً من عباده و ينقطعه عن الامكان و يزيّن قلبه بطراز القوّة و الاطمينان لينصر ربّه بين ملأ الاكوان و اذا اطّلع بما نزل لحضرة السلطان يقوم و يأخذ الكتاب باذن ربّه العزيز الوهّاب و يمشى مسرعاً الى مقرّ السلطان و اذا ورد مقرّ سريره ينزل فى الخان و لا يعاشر مع احد الى ان يخرج ذات يوم و يقوم على معبره و اذا ظهرت طلايع السلطنة يرفع الكتاب بكمال الخضوع و الاداب و يقول قد ارسل من لدى

المسجون و ينبغى له ان يكون على شأن ان يأمر السلطان
بالقتل لا يضطرب فى نفسه و يسرع الى مقرّ الفدا و يقول
اى ربّ لك الحمد بما جعلتنى ناصراً لامرك و قدّرت لى
الشهادة فى سبيلك فوعزّتك لا ابدّل هذا الكأس بكأوس
العالمين لانّك ما قدّرت لها من بديل و لا يعادلها الكوثر
و السلسبيل و ان تركه و ما تعرّض عليه يقول لك الحمد
يا ربّ العالمين انّى رضيت برضائك و ما قدّرته لى فى
سبيلك و لو انّى اردت ان تصبغ الارض بدمى فى حبّك
و لكن ما اردته هو خير لى انّك تعلم ما فى نفسى و
لا اعلم ما فى نفسك و انت العليم الخبير *'

TRANSLATION.

"*This is a copy of what was written on the back of the Epistle to the King.*

'*He is God, exalted is He.*

'We ask God to send one of His servants, and to detach him from Contingent Being, and to adorn his heart with the decoration of strength and composure, that he may help his Lord amidst the concourse of creatures, and, when he becometh aware of what hath been revealed for His Majesty the King, that he may arise and take the Letter, by the permission of his Lord, the Mighty, the Bounteous, and go with speed to the abode of the King. And when he shall arrive at the place of his throne, let him alight in the inn, and let him hold converse with none till he goeth forth one day and standeth where he [i.e. the King] shall pass by. And when the Royal harbingers shall appear, let him raise up the Letter with the utmost humility and courtesy, and say, "It hath been sent on the part of the Prisoner[1]." And it is incumbent upon him to be in such a mood that, should the King decree his death, he shall not be troubled within himself, and shall hasten to the place of sacrifice saying, "O Lord, praise be to Thee because that Thou hast made me a helper to Thy religion, and hast decreed unto me martyrdom in Thy way! By Thy Glory, I would not exchange this cup for [all] the cups in the worlds, for Thou hast not ordained any equivalent to this, neither do Kawthar and Salsabíl[2] rival it!" But if he [i.e. the King] letteth him [i.e. the messenger] go, and interfereth not with him, let him say, "To Thee be praise, O Lord of the worlds! Verily I am content with Thy good pleasure and what Thou hast predestined unto me in Thy way, even though I did desire that the earth might be dyed with my blood for Thy love. But what Thou willest is best for me: verily Thou knowest what is in my soul, while I know not what is in Thy soul; and Thou art the All-knowing, the Informed."'"

Baron Rosen, after quoting the version of Mírzá Badí‘'s mission and martyrdom which I published at pp. 956—957 of my second paper on the Bábís in the *J.R.A.S.* for 1889, observes that, considering the text of the above instructions, and the minute obedience yielded by Behá'u'lláh's followers to his slightest wish, this version is extremely improbable. He says:—"S'adresser au souverain de la Perse, en lui disant 'j'ai un fermân pour vous' etc.,—cela n'est certes pas l'humilité parfaite dont parle l'hérésiarque." The opinion thus expressed by Baron Rosen is entirely borne out by the present work (see pp. 102—105 *supra*), and I am now quite convinced that it is correct. He further adds, "Quant à la date de l'événement, j'ai toutes raisons de croire qu'il s'est passé au *mois de Juillet* de l'année 1869, indiquée par M. Browne."

[1] Cf. p. 104 *supra*.
[2] The names of two rivers in Paradise.

Translation of the Exordium of the Epistle.

١٥٢[1]

"*This is what was revealed in the 'Heykal[2]' for His Majesty the King. 'He is God, exalted is His state [in] Might and Power.*

'O King of the earth, hear the voice of this servant. Verily I am a man who hath believed in God and His signs, and I have sacrificed myself in His way; to this do the afflictions wherein I am (the like of which none amongst mankind hath borne) testify, and my Lord the All-knowing is the witness to what I say. I have not summoned men unto aught save unto thy Lord and the Lord of the worlds. In love for Him there hath come upon me that whereof the eye of creation hath not beheld the like: in this will those servants whom the veils of humanity have not withheld from confronting the Chiefest Outlook bear me out, and beside them He with whom is the knowledge of all things in a Preserved Tablet. Whenever the clouds of fate rain down the darts of affliction in the way of God the Lord of the Names, I advance to meet them; to this testifieth

[1] These numerals, as remarked by Baron Rosen (pp. 146—147), clearly stand for the equivalent letters بها, *Behá*.

[2] Concerning the *Súra-i-Heykal* (of which the *Epistles to the Kings* collectively form only a portion) see note 1 at the foot of p. 108 *supra;* B. ii, p. 954; and p. 149 of Baron Rosen's forthcoming work. My Kirmán MS. lacks this heading, for which the following is substituted:—"This Epistle was revealed in Adrianople specially for His Majesty the King. This servant, the confidential attendant of their Excellencies [apparently Behá-'u'lláh and his sons], sends it for you to peruse. The meanings of sundry Arabic phrases which were in my mind have been written down agreeably to the command of God's Most Mighty Branch [*Ghuṣnu'lláhi 'l-a'ẓam*]." The original from which the Kirmán text and the glosses appended to it (which agree almost exactly with those given by Baron Rosen) were derived would therefore appear to have been communicated to the Bábís in Persia by Áḳá Mírzá Áḳá Ján ("*Jenáb-i-Khádimu'lláh*") at the command of Behá'u'lláh's eldest son 'Abbás Efendí. [See Introduction; Note W, p. 361 *supra;* and B. i, pp. 518—519.]

every fair and rightly-informed person. How many are the nights wherein the wild beasts rested in their lairs, and the birds in their nests, while this servant was in chains and fetters, and found for himself none to succour, nor any helper! Remember the grace of God towards thee when thou wast in prison with sundry others, and He brought thee out thence, and succoured thee with the hosts of the Invisible and the Visible, until the King sent thee to 'Iráḳ[1] after that We had disclosed to him that thou wast not of [the number of] the seditious. Verily such as follow [their] lusts and turn aside from virtue, these are in evident error. And as for those who work sedition in the earth, and shed blood, and falsely consume men's wealth, we are quit of them, and we ask God not to associate us with them either in this world or in the world to come, unless they repent unto Him; verily He is the Most Merciful of the merciful. Verily it behoveth him who turneth towards God to be distinguished in all actions from what is apart from Him, and to conform to that which is enjoined upon him in the Book: thus is the matter decreed in a Perspicuous Book. As for such as cast the command of God behind their backs and follow after their lusts, they are in grievous error.

'O King, I conjure thee by thy Lord the Merciful to regard [His] servants with the gaze of pitiful eyes[2], and to rule with justice in their midst, that God may award His favour unto thee: verily thy Lord judgeth as He pleaseth. The world shall perish with whatsoever of glory and abasement is therein, while dominion remaineth unto God, the Supreme and All-knowing King. Say, Verily He hath kindled the Lamp of the *Beyán*[3], and He will continue it with the oil of ideas and expression: exalted is thy Lord the Merciful beyond this, that created beings should withstand His command. Verily He will shew forth what He pleaseth by His authority, and will guard it with a cohort of the Proximate Angels. He controlleth His handiwork and compelleth His creation: verily He is the All-knowing, the Wise.

[1] i.e. Baghdad.

[2] Literally, "with the glances of the eyes of thy clemency."

[3] Or "of Utterance" or "Revelation."

'O King, verily I was as [any] one amongst mankind, slumbering upon my couch. The gales of the All-Glorious passed by me and taught me the knowledge of what hath been. This thing is not from me, but from One [who is] Mighty and All-knowing. And He bade me proclaim betwixt the earth and the heaven, and for this hath there befallen me that whereat the eyes of those who know overflow with tears. I have not studied those sciences which men possess, nor have I entered the colleges: enquire of the city wherein I was, that thou mayst be assured that I am not of those who speak falsely. This is a leaf which the breezes of the Will of thy Lord the Mighty, the Extolled, have stirred. Can it be still when the rushing winds blow? No, by the Lord of the Names and Attributes! Rather do they move it as they list, [for] Being belongeth not to Nonentity in presence of the Eternal. His decisive command did come, causing me to speak for His celebration amidst the worlds. Verily I was not save as one dead in presence of His command, the hand of thy Lord the Merciful, the Clement, turning me. Can any one speak on his own part that for which all men, whether low or high, will persecute him? No, by Him who taught the Pen eternal mysteries, save him who is strengthened by One Mighty and Strong.

'The Supreme Pen addresseth me, saying, "Fear not; [but] relate unto His Majesty the King what hath come upon thee. Verily his heart is between the fingers of thy Lord the Merciful: perchance He will cause the sun of justice and kindness to dawn from the horizons of his heart." Thus was the command revealed from the All-Wise.

'Say, "O King, look with the gaze of justice upon thy servant; then decide according to the right concerning what hath befallen him. Verily God hath appointed thee His shadow amongst [His] servants[1], and the sign of His Power to the dwellers in the land: judge between us and those who have oppressed us without proof or clear warrant. Verily those who surround thee love thee for their own sakes, while [thy] servant loveth thee for thine own sake;

[1] See footnote on p. 156 *supra*.

nor doth he desire aught save that he may bring thee nigh unto the station of Grace and turn thee unto the right hand of Justice: thy Lord is witness unto that which I say."

'O King, if thou wouldest hear the cry of the Supreme Pen, and the murmur of the Dove of Eternity on the branches of the Lote-tree beyond which there is no passing[1] in praise of God, the Maker of the Names, the Creator of the earth and the heaven, verily this would cause thee to attain unto a station whence thou wouldest behold in existence naught save the effulgence of [God] the Adored, and [whence] thou wouldest regard dominion[2] as a thing of least account in thine eyes, leaving it to him who desireth it, and turning toward a horizon illumined with the lights of [God's] countenance; neither wouldest thou ever endure the burden of dominion, unless [it were] to help thy Lord, the High, the Supreme. Then would the people of the Supreme Concourse magnify thee [saying], "How good is this most glorious state," if thou wouldest [but] ascend thereunto by authority accorded unto thee in the Name of God.

'Amongst mankind are some who say that this servant desireth naught save the perpetuation of his name, and others who say that he desireth the world for himself, notwithstanding that I have not found during the days of my life a place of safety such that I might set my feet therein, but was ever [overwhelmed] in floods of affliction, whereof none wots save God: verily He knoweth what I say. How many were the days wherein my friends were disquieted for my distress, and how many the nights wherein the sound of wailing arose from my family in fear for my life! None will deny this save him who is devoid of truthfulness. Doth he who regardeth not [his] life [as assured] for less than a moment desire the world? [I] marvel at those who speak after their lusts, and wander madly in the desert of passion and desire. They shall be questioned as to that which they have said; on that day they shall not find for themselves any protector nor any

[1] See Ḳur'án, liii, 14.

[2] Or, "the world," for the word ملك bears this meaning also.

helper. And amongst them are those who say, "Verily he denieth God," notwithstanding that all my limbs testify that there is no God but Him, and that those whom He quickened with the truth and sent for [men's] guidance are the manifestations of His Most Comely Names, the day-springs of His Supreme Attributes, and the recipients of His revelation in the realm of creation; by whom the Proof of God unto all beside Himself is made perfect, the standard of the [faith of the] Unity is set up, and the sign of renunciation becomes apparent; and by whom every soul taketh a course towards the Lord of the Throne. We bear witness that there is no God but Him; everlastingly He was, and there was nothing beside Him; everlastingly He will be, even as He hath been. Exalted is the Merciful One above this, that the hearts of the people of wisdom should ascend unto the comprehension of His Nature, or that the understanding of such as inhabit the worlds should rise to the knowledge of His Essence. Holy is He above the knowledge of all save Himself, and exempt is He from the comprehension of what is beside Him: verily in Eternity of Eternities was He independent of the worlds.

'Remember the days wherein the Sun of Baṭ-ḥá[1] shone forth from the horizon of the Will of thy Lord, the High, the Supreme, [how] the doctors turned aside from him, and the cultured found fault with him; that thou mayst understand what is now hidden within the Veil of Light. Matters waxed grievous for him on all sides, until those who were [gathered] round him were dispersed by his [own] command[2]: thus was the matter decreed from the Heaven of Glory. Then remember when one of them came in before the *Nejáshí*[3] and recited unto him a *súra* of the Ḳur'án. He said to those around him, "Verily it hath been revealed on the part of One All-knowing and Wise. Whosoever accepteth what is best, and believeth in that which Jesus brought, for him it is impossible to turn aside from what

[1] i.e. Muḥammad. Baṭ ḥá is here synonymous with Mecca.

[2] Allusion is made to the flight of the persecuted and unprotected Muslims from Mecca in the fifth year of Muḥammad's mission.

[3] *Nejáshí* is a generic name for the Kings of Abyssinia, as *Kisra* is for the Persian, and *Ḳayṣar* for the Roman emperors.

hath been read: verily we testify unto [the truth of] it, even as we testify unto [the truth of] what is with us of the books of God[1] the Protecting, the Self-Subsistent."

'By God, O King, if thou wouldest hear the strains of the dove which cooeth on the branches with varied notes by the command of thy Lord the Merciful, thou wouldest assuredly put away dominion behind thee and turn unto the Chiefest Outlook, the station from the horizon of which the Book of the Dawn is seen, and wouldest spend what thou hast, seeking after that which is with God. Then wouldest thou find thyself in the height of glory and exaltation, and the zenith of greatness and independence: thus hath the matter been written in the primaeval revelation[2] by the Pen of the Merciful One. There is no good in what thou dost possess to-day, for another shall possess it to-morrow in thy stead. Choose for thyself that which God hath chosen for His elect: verily He will bestow upon thee a mighty dominion in His Kingdom. We ask God that He may help thy Majesty to hearken unto the Word whereby the world is illumined, and preserve thee from those who are remote from the region of nearness.

'Glory be to Thee, O God! O God, how many heads have been set up on spears in Thy way! How many breasts have advanced to meet arrows for Thy good pleasure! How many hearts have been riddled for the exaltation of Thy Word and the diffusion of Thy Religion! How many eyes have overflowed [with tears] for Thy love! I ask Thee, O King of kings, Pitier of thralls, by Thy Most Great Name, which Thou hast made the day-spring of Thy Most Comely Names and the manifestation of Thy Supreme Attributes, to lift up the veils which intervene between Thee and Thy creatures, withholding them from turning towards the horizon of Thy revelation; then draw them, O God, by Thy Supreme Word from the left hand of fancy and forgetfulness to the right hand of certainty and know-

[1] i.e. the Sacred books which we now possess, the Gospel.

[2] Literally "*the Mother of Revelation*" or "*of the Beyán*," a phrase evidently copied from the expression ام الكتاب, which occurs in several places in the Ḳur'án (*súras* iii, 5; xiii, 39; xliii, 3, &c.).

ledge, that they may know what Thou, in Thy bounty and grace, desirest for them, and may turn towards the Manifestation of Thy religion and the Day-spring of Thy signs. O God, Thou art the Gracious, the Lord of great bounty; withhold not Thy servants from the Most Mighty Ocean, which Thou hast made to produce the pearls of Thy Knowledge and Wisdom, neither repel them from Thy Gate, which Thou hast opened unto all who are in Thy heaven and Thy earth. O Lord, leave them not to themselves, for they know not, and flee from what is better for them than whatsoever hath been created in Thine earth. Look upon them, O Lord, with the glances of the eyes of Thy favours and bounties, and free them from passion and lust, that they may draw nigh unto Thy Supreme Horizon, and may discover the delight of remembering Thee, and the sweetness of the table[1] which hath been sent down from the heaven of Thy Will and the air of Thy Bounty. Everlastingly hath Thy Grace encompassed [all] contingent beings, and Thy Mercy preceded[2] [all] creatures: there is no God but Thee, the Forgiving, the Merciful.

'Glory be to Thee, O God! Thou knowest that my heart is melted about Thy business, that my blood boils in my veins with the fire of Thy love, and that every drop thereof crieth unto Thee with dumb eloquence[3] [saying], "O Lord Most High, shed me on the earth in Thy way," that there may grow from it what Thou desirest in Thy books, but hast concealed from the sight of Thy servants, save such as have drunk of the *Kawthar*[4] of knowledge from the hands of Thy grace, and the *Salsabíl* of wisdom from the cup of Thy bounty. Thou knowest, O God, that in every action I desire nothing save Thy business, and that in every utterance I seek naught but Thy celebration, neither doth my pen move except I desire therein Thy

[1] Cf. Ḳur'án v, 112, 114.

[2] See note 1 on p. 113 *supra*.

[3] Literally, "the tongue of [its] state" (لسان الحال), which, as contrasted with "the tongue of utterance" (لسان المقال), signifies the words wherewith the state of an inarticulate thing may appropriately be described.

[4] *Kawthar* and *Salsabíl*, the names of two rivers in Paradise.

good pleasure and the setting forth of what Thou hast enjoined upon me by Thy authority. Thou seest me, O God, confounded in Thine earth: if I tell what Thou hast enjoined on me, Thy creatures turn against me; and if I forsake what Thou hast enjoined on me on Thy part, I should be deserving of the scourges of Thy wrath, and far removed from the gardens of nearness to Thee. No, by Thy Glory, I advance toward Thy good pleasure, turning aside from what the souls of Thy servants desire: and accept what is with Thee, forsaking what will remove me afar off from the retreats of nearness to Thee and the heights of Thy Glory. By Thy Glory, for Thy love I flinch not from aught, and for Thy good pleasure I fear not all the afflictions in the world: this is but through Thy Strength and Thy Might and Thy Grace and Thy Favour, not because I am deserving thereof.'"

The Epistle then continues as in the text (pp. 108—151 *supra*).

NOTE Y.

The Martyrs of Isfahán, the martyrdom of Mírzá Ashraf of Ábádé, and the persecutions of Si-dih.

(1) *The Martyrs of Iṣfahán.*

Of the martyrdom of Seyyid Ḥasan and Seyyid Ḥuseyn (called by the Behá'ís *Maḥbúbu'sh-shuhadá* "the Darling of Martyrs" and *Sulṭánu'sh-shuhadá* "the King of Martyrs"), with which the present history concludes, I gave the substance of what I had heard at Isfahán and Shíráz at pp. 489—592 of my first paper on the Bábís in the *J.R.A.S.* for 1889. That account will be found to agree in all material details with the version contained in this work, and, as regards the actual facts of the case, I have but little to add, except that, according to Ṣubḥ-i-Ezel, one of his followers named Mullá Káẓim (of whose martyrdom the Behá'ís make no mention) was put to death in Isfahán at or about the same time (see B. ii, p. 995, note on p. 490).

During my stay in Kirmán, however, I became intimate with a certain Sheykh S—— (not the Bábí courier whom, in Note Z, I have designated by the same abbreviation), a dervish endowed with considerable intellectual gifts not yet wholly destroyed by excessive indulgence in narcotics and stimulants, who had spent the greater part of his life in that eager and restless search after religious novelties called by such as pursue it *seyr-i-ḳulúb* (an expression which I can render but clumsily as "spiritual sight-seeing"), and who, so far as the prevailing antinomianism of his character can permit one to describe him as holding any definite religion at all, was an adherent of the Bábí faith, for which in his youth he but narrowly escaped martyrdom. One evening this Sheykh S——, being in a communicative mood, gave me an account of a conversation alleged to have taken place between himself and the Sháh's eldest son, the Prince Ẓillu's-Sulṭán, relating in part to the martyrdom of these two Seyyids. That Sheykh S——'s story is substantially true I see no reason to doubt, inasmuch as many other things which he related to me have subsequently been confirmed by other testimony, and, so far as I could judge, untruthfulness was not one of his faults. At all events his narrative is too characteristic to be consigned to oblivion, and I therefore give it for what it is worth as nearly as I can remember in his own words.

"When I was at Isfahán," said Sheykh S——, "I was for some time living on the bounty and in the house of one of the Ẓillu's-Sulṭán's attendants, just as I am now living at the expense of Mírzá ——. This man was himself one of the 'Friends' (*i.e.* the Bábís). Through him, as I suppose, the Ẓillu's-Sulṭán learned that I had visited Acre. At any rate, one evening he summoned me into his presence. On entering the room where he was sitting, I halted near the door and made my obeisance. 'Come nearer,' said he. I advanced a few paces, and again halted. 'Nearer,' said he again. In short he continued to bid me approach until I was close to him, when he commanded me to be seated. 'Now,' said he, 'I hear that you have been to Acre. I do not ask whether you are a Bábí or not. A man may go amongst the Jews or the Christians or the Guebres out of curiosity without becoming one of them, and I will suppose that you went amongst the Bábís for the same reason. I ask you, then, being myself curious, what you saw and heard from the time that you entered Acre to the time when you left it two stages behind you?' Seeing his humour, I perceived no better course than to relate to him all that I saw and heard, even as I have related it to you[1]. When I had finished, the Prince said, 'Stand up.' I did so, and he cast over my shoulders a costly shawl, exclaiming as he did so, 'Bravo! You have told me the truth without exaggeration or suppression.' Then he asked me to let him see the epistle (توقیع) with which I had been honoured. I gave it to him, and he read it attentively. When he had finished it he laid it down and remained silent for a while wrapped in thought. Then he said, 'Let me keep this by me to-night: I will return it to you to-morrow.' I accordingly withdrew, leaving the epistle in his hands. On the morrow, when I went to receive it back, the Prince said, 'You have heard, of course, how I killed those two Seyyids here because they were Bábís?' 'I was not in Isfahán at the time,' I answered, 'but of course I heard about it.' 'Well,' said the Prince, 'I will tell you how it happened. The Imám-Jum'a and Sheykh Báḳir owed those two Seyyids money, and coveted their wealth and possessions, wherefore they fell to compassing their death, so that they might plunder their houses and recover the bonds which they had given to them. On their information and complaint I arrested the two Seyyids and cast them into prison, for I feared these doctors of religion, and they had said to me, "Either you will slay these two Seyyids, or you will cease to be governor of Isfahán." On the second or third day after this, in the evening, I, being alone with the *Binánu'l-Mulk* and my secretary, caused the two Seyyids to be brought before me, and thus addressed them:— "I do not wish to kill you. I would not willingly shed the blood of a Seyyid. But I fear Sheykh Báḳir and the Imám-Jum'a. If you will but curse that Seyyid of Shíráz[2], I will at

[1] The substance of Sheykh S —— 's narrative, which I heard him repeat several times, will be found at p. 519 of my first paper on the Bábís in the *J. R. A. S.* for 1889.

[2] *i.e.* Mírzá 'Alí Muḥammad the Báb.

once release you, and thenceforth neither I nor the clergy will have any right to interfere with you further." "We cannot," they replied, "do this thing which you ask of us." I then said, "Look at the matter in another way; either you regard this Seyyid as God, or you do not. If you do not, then curse him. If you do, then he is a boundless sea of light, and your cursing him will no more harm him than casting a dog into the ocean would render it impure." When I had said this, the younger of the two brothers, Seyyid Ḥuseyn, raised his head and answered, "You are a prince and the King's son; such words beseem you not." On hearing these words I was overcome with anger, and, standing up, smote the speaker on the face. Directly I had done so I was sorry, and ordered them to be taken back to prison. As they still refused to recant, they were executed in the Meydán-i-Sháh. Afterwards their bodies were dragged by the feet through the streets and bazaars, and cast out of the gate beyond the city walls.' When the Prince Ẓillu's-Sulṭán had concluded his narrative he swore thrice 'by the death of Jalálu'd-Dawla' ('*bi-marg-i-Jalálu'd-Dawla*')[1] saying, 'for three days after this I could neither sleep nor eat for thinking of those Seyyids.' There was a third brother, younger than the two who were killed, who cursed the Báb, abjured the Bábí faith, and was released."

[1] To swear by the death of any one presumably dear to one's self is a very common form of asseveration amongst the Persians. The oath implies "may So-and-so die if I speak falsely." Hence the dearer the friend whose death is sworn by, the more binding and solemn the oath. This is why a Persian always swears "*bi-marg-i-khudat*" ("by thy death"), never "*bi-marg-i-khudam*" ("by my own death"), for, since one is bound to regard one's own life as of little value, the latter oath would be considered far less solemn. *Jalálu'd-Dawla* is the title of Prince Ẓillu's-Sulṭán's eldest son, who was, till March 1888, governor of Ṣhíráz and the province of Fárs.

(2) *The Martyrdom of Mírzá Ashraf of Ábádé in October* 1888.

Concerning this event, which occurred very shortly after I left Persia, but of which I heard for the first time from General Houtum-Schindler at the meeting of the Royal Asiatic Society on April 15th, 1889, before which I read my first paper on the Bábís, I received on August 3rd a letter from one of my Persian friends at Shíráz dated July 3rd, 1889. Of this letter I published a translation at pp. 998—999 of my second paper. As the matter is of considerable interest and is not likely to be chronicled elsewhere, I think it will not be out of place to reproduce here the original text of the letter, which runs as follows:—

رفیق شفیق بسیار محترم من   از شهادت یکنفر
از اینطایفه نوشته بودید از جنرال شیندلر شنیده اید
تفصیل آن این است   یك بچه از نوکرهای اندرون
نواب ظلّ السّلطان با چند نفر از احباب آشنا شده بود
و آقا میرزا اشرف آبادهٔ اورا باین امر تبلیغ کرده بود
این فقره بعرض شاهزاده ظلّ السّلطان میرسد آن بچه‌را
خیلی اذیت می کنند که راست بگوید ولی مطلب‌را ابداً
ابراز نمیدهد حیله بخاطر آدمهای شاهزاده میرسد یکی
از آنها میرود از چند نفر از احباب میپرسد که آقا میرزا
اشرف کجاست من عیالی در آباده دارم و کاغذی

و پولی میخواهم بتوسط ایشان بفرستم آنها هم این اظهار اورا اعتقاد کرده منزل آقا میرزا اشرفرا باو نشان میدهند چون آقا میرزا اشرفرا می شناسند اورا میگیرند و بحضور شاهزاده می آورند شاهزاده از آقا میرزا اشرف سوال میکند که تو از اینطایفه هستی جواب میدهد من نیستم میگوید اگر نیستی لعن کن جواب میدهد چون بدی آنها بر من ظاهر نشده لعن نمیکنم بالاخره شاهزاده از چند نفر از علما فتوی میگیرد و تلگراف بطهران میکند که اگر این شخص کشته نشود علما و مردم شورش می کنند و علما هم فتوی داده اند خودش هم اقرار کرده که از این طایفه است و برای اسکات مردم قتل او واجب است از طهران هم حکم میرسد که هر طور صلاح است بکنید بعد از آن شاهزاده حکم به قتل آقا میرزا اشرف میدهد از قراریکه شنیدم سر اورا میبرند و بعد اورا بدار میزنند پس از آن جسدش را آتش میزنند *

من خودم با آقا میرزا اشرف آشنا بودم در سال
۱۸۸٤ که در بمبئی بودم ایشانرا دیدم و در آنجا غالباً
همدیگررا میدیدیم گویا عمرش به شصت میرسید آدمی
با فهم و سواد و خوش خط و بسیار نجیب و معقول بود
در سال ۱۸۸٦ که از طهران بشیراز می آمدم باز اورا
در آباده دیدم از هر جهة مرد بسیار خوبی بود *

On August 4th, the day after I received the above letter, I wrote to a friend at Isfahán, on whose kindness I felt sure I might rely, for information which no one was better qualified than himself to give. On October 8th, just a year after Mírzá Ashraf's martyrdom, I received his answer, which bore the date September 6th, 1889. "Yes," he wrote, "it is quite true that Aga Mirza Ashraf of Ábâdé was put to death for his religion in the most barbarous manner in Ispahan about October last. The hatred of the Mullas was not satisfied with his murder, but they mutilated the poor body publicly in the *maidan* in the most savage manner, and then burnt what was left of it."

(3) *The persecutions of Si-dih and Najafábád.*

The same letter from which the above extract is quoted continues immediately as follows:—"Since then we have had two other persecutions of Bábís, one in Sihdih and the other in Nejifabad. In Sihdih, where the Bábí community is small, their houses were burned and their wives and children ill-treated. The men saved themselves by flight to Tehran, and I am told that about 25 of them have just returned to Ispahan and are in the Prince's Stables in *bast*[1]. In Nejifabad there are about 2000 Bábís. They

[1] Sanctuary.

tried the same game with them, but some hundreds of them took refuge in the English Telegraph Office in Julfa, and the Prince [Ẓillu's-Sulṭán] took their part and banished from Nejifabad to Kerbela the Mujtahid who persecuted them. So the result is that they are freer now than they have ever been. I take very great interest in the poor people, not only for their own sakes but for the sake of Persia also, as if liberty is gained for them it will be a great step towards shaking the power of the Mullâs and getting liberty for all. Just before the last persecution of the Bábís the Mujtahids in Ispahan, especially Hájí Nejifi, tried a persecution of Jews also, and threatened Christians with the same. The 13 rules of Omar (I believe, at least, most of them may be traced to him) were enforced for a short time:—(1) That no Jew should wear an *'abá*[1]. (2) That they should wear a mark on their dress. (3) Not to ride any beast of burden in the city. (4) Not to leave their houses on a wet day[2]. (5) Not to purchase merchandize from a Moslem. (6) That when a Jew meets a Moslem he is to salute him and walk behind him. (7) Not to return abuse. (8) Not to build a house higher than a Muslim neighbour. (9) Not to eat in presence of a Muslim during the Ramazán, &c."

On May 16th, 1890, I received from one of my friends in Teherán a letter dated April 13th. Knowing the interest which I took in the Bábís, he was kind enough to include in this letter a brief account of these persecutions, which runs as follows:—

"You have doubtless heard of the late Bábí massacre at Isfahan, and I will only therefore tell you, in case you have not, the principal points. They are inhabitants of a district called Seh-deh, and last summer a number of

[1] A kind of cloak worn over the *kabá*.

[2] All non-Muhammadans are regarded by the Persian Shí'ites as unclean (*najis*), but, as is the case with other impurities, the true believer is only defiled by touching them or their garments when they are moist, for what is dry does not pollute. Hence this enactment, which is generally enforced against the Zoroastrians at Yezd. I have heard of a Zoroastrian being punished with the bastinado for venturing into the bazaars with wet clothes on a rainy day.

them, owing to constant persecution, left their villages and came to Isfahan, whence after a time they returned home, with the exception of a certain number who came to Tehran. On the return of these men to their homes about six weeks ago they were attacked by a mob headed by a man called Agha Nedjefy, and seven or eight of them were killed and their bodies burnt with oil. They then took refuge at the Telegraph Office, and finally, after persistent representations from this [i.e. the British] Legation, have been received by the Deputy Governor. It is hoped that on the Zil's[1] return in a few days they will be able to go home. Agha Nedjefy has been summoned to Tehran and well received. Of course they are said to be Bábis, though there seems to be no real proof that they are of that persuasion. When the murders took place they were under the care of an escort which was intimidated by the mob and left them."

From a comparison of the above extracts it would appear that the Bábís of Si-dih and Najafábád were subjected to two separate persecutions. The first of these, which took place previously to September 1889, seems to have been limited to the destruction of property, and not to have resulted in actual bloodshed. The second, which, according to the last extract cited, must have taken place about March 1st, 1890, was brought about by the return of the fugitive Bábís to their homes, and resulted in the death of seven or eight persons.

Almost at the very time when the second letter from which I have quoted was being written, I heard at Acre some account of the latest phase of this episode. On the last day of my sojourn there (April 20th, 1890) Áḳá Mírzá Áḳá Ján "*Khádimu'lláh*" came into the room where we were sitting, bearing in his hand a letter which had just arrived from Persia. From this letter he read out what purported to be an exact copy of a telegram sent from Teherán by the Prince Ẓillu's-Sulṭán to his deputy at Isfahán. The message was a long one and I had no

[1] *i.e.* the Ẓillu's-Sulṭán, the Sháh's eldest son, till February 1888 Prince-Governor of the greater part of Southern Persia, and still Governor of Isfahán and the surrounding districts.

opportunity of copying it, but its general tenour I remember perfectly well, while some of the expressions contained in it were too remarkable to be forgotten. It contained the most positive orders couched in the most emphatic language to put an effectual stop to these unprovoked molestations of the Bábís. "If you do not instantly restore order and quiet, silence these mischief-makers who disturb the peace of my government, and give efficient protection to quiet law-abiding folks, I will come myself, post, and give you a lesson." Then followed a string of threats and reproaches, ending in these most significant words—"*After all you know me. It is not necessary for me to introduce myself*[1]." That the contents of a telegram sent from the Prince-Governor of Isfahán to his deputy should be known at Acre may appear astonishing, but I have more than once been amazed at the rapidity and completeness with which the Bábís become informed of all that concerns their interests.

The intercession of the British Minister with the Persian Government on behalf of the persecuted Bábís called forth a violent protest from the Teherán correspondent of the *Akhtar*[2]. Of a portion of this article, which was dated Sha'bán 9th, A.H. 1307 (= March 31st, 1890) from Teherán, and appeared in the issue of Shawwál 8th (= May 26th) of the same year, I append a translation.

"Some little time ago troubles arose in Isfahán by reason of an assault made by a party of Jews on a [Musulmán] student [of theology], and the towns-folk attacked the Jews, with whom it went ill. After that again a disturbance occurred in Si-dih of Isfahán, and several of the innovators[3], who were wont to disparage the conduct of the Musulmáns, suffered injury and loss.

[1] آخر مرا میشناسید لازم نیست خودرا معرّفی کنم.

[2] The *Akhtar* (Star) is the chief Persian newspaper, and almost the only one which contains any news as we understand the word. It is published weekly at Constantinople, and has a large circulation throughout the East. Lately, however, it has for some reason been suppressed.

[3] A euphuism for the Bábís, whom other Persians are as a rule very loath to mention by name.

The Imperial Government made strenuous efforts to put a stop to the mischief, and did not allow the flame of that disturbance to spread; but the most astonishing thing is the interference of the English Embassy in such matters, and the submission of the ministers of the Persian Government to such conduct, which oversteps the rights of states and nations, on the part of the afore-mentioned Embassy. What has come to the English Embassy that, in face of the autonomy of the Persian Empire of eternal duration, it should send a special representative to Isfahán for the investigation of this matter, take down the names of these mischievous and seditious innovators, and thus embolden these misleaders of men, who are hostile alike to Church and State, and are, indeed, enemies to the whole human race, in their sedition?

"All these things are the result of the heedlessness of that day when the ministers of state first admitted the interference of foreigners under the guise of benevolent intercession in such contingencies, until now they have changed intercession into arrogance, and benevolence into hostility, and have carried intervention to such a pitch that within the Persian dominions they meddle in a quarrel between two subjects of the Sháh between whom and themselves no sort of connection or relation subsists, and send thither the second secretary of the Embassy to conduct investigations. Yet no one asks of them, 'Sir Ambassador, what concern of thine is it? Should such an event happen in your country, would you allow another to meddle with it? Show us then by what right you have been led to interfere in this matter?'"

On the whole, however, the Bábís are much less liable to suffer molestation now than they were formerly, and not uncommonly the malicious attempts of their inveterate foes the Mullás to inaugurate a persecution prove abortive, as is shewn by the following translation from a letter written to me from Shíráz on October 19th, 1888, by the correspondent whose account of Mírzá Ashraf's martyrdom I have already quoted.

"You asked me concerning the trouble about the Bábís in Shíráz. It was not of such consequence as to be worth writing about. A black maid-servant had stolen sundry articles from the house of Ḳ—— Khán, and, out of mere enmity towards her master, had got possession of a copy of the *Íḳán* which was amongst his books. This she laid before Seyyid 'Alí Akbar, one of the *'Ulamá* of Shíráz notorious for boundless fanaticism. He attempted to induce the authorities of Shíráz to put Ḳ—— Khán and several other persons to death, but the Government paid no heed to his representations, and, indeed, censured and upbraided him. A telegram also came from Teherán sternly forbidding him. When he perceived that he was not supported or countenanced by the Government authorities, he was discomfited and reduced to silence.

"In Bushire also one of the Mullás wished to act ill towards several persons of this sect. *Sa'du'l-Mulk*, the Governor of Bushire, promptly issued an order for the expulsion of the Mullá himself; though at length, by much intercession, it was decreed that he might remain on condition of never [again] meddling in such matters."

An event which took place still more recently in the Russian dominions may perhaps have a salutary effect in checking the ferocious intolerance of the Mullás, at any rate outside Persia. Baron Rosen has described this occurrence, from notes made on the spot by M. Toumansky, in connection with two epistles from Behá to the "revelation" of which it gave rise. This account, together with the text of these epistles, will be found at pp. 247—250 of the forthcoming sixth volume of the *Collections Scientifiques &c.* Availing myself of Baron Rosen's generous permission to make full use of his still unpublished work, I conclude this note with a translation of his narrative.

"At 7 a.m. on September 8th (August 27th, old style) 1889, two fanatical Persian Shi'ites, Mash-hadi 'Alí Akbar and Mash-hadí Ḥuseyn, threw themselves, dagger in hand, on a certain Hájí Muḥammad Riẓá of Isfahán, who was peaceably traversing one of the most frequented streets of 'Ishḳábád, and inflicted on him 72 wounds, to which he succumbed. Hájí Muḥammad Riẓá was one of the most respected of the Bábís of 'Ishḳábád. The crime was perpetrated with such audacity that neither the numerous witnesses of the occurrence, nor the constable who was on the spot could save the victim of this odious attack. The assassins yielded themselves up to the police without any resistance; they were placed in a cab and conveyed to the prison. During the transit they fell to licking up the blood which was dripping from their daggers. The examination, conducted with much energy by the military tribunal, gave as its result that Muḥammad Riẓá had fallen a victim to the religious bigotry of the Shi'ites. Fearful of Muḥammad Riẓá's influence, the Shi'ites of 'Ishḳábád, acting in accordance with the orders of Mullás who had come expressly for this purpose from Khurásán, resolved to cut short the Bábí propaganda by killing Hájí Muḥammad Riẓá. Knowing well, however, that the crime would not remain unpunished, they left it to chance to determine what persons should sacrifice themselves for the Shi'ite cause. Thus it was that the individuals named above became the assassins of Muḥammad Riẓá, who had never injured them in any way. The sentence of the tribunal was severe: 'Alí Akbar and Ḥuseyn, as well as two of their confederates, were condemned to be hanged, but the penalty of death was commuted by His Majesty the Emperor to hard labour for life.

"This sentence was hailed by the Bábís with an enthusiasm easy to understand. It was the first time since the existence of the sect, *i.e.* for nearly fifty years, that a crime committed on the person of an adherent of the new religion had been punished with all the rigour of the law. The impression produced on the chief of the sect, Behá, appears to have been equally profound. The two *revelations* which we shall submit to the reader sufficiently prove this. They are also interesting from another point of view: they are almost the only Bábí documents of which we can understand all the meanings, all the allusions."

NOTE Z.

ZEYNU'L-MUḲARRABÍN, HIS COLOPHONS, AND THE LIGHT THROWN BY THESE ON THE BÁBÍ METHOD OF RECKONING TIME.

The information which I possess about Zeynu'l-Muḳarrabín the Behá'í scribe (or, as he prefers to call himself,

Ḥarfu'z-Zá "the Letter Z") is, unfortunately, very scanty. Before I visited Acre, I had heard his fame in Kirmán, but all that I learned definitely about him was that his real name was Zeynu'l-'Ábidín; that he had resided for many years at Mosul; that all the best and most correct manuscripts of the sacred books were written or revised by him; and that Sheykh S*****, the Bábí courier mentioned at pp. 496—498 of my first paper in the *J. R. A. S.* for 1889, visited him yearly on his return journey from Acre to Southern Persia.

During my stay at Acre in April 1890 I learned that he had resided there for some years, but I did not see him, at any rate to my knowledge. Many manuscripts were, however, lent me to read while I was there, and all of these, so far as I remember, were written by his hand. From some of these I transcribed the colophons of which I shall speak directly. Two manuscripts written by him were given to me on my departure from Acre, *viz.* the present history, whereof the text is now offered to the public in *fac-simile,* and a copy of the *Íḳán.* His industry must be prodigious, the aforesaid MS. of *Íḳán*, for instance, being, as stated in the colophon, the 67th copy which he had transcribed! The present history, being written to some extent for general circulation, is dated only in the Muhammadan fashion; but all MSS. of the sacred books proper are also dated according to the Bábí method. Though I have not ascertained exactly when Zeynu'l-Muḳarrabín came from Mosul to Acre, it appears from the colophons directly to be quoted that in A.H. 1296 (A.D. 1879) he was still at the former place, and that in A.H. 1305 (A.D. 1887—8) he was already at the latter.

Of the Bábí system of reckoning time, and of the names applied to the days and months, I gave an account at pp. 921—922 of my second paper in the *J. R. A. S.* for 1889. Being uncertain as to whether these names had been fixed by the Báb himself or by the Behá'ís, I was careful to enquire about them from Ṣubḥ-i-Ezel, not telling him, of course, what I had heard previously. He wrote down their names for me, and this list which he gave me I here reproduce. It will be found to correspond with the information obtained from the Behá'ís, save that the 8th and 9th months are transposed; and from this I assume that these names were fixed previously to the schism, probably by the Báb himself. Gobineau also, in his translation of the *Kitáb-i-Aḥkám*, mentions the month "*Alâ*" as the last of the 19 months of the year.

List of the 19 Bábí months in order, as given by Ṣubḥ-i-Ezel.

١ بهاء	٧ كلمات	١٣ قدرت
٢ جلال	٨ اسما	١٤ قول
٣ جمال	٩ كمال	١٥ مسائل
٤ عظمت	١٠ عزت	١٦ شرف
٥ نور	١١ مشيت	١٧ سلطان
٦ رحمت	١٢ علم	١٨ ملك

١٩ علاء

As the year contains 19 months, so does the month contain 19 days, and the same names therefore serve for both[1]. Provisionally, however, the following new nomenclature has been applied to the old week of seven days:—

Sunday, يوم الجمال. Wednesday, يوم العدال.

Monday, يوم الكمال. Thursday, يوم الاستجلال.

Tuesday, يوم الفضال. Friday, يوم الاستقلال.

Saturday, يوم الجلال.

[1] The analogy between this and the system of nomenclature in the Zoroastrian calendar is very remarkable.

Of this arrangement Ṣubḥ-i-Ezel said nothing, so that it may possibly have originated with the Behá'ís. I now proceed with the transcription and translation of three colophons copied by myself at Acre from manuscripts written by Zeynu'l-Muḳarrabín, concluding with a fourth appended to the MS. of the *Íḳán* above mentioned.

1. Colophon from a MS. written at Mosul in A.H. 1296 (= A.D. 1879).

فرغ من كتابته كاتبه المسكين حرف الزاء فى يوم
الاستجلال يوم القدرة من شهر العظمة من سنه ۳٦ البهى من
الواحد الثانى من ظهور نقطة البيان روح ما سويه فداه
مطابقاً للسابع من شهر جمادى الثانية من شهور سنه ۱۲۹٦ ست
و تسعين و مأتين بعد الالف من الهجرة النبوية على مهاجرها
الف سلام و تحية و كنت فى الحدباء و هذه هى النسخة
السابعة التى وفقنى الله لكتابتها بهذا الترتيب و الحمد لله
اولاً و آخراً و باطناً و ظاهراً *

"There ceased from the transcription of this its poor writer the Letter Zá on the day of *Istijlál* [Thursday], the day of *Ḳudrat* [the 13th day] of the month *'Aẓimat* [the 4th month] of the 36th year, [that is the year] *Bahí* [the seventeenth] of the second *Váḥid* after the manifestation of the Point of Revelation [i.e. the Báb] (may the life of all beside him be his sacrifice), corresponding to the 7th of the month Jemádí II of the months of the year 1296, six and ninety and two hundred after the Millennium of the Flight of the Prophet (upon its fugitive be a thousand salutations and greetings). And I was [at this time resident] in [Mosul] *al-Ḥadbá*[1]. And this is the seventh copy which God hath helped me to write according to this arrangement. Praise be to God first and last, inwardly and outwardly."

2. Colophon from a MS. written at Acre in A.H. 1305 (= A.D. 1887).

فرغ من كتابة هذا الكتاب المبين كاتبه المسكين حرف الزآء يوم الكمال يوم العلم من شهر العزة من سنة ٤٤ الواو من الواحد الثالث مطابقاً للمستهل من شهر محرم الحرام سنة ١٣٠٥ فى مدينة ع و الحمد لله كما هو اهله *

"There ceased from the transcription of this perspicuous book its poor writer the Letter Zá on the day of *Kemál* [Monday] the day of *'Ilm* [the 12th day] of the month of *'Izzat* [the 10th month] of the 44th year [that is the year] *Váv* [the sixth] of the third *Váḥid*, corresponding to the *Mustahall*[2] [first] of the month of *Muḥarram* the sacred [A.H.] 1305 in the city of *'Ayn* [*'Akká* or Acre]. Praise be to God as beseems Him."

3. Colophon from a MS. written at Acre in A.H. 1306 (= A.D. 1889).

فرغ من كتابة هذا الكتاب المبين كاتبه المسكين حرف الزآء يوم الجمال يوم العلاء من شهر الملك من سنة ٤٥

[1] See note 2 on p. 139 *supra*.

[2] This word I misread and transcribed as مستهد, which gives no appropriate meaning. To the kindness of Baron Rosen I am indebted for the correction here made, which is evidently needed.

الابد من الواحد الثالث مطابقاً لستّ بقين من شهر جمادی
الثانیه سنه ۱۳۰۶ه من الهجرة النبویة علی مهاجرها الف سلام
و تحیّة و الحمد لله الّذی وفّقنی لاتمامه حمداً یلیق لساحة
قدسه * فی مدینة ع نمره ۱۰

"There ceased from the transcription of this perspicuous book its poor writer the Letter Zá on the day of *Jemál* [Sunday] the day of *'Alá* [the 19th day] of the month of *Mulk* [the 18th month] of the 45th year [that is the year] *Abad* [the seventh] of the third *Váḥid*, corresponding to the twenty-third of the month of Jemádí II in the year 1306 after the Flight of the Prophet (upon its fugitive be a thousand salutations and greetings). Praise be to God who hath helped me to complete it, such praise as is worthy of the court of His sanctity.

In the city of 'Ayn [*'Akká*]. Number 10."

4. Colophon from my MS. of the *Iḳán* written at Acre in A.H. 1306 (= A.D. 1889).

فرغ من کتابته کاتبه المسکین حرف الزّاء لیلة الجمال
لیلة المسائل من شهر الشّرف من سنه ۴۵ه الابد من الواحد
الثالث موافقة لاحدی عشرة خلت من شهر جمادی الاولی
من شهور سنه ۱۳۰۶ه من الهجرة النبویّة علی مهاجرها الف
سلام و تحیّة و الحمد لله الّذی وفّقنی لاتمامه حمداً یلیق
لساحة قدسه * نمره ۶۷

"There ceased from the transcription of this its poor writer the Letter Zá on the night of *Jemál* [Sunday] the night of *Masá'il* [the 15th day] of the month of *Sharaf* [the 16th month] of the 45th year [that is the year] Abad [the seventh] of the third *Váḥid*, corresponding to the eleventh of the month of Jemádí I of the months of the year 1306 after the Flight of the Prophet (upon its fugitive be a thousand salutations and greetings). Praise be to God who hath helped me to complete it, such praise as is worthy of the Court of His sanctity.

Number 67."

For the further elucidation of the matter I here reproduce the single Bábí colophon which I was able to cite in my second paper in the *J. R. A. S.* for 1889 (p. 922).

5. Colophon from a Commentary on the *Kitáb-i-Aķdas* seen at Shíráz in April 1888.

حرّره فی یوم الکمال [من][1] یوم العلاء من شهر النور

من سنة البدی[2] من الواحد الثانی سـ۱۲۹۶ـه *

"He wrote it on the day of *Kemál* [Monday] the day of *'Alá* [the 19th day] of the month of *Núr* [the 5th month] of the year *Badí* [which would be the 16th year, but, for the reason given in the footnote, there can be no doubt that this is a mistake for *Bahí*, the seventeenth year] of the second *Váḥid*, A.H. 1296."

From the above colophons we perceive that, besides the division of the year into 19 months of 19 days each, the years elapsed since the 'Manifestation' are also arranged

[1] *sic* in copy, but from analogy the word من appears redundant.

[2] This is evidently a mistake for البهی, for, as we see from the first colophon quoted in this note (*supra*, p. 415), the 13th day of the 4th month of the year *Bahí* (*i.e.* the 36th year of the '*Manifestation*,' or the 17th year of the second *Váḥid* of nineteen years) fell in A.H. 1296, the same year in which this colophon was written; and in all that relates to the Bábí method of reckoning time Zeynu'l-Muķarrabín's authority is incontrovertible.

in *Váḥids* or cycles of 19, and that to each year is given a name[1] which, by the sum of its component letters, indicates the position of the year in its own *Váḥid, e.g.*—

The 36th year after the Manifestation is called "the year *Bahí* [ی + ه + ب = 10 + 5 + 2 = 17] of the second *Váḥid*" [19 + 17 = 36].

The 44th year after the Manifestation is called "the year *Váv* [و = 6] of the third *Váḥid*" [(2 × 19) + 6 = 44].

The 45th year after the Manifestation is called "the year *Abad* [د + ب + ا = 4 + 2 + 1 = 7] of the third *Váḥid*" [(2 × 19) + 7 = 45].

The general arrangement of the Bábí calendar is now sufficiently clear, and, inasmuch as all Bábí colophons would appear to give the Muhammadan date as well as the Bábí date, this is perhaps all that we need know. Nevertheless, since MSS. may subsequently be discovered in which the date is given according to the Bábí method only, and since the matter is one calculated to arouse our curiosity, I feel impelled to discuss two questions which must be solved ere we can feel that we have fully mastered the problem before us.

These questions are :—

(1) From what fixed point does the reckoning begin ?

(2) Does the year consist of 361 (*i.e.* 19 × 19) days only, or is any system of intercalation adopted to keep it in correspondence with the solar year ?

[1] That some special method of enumerating years was employed by the Bábís I conjectured in my second paper in the *J. R. A. S.* for 1889 (p. 922, note 1), but, having only one colophon before me, I altogether failed to understand its application, or to perceive that the *numerical value*, not the *meaning*, of the name of each year was the true guide to its position in the *Váḥid* or cycle of years. Hence I failed to see that *Badí* (بدی) was a mere numerical expression or chronogram, and, imagining that it meant "*first*," vainly perplexed myself over the chronological difficulties involved in this supposition. However, as I have already pointed out, *Badí* in this colophon is clearly a mistake for *Bahí* (بهی), so that I might have failed to deduce the truth even if I had guessed it.

Before discussing these questions further, let us see what is said on the matter (1) by the Báb in the Persian *Beyán*, and (2) by Behá'u'lláh in the *Kitáb-i-Aḳdas*.

(1) Ordinances of the Báb concerning the arrangement of the calendar.

[From the Persian *Beyán*.]

الباب الثّالث من الواحد الخامس * فی بیان عرفان السّنین و الشهور *

ملخّص این باب آنکه خداوند عالم خلق فرموده کلّ سنین‌را بامر خود و از ظهور بیان قرار داده عدد هر سنین‌را عدد کلّ شیٔ و انرا نوزده شهر قرار داده و هر شهریرا نوزده روز قرار فرموده تا آنکه کلّ از نقطه تحویل حمل تا منتهی الیه سیر او که بحوت منتهی گردد در نوزده مراتب حروف واحد سیر نمایند و شهر اوّل‌را بهاء و آخررا علاء نامیده . . . . . .

و شهر اوّل شهر نقطه است و شهور حیّ در حول او طائف و مثل او در بین شهور مثل شمس است و سائر شهور مثل مرایائی است که ضیاء آن شهر در آنها مشرق شده و در آنها دیده نمیشود الا آن شهر و از خداوند

شهر بهآء نامیده بمعنی آنکه بهآء کل شهور در آن شهر
است و آنرا مخصوص گردانیده است بمن یظهره الله و
هر یومی از آنرا بیکی از حروف واحد نسبت داده و
یوم اوّل که نوروز است آن یوم لا اله الّا الله هست
مثل آن یوم مثل نقطه است در بیان که کلّ از آن
خلق میشوند و بسوی او عود مینمایند و مظهر آنرا در
نقطهٔ بیان ذات حروف السبع قرار داده و آنرا در این
ظهور عرش من یظهره الله قرار فرموده الخ

"*The third chapter of the fifth Wáḥid. In explanation of the knowledge of the years and the months.* The quintessence of this chapter is this, that the Lord of the Universe hath created all the years by His command, and by the manifestation of the Beyán hath appointed 'the Number of All Things' [361 = 19 × 19] as the number of every year, and hath appointed it [to consist of] nineteen months, and hath appointed each month nineteen days; that all may advance through the nineteen degrees of the 'Letters of the Unity' from the point of entrance into [the sign of] the Ram to the limit of its course which terminates in [the sign of the] Fish. And He hath called the first month *Behá* and the last *'Alá*. . . . . .

"And the first month is the month of the 'Point,' and around it revolve the months of 'the Living' [حی = 18]; and it is like unto the sun amidst the months, the other months being like mirrors wherein shineth forth the light of that month, and wherein naught is seen save that month. And it hath been named by the Lord 'the month of *Behá*' [*i.e.* splendour or brightness] in this sense, that the brightness of all the months is in that month. And [God] hath set it apart for 'Him whom God shall manifest,' and hath assigned every day of it to one of the 'Letters of the Living.' And the first day [thereof], which is the *Nawrúz*, is the day of 'there is no god but God'; the like of that day is as the 'Point' in the *Beyán*, from which all are created, and unto which all return. And He hath made the manifestation thereof in the 'Point of the Beyán,' the 'Person of the Seven Letters,'[1] and hath made it the throne of 'Him whom God shall manifest' in this manifestation."

The fourteenth chapter of the sixth *Váḥid* is entirely devoted to the glorification of the *Nawrúz* and the description of the ceremonies and rejoicings with which it should be observed. This ancient festival, here called "the day which the Lord of the Universe hath set apart for himself amidst the days, and hath named 'the Day of God'" (*Yawmu'lláh*), is defined as "the day when the sun passes from the sign of the Fish into the Ram," and it is ordained that the actual moment of this passage "whether it occur during the night or during the day" shall be the signal for the inauguration of these ceremonies.

(2) Ordinances of Behá'u'lláh concerning the arrangement of the calendar.

[From the *Kitáb-i-Aḳdas.*]

ان يا قلم الاعلى قل يا ملأ الانشاء قد كتبنا عليكم
الصّيام فى ايّام معدودات و جعلنا النّيروز عيداً لكم بعد اكمالها
كذلك اضائت شمس البيان من افق الكتاب من لدن
مالك المبدء و المآب ان اجعلوا ايّام الزّائدة عن الشّهور

[1] See p. 230 *supra*.

قبل شهر الصّيام انّا جعلناها مظاهر الهآء بين اللّيالی و الايام لذا ما تحدّدت بحدود السّنة و الشّهور ينبغی لمن فی البهآء ان يطعموا فيها انفسهم و ذوی القربی ثمّ الفقرآء و المساكين و يهلّلن و يكبّرن و يسبّحن و يمجّدن ربهم بالفرح و الانبساط و اذا تمت ايّام الاعطآء قبل الامساك ليدخلن فی الصّيام كذلك حكم مولی الانام ليس علی المسافر و المريض و الحامل و المرضع من حرج عفی الله عنهم فضلاً من عنده انه لهو العزيز الوهّاب تلك حدود الله الّتی رقمت من القلم الاعلی فی الزّبر و الالواح تمسّكوا باوامر الله و احكامه و لا تكونوا من الّذين اخذوا اصول انفسهم و نبذوا اصول الله ورائهم بما اتّبعوا الظّنون و الاوهام كفّوا انفسكم عن الاكل و الشرب من الطّلوع الی الافول ايّاكم ان يمنعكم الهوی عن هذا الفضل الّذی قدّر فی الكتاب *

"O Supreme Pen! Say, 'O concourse of creation, We have ordained unto you the fast during [a] limited [number of] days, and We have appointed the *Nawrúz* as a festival unto you after the completion thereof; thus doth the Sun of Revelation shine forth from the horizons of the Book on the part of the Lord of origin and return. Place the days which are in excess over the months[1] before the month of fasting; verily We have made them types of the [letter] *Há* [= 5] amongst the nights and the days, therefore were they not included within the limits of the year and the months. In them it is incumbent on those who are in *Behá* to feed themselves and [their] relatives, then the poor and the needy, and to confess and magnify and glorify and praise their Lord with joy and gladness. And when the days of giving before [the days of] abstinence are ended, let them enter upon the fast. Thus ordaineth the Lord of men: there is no obligation [to fast] on the traveller, on him who is sick, on the pregnant woman, or on her who giveth suck; these hath God excused as a favour on His part; verily He is the Mighty, the Bountiful. These are the ordinances of God which have been written by the Supreme Pen in the books and the epistles: hold firmly to the commands of God and His ordinances, and be not of those who adopt their own principles and fling God's principles behind them for that they follow imaginations and fancies. Abstain from eating and drinking from dawn till sundown; beware lest lust withhold you from this favour which hath been decreed in the Book.'"

From all this it would seem that the restoration of the old Persian solar year in place of the Arabian lunar year; the solemn sanctioning of the great national festival of the *Nawrúz*, which corresponds with the beginning of this solar year, the quickening of the earth after its winter's torpor, and the entry of the Sun into the sign of Aries; the division of the year into 19 months of 19 days each; and the nomenclature certainly of some and probably of all of these months were integral portions of the system devised by the Báb; while the provision of the five intercalary days (corresponding to what the Muhammadans call خمسهٔ مسترقه "the stolen five") and the enactments relating to their observance were supplementary details introduced by Behá. The fast of one month of 19 days (or, in the case of those who have not reached maturity, 11 days,

[1] *i.e.* the days required to bring the Bábí year of 361 (19 × 19) days into correspondence with the solar year.

"according to the number of هو") is also enjoined in the Persian *Beyán* (*Váḥid* viii, *ch.* 18), but the month does not appear to be there specified, though in the *Kitáb-i-Aḥkám* (Gobineau, p. 525) the month of *'Alá*, the last in the Bábí year, is appointed for it. The only part of the Bábí calendar as it at present exists with which Behá can be credited (and that not certainly) is the introduction of the intercalary days needed to bring the Bábí year into correspondence with the solar year. It is evident, moreover, that only so many of these five intercalary days are to be used as may be necessary to bridge over the interval between the last day of the month *'Alá* and the *Nawrúz*.

Lastly it is clear that the Bábí era commences not, as we might *primâ facie* have expected, on May 23rd A.D. 1844 (see p. 3 and note, and pp. 221—226 *supra*), but on the *Nawrúz* of that year (A.H. 1260), which, according to the *Násikhu't-Tawáríkh*, fell on Wednesday the last day (*salkh*) of Ṣafar (Wednesday, March 20th, A.D. 1844). We can easily verify this by working out the dates in the above colophons. Let us take one only, the first, as an example. In it the Bábí date is the 13th day of the 4th month of the 36th year, *i.e.* (3 × 19) + 13 = 70 days after the *Nawrúz*, which always falls on or about March 20th. Seventy days from this brings us to May 29th (11 days in March + 30 in April + 29 in May = 70 days). Looking out the Muhammadan date in the colophon (7th of Jemádí II, A.H. 1296) in Wüstenfeld's tables we find that it does actually correspond with May 29th, 1879. The Bábí year being, like our own, solar, is easily calculated by counting the number of complete years which have elapsed since March 20th A.D. 1844, the commencement of the era. In this case, for instance, the 35th year terminated on March 19th, A.D. 1879 (1844 + 35), and the 36th year therefore extends from March 20th, 1879 to March 19th, 1880.

INDEX.